THE SUN
WON'T COME OUT
TOMORROW

THE SUN WON'T COME OUT TOMORROW

THE DARK HISTORY OF AMERICAN ORPHANHOOD

KRISTEN MARTIN

BOLD TYPE BOOKS

NEW YORK

Bold Type Books
Hachette Book Group
1290 Avenue of the Americas, New York, NY 10104
www.boldtypebooks.org
@BoldTypeBooks

Printed in the United States of America

First Edition: January 2025

Published by Bold Type Books, an imprint of Hachette Book Group, Inc. Bold Type Books is a co-publishing venture of the Type Media Center and The Basic Books Group.

The Hachette Speakers Bureau provides a wide range of authors for speaking events. To find out more, go to hachettespeakersbureau.com or email HachetteSpeakers@hbgusa.com.

Bold Type books may be purchased in bulk for business, educational, or promotional use. For more information, please contact your local bookseller or the Hachette Book Group Special Markets Department at special.markets@hbgusa.com.

The publisher is not responsible for websites (or their content) that are not owned by the publisher.

Library of Congress Cataloging-in-Publication Data has been applied for.
ISBNs: 9781645030348 (hardcover), 9781645030362 (ebook)
LSC-C

Printing 1, 2024

For my brother, John

In memory of our parents, Robert and Amelia

*Happily, for the busy lunatics who rule over us,
we are permanently the United States of Amnesia.
We learn nothing because we remember nothing.*
—GORE VIDAL, *IMPERIAL AMERICA*

*Most kids have folks to teach 'em things but we're just
orphans and it's the hard-knock route for us.*
—*LITTLE ORPHAN ANNIE* COMIC STRIP, NOVEMBER 22, 1924

CONTENTS

Contents

Introduction

AMERICANS LOVE ORPHANS

A mericans love orphans. As children, we meet them in our books, comics, movies, television shows, musicals, theme parks, and even dolls. We know their stories well: The scrappy prankster sasses his aunt, convinces other boys to whitewash her fence, witnesses a murder, and hunts for treasure. The spunky little girl with the corkscrew curls says good-bye to the hard-knock life of a New York City orphanage and hello to a rich new daddy, reminding us that the sun will come out tomorrow. Four siblings find an abandoned boxcar in the woods and make it their new home; later they solve mysteries all by themselves.

As we grow older, orphan stories grow with us. Five siblings band together when their parents die in a car crash and they grow up too fast, treating us to after-school specials. An autodidact genius janitor at MIT undergoes court-ordered therapy after assaulting a police officer and comes to terms with the emotional baggage of being abused by his foster father. A girl's mother dies in a car crash, and she is sent to live in an orphanage, where she learns chess from the custodian and develops an addiction to the tranquilizers she is drugged with; later, as a chess champion, her addiction deepens.

We all know the arc of an orphan story. Step one: While the child is still too young to form distinct memories of them, their parents die in an untimely fashion. Step two: Orphan acquires caretakers who amplify the world's cruelty. Step three: Orphan escapes and goes on an adventure, encountering the world's vast possibilities.

Sometimes the parents aren't dead—instead, the child has been abandoned, making them a foundling, like Punky Brewster, played by the adorable pigtailed Soleil Moon Frye on the mid-1980s NBC sitcom. Punky finds a new father in the manager of a Chicago apartment building she squatted in after her mother deserted her. Sometimes only one parent is missing, as in Mark Twain's *The Adventures of Huckleberry Finn*—Huck's father, the town drunk, is still alive.

There are proportionally far more orphans in American pop culture than there are in American life. One reason why: orphans are expedient protagonists. They come with built-in conflict, necessary for setting any story in motion. And since fictional orphans are free from the close watch of parents, they're afforded more freedom, allowing them to go on adventures full of intrigue that keep us rapt. These stories allow the children who consume them to encounter the worst-case scenario of becoming an orphan—becoming that vulnerable, abnormal figure—without grappling with what it actually feels like to lose their parents. The focus on the adventure gives orphanhood a silver lining, wherein losing your parents becomes both palatable and strangely covetable.

Orphan stories are not meant to represent real orphanhood because they're most concerned with the orphan as a symbol. But I am not a symbol: I am a real person whose parents both died when I was still a child.

Of course, I felt no kinship with popular orphan characters because my situation differed dramatically from theirs. My story wasn't the kind that was represented in books and on screens, perhaps because it was too sad, too steeped in the kind of grief that we find hard to look at head-on. My parents' deaths didn't set me free to explore the world, or leave me vengeful, or turn me into a damaged genius. But orphan narratives have unconsciously governed what others assume about me—that I must have been a pitiful figure, alone in the world without any relations willing to care for her, who had to gather the gumption to strike out on her own journey.

A few years ago, I started wondering why these narratives were so popular. I felt that the prevalence of orphan stories wasn't just about providing plot and character shortcuts. And the more that I realized how much our favorite orphan stories get wrong about American orphanhood—not just my own experience of losing my parents but also the history of our country's policies toward dependent children—the more I wondered why we cling to these myths.

The gap between the stories we tell ourselves about orphans and the lived experiences of those children reveals the narrative that America wants to construct about itself: we are a nation that values the nuclear family, rallies around children in need, and believes all young people have promising futures. In reality, the history of how our country has dealt with dependent children is full of classism, racism, and hypocrisy fueled by capitalism and moral panics, where only some are deserving of strong familial ties. This book will take you inside the history of orphanhood in the United States, from the 1800s to the present, to set the record straight.

Until I started researching this book, I had never associated myself with the label "orphan" because of the cultural baggage it carried. As a teenager, I recoiled from the term so much that I wrote my personal statement for college about it, referencing an apocryphal quote from the philosopher and theologian Søren Kierkegaard as only a pretentious seventeen-year-old can: "My parents died within two years of each other when I was twelve and fourteen. That simple fact legally transformed me from daughter to orphan, an unfortunate label. As Søren Kierkegaard wrote, 'Once you label me, you negate me.' The label orphan negates my parents as well."

Looking back now, I realize that as a teenager, I was terrified of being seen as a walking memento mori: the girl whose parents had died. I was terrified of being pitied, because pity would mark me as outside the norm, inferior to my peers. But mostly, I was terrified of publicly slipping into the abyss of my loss. In order to keep living, I needed to tamp down my grief, to keep acting like I was the same girl I had been before I had seen my mom in her coffin, done up by the mortician with too much blush, wearing a blue silk dress; before I had seen my father's coffin lowered into the same grave two years later.

Before my parents died, my family lived a solidly middle-class existence on Long Island, New York, in the same house my mom had grown up in.

My dad, Robert, was a lieutenant in the New York Police Department—he worked mostly behind a desk in the Auto Crime Division of the Organized Crime Control Bureau in Queens, a short drive away from our house in West Hempstead, and was home most nights by 5:30 p.m. for dinner. My mom, Amelia, stayed at home and filled her life with cooking, cleaning, shopping, reading, and serving as PTA president. Dad coached my older brother John's Little League team; Mom drove me to dance classes twice a week.

Then, in fall 2001, about a month after 9/11, my parents called a family meeting—an unprecedented event. We were not the kind of family that talked forthrightly about problems. We were not the kind of family that had problems, not big ones. Or at least it didn't seem that way to twelve-year-old me.

As we sat on the beige sectional couch in our living room, Mom explained that the pneumonia she had over the summer—the illness that made her hack phlegm into the sink while she brushed her teeth in the morning and shiver under the covers when it was ninety degrees outside—masked something more serious. She talked about the bronchoscopy the doctor had done and what it found: she had lung cancer. Then Dad explained that his prostate cancer was no longer in remission. Up until then I hadn't even consciously understood that Dad had had cancer; I was only eight when he was diagnosed in 1997, and I don't remember my parents ever using the C-word to explain why Dad took time off from work that year. They said they would both start chemotherapy soon. Mom had already shopped for a dark brown wig with her hairdresser. "We got one that looks just like my real hair, Kris," she told me that night.

Just three months later, Dad sat John and me down on that same couch as soon as we walked in the door after school and told us that Mom had died. It was January 4, 2002—our first day back to school after the winter break. Mom had died early that morning; she was only forty-nine. The chemo she had undergone in the fall wasn't effective at controlling the spread of her advanced-stage lung cancer, and by early December she had metastases that compressed her spinal cord and kept her from walking. She realized this with terror one morning when she tried to get out of bed to drive John and me to school and crumpled to the floor. That day, Mom went to the hospital. She would never make it back home.

My first thought upon hearing that Mom was dead was *Why did Dad wait so many hours to tell us?* But then he said, "Mom would have wanted you all to stay at school." During her time in the hospital, when she was laid up in a narrow bed, totally out of it with fever, needing her lips moistened with a sponge swab, she always asked Dad if John and I were doing our homework.

I was sitting on that same couch two years and two weeks later, on January 18, 2004, when my aunt Nancy told me that Dad had died. His health had started to decline a few months after Mom died; he was in the hospital for more than a month in fall 2002 because of the pain his prostate cancer caused, and by the end of fall 2003, metastases in his skull were causing his vision to fail. A few days before he died, Dad fell down the stairs on his way from his bedroom to the living room. It was a snow day, and John and I were home from school watching *Edward Scissorhands*. Dad hit his head on the landing, went unconscious, and never woke up. He was fifty.

My parents' deaths irreparably cleaved my life in two: before was the seemingly impregnable safety and love of a nuclear family in the Long Island suburbs; after was a grief that felt impossible to speak in a culture that still refuses to look head-on at death and mourning.

The only way I related to the orphans I had read about and seen on TV and in movies was that I worried about being viewed as an outsider, the worst thing to be in high school. But that concern was overwhelmed by the reason it existed: my parents were gone. I didn't just miss parental love and my comfortable place in a family; I missed my specific parents. Unlike most popular orphan characters, I wasn't too young to remember my parents. I knew their physical realities well. I knew my mother's cigarette-rasped voice, the bleach-stained black stirrup pants she liked lounging in, her long, tanned fingers flipping the pages of a *Redbook*. I knew my father's predilection for Vans sneakers because they had no arches; his freckled arms cradling an acoustic guitar; his tube of Vaseline-brand lip balm in the pocket protector he slipped into his short-sleeve button-down shirts. I desperately missed these signs of their lives—of them being alive—and I missed how they cared for me, raised me.

When my parents were sick and after they died, my extended family stepped up to act in loco parentis. Grandma Martin moved in when my mom entered the hospital in 2001. My other grandma, my mom's mom, whom we called Nanny, had always lived with us—the house I was raised in was orig-inally her house, and my parents bought it from Nanny after Papa died the year before I was born. She kept her bedroom, where she spent most of her days chain-smoking, knitting slippers, and watching reruns of *Matlock* and *Columbo*. Nanny is the reason why I didn't make my own bed, do laundry, or fix myself breakfast until I was a teenager. My father's younger sisters—Mary Ellen, Joan, Alice, and Nancy—visited Long Island on the weekends when he was sick and after he died, helping my brother and me study, driving us where we needed to go, loading us up with groceries. For the first couple of months after Dad's death, I had imagined this state of affairs would persist, at least to see me through my last three years of high school. John was headed to college that fall—he had managed to send off his applications in Dad's last months and get scholarships to attend Syracuse University.

In his will, my father named his sisters Mary Ellen and Alice as guardians for John and me. Along with my father's other sisters, they decided that keeping two women in their eighties who had never had driver's licenses in charge of two suburban teenagers wasn't sustainable—a rational judgment, as both of my grandmothers would fall into ill health by the time I was a freshman in college. A plan was hashed out: in summer 2004, John and I would move to central New Jersey to live with Aunt Alice, Uncle Joe, and their two kids. It wouldn't make sense for us to live with Aunt Mary Ellen, an extremely busy physician who was single and lived in a loft in Philadelphia. Aunt Alice's house would be the closest to what we had known on Long Island. John would go away to Syra-cuse, and I'd go to the same Catholic high school as my cousin Matt.

At Aunt Alice's, I shoved all of my grief and anxiety down. If you had known me in high school, you would not have suspected the trauma I had recently gone through. I got straight As in my honors and AP classes, wrote for and edited the newspaper, played first-chair clarinet in band, and volun-teered with the Christian Social Action Club. I spent hours each week at my new dance studio, preparing for competitions. I made new friends, to whom I never mentioned my dead parents, and stayed close with my old ones, to whom I rarely mentioned my dead parents. I got into an Ivy League university early decision. My story was far from those of fictional American orphans—and, as I would come to learn, from what many other real orphans have endured.

As I deconstruct our favorite orphan narratives and reconstruct history, I will tell the stories of children who did not have my same advantages. These stories will illuminate that while the United States has changed its methods for handling the dependent children we have considered "orphans"—from the dual rise of industrial capitalism and institutionalization during the 1800s, to the orphan trains that ran from the mid-nineteenth through the early twentieth centuries, and finally to the development of modern, state-sponsored foster care—the classist, racist, and religious biases that rule child welfare have largely remained the same.

As I take you through each era, I'll start first with the stories we want to tell ourselves about orphans—the stories we perpetuate in literature, television, and film. After breaking down what makes these stories so appealing and how they encourage us to look away from the truth, I'll correct the record by unpacking the real history of orphans in the United States. And I'll tell my own story of orphanhood throughout.

In this book, an orphan is not just a person like me, whose parents both died before I turned eighteen. I'm what's called a "full orphan"; the only other American full orphan I have ever met is my own brother. While working on this book, I spent hours digging around on federal government websites, searching for statistics on how many other full orphans there are in the United States. It turns out that no government agency—not the Census Bureau, not the Children's Bureau, not the Centers for Disease Control and Prevention—keeps a precise count of the number of children with dead parents. The absence of such an official tally struck me as strange and further highlights the disparate amount of attention that pop culture pays to orphanhood.

The closest estimate of American full orphans that exists comes from the Census Bureau's Survey of Income and Program Participation (SIPP). The SIPP is a longitudinal survey of a set of nationally representative households that collects data about income, jobs, and eligibility for and participation in social programs, as well as some other demographic information.[1] In 2014, it started asking respondents if their parents were living, and if they weren't, when they died, in search of a link with socioeconomic status and race.[2] The survey's 2021 data estimates that only 0.3 percent of Americans lose both their parents by age eighteen.[3] As applied to the 2021 total child population of 72.8 million, that makes for only about 218,400 full orphans.[4] Like most orphans worldwide—and like my brother and me—most of these children live with other family members.[5]

The fact is that full orphanhood has always been relatively rare and that most of the children we're talking about when we're talking about orphans had one or two living parents but were separated from them, either voluntarily or involuntarily. This was true even in the nineteenth century, when life expectancy was low, maternal mortality rates were high, and orphanages were common. Yet, surprisingly, only about a quarter of children in nineteenth-century orphanages had lost both their parents; more than half had one living parent, and a fifth had two living parents.[6] Desperately poor parents left their children at orphanages in times of need, usually temporarily.

The orphanage era blossomed in the early nineteenth century in response not just to a growing number of dependent children whose parents couldn't manage to take care of them alone but to a moral panic over poverty. While poor adults were blamed for their circumstances, their children were deemed innocent and deserving of charity. Religion—the cure for moral ills and savior of innocent souls—was at the heart of the establishment of orphanages, which largely served only white children. Black children were enslaved in southern states, and Black orphans were largely shunted into poorhouses in free states. Meanwhile, Christian missionaries established residential schools where Native American children who had been forcibly removed from their families and tribes were "civilized," given Anglo names, forced to speak English, and subjected to cultural genocide.

In the mid-1800s, a Protestant minister turned philanthropist named Charles Loring Brace began criticizing the practice of warehousing children in highly regimented orphanages. In 1853, he founded the Children's Aid Society in New York and popularized the practice of sending city children in need of homes and jobs off on "orphan trains" to rural areas, often to newly established railroad towns in the Midwest, where they would essentially be auctioned off to families looking for farmhands and domestic workers. The practice of "placing out" children via orphan train was a social engineering experiment that sent approximately a quarter million poor urban children to barely vetted families in rural areas all over the United States from 1854 to 1929.[7]

Over the course of the first half of the twentieth century, orphanages fell out of favor, and foster care became the predominant solution for caring for dependent children. Today, about 600,000 to 650,000 children spend time in foster care each year.[8] We view them as "social orphans" or "the orphans of the living"—almost all the children in foster care have living parents, and poverty remains a driving force behind family separation by state-run child-protective systems.

In 2022, the most recent year for which federal data is available, 62 percent of the approximately 186,600 children who entered the foster care system were removed from their parents because of neglect, a loosely defined category that varies by state. Frequently, conditions of poverty are construed as conditions of neglect—think of a child who comes to school in dirty clothes because their parent can't afford to go to the laundromat or a child left alone in their apartment while a parent works because they can't afford a babysitter. Physical abuse—what we might imagine to be the most common cause of child removal—was cited in only 13 percent of cases. And only 1 percent of children who entered foster care (about twenty-five hundred children) entered due to parental death. The only reasons less common were children being voluntarily relinquished (about nineteen hundred children) and a child's own alcohol abuse (about eight hundred children).[9]

The risk of being sent to foster care by the child protective services system is not distributed equally. Researchers estimate that over half of Black children in the United States will be subjected to investigations by child protective services agencies.[10] This corresponds with the fact that Black children are overrepresented in foster care, making up 23 percent of the total number of foster youth, versus about 15 percent of the total child population.[11] White children are vastly underrepresented. This completely flips the script set in the 1800s, when Black children were almost entirely excluded from institutions.

You might expect orphanhood and adoption to be closely intertwined. But historically speaking, most of the children this country has considered to be orphans have not been adoptable—they still had parents, and their parents maintained legal custody rights over them. Our country has only been in the business of creating legal orphans—terminating the parental rights of children in foster care to make them adoptable—for the past few decades. This parental death sentence is the ultimate separation of "deserving" children from their "undeserving" parents, who are mostly guilty of being poor. Permanently severing familial ties takes to an extreme the logic that individual adults—and not society at large—are to blame for conditions of poverty. Our country has held fast to this fallacy for more than two centuries.

The orphan has always been treated as a symbol and a cipher in our culture, down to whom we consider to be an orphan. We label certain children as "orphans" in order to excuse taking them away from their families; we label others as "orphans" in order to construe them as objects of pity deserving of new families. In an orphan narrative, the orphan's circumstances always represent what we fear. We work out those fears—of poverty, of neglect, of abuse, of crime—through the orphan. When the orphan finds a new, "better" family, we feel safe. When children's parents have actually died, like mine did, we refuse to sit with their grief. Instead, we've been content to rehash the same sunny stories about orphans over and over again, to the point that we've largely ignored the dark truth of how America has always treated its most vulnerable children.

Looking closely at the gap between stories we want to tell ourselves about dependent children and the lived experiences of those children reveals the myths that America wants to construct about itself. Inside the history of America's orphans lies the history of American childhood, the American family, American poverty. It's past time that we face that history. The classist, racist, and religious forces that made children vulnerable to family separation in the 1800s are still driving the system today. I wrote this book to unpack why we keep telling ourselves the same fictitious stories and to show how American child welfare has been broken from the start.

I used to hate being labeled as an orphan because that one word wrested control of my own personal narrative away from me, coloring it with tropes drawn from fiction that morph fact through a funhouse mirror. This book interrogates how we flatten individuality by shoehorning the diversity of human experience into the shapes of stories we are most comfortable with. My life and my loss are not representative of American orphanhood insofar as no one story can truly stand in for a larger whole. But in telling my own story and the oft overlooked stories of orphans throughout history, I hope to push back against the forces that make us gravitate toward the singular narrative and, in doing so, to help us imagine a more just future for vulnerable children and families.

ONE

ORPHANAGES

Chapter One

It's the Hard-Knock Life

A nnie is *the* American orphan. It is her mop of curly red hair that we think of first when we hear the word *orphan* and her songs of hope and defiance that get stuck in our heads. Her experience of living in Miss Hannigan's house of terror—scrubbing the stairwell on hands and knees, consoling the younger girls in the crowded dorm, and eventually escaping her grim fate thanks to the generosity of "Daddy" Warbucks—has become our blueprint for the orphanage narrative. More than a narrative though, Annie's story has calcified into American allegory: she's our every-orphan, a stand-in for the can-do resilience and pluck we demand of the most vulnerable children in our country.

We first met Annie one hundred years ago, when artist Harold Gray introduced her in his August 5, 1924, *Little Orphan Annie* comic strip in the *New York Daily News*. But for most of us, the Annie we think of is not Gray's girl with her creepy oval voids for eyes but the adorable orphan in her red dress with the white collar from the 1977 Broadway musical *Annie*. That role was originated by Andrea McArdle, a feisty little girl in a tightly curled wig, belting about how "just thinkin' about tomorrow / clears away the cobwebs and the sorrow / 'til there's none."[1] (Sarah Jessica Parker later got her big break at thirteen when she took over the part.) In the musical telling, Annie was left as a foundling on the front steps of the New York Municipal

Orphanage as an infant and lived there until she was rescued by billionaire Oliver Warbucks at age eleven, amid the Great Depression. "Daddy" Warbucks promises to find her real parents, setting J. Edgar Hoover's Federal Bureau of Investigation on the case and announcing a $50,000 reward on the radio, which leads to a scam uncovered by (literally) President Franklin D. Roosevelt and his Secret Service. Annie then lives happily ever after in the luxury of the Warbucks mansion.

Or maybe we all think of freckled, button-nosed Aileen Quinn's take on Annie—she beat out nine thousand other little girls to star in the 1982 movie adaptation of the musical.[2] I can't remember ever sitting down as a child to watch the entirety of that movie, where Carol Burnett plays Miss Hannigan, the cruel, alcoholic head of the orphanage, who conspires with her good-for-nothing brother Rooster (Tim Curry) and his partner Lily St. Regis (Bernadette Peters) to kidnap Annie. I don't think I ever even saw the 1999 made-for-TV Disney remake (another star-studded cast, featuring Kathy Bates, Audra McDonald, Alan Cumming, and Kristin Chenoweth).

But, being an American child, I absorbed Annie osmotically. The Shirley Temple–esque scene of Annie and "Daddy" Warbucks descending his mansion's marble staircase and tap dancing lives rent-free in my head. I have vague memories of hearing about the search for the little girl who would play Annie in the Disney TV movie in the mid-1990s, where thousands of children a little older than me sang bars of "Tomorrow" for a chance to be chosen as the chosen orphan. When I was nine, I would come home from school to watch MTV's *Total Request Live* and catch the music video for Jay-Z's "Hard Knock Life (Ghetto Anthem)," which opens with a pitch-skewed sample from the *Annie* musical. At sixteen, a few years after I became an orphan myself, I ate overpriced Twizzlers and watched my youngest cousin, Lucas, perform in *Annie Jr.* with the Staten Island Children's Theater Association on a high school stage. I didn't think about my own experience as Lucas sang a solo as Bert Healy, the radio host who croons "You're Never Fully Dressed Without a Smile" after "Daddy" Warbucks offers his reward. After all, Annie was nothing like me—she is a girl who never knew her parents, a girl who exists primarily as a symbol of optimism, not grief.

Even now, Annie won't leave me be: my cousin Matt's daughter, then five years old, loved the *Annie Live!* special that ran on NBC in December

2021, and her mom posted snippets of her singing "Tomorrow" on Instagram Stories. On a recent flight to Nashville, I sat next to a young mom and her almost-three-year-old daughter who proclaimed *Annie* to be her favorite movie and warbled out "Tomorrow" for me as I smiled and stuffed down the urge to tell them that I was writing a book about how and why we can't stop telling ourselves Annie's story.

The privations of the orphanage have long loomed large in American popular culture—our cultural fixation on orphanages has outlasted the primacy of institutional care for orphans by more than eighty years. All orphanage narratives owe something to Annie, in all the different permutations of how her story has been told, from the eighty-five years the *Little Orphan Annie* comic strips ran, to the radio drama series of the same name that aired from 1930 to 1942, to the first movie treatments in 1932 and 1938, to that 1970s Broadway musical and those 1980s and 1990s movie adaptations, to the modernized 2014 remake produced by Will Smith and Jay-Z and the 2021 NBC live musical, both of which featured a Black girl in the starring role.

Annie's grit and resilience in the face of being parentless, poor, and mistreated—and her rescue by the ·benevolent and filthy rich "Daddy" Warbucks—promotes the idea that there are individual solutions to the problem of orphanhood. With the right mind-set and the right bank account, you can "clear away the cobwebs and the sorrow" without worrying about the societal issues that necessitated orphanages in the first place. The reality is that harsh, regimented orphanages were the product of religious and societal philosophies about the best way to help the "deserving poor," children were largely powerless over their own fates, and no amount of individual charity could rescue dependent children.

Given that Annie the musical-movie has become our paradigm for orphanage stories, it's odd that in its source material, Annie spends almost no time at all in the orphanage. A mere week after *Little Orphan Annie*'s premiere in the *New York Daily News*, Annie already makes it out of the orphanage—she calls it the "home," always with scare quotes to emphasize how little of a home it truly is.[3] She is taken out on trial by Mrs. Warbucks—yes, in the comics, there's a Mrs. Warbucks. We don't even meet her husband, Oliver "Daddy" Warbucks (again, always with the scare quotes), for a month and a half.

But back to the "home" for a moment. Annie, ten years old in the comics, has lived there since infancy. There's no drunken, flamboyant Miss Hannigan here—instead, there's Miss Asthma, a crone who dresses plainly in a collared shirt and a long black skirt, with glasses perched on her witchy nose and her hair pulled into a severe bun. If *Little Orphan Annie* has anything to say about orphanages, it is expressed through Gray's characterization of Miss Asthma. He casts her as an example of all that is wrong with institutions of charity, which pat themselves on the back for giving the poor the bare minimum of shelter and food while bending over to kiss the feet of their rich benefactors. The very first line of the debut strip comes from Miss Asthma, wagging her finger at Annie, reminding her to be thankful for charity: "I hope you'll always remember what a lot we've done for you here—you have been sheltered, clothed and fed since you were a baby entirely by charity—you should be very grateful."

Annie's reaction to Miss Asthma's admonishing, muttered to herself as she kneels to scrub the floors with a brush, speaks to how we think of orphans (and orphanages) in the popular imagination. They are pitiful figures who exist only to work for their cruel overseers and pine for a new family. Their original parents, dead or otherwise vanished, typically merit no concern, or grief. When Annie is introduced, she wants, first and foremost, to be adopted. Without a family, she feels worthless: "When she keeps reminding me I'm an orphan and that I'm a charity girl it makes me <u>hate</u> her and <u>hate</u> the 'home' and <u>hate</u> myself too for being so poor—gee, I wish some nice folks would adopt me—then I could have a real papa and mama like other kids."

This isn't the spunky Annie we would come to know and love, a symbol of American stick-to-itiveness. It's an Annie beaten down by a "home" that only feeds her mush and milk and subjects her to constant toil (in the very next panel, she's standing on a chair to scrub a basin full of dishes)—work that isn't softened by anyone's love. Annie doesn't even know that she had any parents before entering the orphanage. When she overhears Miss Asthma speaking with Mrs. Warbucks (a trustee) about her file one week later, it is the first time she has ever thought of herself as having "a history with parents in it and everything. . . . I never could be sure whether orphans ever had any parents—I can't remember any." Of course, Miss Asthma slams the door before Annie can hear more about her parentage, and she won't be able to access her records until she's twenty-one. "Isn't it funny to be someone but not know who?" Annie wonders, but the thought doesn't linger. She doesn't long for her parents or yearn to understand where she came from—she's just Annie, no surname, a blank canvas for Gray to paint his allegory on.

From our first introduction to her, then, Annie's main problem is the hold that mean old Miss Asthma has over her due to her parentless, impoverished state. The solution to her problem is adoption by "nice folks"—people who make the individual decision to share their wealth and love by rescuing a "charity girl" like her. In order to win over those folks, Annie needs to show hope and determination, to be resilient above all. This portrayal of Annie's problem and solution remains constant throughout the many iterations of her story and has twisted our imagined reality of orphanhood for generations. Each time we regurgitate Annie's story, we allow ourselves to believe the orphan's struggle is one with individual causes and individual answers. In doing so, we overlook the systems—economic, religious, political—that have made orphans out of real children like Annie and that continue to control their fates. Our preference to buy into Annie's version of orphanhood at the expense of sitting with actuality speaks to how we as Americans value individualism and fail to grasp the need for societal interventions for systemic harms.

In 1951, after more than twenty-five years of conjuring up adventures for Annie, Gray claimed that he had based her on a child he met in Chicago. "She had common sense, knew how to take care of herself," he said. "She had to. Her name was Annie."[4] His choice to make this street-smart, independent girl the star of his breakout comic was a narratively savvy one. "At the time, some 40 strips were using boys as the main characters; only three were using girls," Gray said. "I chose Annie for mine, and made her an orphan, so she'd have no family, no tangling alliances, but freedom to go where she pleased." Of course, writers had long been using orphans as protagonists for exactly these reasons—and Gray was likely more influenced by the writers that had come before him than by some apocryphal street child.

Gray may have been inspired to name his comic's heroine Annie by James Whitcomb Riley's 1885 poem "Little Orphant Annie" (yes, orphant). Originally titled "The Elf Child" and written in an Indiana dialect, Riley's poem depicts an orphan girl who spends her days working as an indentured servant and her nights telling moral stories for the children of her employers:

> *Little Orphant Annie's come to our house to stay,*
> *An' wash the cups an' saucers up, an' brush the crumbs away,*
> *An' shoo the chickens off the porch, an' dust the hearth, an' sweep,*
> *An' make the fire, an' bake the bread, an' earn her board-an'-*
> > *keep;*
> *An' all us other childern, when the supper things is done,*
> *We set around the kitchen fire an' has the mostest fun*
> *A-list'nin' to the witch-tales 'at Annie tells about,*
> *An' the Gobble-uns 'at gits you*
> > *Ef you*
> > > *Don't*
> > > > *Watch*
> > > > > *Out!*

This idealization of child labor became a popular poem for schoolchildren to memorize and recite well into the twentieth century, and it would have been familiar for readers of Gray's comics. It was even made into a silent film featuring Riley in 1918.[5] Riley—known as "the poet of the common people"—based his poem on a real orphan girl, but fiction soon took over her story, down to her name, Allie, which was transposed to "Annie" in a typesetting error.[6] The real girl was Mary Alice "Allie" Smith, who in the 1850s was indentured to Riley's parents in Indiana, working as a servant to earn her keep—an all-too common practice at the time.[7] Allie's parents might or might not have died when she was a child, but in any case, both in real life and in the poem, she was never placed in an orphanage like Gray's Annie.[8]

Gray's biggest acknowledged influence for Annie is, unsurprisingly, Charles Dickens, who set the beats of the melodramatic orphan narrative in the 1800s with his Victorian social novels. In 1938, Gray told an interviewer, "You can take Great Expectations or any Dickens book and put in running water and a telephone and you have Annie in a modern setting with a sound story."[9] For the picaresque *Little Orphan Annie*, Gray swapped the state-sponsored baby-farm-run workhouse of *Oliver Twist*, where little Oliver toils unraveling oakum for navy ships and must beg for more gruel, for a charity-run orphanage, where the children serve as little housekeepers and subsist on mush and milk. (*Oliver Twist* would perhaps inspire the creators of the *Annie* musical too—it was made into a musical in 1960 and then a movie in 1968.)

Like Dickens, Gray used Annie's orphan status to explore social conundrums—but from an American standpoint. In Annie's world, nouveau riche folks of the Roaring Twenties like Mrs. Warbucks, with her turned-up nose and long string of pearls, are greedy phonies. Mrs. Warbucks takes Annie in from the orphanage only to show off to the "real society crowd" and constantly threatens to send her back.[10] (The allegorical name Warbucks itself is like something out of Dickens: in an early strip draft that never ran, a maid explains to Annie that the couple was poor until 1917, then made their fortune selling munitions to Uncle Sam in World War I.)[11] Annie, who has nothing, not even a family, is regularly shown to be more charitable than Mrs. Warbucks. After giving up her coat to the son of a down-on-his-luck man, Annie quips, "Gee, doing something for somebody makes me feel so warm inside I don't need a coat."[12] Later, when she is back on the streets and rescues a mutt puppy—the famous Sandy—from a group of boys who are beating it, a cop says, "Bless 'er heart, the little saint."[13]

That Gray cast an industrial capitalist as the kindly benefactor and patriarch of his strip further speaks to the economic and political propaganda he embedded in *Little Orphan Annie*. When the strip began, Gray was a populist who promoted the ideals of self-reliance and hard work above all.[14] Though Annie is poor, Gray portrays her as capable of taking care of herself and making her own money when she needs to, thanks to her bootstrapping grit. Oliver "Daddy" Warbucks may be filthy rich, but to Gray he's a worker who has leveraged the free market and—crucially—has stayed in touch with his working-class roots. "Daddy" prefers to wear slippers and shirtsleeves around the house and beats up a loan shark in order to help the Fairs (again with the allegory), an old, important family who are at risk of losing their home.

But while "Daddy" instantly takes to Annie, his role as father always comes second to his business empire and his love (like Gray's) of the free market. He leaves for a business trip in Siberia just a month after he first meets Annie, and Mrs. Warbucks promptly deposits her back at the "home." Gray initially wanted to have Annie remain in the care of "Daddy," but his editor, Joseph Medill Patterson, wanted her to stay a poor orphan.[15] They compromised that "Daddy" Warbucks would indeed take in Annie but would regularly disappear, orphaning Annie again and again, only to return every time to rescue her. This set the blueprint for the many remakes of Annie's story—we want Annie to stay a young orphan who is saved in a fairy-tale ending, and we want to see her get saved over and over again. In the process, we are content to ignore the real history and contemporary experiences of children like Annie, who are not so easily "saved."

It's true that when all is going well for Annie, the storylines are boring, lacking tension and coasting mostly on moral lessons. The appeal of both the comic strip and the radio show based on it, which aired in the 1930s and was later immortalized in *A Christmas Story*, lies in the dangerous adventures that Annie and her dog Sandy undertake outside the oppressive orphanage and the supervision of adults.

Even so, Annie's adventures are themselves repetitive. She spends about six months at a stretch off on her own with Sandy, occasionally landing back in the "home" (at one point she saves all the other orphans there from a fire while Miss Asthma flails), working to help others and making ends meet for herself while standing up for fellow little guys. In one plotline, she even makes friends with a city alderman and helps free an Italian immigrant who has been wrongly accused of stealing—totally normal for a ten-year-old. She works variously as a shopkeeper, a waitress, a circus performer, and a newsgirl and almost never attends school. Bad guys abound, and Annie is kidnapped a few times, always to be rescued by "Daddy," who sticks around for a month or two before being called off again on business.

As the strip entered the mid-1930s, when Franklin D. Roosevelt was in office and enacting the New Deal, Gray took it down a more conservative path. Gray privately called FDR a communist and thought that the social welfare of the New Deal would crush the economy.[16] Instead of loan sharks and crooked bankers, the new bad guys are incompetent bureaucrats and corrupt union presidents. Even "Daddy" Warbucks's vanishings take on a political bent—he dies of a mysterious illness caused by "the climate" in 1944, when FDR was seeking a fourth term, saying, "I've lived my life according to my time and generation . . . probably it's <u>time</u> for me to go!" When FDR himself died in 1945, Warbucks unsubtly came back to life, having faked his own death.[17]

Of course, subtlety was never Gray's pursuit. Beyond the fact that he was writing for children in an art form that depends on caricatures, Gray's goal with *Little Orphan Annie* was not to explore the social issue of orphanhood in America but to spread a political message about individual autonomy. If Gray had actually taken the time to study orphanages and how American children ended up there, he would have had to grapple with the limits of self-determination in an industrial capitalist society.

———

Gray died in 1968, so he didn't live to see his conservative comic strip turn into a paean to FDR in the form of a Broadway musical. The theatrical performance was designed as nostalgia for the good old days of the New Deal. *Annie* was the brainchild of its lyricist and original director, Martin Charnin, who saw the potential for a production in the original comic strips after stumbling upon a compilation of them in a bookstore in 1972.[18] But along with composer Charles Strouse and writer Thomas Meehan, Charnin completely reinvented Annie. On the eve of the show's Broadway debut in 1977, Charnin told the *New York Times*, "Notice we don't call our show 'Little Orphan Annie.' We call it 'Annie.' We want to distinguish between Gray's view and ours." He emphasized that his was not a comic strip musical like *Lil' Abner* but an original musical inspired by the comic strip, without a single line borrowed from its source. (This isn't true, of course—one of the early comics contains the line "It's the hard-knock route for us," and the musical includes Annie's catchphrase "leapin' lizards!")[19] Still, if the goal of the comic strip was to spread the very American message of self-determination, the musical would become an argument for the equally American message of optimism, one that still ignored the bigger picture in favor of spinning an individualist fairy tale.

Among the distinctions from Gray's vision: the only characters Charnin, Strouse, and Meehan kept were Annie, Sandy, and Warbucks, though regrettably the 1982 movie reintroduced two Warbucks servants—the Asp and

Punjab—who are racist caricatures. The trio of creators set the show in New York City as opposed to the nameless or made-up locations of the comics. Time-wise, they settled on 1933, during the Great Depression (the musical closes with "A New Deal for Christmas," sung by Oliver Warbucks, FDR, and the rest of the cast).

"At the time that I was writing the musical . . . President Nixon was in the White House, the Vietnam War was still going on, the country was in a deep economic recession, and there was a growing sense of cynicism and hopelessness among millions of Americans, including me," Meehan wrote in a 1977 essay for the *New York Times*. "And it struck me that Annie could in the musical become a metaphorical figure who stood for innate decency, courage and optimism in the face of hard times, pessimism and despair."[20] In other words, like *Little Orphan Annie*, the musical was designed as a not-at-all-subtle American allegory. This time, Annie's resolve to always look on the sunny side was not a plug for free will but a reminder that better days are always just around the corner—or, as "A New Deal for Christmas" puts it, "Those happy days that we were promised / are finally here."

Whereas Gray's comics relied on Annie constantly being orphaned, the Broadway version would find a way to give her a happily-ever-after with Warbucks without flattening the narrative arc immediately—a subplot about finding Annie's real parents. The show opens with Annie in the dreary orphanage, laid up in the crowded dorm with other little girls wearing tattered rags, dolefully fingering the broken locket that her parents dropped her off with. She sings "Maybe," a song of her hopes for her family, a vision of domestic bliss.

Of course, this thread of actually acknowledging Annie's grief and yearning is short-lived. Quickly we're introduced to the wicked Miss Hannigan, hapless spinster proprietress of the orphanage, who demands that the girls constantly tell her they love her. She wakes them up at the crack of dawn to begin scrubbing the place into shape. They set about their work and sing "It's the Hard-Knock Life," whose disturbing lyrics are undercut by the little girls' high-pitched voices and the blares of jaunty horns. "No one cares for you a smidge / when you're in an orphanage!" the girls yell, using mops and buckets as dance props and their beds as gymnastics trampolines. Watching footage of the musical now, I am struck by how bizarre it is that a song about parentless children getting kicked and having empty bellies has been beloved by generations of children.

As in the comics, Annie doesn't spend too much of the musical under Miss Hannigan's thumb. After a brief attempt to run away and try to find her parents, Annie is chosen to spend Christmas with Oliver Warbucks at his mansion. The industrialist quickly falls in love with her. When he buys her a locket from Tiffany's to replace her old broken one, though, Annie bursts into tears, saying it's the only thing she has left of her parents. Warbucks vows to find them with the help of the FBI, and the mansion workers sing "You Won't Be an Orphan for Long," which emphasizes that their employer's wealth and status will make all the difference in the search: "Where other men would call it quits / And disappear / He'll use his fortune and wits / So never fear. . . . You're with a man who always wins / Trust him and he'll prove / Mountains easily move." Again, the problem of orphanhood is presented as being solvable with individual will, wealth, and political favor.

From there, we move on to the $50,000 reward offer on Bert Healy's radio show and Miss Hannigan, Rooster, and Lily's scheme to use their knowledge of Annie's locket to pretend to be her parents. In the midst of all of this, Charnin injects a political plot point: Annie and Warbucks travel to Washington, DC, to meet with FDR, where she sings "Tomorrow" for him, her optimism ultimately inspiring the creation of the New Deal. It's a lot, I know. Roosevelt and the Secret Service later show up at the Warbucks mansion with the news that Annie's real parents are dead—news that is met with celebration, not grief, since this means "Daddy" can adopt her.

To tie everything up with a nice bow, the other orphans are all adopted too by Warbucks's wealthy friends. This admission of the fact that there are many more orphans who need assistance would be welcome were it not simply used to reiterate that the solution to orphanhood is for those among us with more to make the personal decision to "save" those who have less. It's a particularly odd choice in a musical that celebrates the New Deal, the first time our country made steps toward real social welfare for the collective good—a real solution to the real problem of orphanhood.

Despite, or more likely because of, the convoluted and overly pat plot, people ate up this nostalgic, rags-to-riches version of Annie's story—the musical swept the 1977 Tonys, winning best musical, best book, best score, and four other awards.[21] National tours started while the musical was still running on Broadway, and it premiered in the West End in 1978. *Annie* would later get two Broadway revivals, in 1997 and 2012, and become go-to fodder for children's theaters, like the one my cousin was part of not too long ago.

By the time the original Broadway run closed in 1983, the movie version had already hit the big screen—Columbia Pictures paid a record-setting $9.5 million for the rights.[22] The movie would further spread and cement Annie's story as the paradigm of orphanhood and life in an orphanage. It's a story we want to hear: one that makes us feel good about how poor, vulnerable, parentless children used to be treated. Solving their problems is as simple as rich folks choosing to spread some of their wealth; a little social welfare doesn't hurt either but isn't really necessary. The fates of Annie's real parents—their poverty and deaths—don't matter at all.

———

Given the overall optimistic message of Annie, it's not surprising that NBC decided to add it to the network's latest string of live musicals in December 2021. The production, starring Harry Connick Jr. as Warbucks, Taraji P. Henson as Miss Hannigan, Tituss Burgess as Rooster, and Celina Smith as Annie, was updated with a multiracial cast but otherwise hewed closely to the original. It was as though diversifying the casting was the only update the story needed.

As the *New York Times* review put it, "Perhaps it was only proper that this musical about earnest, plain-spoken yearning arrived on TV in 2021"—after all, it was "another challenging year" of a global pandemic.[23] That 120,000 American children had lost a parent or primary caregiver to Covid-19 when *Annie* hit our TV screens was not worth dwelling on.[24] Why worry about the fates of real orphans when the sun will come out tomorrow? It's better to keep telling ourselves this "appealingly simple" story, as the reviewer puts it.

But the true plight of orphans was never as simple as Annie's story. Believing in it for so long has allowed us to overlook the forces that led to the swell of religious-charity-led orphanages that would control the lives of our country's most vulnerable children and their families well into the twentieth century.

Chapter Two

INDOCTRINATING POOR CHILDREN

Perhaps the biggest fiction of Annie's story? The orphanage she escapes is always represented as secular. Her creator, Harold Gray, was himself a practicing Protestant, but while he had no problem spreading moral parables through his comics, he left religion out of the story.[1] When Martin Charnin, Charles Strouse, and Thomas Meehan updated Annie's story for the Broadway stage, they transformed the "home" into the fictional New York City Municipal Orphanage, a name that implies public funding and oversight.[2] Somehow it makes more sense that drunken, flamboyant Miss Hannigan operates under the radar of city bureaucracy rather than private benefactors, religious or not.

Setting an orphan narrative in a religious institution can be a tricky business that risks narrowing your audience, either by alienating members of other sects or offending believers themselves. But the secularization of these institutions in stories from *Little Orphan Annie* to contemporary American children's books like T. J. Klune's 2020 *New York Times* best seller *The House in the Cerulean Sea* is an odd—and total—revision of history. From the start, American orphanages were predominantly run by religious groups that felt a vocational call to care for parentless and needy children. By the mid-nineteenth century, as a series of epidemics, the Civil War, and swells of immigration and population growth born of the rise of industrial capitalism left more children in need of care, Catholic orders and Protestant-run charities were opening orphanages at a rapid clip. They served not only actual orphans whose parents had died but far more poor children with living parents, and they did so not just out of charitable benevolence but to propagate and preserve religious culture.

The history of orphanages in the United States is inextricably bound with religious charity. It was privately run and funded religious charities that first stepped in to care for dependent children, a fact that would have huge repercussions for the delayed and piecemeal development of American social welfare policy. Some of the religious charities founded in the 1800s still exist today, having adapted with the times to change their purview to foster care. They see their involvement in this space as traditionally guaranteed and sacrosanct.

Obviously, orphans have always existed in America because there have always been children who lose their parents before they reach adulthood. In the colonial period, orphaned children typically would have been taken care of by extended family members or apprenticed or indentured in the community—put to work for their keep.[3] This was well before children were seen as anything more than small adults who acted as a key source of labor within families.[4] Children were still commonly indentured throughout the nineteenth century, as evidenced by James Whitcomb Riley's "Little Orphant Annie" poem.

Still, about half a dozen orphanages opened in the 1700s, all but one of them operated by religious charities. The first orphanage in what would become the United States was established in 1729 New Orleans by a French convent of Ursuline nuns. The orphanage served a group of Catholic children whose settler parents died while fighting the Native Americans whose land they occupied.[5] On the Protestant side, one of the earliest orphanages has a more notorious legacy. In 1738, Reverend George Whitefield founded Bethesda Orphanage south of Savannah, Georgia. Whitefield was one of the leaders of the evangelical First Great Awakening, a revivalist

Protestant movement that spread through theatrical, extemporaneous preaching. Bethesda, Hebrew for "house of mercy," was to serve both actual orphans and poor children who Whitefield deemed would be better off in his institution even if they had families.[6] He hoped to convert the children to Methodism and train some for ministry. In other words, even one of the very first orphanages was in the business of separating families and inculcating children. When the cost and maintenance of running Bethesda outpaced both Whitefield's fund-raising abilities and what hired servants could manage, Whitefield successfully advocated for reintroducing chattel slavery to Georgia, where it had been deemed illegal years earlier.[7] Slave labor would make it possible to care for dependent white children.

In the nineteenth century, a perfect storm of conditions left behind a sizable population of children in need of care and led to a proliferation of orphanages. The first impetus was a series of epidemics that orphaned children all over the country. In 1793, yellow fever broke out in Philadelphia, killing about 10 percent of the city's population.[8] The outbreak led to the 1797 founding of the city's first private orphanage, the Catholic St. Joseph's Orphan's Asylum, which sat just a block away from a potter's field, where victims of the epidemic were buried alongside Revolutionary War soldiers.[9] Cholera, meanwhile, hit the United States in successive waves throughout the mid-nineteenth century, each outbreak killing between 5 and 10 percent of the population in major cities.[10] Up until the Civil War, when 750,000 men died in battle, leaving behind widows and half orphans, the cholera epidemics are estimated to have spurred the creation of the largest number of orphanages.[11]

But even though mortality rates were high and life expectancies were low throughout the nineteenth century, the growth of the orphanage can't just be chalked up to parental death. During the period when orphanages were most common, the majority of children who ended up in them weren't actually full orphans at all—a fact that shocked me at first because my experience of the label "orphan" is so colored by our stories about helpless, parentless children. Instead, during the nineteenth century, the majority of children in orphanages had one or two living parents who were simply too poor to take care of them, a situation that only became more common as time wore on. By 1890, less than a quarter of children who lived in what the US Census

called "benevolent institutions"—organizations "devoted to works of benefi-
cence . . . some which receive no compensation for the service rendered other
than that derived from gifts"[12]—were full orphans; about a fifth had two
living parents, and more than half had one living parent.[13] During the 1930s,
when the number of orphanages in America peaked at approximately sixteen
hundred, only about a tenth of institutionalized children were full orphans.[14]
The growth of the orphanage was the product of more and more people fall-
ing into desperate poverty.

It's especially notable, then, that in most of our favorite orphan stories,
the protagonists are actual orphans with dead parents. In the musical *Annie*,
the plot hinges on the search for the parents who left Annie at the orphanage when she was a baby—and the revelation that they are actually dead. It
beggars belief that Annie is a full orphan in the early 1930s, when the vast
majority of children in orphanages had living parents. We prefer the back-
story of parental death to a reality where parents are unable to care for their
own children. The potency of this fantasy, where children end up institutionalized because their parents have died, speaks to how much we want to avoid
thinking about the desperation that poverty wreaks.

By the turn of the nineteenth century, the early stages of industrial capitalism
were beginning to upend and reorder society, landing many Americans in
poverty and creating more dependent children. Wage labor spread, meaning
that instead of working as independent craftsmen or farmers, many Americans were employed by others for the first time.[15] An oversaturated labor
market and weak unions kept wages low. To make matters worse, work was
often only available seasonally, and mechanization threatened some trades.[16]

Industrialization also spurred mass immigration, exploding the country's population from thirteen million in 1830 to sixty-three million in 1890,
nearly a fivefold increase. People migrated into cities, swelling urban populations and further surfeiting labor markets, which drove wages even lower
and made employment even more precarious. In New York City alone, the
population grew from approximately sixty thousand in 1800 to half a million
in 1850, with nearly a quarter million foreign-born residents.[17] Immigration
and migration also took people away from the families and communities that

could care for their children in a time of need. If in 1850 New York City, say, your husband died, and you were not able to earn enough to support your children, you likely couldn't ask a relative for help. Instead, you'd turn to one of the city's orphanages.

Nationwide, orphanages were opening at a rate that proportionally outpaced population increases, growing from about 30 institutions in 1830 to more than 550 institutions in 1890.[18] But they weren't the only kind of isolationist institution that grew during the nineteenth century. During the Jacksonian era, roughly from the early 1820s to 1840, Americans reacted to the changes brought by industrial capitalism by segregating societal "deviants"—anyone who fell outside the norm, namely the poor, criminals, and the insane. These groups were institutionalized in their respective, dedicated asylums: the poorhouse, the penitentiary, and the insane asylum.[19] The term *asylum* emphasized that the "inmates" locked up inside were deemed unable to care for themselves. Early-nineteenth-century Americans were acting on their fears in a moral panic, attributing the new "disorder" of society not to the forces of the market-driven economy, which left wage workers vulnerable to poverty and caused them to pack into cities to find work, but to a lack of willpower. But while penitentiaries, poorhouses, and insane asylums were meant to punish adult "deviants," poor children were seen as requiring special protection—both from the society around them and from their own parents. Many orphanages during this time called themselves orphan "asylums," pointing to a contradiction at the heart of their work. An asylum both provides refuge and assumes a need for reform.

The distinction between the "deserving" and "undeserving" poor created a special motive for charity toward orphans and dependent children. The "undeserving" poor were seen as "able-bodied" and capable of working but too lazy or undisciplined to do so. The "deserving" poor, on the other hand, were those who could not work and therefore were deemed worthy of assistance, specifically elderly widows, the ill, and the very young.

Children in particular were "deserving" because, over the course of the nineteenth century, they came to be seen as innocents, blameless for the moral flaws of their poor parents.[20] The new presumed purity of children was a huge divergence from the Puritan conception that even children were marred by original sin and predestined for hell, though some portion of them would be "elect"—blessed and saved by God. In 1864, when prominent educator and Presbyterian Catharine E. Beecher wrote *The Religious Training of Children in the School, the Family, and the Church*, she claimed that children were not constrained by original sin. Instead, their souls and minds were tabulae rasae, and it was a (middle-class) mother's job to educate them spiritually and stimulate them intellectually.

In the process, upper- and middle-class families went from valuing their children's economic potential as laboring contributors to the household to prizing their children for their innocence, purity, and kinship bonds. Children became what sociologist Viviana Zelizer has pithily termed "economically 'worthless' but emotionally 'priceless.'"[21] The new value of childhood spurred charity for poor children, too, who were not only innocent and priceless but malleable. While charity workers may have given up on trying to reform "undeserving" poor adults, poor children stood a chance of not suffering their parents' fates if they had a change of environment to an orphanage, where their moral character could be shaped.

The rise of orphanages in the United States would not have occurred were it not for religious belief and the charity born of it. States and local governments didn't start passing laws about children's welfare or opening public orphanages in earnest until after the Civil War, and by then they were far outnumbered by private, religious orphanages. The federal government, meanwhile, did not take the first steps toward getting involved in child welfare until after the turn of the twentieth century, and not until the New Deal in the 1930s would federal policy actually begin to make an impact on the lives of poor children and their families. In the vacuum created by the lack of government care, religious charity stepped up.

The vast majority of the orphanages that opened in the 1800s were run by religious charities, and nearly all were run by either Protestant groups, which founded about 280, or Catholic orders, which led the charge with about 350. Jewish groups opened orphanages to care for their own children as well, but there were only about twenty-one of these around the country in the 1800s.[22] Even supposedly "nonsectarian" private orphanages were anything but. They were actually Protestant run but pooled the resources of churches and voluntary groups that practiced different flavors of Protestantism—like Methodists, Presbyterians, and Episcopalians working together.[23] Children at these orphanages were ultimately inculcated with generic Protestant teachings.

Nineteenth-century Protestant orphanages mostly came to be because of the voluntarism of middle- and upper-class Christian women, who saw it as their duty to help those who had not been so blessed.[24] Charitable work—especially serving orphans and poor children—was part of women's rightful sphere, in no small part because it extended their role as mothers, a role that only grew in importance as children became more "innocent" over the course of the century.

The story of New York City's first private orphanage, the Orphan Asylum Society, exemplifies how middle- and upper-class Protestant women banded together to establish institutions to care for full orphans, the children of widows, and poor children. The woman who spearheaded the founding of the Orphan Asylum Society, the Scottish-born Presbyterian philanthropist Isabella Graham, was herself a widow. After her husband's death, Graham settled in New York because she believed "that America was the country where the church of Christ would eventually flourish."[25] In 1797, she and a group of similarly faithful women started a society to support poor widows and their children. By 1806, Graham had taken in six orphans whose widowed mothers had died, and she enlisted her daughter Joanna, as well as Eliza Schuyler Hamilton—yes, of the Schuyler sisters; yes, the widow of the orphan Alexander Hamilton—to help her establish the Orphan Asylum Society in Greenwich Village.[26] When orphanages fell by the wayside in the mid-twentieth century, the society adjusted its purview to foster care and, in 1977, changed its name to Graham Windham, as it exists today. Graham Windham boasts of its early history on a website that capitalizes on the popularity of the musical *Hamilton*: "215 years later, Eliza Hamilton's orphanage—now a family services agency called Graham Windham—is still helping kids get their shot."[27]

Catholicism, meanwhile, has always emphasized that the poor are the most marginalized, and their need should be put first. At the Catholic high school I attended after my parents died, this kind of service undergirded my education to the point that, in order to be inducted into the National Honor

Society, I had to complete at least a hundred hours of volunteering each year. I packed brown bag lunches for homeless shelters, organized hand-me-downs in a local parish's donation closet, and plated spaghetti dinners at fund-raisers for children with terminal illnesses.

Tending to the needs of poor, innocent children, with or without living parents, perfectly meets the Catholic service rubric. Like Protestant orphanages, Catholic institutions were run primarily by women. The Catholic women were not well-to-do wives and widows but religious sisters who had taken vows committing themselves to poverty, chastity, and obedience in the service of God, furthering the mission of Jesus Christ.

The first American congregation of sisters, the Sisters of Charity, was founded by Elizabeth Ann Seton in Maryland in 1809 and modeled after Saint Vincent de Paul and Saint Louise de Marillac's French order Daughters of Charity.[28] Like the Daughters of Charity, Mother Seton's sisters dedicated themselves to caring for the poor. Soon this mission included serving orphans specifically. In 1814, Mother Seton sent three sisters to Philadelphia to care for children at a local orphanage.[29] The pattern would repeat in 1817, when another trio of sisters established the Roman Catholic Orphan Asylum in New York City. Over the course of the nineteenth century, communities of the Sisters of Charity would open several more orphanages across the United States—and, notoriously, an institution for foundlings that became the Catholic answer to Protestant-run orphan trains.[30] An added benefit of having nuns like the Sisters of Charity run Catholic orphanages was that, unlike the superintendents at Protestant orphanages, they didn't expect to be paid, helping stretch budgets. In the early years of the boom, funding for both Catholic and Protestant orphanages came primarily from congregants' and wealthy community members' donations.[31]

Yet religious beliefs and altruism weren't the only things driving Protestants and Catholics to care for poor and orphaned children. By running orphanages, they also reproduced and protected their values, indoctrinating the wards under their care and making sure that Catholic children stayed Catholic and Protestant children stayed Protestant—a mission especially relevant for children who had been separated from their parents' religious tutelage.

At the time, Protestantism was the default religion in the United States, and anti-Catholic sentiment was strong throughout the nineteenth century and further inflamed by anti-immigrant animus as waves of Catholics—like my own ancestors—from Ireland, Italy, and elsewhere flocked to the country. It's not surprising that many Protestant orphanages attempted to isolate, convert, and Americanize poor Catholic children at their institutions.[32] This only strengthened Catholics' motivations to open more institutions to serve their own poor and parentless children in an effort to protect their souls. The competition between Protestants and Catholics over who got to minister to the needs of vulnerable children was constant throughout this era. Both Protestants and Catholics continued establishing more orphanages in the 1890s to make sure that *their* poor children wouldn't end up in the others' hands.[33] While charity might have been the overt justification for opening orphanages, the opportunity to exert religious control over dependent children was undoubtedly a strong motive.

In fictions like Annie's, a life at the orphanage is primarily one of deprivation. Without parents or a family to speak of, children suffer from a lack of love and belonging. That foundational deprivation is compounded by all the other things they experience—from lack of sufficient food to eat to chores they are forced to complete.

This is one arena where our cultural imagination isn't too far off the mark. As much as orphanages in the nineteenth century tried to portray themselves as large family homes, institutions could never meaningfully stand in the place of a real home or real family. Instead, they were heavily regimented places where children were treated not as individuals but as cogs in a machine, especially at Catholic orphanages, which on average had about 140 children in care at any given time.[34] This kind of congregate care meant that the day to day followed a rigid pattern, with little room for deviation.

Daily life at a religious orphanage in the nineteenth century went like this: Every morning before the crack of dawn, you'd be woken up in a large dormitory, where you slept in rows of small beds among dozens of other children. Even if the orphanage was coed, you would often only interact with children of your same sex. If you were little, the bigger kids might help you wash up (not a full bath, as that was a once-weekly group event with shared water) and dress in your rough, scratchy uniform to get ready for prayers. At the Catholic St. Vincent's Orphan Asylum in Philadelphia, you'd attend a full mass in German every morning.[35]

Then you'd file out of the chapel to eat your first meal. The mush and milk that Annie eats at "the home" in the comics and the gruel that Oliver Twist infamously begs for more of are not bad estimations of what you might have been fed at breakfast, lunch, and dinner. Orphanages mostly served food that was cheap and easy to make in large quantities and did not necessarily meet children's nutritional needs. Not until toward the end of the nineteenth century might you start to regularly encounter vegetables in orphanage dining rooms. Meat and fish made limited appearances at dinner time, often in the form of thin soups. Before and after meals, you'd pray, but in many institutions, you would have to remain silent while you ate.

While stories like Annie's tend to leave education out of the picture—in the comics, the redhead never seems to attend school, whether inside or outside "the home"—schooling was actually how residents at orphanages spent large chunks of their days. You'd likely attend school inside the orphanage, especially if the institution was anything other than Protestant. In the mid-nineteenth century, many states had public schooling systems, but those schools were still reflective of the dominant Protestant society at large. Catholics were especially wary of public school, and the religious sisters who ran the orphanages were also tasked with teaching their charges. In the orphanage, you would learn how to read, write, and do basic arithmetic—and, most importantly to the charities funding your education, you'd get moral and religious training to shape you into a good Protestant, Catholic, or Jew.[36] Your schooling would probably stall out at the elementary level, though this was true for most American children at the time.

Outside praying, eating, and learning, you wouldn't have much time for anything other than chores, and the people who ran orphanages liked it that way: if they kept you busy, you'd have less idle time to get into trouble. Your chores would also help keep the orphanage running; essentially, you earned your keep by dusting, sweeping, and scrubbing floors (yes, as in "it's the hard-knock life"), mending and washing uniforms, and helping cook and serve meals. This kind of work was part of your training, especially if you were a girl who was expected to become a domestic servant and later a housewife. If you did have the time and energy to step out of line, you'd be subjected to corporeal punishment—a paddling or whipping, most likely. Given that you would have been among society's most powerless—a child with either no parents or poor parents, with no means to stand up for yourself—and that the outer world would have seen your caretakers as benevolent and selfless, you were especially vulnerable to abuse.

At its best, life at an orphanage in the nineteenth century was regimented; at its worst, it was nightmarish. But for the vast majority of children, it was temporary, only lasting one to four years on average, not their entire childhoods—another departure from some of the tales we know.[37] You might at first think that this brief stay can be chalked up to the fact that children in orphanages were just waiting for adoptive parents to save them à la "Daddy" Warbucks, but this, too, is a myth. Adoption as we now know it was not much practiced before the 1920s, and at any rate most children in orphanages weren't available for adoption. Their living parents maintained guardianship. Parents visited their children in the orphanage as frequently as they were allowed, wrote letters to caretakers and managers to keep tabs, and often paid small fees for room and board in what amounted to child support given directly to private orphanages.[38] In other words, many orphanages preserved rather than severed family ties. Most children would return home as soon as their parents or other family members could afford to care for them again (or, more grimly, as soon as the children themselves were old enough to work and contribute to the household finances).[39]

My own imagination had been so skewed by popular culture that I was surprised to learn that most children only spent a couple of years in institutions before reuniting with their families. When my parents died, I had assumed children who had no families at all—no parents, no grandparents, no aunts or uncles or older siblings—ended up in orphanages and had no means of leaving until they were adopted or came of age. I had been so steeped in narratives about orphanages by that point—and so sheltered as a middle-class white kid on Long Island—that I assumed the institutions still existed and that my brother and I would have ended up in one if we had been so unlucky as to have no familial protectors. Foster care was only a dim, mushy entity in my mind back then and was certainly not a system I imagined myself getting mired in.

My ignorance makes sense when you consider the big cultural myths about orphanages—that they were secular, state-run institutions; that the children within them were actually parentless—and what those myths are designed to conceal. The reality is that from the late eighteenth century through the mid-twentieth, when the last orphanages finally closed their doors, these institutions were primarily in the business of providing temporary relief for poor families by caring for their blameless children and, in the process, inculcating them religiously.

I think we prefer narratives where the children in orphanages are actual orphans with no chance of reuniting with their families because we abhor the concept of parents voluntarily leaving their children at institutions. Part of this can be explained by our tendency to apply modern ideas about childhood and the nuclear family to a historical period where they don't belong. Yet, even in the nineteenth century, many people assumed the worst of the poor parents who utilized orphanages. They were thought to be "undeserving" and unfit, having brought their dire circumstances on themselves.

But leaving a child behind wouldn't have been an easy choice for any of the parents who deposited their children in the foyers of religious orphanages. Asking for this kind of help would have been a last resort. Still, for many poor parents, religious orphanages would have at least ensured that their children were housed, fed, and educated and that they could stay involved in their children's lives. It was the best option in a sea of bad ones, the worst of which was handing over your children to the poor law authorities, who would remand them to the poorhouse.

I had always thought of poorhouses—also known as almshouses—as British institutions. In my imagination, they were part of the system of punishment for paupers that Charles Dickens focused on in his fiction, from the workhouse where Oliver Twist suffers to Marshalsea, the Southwark, London, debtor's prison in which Amy Dorrit grows up and where Dickens's father was incarcerated when Charles was a boy. But America borrowed from the British model of poor laws and poor relief, and poorhouses were part of American life even before the country's founding, serving as a deterrent to and punishment for poverty.[40]

Unlike orphanages, poorhouses were established not by private, religious charitable groups but by local governments, which funded them through taxes.[41] They existed as part of a spectrum of solutions to the problem of poverty in the eighteenth and nineteenth centuries and were an extreme option, locking away the "undeserving" poor and segregating them from the rest of society. On the other end of the spectrum, most cities and states also provided what is known as "outdoor relief" to the poor, which is essentially what we would today call "welfare"—a form of public assistance meant to help the very poor.[42] In some places, outdoor relief might have come in the form of actual money; in others, it might have been food or fuel. Everywhere, it was meant to keep people in their homes and communities, "outdoors," rather than making them fully dependent on public relief "indoors" at poorhouses.[43]

As the social problem of poverty grew in the nineteenth century, and as attitudes about the "deserving" and "undeserving" poor deepened, outdoor relief became more controversial.[44] Those who were more well-off often blamed outdoor relief for supporting, on the backs of taxpayers, the lifestyles of lazy people who didn't want to work—an attitude that still exists today. Poorhouses presented themselves as the best way to aid the destitute because they were at once a source of relief and a source of punishment.[45] The food, lodging, and quality of life offered at the poorhouse couldn't be *too* good, because it would encourage more people to apply for relief and foster idleness and dependence. But life in the poorhouse couldn't be too harsh, either, because some of the people who ended up there were "deserving" poor who truly needed help and could not work. Even so, authorities expected people in poorhouses to be productive, to essentially keep the institutions running through their labor.[46] Not unlike prisons—their institutional cousins—poorhouses always had contradictory purposes and goals, and for this reason they were doomed to failure.[47]

A major reason why poorhouses failed? They lumped together all sorts of people under the same roof—elderly widows and people experiencing serious mental illness, alcoholics and sex workers, people who were experiencing a gap in available wage labor and people who were unable to work due to disability, and, worst of all, children.[48] In 1857, the New York State Legislature called public poorhouses "the worst possible nurseries; contributing an annual accession to our population of three hundred infants, whose present destiny is to pass their most impressionable years in the midst of such vicious associations as will stamp them for a life of future infamy and crime."[49] Since poor children were beginning to emerge as redeemable and impressionable beings who needed to be nurtured in the right environment, the idea that they would be contaminated by the derelict population of the poorhouse became unacceptable.

When state and local governments finally started taking some responsibility for child welfare toward the end of the nineteenth century, it was the result of an uproar brought on by the presence of "innocent" children in public poorhouses. But because private, religious orphanages were already dominant and well established in most places across the country, public officials stepped into a tricky situation. If they wanted to get children out of poorhouses and into institutions that were more suitable for their care—orphanages—they would have to either establish their own publicly funded orphanages or subsidize private orphanages. The latter option made more sense in places that already had a robust religious orphanage apparatus, but it also put states in the business of being responsible for the religious upbringing of children—in violation of the separation between church and state.[50]

The conundrum of public money for religious inculcation was at its most extreme in New York State. In 1875, the state legislature passed what came to be known as the Children's Law, which prohibited the placement of children in public poorhouses and mandated the removal of the approximately three thousand children already in them.[51] Instead, children should be placed at public expense in orphanages that matched their parents' religions—a stipulation that caused the number of private religious orphanages and the populations of children within them in the state to balloon even further. Orphanages received per capita payments from local governments, which essentially encouraged them to take in more children for more public money. The statewide orphanage population swelled from about twelve thousand to twenty-three thousand children after the first decade of the law's enactment, with one out of every one hundred children living in orphanages by the 1890s.[52] In New York City, the effect was especially dramatic: in the 1890s, one in every thirty-five children in the city lived in an orphanage.[53]

In New York and across the country, though, the only children deemed "innocent" and "deserving" enough to be served by orphanages were white children. For most child-saving charities, Black children were considered irredeemable—that is, if they were thought of at all. In much of the country, even as white childhood became imbued with special meaning, Black children weren't considered children. They weren't even considered human.

Chapter Three

BLACK CHILDREN, WHITE PROPERTY; BLACK ORPHANS, WHITE SAVIORS

When NBC's *Annie Live!* chose Celina Smith, a twelve-year-old Black girl from Atlanta with a booming voice, to play America's favorite orphan in 2021, critics lauded the bigger-picture meaning of the casting.[1] In *Variety*, Daniel D'Addario wrote that the choice "suggests a broadening in the number of children who can see themselves at the center of the story, singing and dancing and looking forward to tomorrow. This 'Annie' treats its Annie being Black (and her savior "Daddy" figure being white) as matter-of-fact. This is so inherent in the story that it needn't be dealt with further."[2]

If you looked through this colorblind lens, it was progress that America could imagine a little Black girl as Annie. It was progress that a little Black girl could rise from the "empty belly life / rotten smelly life / full of sorrow life / no tomorrow life" to be clad in the chosen orphan's signature red dress, her dark brown hair in ringlets, adorned with a big red bow. The diverse casting promoted equal opportunity optimism for all little girls who have longed to sing "Tomorrow" regardless of their skin and hair color.

In casting a Black girl to play the character we all think of as a pale-skinned redhead, *Annie Live!* wasn't making a point as consciously political as, say, that of *Hamilton*. But *Annie* the musical does potently propagandize American history. We tend to forget this, because *Annie* is fully engrained in American pop culture to the point that we scarcely think about the musical's underlying messages about orphanhood and family, focusing instead on its general sunny outlook on life. That's why the commentary on *Annie Live!* mostly revolved around what it meant for a Black girl to play the *role* of Annie rather than what it meant to imagine that a Black girl could have historically *been* an orphan like Annie. But if Annie is a symbol, a Black Annie is even more symbolic: of resolve and individualism, yes, but also of a world where opportunity and the hope of a better life are open to all. That world has never existed.

Retconning the story to make it seem like orphanages were integrated in the 1930s—and that transracial adoption was so acceptable as to be unremarked upon—serves to further obscure an aspect of American inheritance that we desperately need to acknowledge: throughout our history, Black children have always been considered the least deserving of having a family, the least likely to be seen as symbols of innocence and potential. America has a long and ongoing legacy of separating Black children from their parents that began during slavery, a legacy that is all too convenient to ignore when watching a talented kid like Smith render inclusive the same old story of resilience and optimism we want to hear.

I have started my history of orphanhood in America with the development of private religious orphanages in the 1800s, but I could have turned back the clock even further, to 1619, when the first ships of enslaved Africans reached the shores of colonial Virginia. Social work scholars Andrew Billingsley and Jeanne M. Giovannoni assert as much in their landmark 1972 book *Children of the Storm: Black Children and American Child Welfare*—the first-ever consideration of child welfare from a Black perspective. "In one sense it might be said that until 1865 slavery was the major child welfare institution for Black children in this country, since that social institution had under its mantle the largest numbers of Black children,"[3] they write.

Not only did chattel slavery "care" for the greatest number of Black children until the end of the Civil War, but it also gave the religious groups that established orphanages an out. Because orphanages were first developed when slavery was the law of the land, charitable institutions could serve poor white children—including European immigrants—without ever imagining that Black children might need their services. They never had to think of Black children as "orphans." "This factor alone," Billingsley and Giovannoni write, "ensured an inherently racist child welfare system."[4]

In calling slavery a child welfare system, Billingsley and Giovannoni don't mean to suggest that it protected Black children who were poor or vulnerable or in need of families. On the contrary, whereas some private orphanages sought to preserve white immigrant children's religious and cultural heritage—and to preserve their families by providing them with charity at a time of acute need so that they could later reunite—chattel slavery served as a means of intentional, forcible family separation and destruction. We can draw a line connecting this history and the way Black families experience our current child welfare system. As Black legal scholar and sociologist Dorothy Roberts—one of the most prominent voices challenging the status quo of the US child welfare system—argues, "Since its inception, the United States has wielded child removal to terrorize, control, and disintegrate racialized populations. . . . Today's child welfare machine, which systematically demolishes Black families, can trace its roots directly back to these practices designed to uphold racial capitalism over the course of US history."[5] Racism, in other words, is at the core of how our child welfare system was designed—a system that Roberts calls "rotten at the root."[6]

Chattel slavery turned Black children into white property. White slaveholders gained legal rights to enslaved people's children by way of a perversion of familial inheritance. Whereas English common law had dictated that children inherited their status from their fathers, in 1662 the Virginia colony passed a law that held that an enslaved woman's children would inherit her status at birth.[7] In other words, the state of being enslaved passed matrilineally, which was unusual in a patriarchal society like colonial America. Black children could become slaves—could become white people's property—from the moment of their birth.

This meant two crucial things for slaveholders. First, the law, which other colonies adopted, incentivized white men to rape the Black women they enslaved, since the progeny of such sexual assaults would become their property, enriching them further. This kind of totalizing dehumanization would have been bad enough, but slaveholders were not content to merely keep the enslaved children that they created via rape. Instead, to slaveholders, the children their enslaved women bore were pawns, not people. Owners sold children for cash and bequeathed them in their estates.[8]

Slaveholders didn't just sell family members away from each other to profit—they did so to foment fear, to punish, and to keep their property in line. Slaveholders who suspected potential rebellion or that their slaves might run away could threaten to sell the children that they—and not those children's enslaved parents—had legal right to.[9] "Family was one of the few bright spots in the long night of slavery, and the auction was the event that ripped enslaved families apart," writes historian Anne C. Bailey in "They Sold Human Beings Here," part of the *New York Times Magazine*'s "1619 Project," which in 2019 marked the four-hundredth anniversary of chattel slavery in America. "The very prospect of it cast a specter over the enslaved population like a slowly dilapidating roof: At any time, it could come down and destroy the inhabitants of an already-fragile dwelling."

In fact, in *The Negro American Family*, sociologist and civil rights activist W. E. B. Du Bois writes that the three "essential features of Negro slavery in America" were "1. No legal marriage. 2. No legal family. 3. No legal control over children."[10] Because enslaved Black people had no rights to stay together as a family, and because slaveholders saw them as capital, children were constantly separated from their families when they or their parents were sold away from one another. From about 1760 to 1860, 1.2 million enslaved people—including children—were sold in the United States.[11] Just in the Upper South—made up of Delaware, Maryland, Kentucky, Virginia, Tennessee, and North Carolina—approximately one-third of enslaved children were separated from their families.[12]

Historian Heather Andrea Williams's book *Help Me to Find My People: The African American Search for Family Lost in Slavery* records the ravages of these separations. Williams scoured newspaper ads placed by formerly enslaved people after Emancipation requesting information on their lost family members, as well as diaries, slave narratives, letters, and public records, to bring to life the grief, yearning, and other emotions that stemmed from the white decimation of Black families. "What amounted to a business transaction for owners could be a traumatic and defining experience in an enslaved child's life," Williams writes in prefacing the story of Kate Drumgoold, whose owner sold her mother to pay a substitute to serve for him in the Confederate Army during the Civil War—a particularly craven act. Drumgoold later recalled, "My mother was sold at Richmond, Virginia, and a gentleman bought her who lived in Georgia, and we did not know that she was sold until she was gone; and the saddest thought to me was to know which way she had gone, and I used to go outside and look up to see if there was anything that would direct me, and I saw a clear place in the sky, and it seemed to me the way she had gone, and I watched it three and a half years, not knowing what that meant, and it was there the whole time that mother was gone."[13] As Williams writes, Drumgoold's childhood ritual of looking up at the sky for her mother is one of mourning, "a practice infused with hope and a touch of magical thinking that allowed her to believe her mother was in the sky and would return just as suddenly as she had disappeared."[14]

While Drumgoold did not witness her mother's disappearance—her sale to another slaveholder—other Black children would forever be seared by the memory of themselves or their parents being sold away from each other at auction. When Charles Ball was four, his owner died in Maryland, and his entire family was split up at the auction block. As Ball wrote in a slave narrative in 1837, "My poor mother, when she saw me leaving her for the last time, ran after me, took me down from the horse, clasped me in her arms, and wept loudly and bitterly over me." His mother's new owner "snatched me from her arms, handed me to my master, and seizing her by one arm, dragged her back towards the place of sale. My master then quickened the pace of his horse; and as we advanced, the cries of my poor parent became more and more indistinct. . . . I never again heard the voice of my poor mother."[15] Fifty years later, Ball wrote, "the terrors of the scene return with painful vividness upon my memory."[16]

If our society doesn't want to dwell on the concept of poor white parents voluntarily leaving their children at orphanages, accounts of the forcible separations of enslaved Black parents from their children are almost too much to bear. They are a reminder of the worst of human cruelty, of the total lack of agency and humanity afforded to Black people for most of American history.

We don't typically grapple with this history. We scarcely teach our children about what life was really like for enslaved Black people at all, let alone how common it was for families to be separated at the auction block.[17]

Perhaps this sort of limited-at-best education is why we pretend that it is not in our country's legacy to separate children from their families. The thesis of gender studies scholar Laura Briggs's 2021 book *Taking Children: A History of American Terror* is that, in fact, doing so "may be as American as a Constitution founded in slavery and the denial of basic citizenship rights to Native people, African Americans, and all women."[18] Children were taken under slavery "in a very brutal kind of political punishment, a symbolism—and reality—that is meant to be starkly tangible, crude, and cruel."[19] Splitting enslaved families apart did not just lead to grief and pain for individuals. It was part of what Briggs calls "a sadistic political grammar." As she points out, "There is a reason why 'forcibly transferring children of the group to another group' is part of international law's definition of genocide. . . . Stripping people of their children attempts to deny them the opportunity to participate in the progression of generations into the future."[20]

While the separation of enslaved families was normalized in America for more than two hundred years, by the mid-1800s abolitionists were forcing the country to recognize just how cruel and inhumane the practice was. In fact, harping on how slavery tore families apart was a successful abolitionist tactic. Harriet Beecher Stowe's 1852 novel *Uncle Tom's Cabin*—which Abraham Lincoln apocryphally claimed sparked the Civil War—famously includes an etching titled "The Separation of Mother and Child."[21] It depicts an anguished Black mother grasping after her son as a white man pulls him away from her at an auction; the boy stumbles back, reaching out toward his mother, while a white man in a top hat and tails, cigar in his mouth, watches dispassionately. It's the sort of image that other abolitionists regularly featured in their pamphlets and newspapers to drive home the horrors of slavery.[22]

Among the most prominent and dedicated abolitionists were the Quakers, whose religious beliefs dictate that all people are equal. Quakers are members of the Religious Society of Friends, a historically Protestant sect that experienced intense religious persecution in England because their belief that the spirit of God dwells within each person was considered heretical.[23] In the seventeenth century, many Quakers settled in the Pennsylvania colony, which was founded by prominent Quaker William Penn. Though it was common for Quaker colonists to own slaves in the 1600s and 1700s, they were also the earliest group to register antislavery beliefs in colonial America. In 1688, a group of Quakers in Germantown, Pennsylvania, published the first abolitionist protest by a religious body, with a petition that used the biblical golden rule to argue for equal human rights.[24] The document also specifically objected to how slavery tore families apart: "Pray, what thing in the world can be done worse towards us, than if men should rob or steal us away, and sell us for slaves to strange countries; separating housbands from their wives and children."[25]

Quakers weren't just outraged by how slave auctions disrupted Black families. They were also moved by the plight of vulnerable Black children in free states. Even in states where slavery was abolished early and Black people were nominally free, Black children lived under segregation and were regarded with intense racist animosity that fueled early-nineteenth-century hunts for fugitive slaves and antiabolitionist race riots.[26] This racism extended to the provision of charity toward so-called orphans. Derelict Black children could be admitted to the publicly run almshouses in free states—the same almshouses that aroused outcry when it came to considering the plight of poor white children—but were barred from almost all private orphanages.

One of the first orphanages that did accept Black children, the Association for the Care of Colored Orphans, was founded in Philadelphia in 1822 by a group of Quaker women.[27] In its annual reports, the association referred to the orphanage as a "family," boasting a homey, rather than institutionally regimented, atmosphere.[28] The fifth such report invited donors to "come and witness for themselves, how much comfort and enjoyment their liberality has provided for these poor orphans, and contrast their present appearance in their neat school rooms or pleasant play-ground, with the suffering and destitution which would have probably been their lot, had not this home been provided for them."[29] These Quaker women were moved by the same ideas about orphanages representing a healthy, morally upright environment for destitute children as the Protestants and Catholics. The difference was that their religion dictated that Black children were "deserving."

The most famous—and infamous—Quaker orphanage exclusively for Black children was the similarly named Association for the Benefit of Colored Orphans, also known as the Colored Orphan Asylum (COA), founded in New York City in 1836. The story of the COA's founding has varied depending on who is telling it but goes something like this: In 1834, Anna H. Shotwell and her niece Mary Murray, both Quakers, were walking in lower Manhattan when they came upon two small Black children who were either playing or huddling sadly on the steps of a dilapidated house.[30] The children were "dirty, unkempt," as a centennial history of the COA put it.[31] Shotwell and Murray found out that they were orphans (or perhaps the children of fugitive slaves) being cared for by a woman (whose race varies from Black to white in historical recollections) who was trying to keep them out of the almshouse.[32] Shotwell and Murray emptied their pockets, giving the woman money to support their care. When the Quakers visited again a few days later, the woman was caring for six Black children, who all appeared clean and happy—their money had made a real difference.

This singular act of charity inspired Shotwell and Murray—daughters of founding members of the New York Manumission Society, alongside Alexander Hamilton and other wealthy white men—to establish their association two years later.[33] Twenty-three other women joined them as founding managers; two-thirds were Quakers, and the remainder Presbyterians and Episcopalians.[34] The orphanage itself wouldn't open until 1837—the women managing it struggled to find anyone who would rent them a home in which to care for Black children.[35] They ended up buying one on 12th Street between Fifth and Sixth Avenues, and that summer eleven children who had been living in the cellar of an almshouse moved in. Like most other orphanages, the COA would go on to admit full orphans and half orphans, as well as children who were abandoned and neglected, poor children dropped off by their parents, and some former slaves.[36] The managers drew the line at vagrant children they deemed to be bad influences and capped the admission age at eight because they felt older children would be harder to rehabilitate. Even for the Quakers, not all Black children were deserving.[37]

In fact, what animated the COA was not just a staunch abolitionist spirit but white saviorism. Though the managers of the orphanage were abolitionists themselves, they took pains to distance the COA from the abolitionist movement, writing in their first annual report that they would remain "entirely independent of the exciting questions that have lately agitated the public mind, in relation to the colored race."[38] They chose this "independent" pose cynically, in order to appeal to the largest number of potential donors, including wealthy white men who had profited from slavery but were dedicated philanthropists.[39] In fact, among the COA's funders was John Jacob Astor, the first multimillionaire in the United States and namesake of the Astoria neighborhood of Queens, Astor Place in Manhattan, and the Waldorf-Astoria Hotel.[40] Astor made his fortune in the fur trade and slave cotton.[41] And while the COA admitted recently emancipated children, it specifically left those children's stories out of its annual reports to avoid the impression that the orphanage sought to shelter runaway slaves.[42]

While white men who worked on Wall Street—itself historically intertwined with slavery as the site of New York's slave market—managed the orphanage's finances, white women managed the children in the orphanage.[43] As was the case with the well-to-do women who helmed the day-to-day operations at Protestant orphanages, working with children at the COA was a societally acceptable way for middle- and upper-class Quaker women to make a mark on the world outside their domestic spheres, precisely because doing so required drawing on their maternal instincts as well as their religious beliefs. Whereas the female leaders of religious orphanages that served white children looked upon the orphans they served as needing moral molding, the white women who ran the COA added a potent dose of white paternalism to their work. These women adopted a white savior stance, believing that they—and not Black people themselves—knew what was best for Black children. The COA's managers felt that in order to tend to their charges' moral and religious education, they needed to isolate them from the Black community.[44] The orphanage's determination to keep out Black influence stemmed from the fact that its managers believed many in that community to be immoral—bad influences, just like the "depraved" older children they kept out.[45]

The carefully controlled, isolating environment of the orphanage— as well as the practical education imparted and religious morals imposed there—would allow these white women to rehabilitate these poor Black children, to essentially assimilate them into Anglo-Saxon culture. But, as Billingsley and Giovannoni argue, this was a futile task: "Whatever education, religion, discipline, and an acceptance of popular morality might do for his soul, they could not change the color of the Black child's skin; and that was the source of his problems. . . . [B]ecause he was Black, however well he learned his lessons in the orphanage school for the colored, he would be refused admission to some states and denied the ballot in most others."[46] A Protestant orphanage might have been able to take a poor Catholic child whose family had emigrated from Europe and make her "American." But when the wards of the COA were turned out for indenture or otherwise left the orphanage, they reentered a world that barely considered them to be human. Individual charity focused on "rehabilitating" individual children would never truly work without societal reforms.

The racism of the outside world encroached upon the orphanage in the form of a violent mob in July 1863, as part of New York City's Draft Riots. The COA had moved twenty years earlier to a larger building, a four-story Greek revival with two wings, on Fifth Avenue between 43rd and 44th Streets, and in 1863 more than two hundred children were living there.[47] The United States was by then two years into the Civil War. In March of that year, Congress had passed the Enrollment Act—the nation's first draft—to replenish the Union Army.[48] Notably, the act conscripted not just able-bodied male citizens between the ages of twenty and forty-five but also male immigrants who fit those parameters and had applied for citizenship. Wealthy men could avoid fighting by paying $300 for a commutation or up to $300 for a substitute to serve in their places. Though Black men fought for the Union—including several former inmates of the COA—they were excluded from the draft because they did not have citizenship.[49]

The Enrollment Act was especially hated by Irish immigrants in New York, most of whom could not afford to pay for a substitute or commutation. The Irish already saw Black New Yorkers as competition for menial labor jobs, and with the Emancipation Proclamation going into effect in January of that year, they feared a flood of freed slaves taking over their jobs—a fear the Tammany Hall Democrats and antiwar newspapers stoked.[50] When the first draft lottery in New York City was finally called in July 1863, it inflamed the Irish population's tense hatred for Blacks like a lit match to tinder. The result was a five-day riot, with hundreds of white men and women targeting Black people with the intent to kill.

On the first day of rioting, a mob descended upon the COA, yelling, "Burn the niggers' nest."[51] African American historian William Seraile argues that the mob stormed the orphanage "because the majestic building underscored the success of blacks over the Irish. The children had clean linen to sleep on, food was plentiful, and meals were regular. The Irish complained that the wives and daughters of New York's swells provided them with the comforts of life."[52] In board meeting minutes compiled shortly after the riot, the COA managers recorded the horror and damages of the scene: "Some 500 of them entered the house. . . . After despoiling it of furniture, bedding, clothing & etc.—they deliberately set fire to it, in different parts—simply because it was the home of unoffending colored orphan children."[53] The building burned down, but the mob's thirst for blood was thwarted—all 233 children escaped. The children and their guardians somehow made it to a police station about ten blocks away, where they remained for three days before traveling by boat to Blackwell's Island—the notorious home of an almshouse, workhouses, prisons, hospitals, and an insane asylum—under police escort.[54]

In late July, the *New York Times* printed a letter to the editor that captured public opposition to the COA reestablishing itself on Fifth Avenue:

I am in favor of rebuilding the Asylum, but doing it in a suitable location. This building has been recently burned by a mob; who can tell when the next asylum, on the same spot, may follow suit? Better build at a distance from the mob, where they would not be likely to go, and out of this county. . . . We have had abundant proof—recently and years ago—that this City and County are very unfavorable places for institutions like this,—and the officers of the Asylum, knowing this, would be acting as accessories, if the building were again fired by a mob.[55]

It is remarkable that this letter writer blames the COA managers, and not racism, for the possibility that the orphanage would once again be vulnerable to arson. At any rate, the COA ended up bowing to public pressure and relocating to Harlem, eventually settling into a newly built home on 143rd Street between Amsterdam and Broadway. The Harlem location, where the COA would remain until a 1907 move to the Riverdale section of the Bronx, was only three blocks away from Alexander Hamilton's historic home.[56]

After the war, most orphanages were in no hurry to welcome Black children into the fold. Even in the North, they largely continued with their missions of rescuing poor white children and preserving their culture and religion (for the Catholics) or attempting to Americanize them (for the Protestants). In the South, some Black communities supported small orphanages, like the Reed Home and School in Georgia, founded in 1884 by a woman who had studied at the historically Black Atlanta University.[57] Unlike the large, regimented orphanages in New York City, these Black-run orphanages were more like boarding homes and served small numbers of children.

The fact was that after the war, Black children did not suddenly become symbolically innocent and deserving in the eyes of most Americans, especially in the South. Instead, they continued to be valued mainly as a source of free labor. Many former slave owners coerced newly freed parents who were struggling financially into agreeing to leave their children with them. Without the means to care for their children, freed parents hoped that their former mistresses would provide for them.[58] These Black parents were acting out of a similar desperation as the poor white parents who left their children at orphanages. The difference was that for Black parents, a country that had denied them personhood had all but guaranteed their poverty.

Adding to former slave owners' de facto practice of coercing newly freed parents to leave their children behind was a de jure campaign to keep Black people bound. Many Black children were functionally re-enslaved by their owners thanks to the Black Codes that passed in several states in 1865 and 1866. These laws were designed to restrict the freedom of Black people by placing limits on their ability to own property, lease land, conduct business, and move freely in public places. They also perverted the apprenticeship laws that already existed to yet again break up Black families, deeming that Black children whose parents were "unfit" were essentially orphans whom local authorities must have apprenticed, or "bound out," to white masters or mistresses.[59] In other words, for Black children in the Reconstruction era, the label "orphan" was merely an opportunity for white people to functionally turn them back into property.

Even the Freedmen's Bureau, established by Congress as a bureau within the War Department to materially aid newly freed Black people and refugees, to provide transportation to assist families in reuniting, and to manage apprenticeship disputes, was no help to these children and families.[60] In fact, the bureau participated in the placement of Black children with white planters. If the bureau determined that children were "orphans" or had been abandoned, it often chose to apprentice them out to white masters and mistresses, where they would remain until they were eighteen or twenty-one.[61] In the process, the Black Codes and the Freedmen's Bureau continued the separation of Black families well after the end of the war. As historian Stephanie E. Jones-Rogers points out, "Beyond ignoring the often tragic reasons for a freed parent's absence and placing a white southerner's need for labor over a black parent's love, these decisions also dismissed bonds of kinship between children and extended family members who were capable of giving them safe and comfortable homes."[62] But the safety and comfort of Black children scarcely mattered, even at a time when the American public was newly concerned with the maltreatment of white children.

Chapter Four

THE DAWN OF CHILD ABUSE AND THE PROGRESSIVE CAMPAIGN TO SAVE CHILDREN

In April 1874, a case of child abuse came before the Supreme Court in New York City that scandalized and galvanized the public. A nine-year-old girl named Mary Ellen Wilson took the stand dressed in calico with a gash on her face. She testified that Mary Connolly—a woman who had indentured her at eighteen months old after her impoverished mother was widowed and relinquished her to the city's Department of Charities and Correction—whipped her near daily, slashed her face with an open pair of scissors, and locked her up in the apartment to the extent that she had "no recollection of ever being on the street in [her] life."[1] Mary Ellen told the court, "I have never been taken on my mamma's lap and caressed or petted. I have never dared speak to anybody, because if I did I would get whipped."[2]

The girl's case reached the authorities only because a Methodist missionary worker named Etta Angell Wheeler had been visiting an elderly woman who once lived in a tenement apartment next door to the Connollys. The elderly woman described hearing Mary Ellen's wails for years and told Wheeler she could not die with a clear conscience unless something was done for the child.[3] Wheeler managed to corroborate the woman's account when Mary Connolly answered the door for her in December 1873. "While still talking with the woman, I saw a pale, thin child, barefoot, in a thin, scanty dress so tattered that I could see she wore but one garment besides," Wheeler later wrote of this encounter. She described Mary Ellen as a "tiny mite, the size of five years, though, as afterward appeared, she was then nine. . . . But the saddest part of her story was written on her face in its look of suppression and misery, the face of a child unloved, of a child that had seen only the fearsome side of life."[4] It didn't seem to matter to the authorities that Mary Connolly was in violation of her indenture agreement, which stipulated that she report on the child's condition yearly to the Department of Charities and Correction—the branch of city government in charge of almshouses, prisons, public hospitals, insane asylums, and the public indenture system.[5]

Wheeler eventually appealed to Henry Bergh, founder of the American Society for the Prevention of Cruelty to Animals (ASPCA), who took on the case personally even though the subject of abuse was a human child. This would become the stuff of legend, with the mythical invention that Bergh intervened because Mary Ellen was "a member of the animal kingdom" and therefore entitled to protection by the ASPCA.[6] In fact, Bergh had been reluctant to widen his philanthropic efforts toward children in the past but had somewhat recently petitioned the court to remove a child from an abusive caretaker who lived near the ASPCA offices after several neighbors reported the maltreatment to him.[7] Wheeler may have gotten the idea to contact Bergh about Mary Ellen after reading about that 1871 case in the newspapers. There was simply no one else for her to appeal to because there was no comparable association for child protection at the time—a damning fact in and of itself.

After an ASPCA investigator verified the abuse, Bergh had ASPCA attorney Eldridge T. Gerry petition to remove Mary Ellen via the ancient writ *de homine replegiando*—against unlawful detention—so she could testify before the court.[8] By the end of April 1874, Mary Connolly would stand trial and be found guilty of felonious assault and battery after a jury deliberated for just twenty minutes. The judge sentenced her to a year of hard labor.[9] Meanwhile, Mary Ellen became a ward of the state and was placed in Sheltering Arms, an institution for destitute and orphaned children, where she lived with older girls, "some of them wayward," a situation Wheeler found "most unsatisfactory."[10] Wheeler eventually convinced the judge to allow her mother, who lived upstate, to care for Mary Ellen.

That Wheeler's husband, Charles, was a reporter may have helped the case gain attention—it quickly became a story big enough to warrant more than a dozen detailed articles in the *New York Times* and other newspapers.[11] The reporting fed public interest, which spurred further journalistic commentary. In their second story on the case, the *Times* noted that "quite a number of persons, including several ladies, were attracted to the court by the publicity which had been given to the proceedings on the previous day, all of them evidently deeply sympathizing with the little neglected waif." By then, several people had already offered to adopt the child. The *Times*'s reporter initially described Mary Ellen in the phrenological manner that was popular at the time, calling her "a bright little girl, with features indicating unusual mental capacity, but with a care-worn, stunted, prematurely old look." Within a few days, some "humane ladies" had provided Mary Ellen with a new wardrobe, and the *Times* opined that she appeared "several years younger."[12] Both descriptions indicated that Mary Ellen was a little white girl worthy of saving, worthy of the public's care and love.

The case of Mary Ellen Wilson came at just the right time to spur the beginnings of child protection and child welfare as we know them today. Of course, children were being abused long before 1874. But the idea that children had rights—and that they were worth more to their families than their potential as contributors to the household economy—had only recently taken hold. Contributing to this new view of "priceless" childhood was the fact that children had a better chance of surviving past age five in the 1870s than they did earlier in the century.[13] With children living longer, it wasn't a stretch to believe that they warranted special shielding from maltreatment to further preserve their lives. And just as poor children had benefited from ideas around their "priceless" nature, the upper classes began to impose their morals around child rearing and the institution of the family on the poor as well. On the one hand, this helped protect poor children from abuse. On the other hand, parents of all classes could no longer freely choose how to raise and discipline their offspring within the walls of their own homes without the specter of outside judgment and intervention.[14]

It wasn't just the timing of Mary Ellen's case that allowed it to shift the public consciousness of child maltreatment. In the 1870s, other cases of even worse treatment—including of a child dying at the hands of his parents—were publicized in newspapers but met with little public outcry.[15] What made Mary Ellen's plight especially appealing? For one, she was functionally an orphan, vulnerable and pitiable, a tiny little white girl so obviously unloved and maltreated that she pulled at the heartstrings of "humane ladies" who were better off than the poor and unmotherly Mary Connolly. She was, in other words, an early archetype for Annie—especially after she underwent her makeover from "stunted" dirty child in rags to posing for portraits in frilly Victorian finery.[16]

The fact that Mary Ellen was nominally under the not-so-watchful eye of the Department of Charities and Correction as an indentured child further motivated the public to take up child abuse as a cause. Clearly, the city wasn't doing enough to supervise indenture placements. An April 1874 *New York Times* article likened the system to child slavery, arguing that surely many "waifs" like Mary Ellen were at risk of abuse:

> The terrible suffering that was crammed, in the case of Mary Ellen, into six years of what we call "happy childhood," makes us shudder over the possibilities of infantile sorrow that attend the career of the little waifs of our City population.
>
> For there is nothing to lead us to conclude that this is an isolated case. The Commissioners of Charities keep up a well-stocked child market, and anybody removed above the level of pauperism has only to go through the formality of signing an indenture to obtain the desired quantity of human flesh, on which to work experiments, brutal or otherwise. . . . The Commissioners of Charities have no agencies for checking abuses like this, and the costly machinery which we provide for the purpose of stopping the growth of pauperism and mendicancy may thus be converted into a very powerful stimulus of both.[17]

The lack of trust in the public system to protect "waifs," rooted in a not-so-subtle moral panic about poverty, pointed to a gap that needed filling. The first child protection organization, the New York Society for the Prevention of Cruelty to Children (NYSPCC), founded by Bergh and Gerry in December 1874, sought to fill that gap. The organization, which ran on charity but had the right, granted by the state legislature, to forcibly remove children and to arrest and prosecute abusive parents, quickly inspired other societies for the prevention of cruelty to children (SPCCs) nationwide; by 1910 there were more than two hundred.[18]

The acknowledgment of child abuse as a social problem led to a sea change in child welfare. In the past, children ended up in orphanages because their parents had either died or, more commonly, made the decision to leave them there in periods of distress. In other words, in a sense, the family remained in control of itself, though the religious bodies that ran the orphanages had latitude in the degree to which parents could see their children at the orphanage or regain physical custody when their crises had passed. It's true that before the dawn of the SPCCs, there had always been the possibility that local police or judges could remove children from their parents. But such cases made up a tiny proportion of the population in orphanages, and often local authorities were merely acting on behalf of the children's families rather than actively removing them from their parents.[19]

The creation of the SPCCs marked the beginning of family policing, where outside actors, largely from the upper classes, would get to decide which families deserved to stay together and which should be broken up. The poor were the most vulnerable to forcible family separation. In the process, society made a whole new kind of orphan. And after the turn of the century, a new argument would coalesce about what the country should do about these orphans once they had been "saved."

When the NYSPCC convened, its founders argued that the best way to prevent cruelty against children was to police and prosecute adults. Their law enforcement approach is reflected in the mission statement that Gerry wrote in December 1874, which declared the society's purpose was to "rescue little children from the cruelty and demoralization which neglect, abandonment and improper treatment engender; to aid by all lawful means in the enforcement of laws intended for their protection and benefit; to secure by like means the prompt conviction and punishment of all persons violating such laws and especially such persons as cruelly ill treat and shamefully neglect little children of whom they claim the care, custody or control."[20] The NYSPCC essentially acted as a specialty police force dedicated solely to the enforcement of criminal laws concerning "little" (innocent and precious) children, just as the ASPCA was dedicated to investigating and arresting people who violated laws against animal abuse. NYSPCC agents wore badges that identified them as members of what was colloquially known as the Gerry Society. Their daily work was not unlike that of modern-day child protective services caseworkers: they received complaints of abuse against children, investigated those complaints, made arrests, and brought prosecution against law offenders. A major difference was that the NYSPCC was not officially a part of the government and functioned as a private charity.[21]

The NYSPCC also actively sought to shape society through lobbying for the passage of new state laws concerning not just physical abuse but a wider remit of maltreatment and moral concerns. An 1876 law prefigured the modern meaning of "neglect" in requiring that guardians feed, clothe, supervise, and provide medical care for children.[22] There were laws regulating child labor—an 1886 law limited the child workweek to sixty hours (!) and barred employment of children in sweatshops and factories.[23] There were laws prohibiting the sale of intoxicants, guns, and tobacco to minors, regulating "obscene material," and preventing children from living in "drug dens and houses of prostitution"—nods to the temperance movement and moral reforms of the late nineteenth century.[24]

Animating all of this legal lobbying was not just a concern that children were experiencing cruel treatment at home, in the workplace, and in their communities but a fear that children in particular were at a risk of growing up to become deviants if they were exposed to the wrong kinds of environments—not just factories, sweatshops, and "drug dens" but, in many cases, their poor parents' homes.[25] Indeed, in its first annual report, the society made its bias against the poor clear, writing that its goal was "to seek out and to rescue from the dens and slums of the city those little unfortunates whose childish lives are rendered miserable by the constant abuse and cruelties practiced on them by the human brutes who happen to possess the custody or control of them."[26] The idea that poor parents were brutish people who only "happened" to have custody of their children made it easy to imagine that that custody could and should be easily severed.

Underneath the fear of child deviancy were class and ethic anxieties that sprang from how rapidly American life had changed over the course of the nineteenth century. After the Civil War, as the Second Industrial Revolution gathered steam and immigration skyrocketed, the national character shifted from small-town, largely rural communities to urban centers jammed with European immigrants and people from all over the country seeking factory work.[27] In New York City in particular, as the population grew, poverty became concentrated in slums and cramped tenements like the one the Connollys lived in. Native-born Protestants from the middle and upper classes saw their less fortunate, newcomer neighbors as the source of all the city's disorder—they were boisterous people who fought and indulged in drinking, uninhibited sex, and gambling, and their children seemed destined to repeat their uncouth ways if they were not saved.[28]

Unsurprisingly, both of the NYSPCC's founders were politically conservative, wealthy elites whose families had been in the United States since at least the early 1700s. Bergh's father owned a shipyard, and his biographer described him as having been born "into the landed aristocracy of New York's hard-working tradesmen," a hilarious oxymoron.[29] Gerry's background was even more illustrious—his namesake grandfather signed the Declaration of Independence and was vice president under James Madison.[30] That these men in particular took up the mantle of preventing cruelty to children in New York City meant that their goal was never solely about helping those "innocents." The children were a means to a larger end: social control via punishing adults, particularly poor immigrant parents.

Other SPCCs that took inspiration from the Gerry Society in the late 1800s sought to police families in a subtler manner. Founded in 1878, the Massachusetts Society for the Prevention of Cruelty to Children (MSPCC) developed a reputation for focusing on preventing such cruelty before it occurred—rather than punishing it after the fact—through an early form of social work.[31] Unlike the NYSPCC, which was founded and run by wealthy men, the MSPCC was heavily influenced by upper-class philanthropic women—the same sort of women who earlier in the century had been behind the founding of many Protestant orphanages. As some of their peers were advocating for women's suffrage toward the end of the nineteenth century, more conservative upper-class feminists focused on moral reforms like the movement against corporal punishment that grew out of new ideals of child rearing.[32] That the women who steered the MSPCC's board would advocate for a more maternal approach to child rescue makes sense.[33]

Still, the MSPCC limited the role of agent to men only. Agents ventured out onto the streets looking for children who were subjected to maltreatment, broadly defined—dirty children begging or peddling, or roaming Boston without shoes, for instance.[34] When MSPCC agents conducted home investigations in order to corroborate complaints, they weren't looking solely to have the adults at fault arrested. In many cases, they approached investigations like amateur social workers, following the "friendly visitor" tradition that Etta Angell Wheeler herself was practicing as a Methodist missionary.[35] "Friendly visitors" had no special training—they were charitably minded wealthy Christians who volunteered to help the poor, sick, and elderly by spending time with them in their homes, serving as moral role models.[36] Clearly, "friendly visiting" wasn't effective at actually remediating poverty, because it treated poverty as an individual failing that could be solved with good Christian advice.

The MSPCC and other child-protective societies that followed a preventative rather than punishment-centered philosophy, however, combined coercion with the "friendly visitor" approach. In an 1881 report, an MSPCC agent explained how they would use threats of arrest and prosecution to get parents to change their ways: "Many cases occur where the proof of neglect may not be sufficient to enable us to take the children, and where, if the parents will abandon the habit of drinking, it is better for them to remain. In these cases, with persuasion and warning, the parents are put on probation, recognizing always the parental rights."[37] The fact that this example focuses on supposed intemperance is telling, because drinking was a major bugaboo for the MSPCC, especially when it came to Irish immigrants indulging in beer or Italians in wine.[38] To the society, alcohol caused abuse, and any level of drinking was a symptom of depravity, creating an unfit home for children. Cultural norms—except those of native-born Protestants—did not matter to the MSPCC.

Whether they erred on the side of policing or prevention, SPCCs nationwide intervened in family life in an unprecedented manner. In the past, charities only got involved with families after the families themselves had sought assistance. Now, privately run charities rather than publicly elected officials were attempting to supervise and control what went on behind closed doors. In some cases, this kind of interference no doubt helped children who were suffering from grave maltreatment, like Mary Ellen Wilson. In others, though, SPCCs meddled in families because of xenophobic and classist beliefs. And as was the case with orphanages, only white children—or the children of European immigrants who could *become* white via Americanization—were considered worthy of saving, even after the Civil War. After all, if children were removed from their parents, they were liable to end up in orphanages anyway, and most still only served white children.

By the turn of the century, the fears that had catapulted the SPCC movement in the 1870s had only gotten worse. In his critical interpretation of the history and evolution of American social work and social policy, *The Altruistic Imagination*, John Ehrenreich calls the tumult of the last three decades of the nineteenth century "the chaos of the new industrial order."[39] Postwar, the Industrial Revolution was in full swing, and several related factors contributed to the chaos. First, there was the swelling population that resulted from industrialism and was driven by immigration and urbanization. That population experienced massive and previously unknown income inequality—this was the Gilded Age era of robber barons and unchecked capitalism. In response, the working class fought for their rights in a series of bloody strikes, and some supported radical ideas like nationalizing the means of production.[40] Amid all this labor strife, the country underwent a trio of economic depressions in the 1870s, 1880s, and 1890s.

In response to all this upheaval, Ehrenreich notes, "fear of endemic disorder and unrest, loss of confidence, generalized anxiety, were widespread."[41] The solution of upper-class religious charity to the poor, as had been de rigueur throughout the century, would no longer suffice to tackle this level of disorder; nor would "friendly visiting." A new, stronger form of control needed to be foisted upon the poor and working classes to stabilize society. The result was the Progressive movement for social reform and the professionalization of social work.

Ehrenreich argues that Progressivism was led by members of a group that he and his former wife, Barbara Ehrenreich, coined as the "professional-managerial class"—a new middle class made up of college-educated, salaried employees who replaced the independent businessmen, farmers, and professionals of the "old" middle class.[42] The professional-managerial class's new position of economic stability seemed especially vulnerable when faced with the possibility of mass unrest. At the same time, they saw an opening for control. Industrial capitalism may have upended the country, but it also led to economic surpluses in the coffers of both the public sector and private hands like those of the Rockefellers and Carnegies, who had started foundations to cleanse their reputations. As Ehrenreich points out, that money led to "the possibility (as well as evidently the necessity) for long-term economic and social planning, for the refinement of management and the rationalization of production and consumption"—and the need for people to take on the responsibility for all that refinement, regulation, and rationalization.[43] The Progressives were precisely those people.

A subset of Progressives was concerned with social policy and social justice—especially as it concerned immigrants, the poor, and their children—inspiring a new kind of social work just as a spirit of reform was sweeping the country. Politicians were enacting reforms of capitalism at the national level via the expansion of the regulatory state, from President Theodore Roosevelt's Pure Food and Drug Act (which created the institution that would eventually be known as the Food and Drug Administration) to President Woodrow Wilson's Federal Trade Commission, and at the level of the state via the passage of labor laws.[44] Social workers, meanwhile, sought to intervene at the level of the community and the family. And whereas in the past social work was practiced by amateur wealthy women like Etta Angell Wheeler and the board members of the MSPCC, the new social work of the early twentieth century would be a rational science, scientific methods being one of the main ways Progressives pushed "progress."

But social work faced an uphill battle to professionalization and rationalization, predominantly because, as in its "friendly visitor" past, it was a field dominated by women. As members of the professional-managerial class, the early female social workers like Jane Addams and Jessie Taft were motivated by more than the Christian call to service that prodded Protestant and Quaker women into charity work in the mid- to late 1800s. These twentieth-century women were college educated, but, as Ehrenreich notes, they lived in "a world that offered few practical outlets for their knowledge and skills—women caught in what Jane Addams called the 'snare of preparation.' They were socially concerned in a world that barred women from participation in the political process, and well prepared for traditional domestic roles in middle-class families, which seemed, to them, empty and oppressive."[45] Social work was an acceptable field for such women, just as charity work had been for women throughout the nineteenth century, because it was in many ways an extension of the domestic sphere.

Early social workers like Addams focused on a social reform model, one that believed in prevention first and foremost, not unlike the MSPCC did. This approach itself was a reaction against the scientific charity movement of the end of the nineteenth century, wherein charity organization societies (COSs) tried to rationalize almsgiving. One of the movement's goals was to weed out "unworthy" poor who were supposedly gaming the system by asking for aid at multiple charities at once—something that was possible thanks to the postwar proliferation of philanthropic organizations. A COS would bring local charities together into cooperatives, and COS workers—including "friendly visitors"—would investigate applicants for charity to assess if they were of the "worthy" or "unworthy" poor before distributing aid.[46]

Addams and other members of the professional-managerial class found the COS approach to be paternalistic and looked to the settlement houses that were popping up in London as a different model of working with the poor. The idea behind settlement houses was that young middle- and upper-class women and men would "settle" as "residents" in poor urban neighborhoods, serving as good neighbors to the poor by both teaching and learning from them about what their needs were and how they could best be supported.[47] In 1889, Addams, along with Ellen Gates Starr, opened what would arguably become the most famous of the settlement houses, Hull-House, on Chicago's Near West Side, in a neighborhood densely populated by European immigrants.[48] In living among the poor and the immigrants, Addams and other residents of settlement houses came to understand that the distinction between the "deserving" and "undeserving" poor was nonsensical and that poverty was the result not of individual moral failure but of environmental and systemic factors.[49] Hull-House sought to ameliorate and prevent poverty among the working class through means like running an employment bureau, offering meeting space for trade unions, and teaching cooking, sewing, and technical skills.[50]

But Hull-House was also enacting its own form of social control. On the one hand, Hull-House hosted cultural clubs for a wide range of ethnicities to support the cultural traditions of its neighbors. On the other hand, it sought to Americanize those same immigrant neighbors, enacting Addams's idea that "a much larger number of immigrants could be taken care of in this country and assimilated to advantage than was being done now."[51] Addams also promoted eugenic ideas, supporting the confinement of "feeble-minded" women to inhibit them from having children. In her book on prostitution and vice, Addams connected eugenics to children's rights: "When this new science makes clear to the public that those diseases which are a direct outcome of the social evil are clearly responsible for race deterioration, effective indignation may at last be aroused, both against preventable infant mortality for which these diseases are responsible, and against the ghastly fact that the survivors among these afflicted children infect their contemporaries and hand on the evil heritage to another generation."[52]

Unsurprisingly, given her support of eugenics, Addams's ideas on race were also colored by the white supremacy of the era. In 1899, inspired by journalist and activist Ida B. Wells, Addams took a stand against lynching, delivering a speech condemning a mob that had murdered a Black man in Kentucky. But to Wells's consternation, Addams's speech betrayed an assumption that the man had been guilty of rape and that Black men were "bestial" and "uncontrolled."[53] Not until the 1920s and 1930s, when Black Americans migrated to the neighborhood, would they begin to be meaningfully integrated into the programming at Hull-House.

Still, Addams was arguably one of the most prominent and successful children's rights activists of the era, and her work through Hull-House and through lobbying served to make life materially better for children around the turn of the century. Instead of separating families as the SPCCs did, Hull-House provided practical support to keep children at home. Residents ran a nursery and kindergarten and provided child care for working mothers; the complex also hosted Chicago's first public playground.[54] Beyond the

Hull-House complex, Addams was a force behind the movement for juvenile justice, which sought to treat children accused of crimes differently than adults, recognizing that childhood is a distinct developmental phase and that children deserve to be rehabilitated rather than punished. In 1901, she helped found the Juvenile Protective Association, which provided the first probation officers for the first juvenile court in the nation.[55] A few years later, Addams would also become one of the loudest voices against institutionalizing dependent children in orphanages.

In the SPCC era, the question of what to do with maltreated children after they were removed from their families remained open, as illustrated by Mary Ellen Wilson's case. The NYSPCC, for one, considered its job done once children were rescued, and it did not cooperate well with other child welfare charities to secure the futures of children removed from their families. They could be placed in orphanages like Sheltering Arms, from which they might be indentured out to an even worse situation than the one they had been removed from.

But by the turn of the century, Addams and other Progressive activists and social workers committed to the cause of child saving were arguing that heavily regimented, overcrowded orphanages were bad places for children to live and that a carefully supervised system of "placing out" children in loving foster homes ought to be the path forward. As political scientist Matthew A. Crenson argues in his book about the downfall of the institutional era and the makings of the modern American welfare system, *Building the Invisible Orphanage*, "the regime of the asylum" era had "assumed the malleability of individual character and its susceptibility to environmental influences, but the creation of the asylum was an admission that reformers lacked the means to manage the social environment itself." In other words, the people who ran orphanages believed that they could shape dependent children into moral citizens by segregating them from society at large in an artificial environment. On the other hand, he writes, Progressives "proposed to reform society itself in order to create the kind of environment in which to raise upstanding citizens."[56] It was Progressives' belief in their ability to make the world better and safer that led them to propose that orphans and dependent children should be deinstitutionalized—a pendulum swing away from the asylum-era attitude of isolating and protecting such children.

A man who had grown up in the Washington City Orphan Asylum was among the Progressives leading the charge in challenging the thinking of the orphanage era on the national stage. James E. West's widowed mother had left him at the Protestant orphanage in Washington, DC, in 1882, when he was five years old. She needed someone to watch her son while she sought treatment for the condition that had her coughing up blood in a handkerchief—it turned out to be tuberculosis. She'd die in Providence Hospital three months later, leaving West a full orphan.[57]

West would end up spending the remainder of his childhood at Washington City Orphan Asylum, and his early experiences there would shape his later activism against institutionalization. Shortly after West arrived at the orphanage, he complained of leg pain and started limping. The staff accused him of malingering.[58] When they finally took him to the hospital about two years later, he was diagnosed with a tubercular bone infection.[59] He would spend twenty-one months at the hospital, strapped to a wooden frame to straighten his bones for much of that time. The treatment obviously didn't work, and West was declared incurable, his leg permanently impaired.

The orphanage managers didn't want to take him back, claiming they couldn't care for a disabled boy who used crutches—after all, their goal was to find their wards work through indenture, and they doubted they would be able to find a placement for West. Hospital attendees left him on the orphanage stoop, and staff placed him in the sewing room with the girls, because they didn't know what else to do with him. West's life changed when he was almost twelve: one of his mother's friends lobbied the orphanage managers to allow the boy access to an education, and they relented, sending him to the public elementary school across the street for three hours a day. While still living at the Washington City Orphan Asylum, he attended high school, and in his last years of institutionalization, he was a staff member in charge of forty younger boys.[60]

Orphanage life became bearable for West only because he was able to belatedly procure an education, which also allowed him a way out. But the neglect he suffered at the Washington City Orphan Asylum, as well as the lack of individualized care available to children like him at such places, stuck with him. After he left the orphanage, West became a Progressive dedicated to the cause of children's welfare. While working as a lawyer, he volunteered with his church's Sunday school and at the local YMCA and served as the secretary of the Washington Playground Association. Later, he'd serve as Chief Scout Executive of the Boy Scouts of America. In addition to all this work on extracurricular programs for youth, West, like Addams, took up the cause of juvenile delinquents. In 1906, he joined a successful campaign lobbying Congress and President Roosevelt for the creation of the first juvenile court in Washington, DC.[61]

Through his work with *The Delineator*—a monthly women's magazine run by the Butterick sewing pattern company edited by novelist Theodore Dreiser—West would come to lobby against institutionalizing children. During his editorship, Dreiser utilized the magazine to spread consciousness of the plight of children in orphanages. In 1908, he hired West to oversee the magazine's Child-Rescue Campaign, the motto of which was "For the child that needs a home and the home that needs a child."[62]

Each month, *The Delineator* featured the stories and photographs of a couple of children who lived in orphanages and were available for indenture or adoption. "Sometimes they may be orphans. Sometimes they may have mothers or fathers who neglected them," the magazine explained when the campaign launched in 1907. "Always they will have human souls possessed of all the potentiality for making good men and women, provided someone will lend a helping hand along the rough way of life, and through a new, right environment there may be a wonderful development for them in the future."[63] Orphanages were, in the eyes of *The Delineator*, the wrong environment for children. In a later issue, the campaign would challenge readers to assume the duty of saving "waifs" from the regimentation of orphanage life: "Are you content to see these little ones imprisoned in orphan asylums where machine charity clothes them, teaches them by the ticking of the clock, when homes are waiting, empty, to do all this, and add what machine charity can never give—human love?"[64]

Essentially, the Child-Rescue Campaign was trying to challenge the primacy of "machine charity" and the institutionalization of children by establishing its own foster care and adoption agency. Its method would appeal to *The Delineator*'s "million subscribers and millions more of readers," and middle-class women responded in droves.[65] A few months after the campaign launched, Dreiser wrote, "Can it be that the homes of America will open up wide enough to let all the homeless children in? It looks as if they might."[66] But within the first year of the effort, *The Delineator* arranged the placements of only forty-one children—a minute percentage of the one hundred thousand children it estimated lived in orphanages in 1908.[67]

The campaign clearly aspired to more. In the November 1908 issue, alongside ads for W. B. Reduso corsets ("fleshiness need not be unbecoming") and articles with titles like "Crocheted Comfort for King Baby" and "Learning How to Keep House at Columbia," *The Delineator* announced a new National Child-Rescue League.[68] West served as secretary.[69] "We want public sentiment to grow so strong, we want the organized movement to be so overwhelming, that officials and institutions everywhere shall be compelled to recognize institutional life for the child as an unnecessary evil," the magazine proposed. The "duties" of joining the league, which required no dues and was open to all readers, stipulated that members should "exercise a friendly interest in the waifs and children in their community not properly cared for, and bring such cases to the proper local authorities, and to join with us in advocating that the confinement of healthy, normal children in orphan asylums . . . is unnecessary, extravagant, and contrary to the best interests of the child and State."[70] The league, in other words, was essentially devoted to awareness raising among the public, with the added responsibility of referring cases to SPCCs and other local officials.

But to truly spread the gospel of the Child-Rescue Campaign and effect real change in the child welfare system, *The Delineator* needed to do more than just reach the sort of "humane" ladies who had once been invested in Mary Ellen Wilson's court case. This is where West's preexisting connection to President Roosevelt played a crucial role. After the successful creation of the Washington, DC, juvenile court, Roosevelt had personally recommended that the Justice Department appoint West as its judge. When West didn't get the appointment—the attorney general had apparently promised the bench to someone else—Roosevelt told him, "You have got a draft on me any time you want to call."[71]

It turns out that one of the biggest developments in the history of child welfare would result from a former orphanage resident calling in a favor from the president. West, together with Dreiser and seven other men working in child welfare, took Roosevelt up on his IOU in late 1908 with an entreaty to convene a conference at the White House concerning the plight of dependent children.[72] The letter they sent the president quoted back to him his own fearmongering words to Congress in support of special treatment for juvenile delinquents: "No Christian and civilized community can afford to show a happy-go-lucky lack of concern for the youth of to-day; for, if so, the community will have to pay a terrible penalty of financial burden and social degradation in the to-morrow."[73]

The White House conference, held in January 1909, during Roosevelt's lame duck period, would mark the federal government's first tentative step into a system that had previously been the domain of religious charities and state and local charity boards. But for all the groundbreaking recommendations that flowed from it, it did little to materially change the lives of dependent children in the decades that followed.

———

The White House Conference on the Care of Dependent Children had an illustrious guest list, carefully calibrated to include representatives from all the major religions that considered their involvement in child welfare to be sacrosanct. Yes, West and Dreiser and other Progressive activists like Addams, Jacob Riis, and Booker T. Washington were in attendance, and they were the ones who pushed an agenda of deinstitutionalizing child welfare. But the conference was vice-chaired by leaders of religious charities.[74] Thomas M. Mulry, head of the St. Vincent de Paul Society, provided the point of view of the Catholic charities that then ran the majority of orphanages.[75] Julian W. Mack, a judge from Chicago who served on the executive committee of the National Conference of Jewish Charities, represented the Jews.[76] The Protestants—still the dominant denomination in America—had on their side Homer Folks, a sociologist who was then the head of the State Charities Aid Society of New York and had previously worked for the Protestant Children's Aid Society of Pennsylvania, as well as many other attendees who were invited to speak on behalf of Protestant charities.[77] Notably, no one represented the SPCCs, demonstrating a disconnect between the people responsible for policing families and the people responsible for policy recommendations about dependent children.[78]

The recommendations of the conference revolved around the argument that "Home life is the highest and finest product of civilization. . . . Children should not be deprived of it except for urgent and compelling reasons." This was, Roosevelt noted in his letter to Congress on the proceedings of the conference, the "keynote," or central fact that all agreed upon.[79] Poverty alone was not one of those "compelling" reasons—in fact, the conference attendees recommended giving aid to poor families to help them "maintain suitable homes for the rearing of children"—but neglect and abuse were.[80] At any rate, the conference recommended that maltreated children and homeless children should be cared for in "carefully selected" foster homes rather than in orphanages.[81] The orphanages that remained were to operate on the "cottage system" rather than mass congregate care. The plan required that groups of about twenty-five children would be under the care of one or more adults, to somewhat approximate home life. However, clearly few if any actual homes had that child-to-adult ratio.[82]

Aside from these pronouncements about where dependent children should live, the conference-goers came to a series of consensuses on how child welfare charities should be supervised going forward. They proposed state inspection of all such charities, including those that received no state funding; state supervision of the educational work of dependent children, both in institutions and in foster homes; and the requirement of more diligent record keeping by all charities, including the duty to "secure full information concerning the character and circumstances of the parents and near relatives of each child in whose behalf application is made."[83] That some child welfare charities were operating for the better part of a century without this kind of basic oversight and attention to detail seems ludicrous.

But only one proposal made by the 1909 White House Conference on the Care of Dependent Children would actually be put into effect soon after: the creation of a federal Children's Bureau, which was to "collect and disseminate information affecting the welfare of children."[84] At the time, Congress was considering legislation to establish the Children's Bureau, but the bill wouldn't actually pass until 1912, when William Howard Taft was president.

For all its rhetoric, the White House Conference didn't end the institutional era. For decades, dependent children continued to suffer in orphanages, where many experienced worse abuse and neglect than they might have encountered at home. Catholics were especially slow to leave behind the orphanage, not least because many Catholics were too poor to functionally serve as foster parents for other families' needy kids. The fear that Protestants would try to convert Catholic children was still very much alive in the twentieth century, fueling continued institutionalization and indoctrination.

At St. Joseph's, a Catholic orphanage in Burlington, Vermont, nuns and priests abused children through the 1970s—long after Progressive child welfare activists reached their consensus against institutionalization in 1909. As investigative journalist Christine Kenneally writes in *Ghosts of the Orphanage*, "The cloistered and cruel world of the orphanage may seem utterly fantastical, but the events that took place there belong very much to reality."[85] She notes that it was common for nuns to force children to eat their own vomit and to humiliate them by draping damp sheets around them after they wet the bed. Survivors describe nuns and priests hitting them with paddles, locking them in the attic, and pulling them out of bed to sexually abuse them. Harrowingly, Kenneally even recounts allegations of at least half a dozen deaths at St. Joseph's—some seemingly preventable accidents and some alleged murders.

Most of the children who lived at St. Joseph's in the twentieth century had living, poor parents. Some parents left their children in the orphanage's parlor voluntarily, but other children were placed there by social workers who collaborated with Vermont Catholic Charities. Those social workers were the ones who decided which kinds of families were deserving of preservation and which kinds of children deserved to have families.

But if the White House Conference didn't change the lives of the children who would continue to be abused at St. Joseph's for six decades after it convened, its pronouncements in favor of keeping families together and placing children in carefully selected and supervised foster homes also came too late for thousands of other children who were subjected to a Protestant minister's railroad-fueled social engineering experiment.

TWO

TRAINS

Chapter Five

MAKE SOMETHING OF
YOURSELF IN THE WEST

In historical novels about the orphan train era, the streets of mid-nineteenth century New York City are teeming with hawkers selling corn from push-carts, beggars wrapped like mummies in strips of tattered cloth, and barefoot children picking rags from the gutters to sell. If the fictional children have homes and families, they live in tenements that smell of garbage and garlic, sleeping six to a mattress. If they are among the "deserving poor," their parents keep the floor scrubbed and a Bible on the table. Otherwise, they might live in a shanty among chickens and towers of scrap metal, sewing piecework or shin-ing shoes to help their families scrape by. Girls without homes dance on the street or sweep crossings or become sex workers; boys join street gangs and are routinely thrown in the Tombs, the infamous jail in the Five Points neighbor-hood of Lower Manhattan. Whether their work is honest or not, their futures hold no hope for anything but basic survival—that's all their poor parents can achieve, which is why so many of them succumb to the bottle.

It might seem odd that children in the late 1970s, 1980s, and 1990s would want to read scores of books that hashed out such depressing melo-drama. But in each of the books that feature this narrative, the plot suddenly changes after setting this doleful scene, when a Protestant minister named Charles Loring Brace steps in. His charity, the Children's Aid Society (CAS), has a bold plan: to send "street urchins" west on the newly expanded railroads. In the West—the Midwest, really—there is plenty of everything: clean air, apple orchards, real warm beds, and, most importantly, farm families in need of labor and in want of children to love as their own. By living and working among these good, hardy people, the children will have a chance to make something of themselves.

The first novel to sell this story to young readers and renew interest in this slice of American history was James Magnuson and Dorothea G. Petrie's 1978 *Orphan Train*, a title that hits on precisely what makes these stories appealing: the journey that comes after the setup sketched out above and the fact that the children heading west are parentless, due to death, abandonment, or neglect.

Orphans are perfectly suited to pint-size heroes' journeys. Add in the excitement of rail travel west and just enough history to make the stories feel authentic—Brace and the CAS did exist outside the parameters of the novels—and you have a narrative ripe for perpetuating American myths and morals. Which is precisely what the hundreds of books that came after the original *Orphan Train* produce, concealing the dark, seventy-five-year history of placing approximately a quarter million poor urban children with barely vetted families in rural areas all over the United States, creating the blueprint for modern foster care.[1]

I had never heard about this social experiment until I began researching this book. If you learned about the orphan train movement as a child, you almost certainly didn't know about its classist and racist origins or about the trauma it compounded. You most likely read about it not in a textbook but in a novel like Magnuson and Petrie's *Orphan Train*. The term *orphan train* didn't truly exist until the book and the 1979 made-for-TV movie adaptation (which features a young Glenn Close) popularized it.[2] The CAS itself never used it, instead calling its program the "emigration plan" and characterizing its work as "placing out," admittedly less catchy phrases that nonetheless suggest that the majority of the children sent on trains had living parents—they were just desperately poor. Other charities that followed the CAS's lead, like the Catholic New York Foundling Hospital, called them "baby trains" or "mercy trains."

Petrie claims, in a "historical note" at the start of the book, to have researched the history of the CAS trains after meeting a former rider in her mother's Iowa hometown. However, the surge of interest in this fictional version of the movement's history can be attributed to the popularity of its two main components: orphans and the West. In the 1970s and 1980s, new versions of old orphan stories were finding widespread success. The *Annie* musical, for instance, premiered on Broadway in 1977 and went on national tour in 1978. Even *The Adventures of Tom Sawyer* got a musical adaptation in the 1973 film starring Jodie Foster as Becky Thatcher. At the same time, Westerns were as popular as ever. Clint Eastwood's *The Outlaw Josey Wales* hit movie screens in 1976, the same year as John Wayne's last film, *The Shootist*. On TV, there was *How the West Was Won*, which ran from 1977 to 1979.

While orphan train books take place in newly settled railroad towns in the Midwest rather than the Wild West, this too was frontier land. In one book, a train rider even reads Edward Ellis's 1860 dime novel *Seth Jones, or the Captives of the Frontier*.[3] The marketers of 1978's *Orphan Train* were eager to capitalize on the intersection between orphan stories and Westerns—the original jacket copy hypes a "boxcar odyssey," with "abandoned waifs" "rescue[d] . . . forever from the Oliver Twist world of the New York streets. . . . It all adds up to a novel as warm, spunky, and utterly enthralling as *True Grit*."

The original *Orphan Train* fictionalizes the first train trip west by the CAS in 1854, and though Magnuson and Petrie wrote it for children, it focuses not on the perspectives of the twenty-six "orphans" but on that of their twenty-eight-year-old caretaker. Our protagonist is Emma Symns, the sheltered, spinster niece of a fictional minister who is working with Brace. Emma is herself a full orphan—her parents drowned in a freak rowboat accident; her uncle raised her—but the "vagrant" children the society is sending on their way are not similarly parentless.[4] They have most often come to the society's attention via "letters from parents who felt they could no longer raise their children, letters from prisons and hospitals, letters of children driven out of drunkards' homes, boys cast out by stepmothers or stepfathers"—letters Emma answers.[5]

Though Emma is "touched and shaken" by their stories, she initially regards these children as less than human. When one of the "ragged, dirty children" approaches her at the society's office, she finds herself "stiff and weary, as if she were face to face with some wild, untamed creature."[6] Later, in a scene where the children are being "fumigat[ed]" in preparation for the train, Magnuson and Petrie hit the same note of comparing the children of the poor to animals needing domestication, though this time they add a jab at Native Americans. Emma feels "a chill, suddenly, as if these were not children she was watching, not children as she had known them, but wild animals or some savage tribe whose language she'd never been taught."[7] Emma's journey is an emotional one: she both comes to care for her wards and to acknowledge their humanity and falls for a daguerreotypist she meets on the train. Meanwhile, the reader is sold a narrative that portrays the westward trafficking of "untamed" poor "street Arabs" as a project that cultivates them into productive Christian citizens.[8]

Told in a close third person, the novel occasionally moves from Emma's perspective to those of the children but never affords them interiority. Instead, much space is devoted to excitement and adventure along the tracks and to selling the American Dream of the heartland to readers. One child, Liverpool, is a provocateur who has a carnival barker's gift. He furthers the book's propaganda, claiming the trains will deliver them to a life of opportunity: "The West's the place for growin' presidents. . . . If you want to be the man who'll make his mark in the country, you will get up and come with us, for there's lots on the prairie a-waitin' for ya."[9] Magnuson and Petrie lift this speech nearly verbatim from a book Brace wrote about his work with the poor. In a claim that beggars belief, Brace writes that a newsboy was responsible for this colorful oration, which is some 650 words long in total and begins, "Boys, gintlemen, chummies: Praps you'd like to hear summit about the West, the great West, you know, where so many of our old friends are settled down and growin' up to be great men, maybe the greatest men in the great Republic."[10] Clearly the propagandizing of the orphan train era didn't begin with children's books published more than a century later.

The trek to the fictional town of Rock Springs, Illinois, takes up the entirety of *Orphan Train*. Exciting plot points that repeat in later books in the genre include a girl disguising herself as a boy for easier placement, a fire onboard the train, and a runaway slave (who is literally being shipped by train in a pine box) pursued by bounty hunters. Magnuson and Petrie can't stop there: they also include an acting troupe performing an impromptu production of *Uncle Tom's Cabin* in full blackface, a child drowning, and a derailment over the Illinois River. The authors clearly preferred fantastical action to grappling with complex reality.

Orphan Train created the mold for tropes that portray the CAS's emigration plan as Manifest Destiny. The narrative that westward expansion was inevitable and essential is so entrenched that American children are indoctrinated in it through novels as well as textbooks. Aside from a few hecklers who ask the train riders if they are "scairt of gettin' scalped by the Indians" and the daguerreotypist's dreams of getting "pictures of the Indians, the mountains, the sodbusters and the railroad men, trappers and gold hunters" to "record a changing country," there is no Indigenous presence in *Orphan Train*.[11] This is convenient, as it allows for a wholesome portrait of hardworking homesteaders who benevolently open their homes to needy children, ignoring the violence of Native American displacement.

While Magnuson and Petrie's *Orphan Train* is largely forgotten by modern readers, it laid the blueprint for a romanticized narrative that would spawn hundreds more historical novels over the following forty-plus years. Most are written for children, like Joan Lowery Nixon's 1980s–1990s middle-grade series *Orphan Train Adventures*, Jane Peart's 1990s young adult series *Orphan Train West*, and Wendy McClure's 2010s middle-grade series *Wanderville*. Of course, the Boxcar Children, those original fictional railroad-related orphans, have an orphan train link: Book 105 in the series, *The Mystery of the Orphan Train*, unravels the connection between long-lost siblings separated by an orphan train ride to Kansas. An orphan train even makes an appearance in American Girl Samantha Parkington's book series, when Samantha—a rich Victorian-era orphan raised by her grandmother in Westchester County, New York—helps her poor foil, Nellie O'Malley, escape an orphanage that plans to send her west. My Grandma Martin gave me my very own Samantha doll, complete with bedroom set, long before I became an orphan myself. While I read some of her book series, I either skipped the above edition, or the scheme of shipping orphans on the railroad scarcely registered as notable or odd to me.

These offshoots remix the original *Orphan Train* concept for new generations of readers. Joan Lowery Nixon's *Orphan Train Adventures* series, which began publishing in 1987, makes improvements on *Orphan Train*'s model in that it is actually rooted in children's perspectives, including their grief at being separated from their former lives. But, as the series title emphasizes, Nixon couldn't resist casting the forced trips as adventures. In her author's note, Nixon admits as much when she writes, "We chose St. Joseph, Missouri, between the years 1860 and 1880 as our setting in order to place our characters in one of the most exciting periods of American history."

The series follows the Irish immigrant Kelly family, each book zeroing in on one of the six siblings' perspectives. The first, *A Family Apart*, told from eldest child Frances Mary's point of view, tracks the Kellys' experience of being placed by their widowed mother with CAS in 1860 and parceled out to new families in Missouri and the Kansas and Nebraska territories. From the start, Nixon paints the Kellys as "deserving poor" who are victims of circumstance. When one of the brothers becomes a pickpocket, his thievery is portrayed as driven by need. After he is caught by police, Mrs. Kelly appeals to Charles Loring Brace to take her children west, where, she tells them, "You'll have wholesome food, a clean bed of your own, and schooling, and all sorts of fine things, the like of which I could never, ever, give you, no matter how hard we work."[12] Others might feel that an economy and society that has given a poor immigrant widow like Mrs. Kelly no opportunities to keep her children fed, educated, and safe requires systemic reform. Nixon, though, follows Brace's lead and depicts the orphan trains as the only answer for the family.

The Kelly children, of course, feel abandoned, and throughout *A Family Apart*, Frances Mary struggles to come to terms with her mother's choice. The moral of the story is the meaning of sacrifice. By the end of the book, Frances Mary realizes that her mother's decision embodies the idea "that you can love someone or some idea enough to give up something you prize, in order to make people's lives better."[13] Portraying the decision that destitute, immigrant parents made to place their children as one imbued not only with agency but as an expression of love makes trauma palatable.

To this object story, Nixon adds adventurous flair, borrowing plot points from *Orphan Train*. Frances Mary pretends to be a boy so that she can be placed with her youngest brother, having promised her mother that she will look after him. After they are chosen by a Kansas family who host a stop on the Underground Railroad, Frances Mary offers to drive a runaway slave couple in a wagon to their next stop. This plot twist might beat out Petrie and Magnuson's Uncle Tom extravaganza in absurdity but succeeded in rousing the excitement of the original owner of my used copy, who wrote, "Aaaah! What will happen!" when a chapter ends with bounty hunters approaching Frances Mary's wagon.

———

Orphan train fiction for adults is less fantastical but still stretches history for narrative effect. Recently there has been a spate of romances like Jody Hedlund's series for Christian publisher Bethany House, with titles like *With You Always*, which follows a teenage seamstress who leaves New York City on a CAS train and falls in love with a wealthy entrepreneur who is building a town along the Illinois Central Railroad. Orphan trains also make for popular self-published romance fodder, as in Rachel Wesson's series *Hearts on the Rails* and Zoe Matthews's books *An Unexpected Family* and *The Promise of a Family*. That this era has been reimagined as material for storylines about adult love affairs further pulls focus away from the real children whose real lives were forever changed by the orphan train movement.

The most popular adult orphan train book is, of course, the other *Orphan Train*—Christina Baker Kline's 2013 book—which spent four consecutive weeks at the top of the *New York Times* best-seller list and was so popular as to spawn a young readers' edition in 2017.[14] Kline's train rider is Niamh Power, an Irish immigrant who loses her alcoholic father and three siblings in a 1929 tenement fire; her mother, known for her "black moods and rages," survives but is institutionalized.[15] Niamh is nine years old when she rides a CAS train to Minnesota and finds a placement with a couple looking for a free seamstress for their women's clothing business. They don't send Niamh to school, preferring to squeeze as much sewing work out of her as possible, but they do bestow her with the "American" name Dorothy. In this, Kline undercuts both Brace's propaganda and that of earlier orphan train fiction, acknowledging that not all of the adults who took in train riders were offering them loving homes and educational opportunities. But as the plot progresses, Kline takes the melodrama of earlier orphan train fiction up a notch by putting her protagonist through extreme and extended suffering, only to redeem it all with silver linings and a tidy ending.

The trauma begins when the stock market crashes, the clothing business no longer needs Niamh/Dorothy's labor, and the couple disposes of her. The local CAS agent delivers Niamh/Dorothy to a new family that he calls "good country people."[16] He does not care that they live off the grid in a shack and subsist on squirrel stew or that the mother sleeps all day and the children are practically feral. The father rapes Niamh/Dorothy and the mother casts her out in the middle of the night to traipse miles through the snow to a schoolhouse, where she is rescued by a teacher reminiscent of Miss Honey from *Matilda*. Soon she is adopted by a wealthy Protestant couple looking to replace their dead daughter, Vivian, whose name they bestow upon Niamh/Dorothy.

Kline must have chosen to start her story in 1929 to make the interweaving contemporary plotline work: in 2011, Niamh/Dorothy/Vivian, at ninety-one, meets a teenager whose life in modern foster care mirrors her own. But, in reality, 1929 was the very last year that the orphan trains ran, and by then public opinion had largely turned against the experiment. Generations of children had already benefited by being seen as "priceless" by the 1920s, and SPCCs had successfully lobbied to implement child labor laws. In the last years of the emigration plan, only a few states still accepted CAS train parties, and Minnesota was not one of them. Had Niamh actually ridden a train in 1929, she likely would have been subjected to much stricter oversight by the CAS.

Kline's *Orphan Train*—which by now dominates the cultural imagination of the movement—is ultimately fabulist from a historical perspective. But despite its bending of the facts, the moral vision it propagates is as much an American myth as the Manifest Destiny, bootstrap dreams of the 1978 *Orphan Train* and Nixon's *Orphan Train Adventures*. The earlier books glamorized the orphan train movement as bettering the lives of poor children who had no other chance and propagandized the benefits of rural life and a Protestant work ethic. Kline's *Orphan Train* tells a different American story: one of resilience and ultimately redemption. It's an Annie story all over again, this time for adults to buy at a Hudson News in the airport and read rapt on vacation, never questioning the framing of history they're being sold.

From the very first page of *Orphan Train*, Kline paints Niamh/Dorothy/Vivian as a woman of steely resolve who has endured much hardship but never falters. She speaks of the ghosts of those she's lost in her life: "I could take solace in their presence or I could fall down in a heap, lamenting what I'd lost."[17] The only choice is resolve, not indulging in anguish and grief. And while the book does depict its protagonist's losses in great detail, it does not linger on the decades of grief and resignation to the life she was dealt or how she tolerates it. Niamh/Dorothy/Vivian's resilience is rewarded when foster teen Molly—a Penobscot Indian who considers herself an orphan despite having a living mother—comes into her life at its end, allowing her to pass on her story, fill in its gaps, and help Niamh reunite with biological family members she had thought were unreachable. Kline barely touches on Molly's own experience of grief and the abuse and neglect she suffered over nine years in foster care. The fact that Native children are overrepresented in the system and have a harrowing child welfare history all their own goes unmentioned. Molly exists in *Orphan Train* only as a Native version of the magical Negro stock character, coming to the aid of an old woman so her life can be made whole before she dies.

We prefer these inventions to the truth of the orphan train movement, which was, in the end, a social engineering experiment that preyed on some of our most vulnerable, populating stolen land with stolen lives. To acknowledge that reality requires grappling with the fact that we allowed the lives of hundreds of thousands of children to be determined by the classist, racist philosophies of a Protestant minister who was not an elected official. This is the real legacy of our past, one that still colors our child welfare system today, where conditions of poverty are commonly cast as grounds for removal. Many poor children—and especially poor brown and Black children—are still not believed to be able to make something of themselves without losing their families.

Chapter Six

TRAIN CARS FULL OF "DANGEROUS" CHILDREN

The letters are scrawled and scratched on thin paper, their edges tattered. The oldest have been preserved for more than 165 years, filed away in folders and boxes to be accessed by researchers at the library of the New-York Historical Society on the Upper West Side of Manhattan, across the street from Central Park. The letters speak of children who left New York City just as the park was being planned as a tranquil green reprieve from overcrowded streets.

Some of the children had been homeless on the streets of Lower Manhattan; some of their parents had died. All were poor. The Children's Aid Society (CAS) had selected them as participants in a seventy-five-year experiment that would test founder Charles Loring Brace's theories about poverty, work ethic, and the effects of urban versus rural surroundings. They were among the first who rode trains to places like Michigan, Illinois, and Indiana, as part of the "emigration plan" that we now know as the orphan train movement. As in the fictions that the CAS would go on to inspire, Brace's plan promised to rid the city of children who were destined to make up its "dangerous classes." In turn, the children were to be bestowed with opportunities—schooling, fresh open air, farmwork—and the God-fearing, enterprising homesteaders of the developing "West" were to benefit from their labor. The letters, though, tell a very different story.

The children referred to in these letters are now long dead, but as I sat under the library's bright lights and deciphered varied loops and slants of handwriting, I could still feel the urgency of the writers' pleas to the CAS on their behalf. "I have wrote to you several times as regards to my son William W. Tupper," one letter from August 1860 begins. "I wish to ascertain what part of the United States he is residing in and if he is well cared for. I was promised when he was sent away that I would know what place he was to be sent to. He left my house last January and it is as you are aware a long time to wait to hear from him. . . . I feel worried about him, as he was sent away without me seeing him. I would call myself but I am compelled to attend to my work whilst I have it. Please let me know as soon as possible."[1] I couldn't stop thinking about this man, who was living on Ludlow Street, and whether he ever learned where his son ended up. Were they ever able to reconnect? Did this father live the rest of his life ruing the circumstances that had led him to sign his son over to the CAS in the first place?

Another letter, written by a child named George Anderson in Michigan in February 1861, devastated me because of the simplicity of its requests. "My dear mother," the letter begins, in wobbly cursive. "I take pen in hand to let you know that we are all well and hope you enjoy the same blessing. William lives one mile from me. Margrette lives ten miles from me. . . . I would like to have you come out here. There's work enough. If you don't come out here I hope you will write us as soon as you can how old we are. I don't know how old I am."[2] The fact that this letter exists in the archives told me that it never reached its intended recipient, that instead it languished in the offices of the CAS, whose staff couldn't bother to find this child's mother, to answer the basic question of how old he and his siblings were—an utterly foundational piece of self-knowledge withheld. Did George ever find out when he was born? Was he able to keep in touch with Margrette and William, or were the siblings torn further apart as time went on?

Two folders down, I came across another letter about another family dismantled, this one from April 1861, Kalamazoo, Michigan, on behalf of a woman who took one of the train riders, alerting the CAS to a case that violated the rules of the organization's placement agreement: "You gave a girl to

Ms. F. E. Wallbridge. She is loving and beloved, but Ms. W tells me that she cries and worries about the condition of her sister, who is at Prof. U. Gregory's: not sent to school; worked hard; and abused. . . . Something ought to be done about it."[3] Was anything ever done about it? Did the abused sister ever manage to get the education the CAS had promised her? Was the girl who lived with Ms. Wallbridge haunted by her sister's fate—by the utterly arbitrary way she was delivered to a "loving" home, while her sister was "abused"?

Taken one by one, these letters gnawed at me. But the more of them I read, the more I realized that they fit into a pattern that haunted me even more. Year after year, parents in New York City wrote to the CAS searching for information about the whereabouts of their children. Children wrote seeking the most basic information about themselves—how old they were, who their parents were, whether they had siblings, what names they had been born with. Adults and children alike rang alarm bells about placements gone wrong and children abused. And I was all too aware of the gaps in the archival record. For each letter sent to the CAS from a town like Kalamazoo representing a child remembered to history, there were hundreds, even thousands, of children who rode trains from New York City and disappeared—children who ran away from their western placements after a month or a year, children who didn't know how to write and couldn't alert the CAS to the horrors they were experiencing in their placements, children whom the CAS never checked in on after they were selected by "employers" at what amounted to child auctions.

Meanwhile, in their annual reports, the CAS ignored what the letters they received and filed away made so obvious: that the orphan train movement was tearing apart poor families, cutting children off from their roots and the most fundamental sense of who they were and making them vulnerable to maltreatment in faraway places. In the same month that George Anderson wrote to his mother asking how old he was, Brace wrote of the good that the CAS's emigration plan was doing for New York City by ridding it of children like George and his siblings. "The practical importance of such a work as that of our Society can only be made real to the mind by considering how the public would do without it," he wrote in an annual report. "Of the seven hundred odd destitute or orphan children placed, during the last year, by the Society, in country homes, it is a fair supposition that at least one-half, if they had been left in the poverty and temptation of the city, would have become, in some way, burdens or injuries to society."[4] What actually happened to those children once they rode the rails away from New York's "poverty and temptation" mattered less than the fantasy that the moral character of both the children and the city could be improved by their removal.

It was a potent fantasy, one that kept the CAS's emigration plan chugging along from 1854 to 1929 and inspired other charities to follow suit. The dark realities of the orphan train movement were little exposed in its own time, and we have largely forgotten that about a quarter million poor city children were capriciously plucked from the lives they knew and trafficked to developing railroad towns. The fantasy also allows us to ignore the fact that the beginnings of foster care in the United States grew out of fears of and prejudices against the poor—especially the immigrant poor.

Brace's 1861 argument about "destitute" children destined to become "burdens or injuries to society" speaks to the crux of what animated the orphan train movement: moral panic over poverty and vice, which were seen as so linked as to be interchangeable. As industrial capitalism took over and migration to urban centers like New York surged, new social stratifications emerged. The upper classes with generational wealth viewed those who struggled to eke out a subsistence as lacking the discipline needed to bootstrap themselves out of poverty through Protestant work ethic. The epicenter of New York City's moral panic was the Five Points slum, where the poorest of the poor lived. Disdain for the poor was compounded by anti-immigrant, anti-Catholic, and racist animus—the slum was where many German immigrants, Irish Catholics fleeing the potato famine, and free Blacks landed.[5]

This slice of Lower Manhattan, bounded by the Bowery to the east, Centre Street to the west, Canal Street to the north, and Park Row to the south, gained notoriety as the most dangerous part of the city on multiple fronts. Not only was Five Points home to desperately overcrowded tenements where infectious diseases like tuberculosis tore through the population, but it was regarded as a den of vice, debauchery, and deadly violence. An unhinged air of lawlessness hung over the slum, where taverns and bordellos were the only successful businesses and gangs ruled the streets. Five Points' dastardly reputation was so well-known that when Charles Dickens visited America in 1841, he made a point of touring the slum—but not without a police escort. In *American Notes for General Circulation*, published the next year, Dickens described his visit to Five Points as a descent into an alcohol-soaked hell that rendered its inhabitants subhuman: "This is the place: these narrow ways, diverging to the right and left, and reeking everywhere with dirt and filth. . . . Debauchery has made the very houses prematurely old. See how the rotten beams are tumbling down, and how the patched and broken windows seem to scowl dimly, like eyes that have been hurt in drunken frays. Many of those pigs live here. Do they ever wonder why their masters walk upright in lieu of going on all-fours? and why they talk instead of grunting?"[6] That even Dickens, chronicler of inequity and champion of the poor, did not evince sympathy for the inhabitants of Five Points speaks to the disgust and fear that the slum roused in those who were merely tourists, who didn't have to live in those rotting buildings constructed literally over a landfill.

My introduction to Five Points came through watching Martin Scorsese's *Gangs of New York* with my father the year before he died—he deemed it partly educational, since the Catholic Dead Rabbits gang, led by Liam Neeson in the film, did actually exist. *Gangs of New York* opens with a (fictionalized) 1846 brawl between the Dead Rabbits and the Natives gang (based on the real-life Protestant, Know-Nothing nativist Bowery Boys), in which Neeson's character is murdered while his son, Amsterdam, looks on. Amsterdam ends up at a (fictional) orphanage on Blackwell's Island, but by 1862 he's all grown up (now played by Leonardo DiCaprio) and ready to exact revenge by infiltrating the Natives and murdering their leader. The irony that one of the last movies I watched with my father is, at its heart, a gruesome orphan vengeance narrative is not lost on me.

Brace's work both on the real Blackwell's Island and in Five Points galvanized his career in social reform and his focus on children. When Brace came to New York City in 1848 as a twenty-two-year-old to study at the Union Theological Seminary, he experienced a culture shock. He had been raised in Connecticut in a well-connected family. Brace's father was the head of the Litchfield Female Academy, where Catharine E. Beecher and Harriet Beecher Stowe—daughters of Calvinist minister Lyman Beecher—were students; he'd later work as the principal of Catharine's Hartford Female

Seminary.[7] Brace was one of his father's students too—he was homeschooled, fed the classics, Shakespeare, and Latin, which prepared him for study at Yale College.[8] His religious upbringing and the relationships he forged at Yale would inspire him to pursue ministry and eventually lead him to establish the Children's Aid Society and the orphan trains.

Brace was raised Congregationalist, a branch within Calvinism, the religion of the Puritans that preached that "the elect" were predestined for salvation from birth and that children were born damned. But his family attended the North Congregational Church in Hartford, where minister Horace Bushnell bridged the divide between Puritanism and the Romantic ideas of the Victorian era that portrayed children as holy innocents—ideas that Catharine E. Beecher would later spread in *The Religious Training of Children in the School, the Family, and the Church*.[9] Bushnell's sermons on "unconscious influence" and his then revolutionary call to focus on the religious development and "Christian nurture" of children stayed with Brace for the rest of his life.

At Yale, Brace was roommates with John Olmsted, whose older brother Frederick Law Olmsted—the landscape architect who went on to codesign Central Park—became a close companion as well. Frederick, who started his career as a social critic and journalist, prodded Brace to undertake practical social reform work rather than the path of the "minister-philosopher."[10] The Olmsteds also encouraged his path to New York. After graduating in 1846 and spending a year teaching in Connecticut, Brace enrolled at Yale Divinity School but decided to complete his studies at the more liberal Union Theological Seminary, which was conveniently located in New York, where his friends the Olmsteds lived.

In 1849, when Brace became an ordained Congregationalist minister, he began visiting Blackwell's Island weekly to preach to and speak with the people remanded there. Blackwell's—now known as Roosevelt Island—was one of the islands in the East River that New York City used to isolate its destitute, incarcerated, and ill during the asylum era. Owned by the city and overseen by the Department of Charities and Correction, Blackwell's was home to a penitentiary, a hospital for inmates and one for the poor, an insane asylum, and an almshouse. During the Civil War Draft Riots, Blackwell's would serve as the way station for the Black children whose orphanage was burned by a racist mob.

Visiting Blackwell's opened Brace's eyes to the horrid fates suffered by adults who had been "cast out of everything but God's mercy," as he put it in a letter to his father.[11] His time in Five Points alarmed him further. In 1851, he began assisting Reverend Louis M. Pease as a "visitor" for the Five Points Mission, entering the tenements to minister to people he would later refer to as the "squalid poor" and encourage their conversion. In his 1872 book *The Dangerous Classes of New York, and Twenty Years' Work Among Them*, Brace referred to his ministry both on Blackwell's Island and in Five Points as "Sisyphus-like work" that "soon discouraged all that engaged in it."

The growing population of "street Arabs" in places like Five Points was the source of Brace's own moral panic: an 1849 report by the city's chief of police estimated that ten thousand children were houseless and "addicted to immoralities of the most loathsome description."[12] In *The Dangerous Classes*, Brace claimed that these vagrant children were the "class of a large city most dangerous to its property, its morals and its political life." He cast them as "ignorant, destitute, untrained, and abandoned youth: the outcast street-children grown up to be voters, to be the implements of demagogues, the 'feeders' of the criminals, and the sources of domestic outbreaks and violations of law."

If reform of the vagrants, criminals, sex workers, and destitute who ended up on Blackwell's Island was all but impossible, Brace came to see prevention as the path forward: rehabilitating "ignorant" children was the answer to solving the immorality of the city. Brace was animated by the same impulse to isolate children from supposed "deviants" that motivated many orphanages and would later spur on the removal of children from almshouses and the legal lobbying of societies for the prevention of cruelty to children. His method, though, relied on far more radical isolation.

In January 1853, a group of men with whom Brace worked at the Five Points Mission called upon him to lead a new organization, the Children's Aid Society, which would aim to be what Brace called a "grand, comprehensive effort to check the growth of the 'dangerous classes.'" The solution that the CAS proposed was not putting children in regimented orphanages and almshouses, which Brace believed only created more criminals. Brace hated the idea of dependence and thought the "monastic" nature of institutions, which segregated their wards from the real world, made people "indolent, unused to struggle; subordinate indeed, but with little independence and manly vigor."[13] While the CAS did run some institutions, they were built on Brace's preference for bolstering independence in children. The Newsboys' Lodging House, for instance, gave the street children who hawked copies of Joseph Pulitzer's *New York World* and William Randolph Hearst's *New York Journal* (yes, à la the 1992 Disney movie-musical *Newsies*) warm, clean beds to sleep in and hearty meals to eat—for the price of ten cents a night. When the Newsboys' Lodging House opened in March 1854, just six months before the CAS sent its first trainload of orphans west, Brace's plan was "to treat the lads as independent little dealers, and give them nothing without payment, but at the same time to offer them much more for their money than they could get anywhere else. Moral, educational, and religious influences were to come in afterward."[14] Those influences were instilled at the various industrial schools that the CAS ran, which taught boys and girls skilled, "honest" trades like shoe pegging and sewing and instructed them in English and good Protestant moral character.

Still, Brace believed the most efficient way to surround street children with "moral, educational, and religious influences" was to completely change their environment. Sending children via railroad to live with new families would allow the CAS "to so throw the influences of education and discipline and religion about the abandoned and destitute youth . . . and draw them under the influence of the moral and fortunate classes, that they shall grow up as useful producers and members of society."[15] Brace, whose Connecticut childhood instilled in him a love of nature, felt that the countryside was the most salutary place for the would-be "dangerous classes" and that farmers were especially good Christian people. In *The Dangerous Classes*, he wrote of a hypothetical he tested himself with: "'If your son were suddenly, by the death of his parents and relatives, to be thrown out on the streets, poor and homeless—as these children are—where would you prefer him to be placed—in an Asylum, or in a good farmer's home in the West?'" To Brace, the only answer was "the plainest farmer's home rather than the best Asylum."[16]

Brace believed that the most dangerous poor children were the children of immigrants. In fact, the opening of the CAS's first annual report makes clear that the organization was responding in large part to nativist fears.

"This association—the Children's Aid Society—has sprung from the increasing sense among our citizens of the evils of our city," Brace writes.

> Thirty years ago, the proposal of an important organization, which should devote itself entirely to the class of vagrant, homeless and criminal children in New York, would have seemed absurd. There were vile streets, and destitute and abandoned people; but the city was young and thriving. . . . In these considerations one element was forgotten. During the last twenty years, a tide of population has been setting towards these shores, to which there is no movement parallel in history. . . . A portion of this immigration has been good—sober, hard-working people, who have spread over the country and become mingled with our population. Another part has been bad, almost the worst—the off-scouring of the poorest districts and the most degraded cities of the Old World. . . . The children of this class, naturally, have grown up under the concentrated influences of the poverty and vice around them.[17]

In order to prevent children from becoming as "bad" as their parents, they needed to be made American—and Protestant—in the West. Brace claimed that 99 percent of the poor were Catholic and that Catholics were idiotic and devoid of true religion. Brace also claimed he never tried to convert them, though the CAS often placed Catholic children in Protestant homes.[18]

Unsurprisingly, given his attitudes toward Catholic immigrants from the "Old World," Brace also endorsed eugenic ideas. Influenced by his friend Charles Darwin, Brace wrote in *The Dangerous Classes* that the latent forces of "gemmules" (theoretical inheritable particles that were later proven not to exist) from "vicious" recent ancestors were to blame for generational poverty: "certain appetites or habits, if indulged abnormally and excessively through two or more generations, come to have an almost irresistible force, and, no doubt, modify the brain so as to constitute almost an insane condition." He believed these "vicious" gemmules could be overcome by removing a child from "the sensual and filthy ways of her parents."[19]

Notably, Brace was less prejudiced against Black people than Catholics and families where multiple generations were "paupers or prostitutes." He was a vocal abolitionist. But still, the CAS almost entirely left Black children out of the emigration plan. Black people didn't have the freedom or wealth to be even "the plainest farmers" in Brace's idealized version of the Midwest. And certainly, white people couldn't be expected to open their homes to Black children.

Being sent west went like this: CAS agents would assess candidates' worthiness.[20] They made their selections primarily among children who were already living in New York City's orphanages and asylums, but occasionally train parties would pick up houseless children along the way, and agents would neglect to confirm their backgrounds. This was the case with the first CAS journey, which set off from New York on September 28, 1854. Hours before departure, a twelve-year-old vagrant boy called Liverpool (after his hometown), who claimed that he was shipped to the United States as a cabin boy, ran into a CAS volunteer. Without checking into this story, the volunteer dropped Liverpool off at the Newsboys' Lodging House to be transformed from a "walking rag bundle" into a presentable orphan for the people of Dowagiac, Michigan, a railroad town established only six years earlier.[21] Liverpool's story would later be mashed up with that of another street child in James Magnuson and Dorothea G. Petrie's *Orphan Train*.

Ideally, parents or guardians would sign over custody of their children to the society; children who had no such protectors would sign the forms themselves. Older boys were preferred by potential families because they were suitable as farmhands; babies and toddlers were popular with those looking for children to raise as their own (often to replace those who died young, as became a plot point in Christina Baker Kline's *Orphan Train*). Older girls might be chosen for housework but were ultimately harder to place.

One or two agents were responsible for dozens of children, who often weren't told where they were going, lest it make them volubly upset on the ride. The first stop would most often be a railroad town in the Midwest where the CAS had connections, ideally a place flanked by thriving farms, though the CAS would eventually send children to every state in the lower forty-eight except Arizona. Settlers would have known the train was coming, thanks to advertisements like an 1887 Kansas newspaper listing: "The

'Children's Orphan Aid Society of the City of New York,' will the first week in January, 1887, send a company of HOMELESS ORPHAN CHILDREN west. . . . Mr. Schleyit and Mr. McCully will be pleased to meet . . . all who are willing to give one, or more, of these unfortunates a home."[22]

Applicants were vetted by local committees. In the early years, the committees were made up of Protestant clergy; later, CAS agents engaged prominent, longtime citizens of the towns to assess applications. At any rate, the CAS's investigation of people who wanted to take in train riders was cursory at best, and the organization made no effort at matching children to placements that would best suit their needs. Instead, after disembarking, the children were taken to a church, hotel, or hall and displayed to a crowd of adults ready to stick their fingers in strangers' mouths to inspect teeth.

If chosen, a child would be "placed out" to a new family in what essentially amounted to a loose form of indenture, though Brace opposed the legally binding practice. Instead, the CAS placed out children via a verbal agreement between the agent and "employer," as the adults taking in children were known. Employers were also supposed to be given cards that spelled out the terms of the agreement.[23] One 1890 poster explains the terms for taking older boys, the class that the emigration plan was originally predicated on: "Boys fifteen years old are expected to work till they are eighteen for their board and clothes. . . . Boys between 12 and 15 are expected to work for their board and clothes until they are 18, but must be sent to school for a part of each year. . . . Boys under twelve are expected to remain until they are eighteen, and must be treated by the applicants as one of their own children in matters of schooling, clothing and training."[24] The CAS agreement did not grant employers legal custody over train riders. If a child's biological parents were living, they would retain guardianship or sign it over to the CAS. (The CAS gained guardianship of children who had been abandoned or orphaned through the orders of local officials.)[25] Either the child, his or her biological parents, or the new family could dissolve the relationship at any time, at least in theory.[26] Children who weren't chosen would get back on the train; the process would repeat at the next destination. CAS agents might or might not check up every year or two on those left behind.

The flaws of this plan are immediately obvious: the dehumanizing way in which the children were treated, the hands-off screening of potential "employers," the lack of follow-through by CAS. In 1883, an independent investigation for the National Conference of Charities and Correction found that the local committees were feckless in screening families and that barely half of children thirteen and older remained in their placements after three years. While younger children were often taken out of "benevolence," older children were "taken from motives of profit" and often ended up with extremely poor families who did not send them to school and "lived in shanties."[27]

The CAS already would have been aware of how poorly some of its placements turned out due to letters it received from children and "employers," now filed away in the archives. These were not the kinds of letters that the organization highlighted in its annual reports, where it bragged about the success of the program and appealed for more funding. In prefacing a selection of letters in the 1860 report, Brace excused the CAS's lack of supervision over the placements: "Still it is, perhaps, often a favorable indication that we lose sight of them entirely. If they turned out badly, we should be sure to hear enough about them; but, as we are informed by our friends in the West, most of them become entirely absorbed into the community."

The excuse covers up the fact that the CAS's record keeping was disturbingly lax. One record book at the New-York Historical Society library contained haphazardly written notes about the children taken in during the CAS's first year. Many children's pages were mostly blank; others were simply updated with "doing well." Several children's pages indicated that they had run away soon after placement, so the CAS did "lose sight of them entirely," as Brace put it, but this was not a "favorable indication." It is not surprising then that the organization didn't update parents like William W. Tupper's father as to their children's whereabouts—the agents probably didn't know where most of the train riders were.

Brace, though, believed his emigration plan to be a rousing success in terms of reforming the orphan "waifs" into wholesome members of society. In *The Dangerous Classes*, published sixteen years after the first train went west, he wrote, "The boys and girls who were sent out when under fourteen are often heard from, and succeed remarkably well. In hundreds of instances, they cannot be distinguished from the young men and women natives in the villages." He admitted that older boys "leave their places frequently" but claimed that "the great mass become honest producers on the Western soil instead of burdens or pests here, and are absorbed into that active, busy population." Employers who welcomed older boys could keep them for longer, Brace wrote, "by little presents of a calf, or pony, or lamb, or a small piece of land, in giving the child a permanent interest in the family and the farm."

Brace's Manifest Destiny mythmaking rivals that of the hundreds of novels written about the orphan train movement. He wholeheartedly put his faith in the character of the farm folks of the "West," where, he claimed, "there is no harassing 'struggle for existence,'" unlike in Five Points and other slums. In these farm towns, "a little band of young wayfarers and homeless rovers in the world find themselves in comfortable and kind homes, with all the boundless advantages and opportunities of the Western farmer's life about them." There was a limitless number of "comfortable and kind homes" in Brace's mind—he wrote that if the emigration plan could achieve its "full scope, we could take the place of every Orphan Asylum and Alms-house for pauper children in and around New York."

The CAS itself would eventually cringe at its own paltry practices of record keeping and supervision of placements. In 1932, just three years after the trains ceased running, a CAS worker named Helen Baxter wrote in a preface to an agent's recollections of train trips, "Record keeping was in the early days rather casual. . . . Supervision was—well it just wasn't in the early years."[28] That same year, another employee, named Helen Cole, wrote, "Our trustees have no idea of how poor some of our former placing was. They still believe that the majority of placements were highly successful."[29] And riders' own reports would demonstrate how life in the "West" was not all that Brace had it cracked up to be.

———

Most orphan train riders are now dead, but stories shared while they were living highlight how the CAS upended their lives. The orphan train experience was so isolating that many riders believed the journey they had undertaken was the only one of its kind. In the mid- to late 1980s, groups like the Orphan Train Heritage Society of America (OTHSA) began convening rider reunions. Only then did many riders start to learn more about—and come to terms with—the scale of the movement. By that point, all the riders still living were at least in their fifties.

Before their stories died with them, Mary Ellen Johnson, OTHSA's founder, collected hundreds of testimonials from riders and their family members and complied them into six volumes titled *Orphan Train Riders: Their Own Stories*. These books are now distributed by the National Orphan Train Complex, a museum that was founded in Concordia, Kansas, in the early 2000s and merged with OTHSA in 2007. Housed in a 1917 Union Pacific train depot, the complex seeks to keep the history of the orphan train movement alive and help descendants of riders trace their ancestry through the archival records and artifacts it maintains.

In the second volume of *Orphan Train Riders*, Arthur Field Smith, who rode a train to Iowa in 1922, shared what it meant to him to finally—after more than six decades—be in touch with others who had shared his childhood experience. He wrote of meeting a woman at a 1989 OTHSA reunion who recalled a CAS building on Staten Island where they had both spent time: "As Ethel confirmed this slender thread of memory, tears of joy came in a sudden torrent as I tightly held this wonderfully understanding lady. How can I explain just how important such little things are to an orphan who needs so badly to find some roots?"[30] Arthur acknowledged that his experience in Iowa was an unusually lucky one—he was about five years old when he was "placed out," and the family that took him in treated him as a son, not a laborer. They even formally adopted him in 1929. But the bewilderment of being plucked from New York and sent to the Midwest never left Arthur; nor did the longing to understand where he had come from.

Another 1922 rider to Iowa, Alexander Douthit, wrote of having a much rougher experience.[31] He was six years old when he boarded a CAS train, after living in an orphanage for four years with his brother Walter, who was only nine months younger. They had been orphaned in 1918 when their mother died in the flu epidemic; their father had been killed some time before. In Iowa, Alexander and Walter were immediately separated, taken by families who lived in different towns. Walter's new family changed his name to Harold, adopting him as their son. Meanwhile, Alexander's first placement disposed of him after three months when the couple found out they were expecting "a child of their own." He then spent three months with another family before settling in with the Douthits, a farming couple. "It was not a home of family love," Alexander wrote. "My father worked the farm and had no side interest. His belief was that young people were just workers and that he knew all the ways to work. . . . I was really a hired man."[32] But he wasn't a man at all—he was a young boy. One of the few lights in young Alexander's life was that his brother lived close by—within twenty miles—and they got to see each other despite their separation.

Many other riders recalled moving placements frequently in the Midwest. Claretta Miller, too, was separated from her siblings and sent to Nebraska in 1918. In a recollection published by OTHSA in the 1990s, she described being first placed with a large German family who wanted a servant, then shuffled around from home to home, "a lost and lonely little girl," before finding a lasting placement.[33] Josephine Delger, who rode to Fayette, Iowa, in 1911 at age eleven, shared a similar story with OTHSA.[34] She was initially placed with a couple who were looking for a replacement for their dead biological daughter, but the couple decided they didn't want to keep Josephine after a year. She was then moved to a farm, where she was put to work outside. "All I remember is working," she wrote. "I slept in a filthy dirty attic with only straw for my bedding and a feather tick for a cover. I cannot ever remember getting bathed or having my hair washed, other than by a rain shower while working outside."[35] She finally ran away when she was seventeen.

But even if the families they were placed with didn't abuse them or view them solely as sources of labor, the children who rode orphan trains were often shunned by the community. In a 1995 PBS documentary, Alice Ayler, who was sent to Kansas, recalls that she was told she had "bad blood. . . . We kids from New York were of inferior stock." This, of course, is a eugenic idea, one that recalls Brace's theories about "gemmules" and contradicts the notion that the people of burgeoning midwestern farm towns kindly absorbed orphan train riders into their communities.

———

Before his death in 1890, Brace would come to support the passing of new laws against child labor. But as much as he detested the fact that poor children were often subjected to factory labor, he still believed that children should be industrious and possessed of an independent, Protestant work ethic. In *The Dangerous Classes*, Brace wrote that factory work makes a child "weak in body and ignorant or untrained in mind." He disparaged the greed of parents who put their children to work in factories instead of sending them to school and of employers who argued that their wages kept these children's families out of poorhouses. The right kind of work for a child was family farm chores. Brace didn't seem to consider that farm families would be driven by the same greed that he decried in poor city families, that in reality orphans like Josephine Del-ger who were placed on midwestern farms faced long days of extremely difficult physical work, daily beatings, withheld meals, and no schooling.

Despite the fact that many of them were maltreated, the riders who were still alive in the 1990s to record their experiences in the volumes of *Orphan Train Riders* were sent west after the orphan train movement had already been forced to make reforms. When Brace died, his son took over the CAS and developed new methods of oversight, including more stringent postplacement supervision. In the last decades of the emigration plan, par-ties were sent to a dwindling number of states that still allowed the orphan trains—several states passed laws restricting or banning the practice entirely. By the final years of the orphan train movement, only Michigan, Kan-sas, Iowa, Nebraska, and Texas still accepted CAS placements, with much more oversight. The average age of riders dropped, and small children were more likely to be adopted, rather than informally indentured, by their new families—something Brace, who had advocated for country *jobs*, not fam-ilies, had never anticipated.[36] But even with these measures, the movement was increasingly seen as cruel and antiquated.

By 1909, when Theodore Roosevelt convened the first White House Conference on the Care of Dependent Children, the popular conception of child welfare had changed to the degree that the conference's recommenda-tions fully rejected Brace's view of "dangerous classes" of children. Where Brace saw children as "independent little dealers" who were in danger of being tainted by the "vicious" ways of their poor parents, Progressive reform-ers envisioned providing aid to keep poor families together so that innocent children—incapable of looking after themselves—could be protected in the loving embrace of kin. If parents were found to be abusing their children, the children were to be removed to foster families. Yet, unlike in the emigration plan, those families would be carefully chosen, investigated, and checked up on by a new class of professionals: social workers. Modern foster care would go on to develop its own dark reality and would never live up to the ideals of Progressive reformers, but it is nowhere near as capricious and haphazard as the emigration plan.

Like other charities with roots in 1800s orphan care, the CAS still exists because it adapted alongside the changing mores. Nowadays, the CAS has shed its religious past, and while the organization still operates foster care services in New York City, it does not glorify the fact that its founder laid the groundwork for foster care. Instead, the CAS acknowledges on its website that the orphan train movement was "controversial" and "had its pitfalls."

But even while Brace's orphan train vision would come to be judged as social engineering gone wrong, it was extremely influential. Charities nationwide imitated the CAS emigration plan. One, the New York Foundling Hospital, was the Catholic answer to the CAS, ensuring that abandoned babies would sustain the faith across the country.

Chapter Seven

CATHOLIC REMEDIES FOR "FALLEN WOMEN" AND FOUNDLINGS

M ost narratives of the Catholic counterpart to the Children's Aid Society (CAS) begin with the cradle. On October 11, 1869, Sister Mary Irene Fitzgibbon of the Sisters of Charity of St. Vincent de Paul, along with two other nuns, placed a cradle on their stoop on East 12th Street in Manhattan.[1] They had recently moved into the brownstone with a budget of only $5, tasked with saving abandoned infants, or foundlings.[2] Sister Irene was driven by encountering foundlings left on the stoop of St. Peter's Convent, where she had been serving as the superior, and by what she later referred to as a "lengthened record of infanticide" in "each morning's paper"—both symptoms of parents in absolute desperation.[3] That very first night, someone left a baby in the cradle on the stoop.

Starting with the cradle makes for a good story. It casts Sister Irene and her fellow nuns, Sister Theresa Vincent and Sister Francis Liguori, as benevolent heroes rescuing innocent, helpless, "illegitimate" infants from certain death—surely they would perish from exposure if left outside or die by their own poor, disgraced mothers' hands if there weren't a cradle to receive them.[4]

That's the image that Sister Irene wanted to conjure, especially in her own writings about the origins of the organization she founded on East 12th Street, first known as Foundling Asylum of the Sisters of Charity and later as the New York Foundling Hospital.[5] In the Foundling's 1873 annual report, Sister Irene writes,

> There is no class of suffering humanity whose cry for help and life is so sad and touching as the Foundling's. Scarcely has the unfortunate inhaled the vital air, unaware of all of life except its first necessities and sufferings, before its disposal becomes a grievous question with the attendants upon its birth. The doorstep, the street, the sink, the river, the string and the knife, present each a means of riddance to those who, wanting in means or fearing disgrace, sit in foregone and final judgement upon the innocent offspring of passion or poverty. . . . The Sisters have heard this low infantile wail, and are responding to it in the hope and belief that, through the grace of their Master in Heaven, and the aid of His children upon earth, they might be enabled to minister to these unfortunates and vanquish the Tempter.[6]

By portraying foundlings as barely able to catch their first breaths before their lives are in imminent danger—and portraying the sisters as responding to their "low infantile wail"—Sister Irene more than justifies her work. She depicts her charity as engaged in spiritual battle, each baby's cry a siren signaling a war between the devil and God. On the side of the devil is "passion," or sex outside wedlock. On the side of God are those who have been touched by his grace and have responded to his call to live a life of ministry.

Once the Foundling had saved these otherwise forsaken babies and nursed them to good health, it sought to "put them in the way of being brought up virtuously."[7] But how to find suitable homes for foundlings in a city so beset by poverty and desperation that twenty-eight infants were left in the cradle on East 12th Street in the first month of its existence alone?[8]

In 1875, after taking in thousands of abandoned babies and raising some of them to toddlerhood and beyond, Sister Irene modified Charles Loring Brace's "emigration plan" and began "placing out" the Foundling's tiny wards on trains to "the West."[9] While the CAS opted to send older children on trains without researching and preselecting new homes for them, instead holding what were essentially child auctions in railroad towns, the Foundling was thankfully more careful with the fates of its toddlers.

Before sending toddlers off on their train journeys, the organization had agents and local priests screen applicants in the destination town.[10] The Foundling then matched each toddler with a new family, in a process that still prioritized superficiality—maybe an Irish family in Iowa wanted a blonde-haired, blue-eyed girl, and a German one in Illinois wanted a brown-haired, brown-eyed boy—but at least spared the children from being sized up upon arrival. Instead, the toddlers were outfitted with tags that identified them, so they could be correctly deposited with their new families at the end of their journeys, like packages sent in the mail. And the thousands of young children who rode the Foundling's so-called baby trains until they ceased running in 1919 were largely requested by new families in railroad towns for their potential not as laborers but as sons and daughters.[11] An indenture form from 1911 spells out the arrangement: the baby train rider was to be treated as the parents' "own child in every respect" and must be provided with "suitable and proper board, lodging and medical attendance, and all things necessary and fit for any indentured child, and in all respects similar to what would ordinarily be provided and allowed . . . [for their] own children." In addition, the agreement stipulates that the child must be educated in "reading, writing and the general rules of arithmetic" and be brought up "in a moral and correct manner, and in the Catholic faith."[12] In this way, the Foundling's participation in the orphan train movement presaged modern adoption.

But the story of the Foundling is not just a story of baby saving. Inside the story of the Foundling lies a history of punishing and policing sexuality and controlling reproduction. I could not stop thinking about the fact that we are still fighting for reproductive rights and bodily autonomy when I was combing through the Foundling's archives at the New-York Historical Society in June 2022, the same month that the Supreme Court struck down *Roe v. Wade*, ending the national right to an abortion.

The Foundling's history is also emblematic of the religious hegemony at the heart of American welfare. Ultimately, Sister Irene and the nuns, laypeople, and philanthropists who would go on to carry out her vision were in the business of preserving the minority Catholic faith against encroachment by dominant Protestant charities and ensuring that Catholic culture would be perpetuated and reproduced across the United States.[13] If the Protestants had a foundling asylum in New York City, the Catholics had to have one too.[14] And if the Protestants—via the CAS—were sending orphans west on trains, the Catholics would have to do so too.

———

To understand how the Foundling capitalized on the orphan train movement, we need to explore how the existence of foundlings came to be seen as a societal problem in the first place—and what made foundlings different from, and more stigmatized than, orphans. Many of the so-called orphans that we know and love from literature and pop culture, from Oedipus to *Wuthering Heights*'s Heathcliff to Superman and Punky Brewster, are actually foundlings.[15] But the word *foundling* itself carries the root of its difference visibly—a being who is "found," meaning that it had been left or lost. While both orphans and foundlings are parentless, a child becomes a literal orphan, like me, when their parents die, whereas a child becomes a foundling when their parents actively abandon them. Orphans are objects of pity; foundlings are objects of shame.

Though we have contemporary examples of infant abandonment to give us a mental image of the practice, the thought of deserting a newborn—anonymously leaving it somewhere to be found by strangers—still shocks most of us now. The practice is rare: only about a hundred cases occur in the United States each year, but many of them make national news. In August 2022, the *New York Times* ran an article about baby drop boxes, modern versions of the Foundling's cradle.[16] The drop boxes appear similar to the mechanisms by which you can return a library book after hours but are larger and marked with the branding "Safe Haven Baby Box Drop Off." The *Times* reported that three infants had been left in one such box at a fire station in Carmel, Indiana, that spring.

That spate garnered much attention in part because it marked the first time anyone had left babies in the box since it was installed in 2019 and because safe haven laws were newly relevant in the wake of the decision in the *Dobbs v. Jackson Women's Health Organization* Supreme Court case that overturned *Roe*. Safe haven laws protect the practice of infant abandonment, allowing parents to leave babies with trained professionals at designated places like fire houses and hospitals.[17] The laws now exist in all fifty states, but they are relatively new—Texas passed the first one in 1999 in response to thirteen babies being found in trash cans and dumpsters.[18] The Texas law is called the "Baby Moses" law, hearkening back to the biblical story of infant desertion. The baby drop boxes are the product of a movement by conservative Christians to promote adoption as an alternative to abortion.[19] There are now about 150 across the country.[20] In its August 2022 story, the *Times* reported that only twenty-one babies had been left in safe haven drop boxes since 2017.

That the *Times* story on baby drop boxes does not once mention the word *foundling* speaks to how short our historical memory is. In nineteenth-century New York City, stumbling upon a foundling was a common phenomenon, one that didn't demand public sympathy and panic until after the Civil War. Record keeping of the number of infants deserted in New York City during this period is hard to come by, especially since specific institutions dedicated to the care of foundlings didn't exist before the 1860s and because not all babies left on the street ever made it to those institutions. Still, historians estimate that about two thousand babies were received in the city's foundling asylums per year in the early 1880s.[21]

Foundlings were common in this era in part because, though premarital sex was extremely common behind closed doors, it was societally taboo. Foundlings were physical evidence of illicit sexual relationships—the products of "passion," as Sister Irene put it—hence the shame. It may be hard to imagine now, given how much we have expanded our notions of the makeup of a family, but giving birth to an "illegitimate" baby was stigmatized until as recently as the 1970s in the United States, and religious charities built expansive apparatuses to both rehabilitate sinful women and disappear the evidence of their sins.

American ideas about foundlings were initially imported from Europe, where sex outside marriage was similarly scorned. Some foundling asylums in Europe came into existence all the way back in the Middle Ages. By the eighteenth century, the practice of infant abandonment in Europe was so widespread that in cities in France, Italy, and Spain, up to a third of babies were abandoned.[22] Catholic asylums in Italy allowed for anonymous abandonment—they used a so-called wheel system, where a turntable was located in an outdoor niche. People could place a baby on the turntable outside and rotate it indoors without being discovered themselves. The Foundling's cradle (which was eventually placed indoors in a secluded vestibule) and the current baby drop boxes are adaptations of the Italian wheel.[23]

Meanwhile, not until the Industrial Revolution did the United States start to encounter the issue of babies left on stoops and in streets. City living allowed for more anonymity and privacy than the small agrarian communities that were common in the eighteenth century; this privacy in turn made it possible for parents to desert their babies without identifying themselves. The poverty that resulted from the instability of wage labor, as well as the fact that many women worked in domestic jobs where they couldn't bring their babies, also increased the number of infant abandonments in nineteenth-century cities, especially New York.[24]

While women have always had abortions—and though abortion was mostly considered a rational choice in the nineteenth century—then, as now, poor, single women were less likely than their married, higher-class counterparts to be able to afford one.[25] The same goes for access to contraceptives. In a sickening echo of recent Supreme Court comments that suggested safe havens obviate the need for abortion rights, physicians began lobbying for foundling asylums as an alternative to abortion in the 1850s. Physicians felt that abortionists—who were frequently women—were encroaching on their status and authority, even though this was before the dawn of germ theory, when medical practices were barbaric.[26]

Plenty of babies were born out of wedlock in preindustrial America, too, but their conception typically occasioned shotgun weddings.[27] And while there has always been infanticide, the murders that Sister Irene alludes to in her 1873 report are lurid but probably exaggerations—the exceptions rather than the rule. The fact is that in the nineteenth century, abandonment and infanticide were inextricably linked, because whether babies were left on a stoop or actively killed shortly after birth, they frequently met the same fate. Many babies died of exposure from being left out in the cold, improperly bundled, or from baking in the heat.[28]

It's important to note, however, that the overall infant mortality rate in New York City in the late nineteenth century was extremely high. In 1868, the year before the Foundling opened, the Metropolitan Board of Health estimated that a little less than one in four babies died before turning one.[29] Infant mortality rates were abysmal in this era not just because of the practice of infant abandonment but due to the overcrowding and poor sanitation in the city's tenements and slums, like Five Points, that had horrified Brace.[30]

When considering the fact that even babies kept at home with their mothers frequently did not survive their first year, the practice of infant abandonment seems somewhat less coldhearted and helps contextualize why New Yorkers weren't initially shocked by it. But within a few short decades, a perfect storm would lead to the development of foundling asylums. In New York City, the epicenter of the American foundling "epidemic," two Protestant-run foundling institutions, the Infant's Home at the Nursery and Child's Hospital and the New York Infant Asylum, opened in 1865.[31] The public Infant Hospital on Randall's Island opened in 1869, the same year as the Foundling. The confluence of moral panics around the increase in immigration and the overcrowding of the city with the poor, as well as muckraking press coverage (think of Sister Irene's citation of the daily paper listing infant deaths) and changing mores around childhood and child welfare, made foundlings a problem that charities needed to solve. In the process, like orphans, foundlings would become objects upon which society worked out its fears, prejudices, and morals about childhood, motherhood, the family, and class.

In 1869, prior to opening the brownstone on East 12th Street, Sister Irene and two other nuns, Sister Mary Frances and Sister Theresa Vincent, toured Catholic institutions in Philadelphia, Baltimore, and Washington, DC, looking for models. In a diary that Sister Theresa Vincent kept during the journey, she writes glowingly of St. Vincent's Infant Asylum in Baltimore, which hosted a maternity home: "In this Institution are taken poor unfortunate girls who are known to be virtuous but who by some misfortune have fallen. These girls are cared for by kind women during their sickness. They remain to care for their little ones for a time, then commit them to the care of the Sisters while they leave the Institution thanking God for providing them with shelter from the scoffs of a wicked world. This blessing is often the cause of making them love their religion and clinging to it faithfully through life."[32] The "sickness" that Sister Theresa Vincent refers to here is, of course, pregnancy and childbirth. By providing unwed pregnant Catholics with a place to secretly give birth—Sister Theresa Vincent notes that only one nun knew the women's actual names and that they were not allowed to visit their babies after they left—the Baltimore asylum protected their reputations and gave them a reason to "owe" something to the church, namely, their unbending faith and devotion. As I read Sister Theresa Vincent's diary in the New-York Historical Society library, I felt physically ill, horrified by the blithe manner in which she praised a practice that forced women to carry their pregnancies to term, then separated them from their children, and by the tit-for-tat representation of religious charity and faith.

The Foundling would later borrow this model in New York. In 1880, it opened St. Ann's Maternity Hospital, which served unmarried mothers "seek[ing] shelter and seclusion with hope of preserving character and family reputation."[33] St. Ann's was part of a massive complex on the Upper East Side that spanned the block between Lexington and Third Avenues and East 68th and 69th Streets. It was built with the help of a $100,000 state grant in 1870—a bequest made possible by connections to the Tweed Ring in the Tammany Hall Democratic machine.[34] The complex also included a hospital for sick and disabled children, an asylum for "homeless and needy mothers," nurseries where unmarried mothers were compelled to breastfeed both their own babies and another baby for three months after giving birth, a nursery for toddlers, and a kindergarten.[35] In the space of a city block, the Sisters of Charity and the lay doctors and nurses who worked at the Foundling sought to launder the reputations of "illegitimate" mothers and children alike. In the charity's 1882 annual report, Sister Irene noted that "faithful mothers" who remained to nurse babies were "then assisted to procure good homes in service" as a reward for "yield[ing]" to "maternal instinct."[36]

Over the course of the nineteenth century, families adapted from valuing their children's economic potential as laboring contributors to the household to valuing their children for their innocence, purity, and emotional bonds. At the same time, motherhood became imbued with weighty symbolism, and "maternal instinct" became a prescribed part of the woman's role in society. In the mid-1800s, as work shifted out of the home, incomes rose, and mass production made keeping a household easier for upper- and middle-class white women, they became mothers first and foremost.[37] Historian Barbara Welter's landmark 1966 article "The Cult of True Womanhood, 1820–1860" first outlined how upper- and middle-class white womanhood became tied up with maternity and domesticity during this period. Welter draws on the women's magazines of the era to argue that a woman could achieve "True Womanhood" if she demonstrated the "four cardinal virtues" of "piety, purity, submissiveness and domesticity." Together, these virtues "spelled mother, daughter, sister, wife—woman" and circumscribed a white woman of means to "her 'proper sphere,' her home."[38] She would get that home through marriage, and once she was married, she'd of course become a mother. "A true woman naturally loved her children. To suggest otherwise was monstrous," Welter writes.[39]

In this way, mothers who abandoned their babies eventually became the monsters and the scapegoats of the foundling "epidemic." The circumstances that would lead a woman to leave her infant in a cradle like the one at the Foundling—destitution born of limited opportunities for stable work for women, lack of access to abortion and contraception, abandonment by the men who had impregnated them in the first place—weren't the problem. Women were the problem. The very existence of a foundling was evidence of a mother's shunning "True Womanhood."[40] So instead of lobbying for real social welfare, asylums like the Foundling sought to stem the tide of infant abandonment by reforming individual women, just as orphanages and the CAS's emigration plan sought to reform individual children. Hence the focus on compelling women who had "sinned" by giving birth out of wedlock to nurse and "rewarding" them with the opportunity of a job and a reputation wiped clean. "Rarely does such a mother leave the institution, without having bewailed and repented of her fault before God, and without being firmly determined to lead thenceforward, with the Divine assistance, a pure and Christian life," the sisters wrote in a report the year after St. Ann's opened.[41]

Just as Catholics and Protestants played a tug-of-war over dependent children, reforming the souls of "fallen" women was a concern of both sects, because Christians have always considered sex out of wedlock a mortal sin—one that women in particular are shamed for. The most extreme way that both Catholics and Protestants sought to punish "fallen" women was via the Magdalene Laundries.

If you've heard of the Magdalene Laundries, you probably think of them as an Irish phenomenon, perhaps because of recent revelations of the scale of their horrors. In Ireland, these institutions—first operated by Anglicans and later by Catholic orders—were essentially prisons for poor young women who were seen as "promiscuous," either for engaging in sex work or for becoming pregnant outside marriage. Named for Mary Magdalene, the "reformed" supposed sex worker who travels with Jesus and witnesses his crucifixion and resurrection, the laundries forced women to repent via unpaid labor—literally washing dirty laundry, which metaphorically washed away their sins.[42] That some girls and women were sent to the laundries after having been sexually abused underlines how men got off scot-free while women suffered.[43] The injustice is even more unsettling when we consider that some women reported being raped while at the laundries and were forced to give up the resulting babies to orphanages.[44] The Irish Magdalene Laundries operated from the 1700s until the shockingly recent 1996.[45] Some thirty thousand women were imprisoned in the laundries during the nineteenth and twentieth centuries, and mortality rates were high because the women were essentially starved and received little to no medical attention.[46]

Thinking of Magdalene Laundries as solely an Irish problem, one associated with the dominance of conservative Catholicism there, is a way to absolve ourselves of the United States' own crimes against "fallen" women. America, with its purported separation of church and state, has always been more forward-thinking, or so we tell ourselves. But Magdalene Laundries existed in the United States, too, and were operated both by Protestants and Catholics for nearly as long as those in Ireland. As Rheann Kelly, Christina Kovats, and Natalie Medley—members of a group of scholars incarcerated at Indiana Women's Prison—point out in a 2017 commentary for the Marshall Project, the Sisters of the Good Shepherd opened the first American Magdalene Laundry in 1840s Kentucky. They argue that the Kentucky laundry, where "erring and wayward women and girls" were locked away, was in fact the first women's prison in the country.[47] By 1900, thirty-eight Magdalene Laundries were operating in the United States; the last closed in the 1960s.

That the Foundling worked with both "illegitimate" babies and their mothers set it apart from the Magdalene Laundries. Its primary motive was not to punish women for having sex out of wedlock but to use the products of women's sins—their babies—to preserve and spread the Catholic faith through baby trains. At St. Ann's Maternity Hospital, the Sisters of Charity followed the model of the asylum in Baltimore that they had so admired: they used pseudonyms for the unwed mothers in their care to preserve their anonymity and their reputations.

Catholic orders like the Sisters of Charity were galvanized to open institutions for "fallen" Catholic women and their babies because they feared that if they failed to do so, Protestants would serve them instead and seek to convert them. This fear wasn't unfounded and speaks to the same forces that led to the swell of Catholic orphanages in the late 1800s. The increase in Irish immigration during and after the potato famine led to a large population of poor Irish Catholics, especially in New York City, in need of support.[48] Other waves of immigration brought needy Catholic Italians, Germans, and Slavs.

Despite the fact that Catholics were a minority group in New York in the nineteenth century, they made up the majority of the poor and were primarily served by Protestant groups. In New York in 1852, for instance, the Association for Improving the Condition of the Poor, a Protestant organization, estimated that 75 percent of its work was with Catholics.[49] Its leaders saw the children of these Catholics as little more than "accumulated refuse" polluting the city's streets. The similarly anti-Catholic attitudes of Brace and the CAS were even more concerning. As historians Dorothy M. Brown and Elizabeth McKeown write in *The Poor Belong to Us: Catholic Charities and American Welfare*, Catholics saw the CAS as "an unqualified menace that had caused thousands of Catholic children to lose their religion and thus their only hope of eternal salvation."[50] Niamh Power's fictional experience of being converted to Protestantism and stripped of her Irish name in Christina Baker Kline's *Orphan Train* is perhaps one of the least far-fetched plot points in the book.

From the start, Catholic charities had focused on supporting children.[51] But babies were too young for orphanages, which typically served ages three and up. By taking in infants, the Foundling filled a gap and ensured that these children would be baptized into the Catholic faith before they could be claimed by Protestant charities, saving their souls, if not their lives—in the early years, mortality rates were abysmal. In time, hired wet nurses, lactating poor women who were paid to feed and tend to the babies in their own homes, since there was no safe alternative to breastmilk, helped keep more foundlings alive.[52] By the 1880s, the Foundling sent each baby out to wet-nurse within a week of its reception in the cradle. After weaning, the babies would go to live with "boarding mothers" who were paid a stipend in an arrangement very similar to modern foster care. If they lived long enough to become "run-around[s]," the children would be sent back to the Foundling for nursery school. Then they might be chosen to ride a baby train.[53]

Perhaps owing to the minority nature of Catholicism in the United States and to the more careful prematching scheme it used to place toddlers, the Foundling sent far fewer children on trains than the CAS.[54] The Foundling's process for sending children to "the West" followed the basic model that the CAS had laid out, but with the primary goal of finding families, not jobs, for their much younger charges. These families had to be Catholic, first and foremost. Before sending the toddlers off on their journeys, the Foundling sent agents to towns all along railroad lines where Catholic parishes had been established. There, the agents consulted with priests to find parents—most importantly, mothers—who would promise to take their new children to Mass, guide them through their sacraments, and generally bring them up to be pious and virtuous.[55]

Notably, unlike Brace, the Sisters of Charity were not interested in turning the immigrant poor into "Americans." The Catholic communities that the Foundling sent its trains to were often ethnic enclaves.[56] While the Foundling agents placed children in some of the same midwestern states and territories that the CAS frequented, like Kansas and Nebraska, they also sent large parties to Louisiana, which, then as now, had a significant population of Catholic people with French, Spanish, and Creole heritage.[57]

In 1904, this practice of prioritizing Catholicism first and foremost backfired in what the Foundling's archival records refer to as "the Arizona incident." In September of that year, forty children were sent by train to be placed with families in Clifton and Morenci, Arizona—mining towns in what was still just a territory.[58] The toddlers were white, and the families, who had been vetted by a French priest, were Mexican. White Protestant vigilantes responded by kidnapping the children. George Whitney Swayne, the Foundling agent who had accompanied the nuns and children to Arizona, wrote that the white mob accused the local priest, the nuns, and the agent of selling the children and yelled, "'Hang Them' 'Tar and Feather Them' etc."[59]

The "Arizona incident" was splashed across newspaper headlines throughout the United States, from Seattle to San Antonio to Jacksonville.[60] The *New York Times* called the Mexican families "wretched and questionable."[61] The Foundling fought to have the children removed from the Protestants who had kidnapped them and filed a writ of habeas corpus case that eventually reached the Supreme Court. In their decision to reject the Foundling's appeal, the Court doubled down on the racism at the heart of the situation, writing, "The children were distributed among persons wholly unfit to be intrusted [*sic*] with them, being, with one or two exceptions, half-breed Mexican Indians of bad character."[62] The Catholic children were to remain with the Protestant kidnappers.

The "Arizona incident" is a microcosm of the bigoted, sectarian ideologies that ruled—and still rule—vulnerable children's fates. To one side, all that mattered about these children was that they were Catholic; to the other, all that mattered was that they were white. Instead of considering what would be best for the children as individuals, both the Foundling and the mob of white settlers treated them as chits in a power play.

Reading through the Foundling archives, I was struck anew by a divergence between how the charity depicted the experience of young children being "placed out" to new homes in faraway towns and how the riders themselves recalled their experiences in letters and oral histories and at orphan train reunions later in life. As was the case with the CAS, in annual reports, histories, and the press, the Foundling conjures a vision of blissful, wholesome family life for the children it sent on trains, supplanting the families they were severed from early in their lives due to poverty and stigma. In an 1881 report, the sisters write of baby train riders, "As far as could be expected, they have met with parental care and love; and in their innocence fondly imagine that they could have found their lost mother and father. It is most affecting to behold a little troupe starting off for these far-off homes. In response to the question, '*Little one, where are you going?*' the reply inevitably comes, '*To my papa and mamma.*'"[63] An 1893 report is even more high-flying: "Again, the wonderful providence of God shows a special care for these little ones, cruelly deserted by their natural protectors, and kind-hearted strangers are eager to supply the parents' place. To-day, thousands of them are petted and cherished members of happy households."[64]

Of course, not all of the baby train riders were treated with love in their new homes, and not all were content to imagine that their new parents were their "real" parents. The erasure of these children's identities at birth owing to the Foundling's practices of secrecy and protection of birth mothers' identities would haunt many of them later in life. In a 1994 request for information, a woman named Helen Macior, who was born in 1913 and rode a train to Illinois in 1915, writes that she is seeking information simply "to learn who I am."[65] The yearning behind Helen's request for the most basic information about herself, at age eighty-one, gutted me. On another 1994 request form, Marguerite Thomson, who was born in 1906 and rode a train to Nebraska in 1911, writes that she wants more information "to release the emptiness in [my] heart."[66] Marguerite's case represents both the pain of being kept from one's origin story and the fact that some children placed by the Foundling endured horrific abuse, just as CAS train riders did. After her first placement in Nebraska fell apart, a woman took her in. The woman's husband raped her repeatedly when she was twelve years old. She later recalled to a researcher, "I'd wake up in the nighttime and he would be in bed with me. I'd holler to her, and she'd come get me and make him go back to bed. She'd tell me to lock the door, but it didn't do any good."[67]

The tension between the Foundling's desire to keep unwed mothers' identities secret and the desire of former train riders to know about their origins foreshadows a central conundrum of modern adoption: the difficulty that adoptive children face in accessing information about their birth parents. In the Foundling archives, I found document after document that argued for why secrecy is necessary. In a representative letter to the State Board of Charities in 1900, the Foundling pushed back against new regulations that would require it to collect and turn over the most basic information about the parents of the babies left in its cradles and born in its hospital: their names and addresses. The letter argues that, due to the fact that "the vast majority of . . . the children are illegitimate,"

> should the mothers have any reason to apprehend that their names would ever become known to anyone but ourselves, it is extremely doubtful whether they would consent to send their children to the institution. In fact, there is great reason to fear that, rather than do so, they would abandon the children in the street, leaving them to the mercy of any chance passer, or leaving them to die, if they were not discovered and taken care of in time. . . . The names of the parents would become matters of public record, and the unfortunate mothers would be subjected to humiliation, if not to blackmail.[68]

This argument threatened that more foundlings would end up on the streets and likely die if the Sisters of Charity were forced to abandon secrecy. The state board had made the request in order to ensure that the children whose care it was subsidizing with per capita payments were indeed sufficiently "needy"—that their families indeed could not afford to take care of them.

Both representatives of the Foundling and representatives of the state and city governments did not consider that people have rights to self-knowledge. In fact, in a 1903 letter to the city comptroller arguing for the necessity of secrecy, a representative of the Foundling, stoking fear about making birth parents' information public, references a case where a man asked to see his records: "Perhaps you will recall the case of one, King, who recently obtained much publicity by going to the Foundling Hospital and demanding to see the books of the institution concerning himself. . . . The sisters refused to give him the knowledge he sought, and after visits he shot two of them. At the trial of King, he was shown to be insane. . . . King's reiterated cry was that he had a right to know who his parents were and if they had money he should have his rights."[69] Though the Foundling casts King as having mercenary intentions and implies that only an insane person would fight so hard to find out about his birth circumstances, contemporaneous accounts in the *New York Times* paint a different picture. Henry J. King was left at the Foundling when he was a few months old in 1871 and later sent to Maryland. In 1900 he obtained a court order to have the Sisters of Charity show cause as to why they refused to supply him with his records.[70] In July 1902, after years of frustration in his search, King entered the Foundling compound and shot two sisters, both in the arm and one in the torso, before shooting himself. All survived. At arraignment, King told the judge, "This thing preys on my mind, day and night. I cannot work and I cannot sleep; I who thought so much of the Justice of God. All I want is my rights. The law would not help me, and I had to take the law into my own hands."[71]

Though New York State law began to require birth registration in 1881, it was not actually followed in practice until around 1913.[72] It's quite likely, then, that King's birth was never recorded—that the Sisters of Charity truly did not have any official documents to share with him. King was "farmed out," likely via indenture, to a man in Maryland, "with whom he lived for some years," or so the *New York Times* reported. If he had been adopted, though, and if his birth certificate did exist, the law would soon definitively come down against his right to see it.

By the 1930s, when every state had already passed its own adoption laws, and when birth registration was universal, states started to seal original birth records after adoptions.[73] A new, revised birth certificate, listing the names of the adoptive parents, would supplant the original, and only with a rare court order would the adoptee be able to learn who they really were. New York sealed adoptees' original birth certificates in 1935. In 2019, it became one of only nine states to unseal those records, granting adoptees unrestricted access to their original birth certificates after they have turned eighteen.[74]

———

The fact that the Sisters of Charity insisted on secrecy well before the dawn of modern adoption and the accompanying sealing of records and refused to allow anyone—let alone the foundlings themselves—know who the children' birth parents were speaks to how their mission was never purely one of baby saving for its own sake. It's not an exaggeration to say that the Foundling saw the babies left in its cradle or born in its maternity hospital not as individuals with specific histories and agency but as pawns in a larger fight to preserve Catholicism and to police sexuality. By erasing each baby's past, the Foundling erased the supposed sins that had led to its creation. As a blank slate, the baby could be made into a tiny missionary of Catholicism, planted to further grow the seeds of the church in new frontiers.

The Sisters of Charity assumed that every child left at the Foundling came from Catholic parents, but that is a big assumption to make. Their entire scheme was premised on the idea that Catholicism is passed to a child at the moment of birth. In reality, it is a religion that a child has to be actively admitted into via the sacrament of baptism, which a parent must choose for them. It is true that some babies were left in the cradle with notes that made reference to Catholic religion. "With the assistance of Our Blessed Lady I promise to place in the contribution box all I can spare from my earnings," one woman wrote.[75] Another included $2 "to have this child baptized Willie."[76] But other notes were silent on the matter, providing only the child's name ("Augustus, born Oct 16 1870. Be good to my darling!"), and some babies came with no note at all.[77]

When toddlers were sent to new families in railroad towns, they bore new labels: the tags sewn into their dress hems or coats identified them by their names and the names and addresses of their new parents. There is evidence that in freshly labeling toddlers, the Foundling turned some Jewish children into Catholics. One woman believed that her surname at birth was the common Irish Catholic name Ryan, only to find out late in life that it actually was Rubin and that she had been born a Jew (unlike Catholicism, Judaism is conferred at birth, matrilineally).[78]

Eventually, former foundlings themselves would push back against the secrecy that the Sisters of Charity had once forced upon them. In a situation that presaged the CAS riders' reunions, baby train riders began holding their own gatherings in the 1960s. Once they joined together and began sharing their stories, a collective hunger for more information bubbled to the surface.

A woman named Mary Carl Heser Kingdon organized the first reunion in 1962 in Grand Island, Nebraska, seeking to meet others who had ridden to that state on a 1912 Foundling train. In a reminiscence I read in the archives, Mary Carl wrote about what had inspired her to look for other riders. She wasn't even sure where she had been born—she mentioned both Staten Island and Italy—but believed that she was born in 1908 and "orphaned" a few weeks later.[79] Ten years after she was "placed out" with a family in Nebraska, they legally adopted her, and she seems to have had a good experience with them. But she wanted to know more about where she had come from. Mary Carl described visiting New York in 1955 for the primary purpose of finding "the name of my mother and father . . . but at [the Foundling] I got very little information, so I came back to Nebraska no wiser, but still hoping someday to find someone."[80] The reunion she arranged through wire service articles in newspapers and with the help of other riders fulfilled that hope, even if she didn't find a brother or sister.[81] Mary Carl referred to the night spent with about fifty other baby train riders as "the real highlight of my life."[82]

At the Grand Island reunion, some riders brought the clothing they had worn on their train journeys fifty years earlier, with their Foundling identifying tags still sewn in. One woman, Florence Kocian, rode wearing clothing that bore tags for "Jane Dalgleish" and a hat tagged "Florence Smith." Though she was in fact born with the name Jane Dalgeish, her foster mother preferred the name Florence and kept it, exchanging her identity with someone else's as simply as changing her clothes. At the reunion, she met the real Florence Smith, and they hugged.[83] In photos published in newspapers and archived in scrapbooks, the former foundlings, now in their fifties and sixties, wear replicas of their shipping tags and beam.

News of the 1962 reunion set off a cascade of letters from other riders seeking self-knowledge. By the 1980s and 1990s, when Mary Ellen Johnson was gathering oral histories and hosting reunions via the Orphan Train Heritage Society of America, former foundlings were growing impatient in their requests. In 1995, Helen Macior, the woman who had written simply to find out who she was, sent another letter to the executive director of the Foundling—by then a position held by a layperson. "I truly believed Sister Marilda Joseph, yourself and others who promised speedy research and answers to our identity," Helen wrote. "Seven months have elapsed, and nary a word. This in addition to the last 5 years of correspondence. . . . If there is one thing I strongly believe, every human being is entitled to know from whence they came, be it good or bad."[84] This was the last letter from her in the archives, and I wondered if Helen died before she had the chance to access what little information the Foundling likely had about her case.

In another 1995 letter to the director, a woman named Alice Bernard was more forthright with her impatience and anger. "Some of these nuns should have come with us to the public library and vital records bureau to see what we all went through to find a glimmer of hope," she writes. "Sitting at those [microfilm] machines for 5 to 6 hrs. is pretty tiresome for people our age. If they had a little compassion they would realize how much easier [it is] to just give us the information. What are they afraid of, lawsuits? Dead people can't sue."[85]

Now the last of the baby train riders would be more than one hundred years old, if any are still living. The Foundling, meanwhile, lives on. While nuns from the Sisters of Charity sit on its board of trustees, they are no longer involved in the charity's day-to-day operations. Its modern programming includes foster care and a residential "mother and child program" that echoes the original maternity hospital, providing housing and parenting and vocational education for pregnant foster youth.[86] The Foundling no longer operates out of the compound on the Upper East Side—the charity sold it to Donald J. Trump for $40 million in 1985.[87]

If the orphan train era on the whole was a dark period of social engineering in response to moral panics about urban changes, its foundling chapter was the consequence of a culture of repression, stigma, and secrecy. I can't help but feel that so many women did not need to be forced to carry pregnancies to term only to have little recourse but to relinquish their babies. They did not need to be forced to choose between shame and erasure. Their babies did not need to carry out lives chosen for them by nuns and priests and agents who cared most about perpetuating a religion, and they did not need to have their own histories withheld from them in adulthood—all because they were assumed to have been conceived in sin.

Yet the dark history of the Foundling's baby trains still doesn't come close to the most sinister and systematic use of the railroads to erase children's identities. That grim honor goes to our federal government.

Chapter Eight

FORCED ASSIMILATION BY TRANSCONTINENTAL RAILROAD

The self-guided walking tour of the Carlisle Barracks begins at a squat, light gray, stone building. The story goes that during the Battle of Trenton in December 1776, George Washington's patriot troops captured a group of Hessian soldiers—German auxiliaries fighting in the Revolutionary War on behalf of the British. The Americans then supposedly brought some of those Hessian prisoners of war to their barracks in Carlisle, Pennsylvania, which had been established during the French and Indian War twenty years earlier and was being used for the storage of gunpowder and arms.[1] According to legend, in 1777, the captured Hessians built this stone magazine, a warehouse for munitions. It is the oldest structure still standing in the barracks.[2]

I wasn't taking this solo tour because I cared about Carlisle's importance to early American history, though the city is proud that Molly Pitcher lived and died there and relishes its connection to the 1794 Whiskey Rebellion. Nor was I particularly interested in the fact that the grounds that I was walking were now the home of the US Army War College, which prepares senior officers and civilians "to preserve peace, deter aggression, compete below the threshold of armed conflict, and achieve victory in war—with a special focus on Landpower," per its website—though the presence of the army did mean that I needed to pass a federal background check against the National Crime Information Center Interstate Identification Index to be allowed onto the barracks.[3]

I was in Carlisle because I wanted to understand the role this small city twenty miles west of the Susquehanna River had played in tearing Native children from their families. I was at the barracks because they were once home to the federally run Carlisle Indian Industrial School, the notorious Indian boarding school that purported to provide "education" but was, in reality, a place of forced assimilation. From 1879 to 1918, Carlisle sought to break the ties between Native youth and their families and tribes—to essentially render them orphans. The school combined the institutionalization of orphanages with the use of the transcontinental railroad and "placing out" scheme of the orphan trains.

Native children who made railroad voyages to Indian boarding schools like Carlisle took opposite journeys to the orphan train riders sent to live with settlers in the Midwest and beyond. As Native children and "orphans" criss-crossed the country, they were swapping places as pawns in parallel schemes, one designed by the government to kill a culture, the other designed by private religious charities to quell moral panics.

I was standing alone in front of this old stone building on a freezing November day not to marvel at how long it had lasted—it was the only original building left standing after Confederate troops burned the barracks in 1863—but because it was a site where Native children had been abused.[4] With its brick-lined stone walls, the magazine had been a safe spot for housing flammable gunpowder during the Revolutionary War. Those same walls made this building, then known as the Guard House, the location of choice for punishing Carlisle students "whose disciplinary infractions merited confinement."[5]

I had purchased a walking tour booklet at the Cumberland County Historical Society gift shop downtown; there was no information about the Carlisle Indian Industrial School available in the Carlisle Barracks visitors center. I wondered if the US Army War College students and their families who went about their business on campus thought much about what the federal government had done to Native Americans here starting some 140 years earlier. Nearby, a boy of about ten was playing with his small white poodle mix, running around on a pristine green lawn between white colonial-style buildings—buildings where Carlisle's superintendent and teachers had lived. I thought about the Native children who had been imprisoned in the Guard House and wondered if anyone would have been able to hear them cry for help or mercy.

The idea of subjecting children to confinement in a dark and dank place built by prisoners disturbed me. But I was even more disquieted by what I saw in the museum within the stone building, which is now known as the Hessian Powder Magazine. In one small area dedicated to the Carlisle Indian Industrial School, a wall placard seeks to sanitize its history. "Richard Pratt's vision was to provide training for Native American youth who could then sustain themselves in industry, trades and farming," the wall text begins, speaking of the school's founder, an army officer. The narrative ignores why Native American youth would need to "sustain themselves" by working at colonizers' trades rather than perpetuating the ways of life of their tribes, how those youth ended up at Carlisle, and why the federal government found the cause of "training" Native American youth to be so critical.

The museum prefers to avoid such questions, but they are at the heart of why I was visiting. While the federal government abrogated any sense of responsibility toward orphans and poor children until 1909, when the White House held the first Conference on the Care of Dependent Children, it had begun to intervene in the lives of Native children almost a hundred years earlier. In 1819, Congress passed the Civilization Fund Act, which provided federal funding to boarding schools run by religious missionary groups that sought to, well, "civilize"—assimilate and convert—Native children.[6] Carlisle was the first Indian boarding school to be run—not just funded—by the federal government itself.[7] In total, between 1819 and 1969, the federal government supported or outright ran more than four hundred boarding schools for Native children.[8] It did so in an express attempt to dispossess and assimilate Native peoples. The government—aided and abetted by religious groups and the railroad—stole children away from their families and tribes, and stole the children's cultural inheritance away from them, all to further a larger scheme of stealing land.

At the Carlisle Barracks, only a few markers memorialize the Carlisle Indian Industrial School's history, and like the museum placard, they largely ignore a dark reality. But as I walked the grounds, I came upon one that didn't bowdlerize the school's mission. On a stone near what was once the school's hospital, a bronze plaque honors Richard Henry Pratt, Carlisle's founder and first superintendent. The plaque quotes Pratt himself: "The way to civilize an Indian is to get him into civilization. The way to keep him civilized is to let him stay."[9]

This quote, though a damning indication of Pratt's attitude toward Indigenous peoples, isn't even his most infamous. That honor goes to a line from a speech he delivered in 1892, which distilled his assimilationist vision in one sentence: "Kill the Indian in him, and save the man."[10] Like Charles Loring Brace, Pratt believed that a radical change of environment was necessary to wholly remove children from the bad influence of their parents. But unlike Brace, Pratt didn't even believe that those parents were human—they were savages.

The federal government itself now acknowledges that the goal of the Indian boarding schools was to assimilate Native children using "systematic militarized and identity-alteration methodologies."[11] Those tactics included giving Indian children Anglo names and forcing them to speak English instead of their native languages, cutting their hair, stripping them of their tribal clothing and dressing them in "military or other standard uniforms," and forbidding them from practicing tribal religions or taking part in tribal traditions and rituals.[12] Though the US government isn't willing to explicitly admit this yet, all of these "methodologies" meet the definition of cultural genocide—aiming to destroy an ethnic, racial, or national group by dismantling its culture. Indeed, historians and Native activists have long argued that the forced transfer to and assimilation of Native children at Indian boarding schools constituted cultural genocide.[13]

The quotes above come from an investigative report by the Bureau of Indian Affairs that Secretary of the Interior Deb Haaland mandated in 2021 as part of the Federal Indian Boarding School Initiative. Haaland—an enrolled member of the Laguna Pueblo whose great-grandfather was forced to attend Carlisle and grandmother was taken to another Indian boarding school—called for the establishment of the initiative shortly after news broke that the remains of more than a thousand people were found in unmarked graves on the sites of former residential schools in Canada.[14] As Haaland wrote in an op-ed for the *Washington Post*, "The deaths of Indigenous children at the hands of government were not limited to that side of the border." The Federal Indian Boarding School Initiative's mission includes investigating Native children's deaths at government-supported boarding schools, as well as the "lasting consequences" of the schools.[15] The initiative's first report, released in May 2022, officially catalogues for the first time the scale of the federal government's support of Indian boarding schools, as well as the abuses it perpetrated.

The systematic abuses of Indigenous children at boarding schools were designed in the 1800s as a way of solving the United States' "Indian Problem"—the clash between tribal sovereignty and land ownership and American Manifest Destiny. Settlers first tried to tackle the Indian Problem through warfare. The Indian Wars—a series of campaigns against tribes that had been living on the North American continent long before the 1600s—began in the colonial period and spread west of the Mississippi River in the early 1800s. Colonizers' bottomless hunger for Native land on which to settle, cultivate, and mine for natural resources propelled these wars. The only one I remember learning about as a child was the War of 1812, which I was taught was a war between the United States and Great Britain over British interference with American international trade. That's true, but only part of the story: the war was also sparked by America's unrelenting push into Indian territories and Britain's support for tribes that opposed US expansion into the Northwest Territory, and it was fought not just between American and British forces but also between Indigenous allies on both sides (far more supported the British).[16] The War of 1812 ultimately cost tribes millions of acres of land.[17]

In addition to violently driving Natives off their land, some of the Indian Wars ended with treaties by which the federal government essentially stole Native land and relegated tribes to reservations. In total, the United States entered into approximately 368 treaties that govern the federal government's responsibilities toward Native nations, before abandoning the practice of recognizing Native peoples as sovereign nations entirely in 1871.[18] Those treaties, often signed under coercion and fraudulent conditions, and often broken by the United States, are sometimes called "bad paper."[19] All told, tribes ceded approximately one and a half billion acres to the US government through treaties, agreements, and other seizures.[20] Today, tribes that once occupied lands across what is now the United States can only lay claim to approximately fifty-six million acres of reservations and other land trusts.[21] That's only a little more land than what makes up the state of Utah.

In addition to expropriating Native peoples from their land via treaties, Congress passed the Indian Removal Act in 1830, allowing President Andrew Jackson to approve "the exchange of lands with the Indians residing in any of the states or territories, and . . . their removal west of the river Mississippi."[22] The Indian Removal Act applied to the "Five Civilized Tribes"—the Cherokee, Chickasaw, Choctaw, Muscogee, and Seminole nations—which were living in the South. Their land was especially attractive to white settlers because gold had recently been discovered in Georgia.[23] After the Cherokee contested their removal to Indian Territory, US Army forces as well as state militias forced some sixteen thousand Cherokee on the Trail of Tears, a death march that killed approximately four thousand.[24]

All that bloodshed and bad paper still wasn't enough to satisfy the federal government. Solving the Indian Problem for good would mean actually eliminating Native peoples at their roots by taking their children and forcing them to assimilate. The Indian boarding school system was integral to this project.

In fact, the federal government considered funding and running Indian boarding schools to be an economically efficient answer to the Indian Problem. When Pratt asked Secretary of the Interior Carl Schurz for permission to found a school for Native Americans at the then abandoned Carlisle Barracks, Schurz obliged, in part because he claimed that it would only cost $1,200 to send an Indian child to boarding school for eight years, as opposed to $1 million to kill an Indian at war.[25] Schurz was far from the first in the federal government to suggest that cultural genocide was less expensive than plain old genocide. In fact, the United States had been promoting this scheme since its earliest days. The Kennedy Report of 1969, which aimed to investigate the federal government's role in educating Native children, explains that its ultimate goal had always been to eliminate Native culture and steal Native land: "Beginning with President Washington, the stated policy of the Federal Government was to replace the Indian's culture with our own. This was considered 'advisable' as the cheapest and safest way of subduing the Indians, of providing a safe habitat for the country's white inhabitants, of helping the whites acquire desirable land, and of changing the Indian's economy so that he would be content with less land. Education was a weapon by which these goals were to be accomplished."[26]

Boarding schools would make headway toward these goals in important ways. First, the schools would teach Native children to take up the white man's way of life—the "industry, trade and farming" alluded to in the wall text of the Hessian Powder Magazine exhibit—in the process eschewing lifestyles based on nomadism and hunting that tied them to their wide swaths of land. This kind of assimilation and territorial dispossession was promoted by none other than Thomas Jefferson in an 1803 confidential message to Congress, wherein he suggested that the government "encourage [Indians] to abandon hunting, to apply to the raising [of] stock, to agriculture, and domestic manufacture, and thereby prove to themselves that less land and labor will maintain them in this better than in their former mode of living."[27]

The Federal Indian Boarding School Initiative's report confirms that the education at Indian boarding schools largely comprised vocational or industrial training and that child labor was essentially part of the curricula.[28] The samples of schoolwork by Carlisle students that I leafed through in the Cumberland County Historical Society's archives revolved around vocational training to an almost bizarre degree. Spelling tests for first graders used vocabulary from the industrial laundry; seventh-grade math word problems were based on tailoring (e.g., find the distance between brass buttons on a uniform coat); student artwork depicted blacksmithing tools.[29]

Beyond assimilating Native children, the boarding school system physically removed those children from tribal lands, compounding and coinciding with the government's invasion and possession of those lands. By the time Carlisle opened in 1879, Congress was no longer making treaties with tribes, and the tribes that the government had formally recognized were largely relegated to reservations in the West.[30] The children who were forced to attend Carlisle and other Indian boarding schools far from their reservations had to travel long distances across the continent via the newly built, federally subsidized transcontinental railroad, whose construction further encroached on Native land.

As the federal government took land away from Native Americans, it distributed that stolen land to settlers, essentially for free. The 1862 Homestead Act, designed to spur development of the West, granted adults over the age of twenty-one and heads of households allotments of 160 acres of public land in exchange for a minimal filing fee and five years of residence on and cultivation of that land.[31] The act, which was in effect until 1986, eventually applied to public lands in thirty states—essentially everything west of the Mississippi, save Texas, and a number of states east of the river: Wisconsin, Illinois, Michigan, Indiana, Ohio, Mississippi, Alabama, and Florida.[32] It granted 270 million acres of what had once been Native land to homesteaders. In 1887, inspired by the Homestead Act, the Dawes Act imported the practice of breaking up land into individual allotments to Indian reservations, with disastrous results. Not only did the Dawes Act prioritize individual land ownership over tribal communalism, but it allowed for the sale of "excess" reservation land, leading to the government seizure of an additional sixty million acres for homesteaders and others.[33]

Some of the families who accepted orphan train riders were homesteaders, living on land that had belonged to displaced Native Americans.[34] This is exactly what much orphan train fiction, including Joan Lowery Nixon's *Orphan Train Adventures* series, romanticizes. In *A Family Apart*, some of the Kelly siblings live with industrious, abolitionist homesteaders in Kansas who took an allotment on the territory so they would have a voice in making it a free state. One orphan train children's series even includes a book titled *Prairie Homestead*. This makes for potent fantasy that puts a positive spin on the fact that orphan train riders were supplying vital labor to homesteads—settlers relied on the free labor of children in order to cultivate their land and make good on the terms of the Homestead Act.[35]

Meanwhile, Indigenous children—who had been stolen off the reservations their tribes had been relegated to after their land was stolen—supplied physical labor to keep boarding schools running. The Federal Indian Boarding School Initiative's report found that manual labor was rampant and included everything from raising livestock and poultry to making garments to working on the railroad system itself.[36] At Carlisle, students even worked to supply the needs of the Bureau of Indian Affairs, making wagons and harnesses used on reservations.[37] Both sets of children were sacrificed for American Manifest Destiny, but Indigenous children forced to attend boarding schools didn't just lose their families and their childhoods to labor; they were systematically deprived of their heritage.

School officials, federal Indian agents, and scouts—members of tribes who allied and cooperated with the US military—carried out recruitment at reservations, coercing parents and tribal leaders to send their children to Carlisle. Sometimes Pratt himself traveled to recruit students.[38] The alliance between the federal government and missionary groups, established with the Civilization Fund Act, continued when it came to finding Carlisle pupils—in 1880, the commissioner of Indian affairs nominated a reverend who served as the general agent for the Presbyterian Board of Missions to select students from tribes in Colorado and New Mexico. The government bankrolled these trips.

While some children attended schools like Carlisle because their families and tribes thought the education offered would be good for them, many were recruited under conditions that mimicked the trickery surrounding the bad paper that had sequestered Native nations on reservations—they were given a choice that was scarcely a choice.[39] Many others were forcibly removed.[40] This was openly acknowledged at the time: in an 1884 telegram, an Indian agent declared that he would use "severe measures" to recruit Apache girls for Carlisle.[41] Some students were even sent to Carlisle as prisoners of war, or because their parents were prisoners of war.[42] In 1886, after the end of the Apache Wars, when the US government held tribal leader Geronimo and his band captive despite the fact that they had surrendered and were not charged with any crimes, a group of Apache children were forcibly removed to Carlisle.[43]

In total, about seventy-eight hundred children from nearly every Native nation were sent to Carlisle during its nearly forty-year run.[44] The majority of students were between the ages of twelve and twenty when they enrolled, but some were much younger. Enrollment terms lasted three to five years, and some students re-enrolled for a second term.[45] Only 779 students—about 10 percent—graduated from Carlisle.[46] After their studies, they would return to their reservations.

The connection between federal Indian boarding schools and the military was also by design. In fact, Pratt developed the idea of turning unused military properties into Indian boarding schools when he was serving in the army. As a cavalry officer, he had spent 1867 to 1875 in Indian Territory, leading a contingent of freed Black "Buffalo soldiers" and Indian scouts in campaigns to keep Native peoples on their reservations and away from settlers.[47] From 1875 to 1878, Pratt was appointed to guard a group of seventy-two Native prisoners of war at Fort Marion, Florida. The prisoners were warriors from the Cheyenne, Kiowa, Comanche, and Caddo nations, whom the government sentenced to exile for their hostility and continued raiding of settler parties—raids driven by the insufficiency of the provisions the federal government supplied reservations with.[48] The tribal leaders and warriors' journey to prison began with American forces marching them in chains from Fort Sill, Oklahoma, to a railroad station 165 miles away. After a long train journey not unlike the ones that children from their tribes would later experience en route to Carlisle, they were imprisoned at Fort Marion in a pen of about a hundred square feet.[49]

Pratt soon removed these incarcerated warriors' shackles—but not to set them free. He intended to make them into "men," as in his "kill the Indian in him, and save the man" adage. He had their hair cut and made them dress in military uniforms and perform military drills. And in a makeshift school, Pratt allowed local women to teach the men how to read and write in English, furthering their assimilation. At the end of their incarceration, Pratt had convinced about twenty of the Native men to continue their education at the Hampton Institute in Virginia, a government school for Black freedmen.[50] By then Pratt had realized that education needed to be a key component of an assimilationist answer to the Indian Problem, and he wanted to establish his own school that would exclusively serve Natives.

Pratt soon suggested to Interior Secretary Schurz that Carlisle Barracks would be an ideal location for an Indian boarding school. The barracks had been sitting empty since a cavalry school vacated them in 1872; they were located amid "a fine agricultural country and the inhabitants are kindly disposed and long free from the universal border prejudice against the Indians."[51] (Like Brace, Pratt had strong faith in the moral character of rural peoples.) In mid-1879, Pratt, Schurz, and Secretary of War George McCrary collaborated on transferring the Carlisle Barracks from the War Department to the Interior Department, which houses the Bureau of Indian Affairs.[52] That the first federally run Indian boarding school would be established on a former military barracks makes a perverse kind of sense—it marked just the latest battle in a long-running war to decimate Native peoples.

Besides marking the beginning of the federal government establishing its own boarding schools, Carlisle stands out because of how far it was from the reservations of many tribes whose children were forced to attend. The majority of the more than four hundred federally supported Indian boarding schools were located west of the Mississippi, near or on reservations. Oklahoma, the site of what was once Indian Territory, was home to seventy-six boarding schools.[53] On-reservation boarding schools largely drew from individual Native nations, and while life there was heavily regimented and full of deprivation, children were at least physically closer to their families and lived, studied, and worked among tribal peers.

Carlisle was different by design. By removing children as far as possible from their reservations and keeping them at Carlisle for years at a time (visits home were very rare), Pratt hoped to speed assimilation.[54] "I believe in immersing the Indians in our civilization and when we get them under holding them there until they are thoroughly soaked," Pratt told a convention of Baptist ministers in 1883.[55] The orphanage-like institutional environment of Carlisle, where each minute of the children's time was planned and supervised with militaristic precision, was one means of this immersion.[56] Adding to the heavy dose of "civilization" was a scheme that echoes the indenture and "placing out" system key to the orphan trains: Carlisle's "outing" program, whereby children were sent to live with and work for white people in the area. Boys often worked on farms, whereas girls were trained to be domestic servants, replicating the gendered labor divisions of the orphan train movement and furthering the "industrial" education the students received at Carlisle.[57] And as with both religious orphanages and the orphan train movement, religion played a role in the Americanization of Native children—Carlisle students were required to participate in Christian church services, both at school and while on outings.[58]

The first trainload of children to arrive at Carlisle in 1879 were Lakota people of the Sioux tribes, traveling from what was then the Dakota Territory, more than fifteen hundred miles from Carlisle. Lakota children were chosen to kick off the experiment because the government saw their tribe as combative; the Great Sioux War over ownership of the Black Hills, which resulted in the government reaping more Native land and the establishment of the Great Sioux Reservations, was still fresh. An eleven-year-old Lakota boy named Ota Kte, whose English name was Luther Standing Bear, was among the first to make the journey.[59] He later recalled, "I could think of no reason why white people wanted Indian boys and girls except to kill them, and not having the remotest idea of what a school was, I thought we were going East to die."[60]

Even the closest reservations in New York, like the Allegheny Indian Territory, where some Seneca people lived, were still more than two hundred miles away. Pennsylvania itself has never had any federally recognized tribes and is thus home to no reservations, despite the fact that much of the state's land was once inhabited by the Lenape people.[61] Carlisle is located on the unceded territory of the Susquehannock people, who were considered extinct as a tribe by the time Carlisle came to be.[62] The state was thus a perfect location for carrying out Pratt's mission.

Not only was the distance from reservations deliberate, but the mixing of children from different tribes was part of Pratt's design, allowing for more efficient and effective ethnic cleansing. By recruiting from almost every Native nation simultaneously, the school sought to destroy each tribe's culture all at once.[63] It was Carlisle policy to place students in dorms with members of other tribes, meaning that their only shared language would be the English they were forced to learn. This mixing of cultures was part of the blueprint that Carlisle formed for the federal government's Indian boarding school system moving forward. The government went on to establish other military-style, off-reservation boarding schools across the country, like the Tomah Indian Industrial School in Wisconsin, conveniently located off a major railroad line, and the Phoenix Indian Industrial School, which opened at an abandoned military post at Fort McDowell, Arizona.

———

Pratt considered himself a friend to Indians and believed that in teaching Native children how to become white, he was bringing different races into harmony as mandated by the story of Adam and Eve.[64] "The original idea leading to the establishment of the Carlisle Indian school cannot be traced farther back than Adam," Pratt once wrote in a defense of Carlisle. "It is clear that when Adam became the father of mankind there was then established that beneficent principle—the unity of the human race—which through endless difficulties still struggles for supremacy."[65] Of course, in pushing for "the unity of the human race," Pratt really believed that all of humanity must be forced to adopt the white, Christian culture of the late nineteenth century.

If you believe Pratt's propaganda, his "unifying" experiment at Carlisle was a rousing success. From the start, Pratt was eager to show off his English-speaking students in their new uniforms with their new haircuts and new Americanized names, as though a *Pygmalion*-style change of costume and speech evidenced the dismantling of these youths' "savage" upbringing. He arranged for the school's military-style band to play at the 1883 opening of the Brooklyn Bridge and sent 420 students to the 1893 World's Fair in Chicago, where the choir and band performed.[66]

In addition to these very public and performative displays of Carlisle students, Pratt employed a local photographer to capture the students in before-and-after portraits. The first shot was taken upon their arrival, when the youth were still wearing their tribal garb, or "blankets," and the second was taken after the school had cut their hair and clothed them in uniforms. The portraits were published in school publications and sold as cabinet cards to spread visual proof of how Carlisle transformed its students.[67] To many students, these photos represented the painful erasure of their cultures. "We'd lost our hair and we'd lost our clothes," recalled Asa Daklugie, an Apache Carlisle student. "With the two we'd lost our identities as Indians. Greater punishment could hardly have been devised."[68]

One "before" photo from 1880 shows four Zuni students—two boys, two girls—recently arrived from New Mexico.[69] The children appear young, maybe ranging in age from six to ten; the school did not record their ages on their student information cards. Their dark hair reaches past their ears for boys and girls alike. The girls wear striped shawls tied over long dresses, probably made of woven cotton; the boys wear white long-sleeved shirts and dark pants, with patterned kerchiefs tied across their brows.[70] On the back their names are listed as "Teai-e-se-u-lu-ti-wa—Frank Cushing," "Tra-wa-ea-tsa-lun-kia—Taylor Ealy," "Tsai au-tit-sa—Mary Ealy," and

"Jan-i-uh-tit sa—Jennie Hammaker," a simple dash representing the forced imposition of an American name. In the "after," the Zuni children are posed in their new school uniforms.[71] The boys' hair is freshly shorn, and they wear military-style coats with brass buttons. The girls are outfitted in dresses with frilled collars and white pinafores, their hair brushed back. Little Tsai au-tit-sa, now firmly in costume as "Mary Ealy," sits on a wooden swing. In each photo, the children's mouths are flat lines.

Teai-e-se-u-lu-ti-wa would die at Carlisle just one year later. He was one of ten children to die there in 1881.[72] That same year, fourteen students returned home to their reservations due to sickness, and four of them later died. There were only 295 students at Carlisle in 1881, the third year of the school's operation, meaning that more than 3 percent of the student body died that year. Malnourishment, as well as crowded dormitories, cafeterias, and classrooms, meant that deadly infectious diseases like tuberculosis, pneumonia, meningitis, measles, and scarlet fever spread easily among students.[73] All told, 223 Carlisle pupils died while enrolled at the school, and more died shortly after returning home.[74]

When Teai-e-se-u-lu-ti-wa's parents requested that his body be repatriated back to Zuni Pueblo, Pratt wrote to the Office of the Pueblo Indian Agency that it was "not . . . practicable." He instead invited the Zuni Pueblo chiefs to visit the school, noting that when another parent, Chief White Thunder of the Rosebud Sioux, saw his son buried "as our own dead" at Carlisle, "he was satisfied." Tra-wa-ea-tsa-lun-kia also died during his time as a pupil at Carlisle, in 1883, when he was on an "outing" in Schellsburg, some hundred miles west of Carlisle.[75] He had come down with typhoid fever. Pratt instructed for Tra-wa-ea-tsa-lun-kia to be buried in Schellsburg; Carlisle would foot the bill.[76]

Teai-e-se-u-lu-ti-wa was never repatriated to Zuni. I know this because I saw his grave at the Carlisle Barracks, marked by a white stone that bears his English name, Frank Cushing, and his tribe. His remains, along with those of about 180 other deceased Carlisle students, were transferred from their original burial place at the barracks to a new cemetery on the edge of the property sometime around 1929.[77]

The cemetery sits in a bleak part of the barracks, between a busy road and a commissary parking lot studded with rented storage containers. A black metal fence surrounds the rectangular plot of small, uniform white gravestones, a cemetery the US Army describes as "small, orderly, and historical."[78] When I visited, the fence was locked. I looked around for a smooth pebble to place atop the large stone outside the fence that is dedicated to the entire cemetery—when I was a child, I always left rocks on my Papa Dascole's gravestone, having been taught that doing so marks the visit. I settled for a fallen leaf, adding it to the pile of stones, coins, seashells, and dried flowers already there. As I walked around the perimeter, my breath snagged when I noticed colorful artificial flowers decorating some of the graves. A small stuffed dog with bright blue ears sat in the dirt about a foot away from one grave, tossed by the harsh wind. About twenty gravestones were missing, the result of the disinterment and repatriation of remains back to families—a process the federal government began allowing in 2017.[79] Otherwise, if descendants want to visit their dead, they too must travel all the way to the site where their people had been subjected to forced assimilation and pass a federal background check.

Many of the students who survived their time at Carlisle experienced a kind of purgatory, where they were caught between their tribal ways of life and their white education and training. Plenty Horses, a Lakota, suffered exactly this fate. Sent to Carlisle at age fourteen in 1883, he was enrolled for five years, during which time he went on three different country "outings."[80] His trade at Carlisle was farming, but when he left the school, he said, "There was no chance to get employment, nothing for me to do whereby I could earn my board and clothes, no opportunity to learn more and remain with the whites. It disheartened me and I went back to live as I had before going to school." But reintegrating into the Pine Ridge Indian Reservation was not so easy for Plenty Horses. "When I returned to my people, I was an outcast among them," he said. "I was no longer an Indian. I was not a white man. I was lonely."

His conundrum reminded me of the dilemma faced by Black children who had been deemed redeemable by Quaker orphanages—their education, moral and academic, could not change the fact that they lived in a country where many people saw them as subhuman. Assimilation could never make these children white, but instead of attempting to make white Victorian culture more tolerant of difference, both Pratt and the Quakers who ran orphanages for Black children plowed forward with experiments that were bound to fail. Both were motivated by a desire to assimilate children rather than truly consider how best to aid them and their communities.

Plenty Horses spoke about being caught between two cultures while being tried for the murder of army lieutenant Edward W. Casey in January 1891.[81] Plenty Horses shot Casey in the aftermath of the Wounded Knee massacre, where the US Army killed more than 250 Lakota, including many women and children, in 1890.[82] The mass grave in which many of the Lakota dead were buried was still fresh when Casey was sent to negotiate with Lakota warriors, and Plenty Horses said he shot the lieutenant "so I might make a place for myself among my people. I am now one of them."[83] Plenty Horses was acquitted because the court considered the killing to be an act of war. The ruling was expedient in that by declaring that the Lakota had been at war with the United States, the court allowed the soldiers who had killed so many Lakota to avoid charges of murder.

Other Carlisle students did shrug off their tribal cultures upon leaving the school. After graduating Carlisle, Julia Powlas, whose Native name is not recorded, returned to the Oneida Nation and worked as a clerk for the Indian agent in charge of implementing the government's Indian policies on the reservation.[84] She wrote in an 1890 letter to the school that evidences her embrace of "civilization" that she was "married to an educated returned student from Carlisle. . . . We have built a new frame house & have 30 acres cultivated and 60 acres uncultivated. . . . Our people are all civilized & have never seen any one wearing an Indian clothes in our country."[85]

Powlas and her husband were unusually lucky in finding work on their reservation and gaining the support of the presidentially appointed Indian agent, who, like all other agents, was not Native himself. More often, upon returning from Carlisle, Native people found themselves stymied by severely circumscribed opportunities on their reservations, where natural resources were scarce, the land was difficult to cultivate, and the US government maintained control despite treaties that promised sovereignty. Pratt's plan to "keep" Natives "civilized" by "letting [them] stay" did not jibe with the reality that, in the late 1800s, most Native people had no other option but to live on reservations. His frustration with this fact led him to rail against both the reservation system and the Bureau of Indian Affairs, which he saw as a bureaucratic machine that reinforced the segregation of Native people from white culture.[86] (Of course, though he opposed segregation, Pratt didn't believe that Native cultures should continue to exist.) Pratt's vocal—and controversial—position against reservations led to his forced retirement in 1904.

But Pratt was not wrong to believe that true assimilation for Carlisle alumni would not be possible unless they were allowed to continue living in the white American world. As William Little Elk, a Cheyenne who entered Carlisle at age twenty-one in 1881, wrote to Pratt in 1890, "There are great many return children that are going back in Indian ways. Why just because there is no work to do. How we going keep up the way that we have learn. If you want us to do right + want us to become like Whites do something for us."[87]

Jim Thorpe, the school's most famous alumnus, seemed to be one of the few able to integrate into white American society upon leaving Carlisle, entirely because of his athletic prowess. I had heard of Jim Thorpe before, because there is a town named after him in Pennsylvania, in the Pocono Mountains, a place he never lived or visited but where his remains are controversially interred. But if you're more of a sports fan than me and you've heard of Carlisle, it might be because of Thorpe and his coach, Glenn S. "Pop" Warner—the namesake of the nationwide program that allows boys as young as five to compete in tackle football.[88] Warner coached football at Carlisle from 1899 to 1903 and again from 1907 to 1914.[89]

In downtown Carlisle, the only acknowledgment of the school's history is a memorial stone on a manicured historic public square that reads, "In recognition of the athletic achievements of Jim Thorpe, student of the Carlisle Indian School, Olympic champion at Stockholm in 1912, and in 1950 voted the greatest athlete and football player of the first half of the 20th century." When I visited the Cumberland County Historical Society to access the school's archives, its small museum's special exhibition was called "Heart of a Champion: Sports in Cumberland County," with much attention paid to Carlisle athletics, legendary football coach "Pop" Warner, and Thorpe. And at the Carlisle Barracks, Thorpe and Warner are prominently featured in the Hessian Powder Magazine museum; their portraits, along with that of another Carlisle football player, William H. "Lone Star" Dietz, are the only ones featured from the Indian boarding school era in a display titled "I Was at Carlisle." The barracks' main gymnasium has been called Thorpe Hall since 1954, the year after Thorpe died.

Thorpe was raised in Indian Territory in what is now Oklahoma, where the federal government had displaced his tribe, Sac and Fox, from their lands near Lake Huron and Lake Michigan. He was born in 1887 and named Wa-Tho-Huk, which means "bright path" or "path lit by lightning." Thorpe's life was already tumultuous before the upheaval of being sent east. His twin brother, Charlie, died of typhoid fever contracted at an on-reservation boarding school when they were nine years old.[90] His father was a physically abusive heavy drinker who had a second family, and Thorpe ran away from his on-reservation boarding school several times before being sent in 1898 to the Haskell Institute in Kansas, a federal Indian boarding school modeled on Carlisle.[91] He attended Haskell from ages eleven to thirteen and returned home for a few years, during which time he lost his mother, who died in childbirth. His father and new stepmother sent him to Carlisle in 1904, when he was sixteen. Within three months of his arrival, his father died, and Thorpe became an orphan.[92]

In some recollections, attending Carlisle saved Thorpe's life. He was a student at the school on and off between the ages of sixteen and twenty-four, and it was at Carlisle that "Pop" Warner is said to have recognized and honed his athletic talents.[93] Thorpe played left halfback for the Indians' football team, which dominated at the collegiate level against the likes of Harvard and West Point in games seen as symbolically pitting Natives against the white man.[94] Thorpe also played on the baseball team and emerged as an all-around track talent. His 1912 Olympic gold medals were for the decathlon and the pentathlon; he later played both for Major League Baseball and the National Football League.

Making Thorpe the poster child of Carlisle—and casting Carlisle and "Pop" Warner as the saviors of Thorpe's life—is opportunistic, painting a picture of the school as nurturing talent and providing its students with opportunities they wouldn't otherwise have encountered. But doing so papers over controversy surrounding Carlisle athletics that would in part contribute to the school's closing in 1918 and the legacy of athletics in Thorpe's own complicated life. Sports like football were a means of Americanizing Carlisle students just as much as forcing them to speak only English and wear white people's clothes. Lacrosse, a Native sport, was not allowed at Carlisle until 1910. It replaced baseball in a move by Warner to discourage students from playing semiprofessional baseball for pay during the summers—he wanted to push more Carlisle students into going on "outings" to work on farms during summer vacation.[95]

In fact, a few years later, Thorpe's own history of playing summer semipro baseball would lead Olympic officials to strip him of his goal medals—the Olympics then required athletes to be of "amateur" status.[96] Thorpe's medals and records would not be restored until long after his death. "Pop" Warner claimed to not know that Thorpe had played semipro baseball, abandoning him in his moment of need.[97] This betrayal would in turn spark a congressional investigation into athletics at Carlisle. Gus Welch, an Ojibwe, a Carlisle football player, and Thorpe's roommate, was so horrified by Warner's behavior toward Thorpe that he collected two hundred signatures on a petition to the commissioner of Indian affairs, asking for an investigation into misconduct in Carlisle's administration and athletics.[98]

In 1913, the Bureau of Indian Affairs sent an investigator, E. B. Linnen, to look into the complaints; Congress subsequently conducted its own investigation. Welch and other football players testified that Warner was verbally and physically abusive, cursing players out and kicking them.[99] Warner got away with this behavior because athletics had become a cash cow for the school, netting more than $200,000 between 1907 and 1913.[100] In his report, Linnen wrote, "Football and athletics have dominated said school. [A]ll other departments have been made to be subservient thereto."[101] Linnen also found that Warner had essentially professionalized the Indians' team, paying players for their participation, rendering his behavior around the Thorpe Olympics controversy especially hypocritical.

Carlisle never recovered from the abuses of power and mismanagement brought to light by the Bureau of Indian Affairs and congressional investigations. The school shuttered in 1918, and the campus was transferred back to the Department of War, which used it for rehabilitating soldiers returned from World War I.[102] But the federal Indian boarding school system endured long after the experiment at Carlisle ended. Not until 1969, following the Kennedy Report, would the government cease funding and operating the schools, leading to the founding of the Bureau of Indian Education, which transferred educational decision-making to tribes themselves.[103]

The traumatic legacy of Carlisle and the federal Indian boarding school system remains fresh and pervasive. Most Native peoples living now can trace their lineage back to these boarding schools—in 1926, as many as 83 percent of school-age Native children attended them.[104] At federal Indian boarding schools, children endured painful severance from their families and their cultures and were physically abused when they tried to speak their own languages and broke other rules.[105] Solitary confinement, as in the Carlisle Guard House, was a common punishment, as were flogging, slapping, and the withholding of food.[106] As the Federal Indian Boarding School Initiative's report attests, emotional and sexual abuse was also "rampant."[107]

The federal government now acknowledges that the long-term effects of its Indian boarding school system are still being felt in Native communities. In 2018, the Running Bear studies, funded by the National Institutes of Health, found that "American Indians who attended boarding school have lower physical health status," including a three-times higher rate of cancer as compared with nonattendees.[108] Notably, the study found that former boarding school attendees who were over the age of eight when enrolled—as was the case for the majority of the Carlisle students—and were punished for speaking their Native languages had the worst physical health status scores.[109] The detrimental physical health effects are generational too; the Running Bear studies found that children whose fathers attended Indian boarding schools had greater past-year chronic physical health problems than those whose fathers did not attend.[110] Boarding school alumni also face increased risk for serious mental health issues like posttraumatic stress disorder, depression, and unresolved grief.[111]

As Deb Haaland wrote for the *Washington Post*, "We have a generation of lost or injured children who are now the lost or injured aunts, uncles, parents and grandparents of those who live today." In fact, as the government acknowledges, in some families, multiple generations of children were sent to Indian boarding schools in a cycle of separation and trauma. And that cycle did not end when the boarding schools closed. Rather than send Native children to heavily regimented, overcrowded schools, the government instead aided and abetted rampant forced removal into foster care and adoption into white families.

THREE

FOSTER CARE

Chapter Nine

ALL IN THE FAMILY

The first kid I knew who didn't live with his parents was Shawn Hunter, Cory Matthews's best friend on *Boy Meets World*. Like many in the 1990s, I grew up alongside Shawn and Cory, one episode at a time. Though *Boy Meets World* was set in Philadelphia, the white bread world of Cory (the titular boy, played by curly-haired dweeb Ben Savage) felt not unlike my own in the Long Island suburbs. As with the coming-of-age family sitcoms that came before it—notably *The Wonder Years*, a 1960s nostalgia machine that starred Ben's older brother Fred Savage—the series centered on dilemmas faced by middle-class white kids who live in the cushioned shelter of a tight-knit nuclear family. My own family was akin to the Matthewses back then: working father, stay-at-home mother, sitting down for a home-cooked dinner together nightly. The biggest difference between Cory's life on *Boy Meets World* and my own was that I didn't have any friends like Shawn.

Growing up, nearly all of my friends' families were like my own. Most of my friends' moms stayed at home or worked in the kinds of jobs that meant they could still pick up their kids after school and be active in the PTA. One ran a hairdressing business out of a salon her husband built in their basement, and she cut my hair and my mom's for years; later, she'd take my mom wig shopping before she started chemo. Most of the dads worked solid middle-class jobs; several were cops like my dad. I only had one close friend with divorced parents, and she and her mom lived in a house almost twice the size of mine, with a formal living room *and* a den and a jacuzzi tub upstairs. In West Hempstead, there were no trailer parks like the one Shawn lived in; the only apartment buildings I knew of were the ones we passed on the way to Roosevelt Field Mall in the wealthy village of Garden City a few miles away.

This is all to say that Shawn's life even before his parents abandoned him—full of precarity, leaving him rough around the edges from living among bullies and petty criminals in a trailer park, with a huckster father who scraped by on tall tales and a mother who was essentially a nonentity—was foreign to me. I saw Shawn's character through the framework of what my parents referred to as "WT": white trash. They used the code because they knew the term was a slur, one that paints poor white people as worthless and disposable. I was familiar with WT from families on other TV shows we watched, like the Connors on *Roseanne*, the Bundys on *Married with Children*, and, at the extreme end of the spectrum, the redneck Spucklers on *The Simpsons*. The shows made it seem like the poorer you were, the more backward, uncivilized, and "undeserving" you were.

Shawn's characterization on *Boy Meets World* would eventually fit into the grooves of well-worn WT tropes, and those tropes would be used to explain why he didn't get to have a family—not one like Cory's, anyway. Because Shawn's father couldn't hold down a job, because his mother ran away, because they lived in a trailer instead of a house built into the ground—because, essentially, they were poor—they did not deserve to stay together. *Boy Meets World* wants us to believe that Shawn would be better off without his parents in his life, and watching the show as a child, I bought into that notion.

Shawn's character arc follows the script for dependent children's stories that Charles Loring Brace set when he promulgated his theories about the "dangerous classes" and "vicious" gemmules in the mid-nineteenth century, ideas that would be repeated, refined, and eventually revised in orphan train fiction. That Shawn improbably never encounters the child welfare system makes his story even more appealing. For much of *Boy Meets World*, Shawn may be effectively parentless, but he gets the silver lining of a move from "trailer park trash up to decent society," as he says, without encountering the abuse, control, and disorder of the foster care system.[1]

In pop culture, foster care is always—like life in an orphanage or with a poor family—something a character has to escape or overcome in order to have a fighting chance. *Boy Meets World* sidesteps the issue entirely, speaking to how, in the 1990s, we were so afraid of foster care that we preferred to pretend that it didn't even exist. Shawn Hunter—though he was never a foster kid and does not become an orphan until he is over eighteen—is *the* orphan character of 1990s sitcoms.

OK, maybe it seems extreme for me to claim that Shawn Hunter is a paradigmatic orphan character. I'm sure that a lot of people who loved *Boy Meets World* when they were kids would object that my interpretation is not canon. But maybe we don't usually see Shawn as an orphan character because we are so inured to and uncritical of orphan tropes that they barely register anymore. We don't question why we are sympathetic to characters like Shawn, who serve to reinforce conservative, classist ideas about who gets to have a family and allow us to ignore the realities of the child welfare system.

In the 1990s and early 2000s, we got a string of shows that skirted around foster care. They featured characters abandoned by their parents, like Ryan Atwood on *The O.C.*, or outright orphaned, like the Salinger siblings on *Party of Five*, who get a second chance and are absorbed into a perfect middle-class (or better) nuclear family or manage to construct a new family for themselves. Shawn Hunter is just one of the characters of this era onto whom we mapped our morals about poverty, "best interest," and the nuclear family. And he came to embody the stereotypes that have long been the hallmarks of orphan narratives, updated for the 1990s.

Played by a moody Rider Strong, whose floppy, center-parted brown hair, icy blue eyes, and smirk of a smile made him *Teen Beat* foldout poster material, Shawn starts out on the show as Cory's longtime best friend and fellow sixth-grade class goof. Shawn becomes a character in his own right halfway into the first season in order for Cory to learn a lesson from his neighbor and middle school English teacher Mr. Feeny (played by the avuncular William

Daniels) about charity and friendship—a lesson that is centered on a tale by Charles Dickens. Instead of the Dickensian orphan stories—*Oliver Twist, Great Expectations, David Copperfield, Martin Chuzzlewit, Bleak House,* the list goes on—that undergird the characterizations of Annie and so many of our other favorite orphans, here the morals come from *A Christmas Carol,* which features a child who is not parentless but pitifully poor and sick.

Though Shawn is healthy, he is the Tiny Tim of this episode. It's a role assigned to him by Cory when he learns that Shawn's father was laid off from his job. Cory, having not paid attention to Mr. Feeny's lectures on *A Christmas Carol,* looks to make his friend's Christmas less bleak and to be praised for it. He gifts Shawn one of his own presents—an NBA-certified basketball—but Shawn sees through the proffer. "I'd rather have nothing for Christmas than your lousy charity," he yells at Cory, knocking the ball out of Cory's hands and storming out of his backyard.

It's the first time we see the friends fight because of their class differences, a dynamic that will play out again and again in *Boy Meets World,* with Shawn always the one to lash out and Cory always the one to smooth things over. Shawn's central dilemma as a character is between wanting to love his father and resenting him, first for his poverty and later for his absence. Mr. Feeny conveniently appears on the other side of the Matthewses' white fence for lesson time. The aphoristic moral of the story? "A true gift is given with no expectation." Later Cory acts on this advice to save his friendship, putting an extra five bucks toward Mr. Feeny's class Christmas gift in Shawn's name to spare him the embarrassment of looking like "a deadbeat."[2]

Rewatching the series as an adult, I was struck by how transparently *Boy Meets World* codes poverty as laziness, as something shameful to be hidden. But the subliminal messaging of the show shouldn't surprise me. *Boy Meets World* not only reflects the era's dominant perspectives on social class and the nuclear family but helped plant the same ideas in kids' heads. From the start, the series hammered home the central importance of the nuclear family—and the marginality of life outside it. Within the first ten minutes of the first episode, Cory proclaims that he's an orphan with a "rough life" who has been "dumped" by his family because his brother decided to take a date to the Phillies game instead of him. Mr. Feeny sets Cory straight, telling him that his parents are good people and that "their real strength comes from being a family."[3] It's a line that doesn't *really* make sense, that feels almost tautological, but nevertheless bolsters the idea that the nuclear family in and of itself is a good thing that affords those in it strength they wouldn't otherwise have.

Boy Meets World was part of ABC's TGIF lineup in the early to mid-1990s, a lineup entirely dedicated to reinforcing the centrality of the middle-class family. *Boy Meets World* was given a prime 8:30 p.m. timeslot between *Family Matters* and *Step by Step*, two other sitcoms that featured different flavors of families—Black and blended, respectively, recalling *The Cosby Show* and *The Brady Bunch*. *Family Matters*, *Boy Meets World*, and *Step by Step* were all essentially variations on a theme: these parents loved each other, made a decent living, and were respectable community pillars. If their kids fought or they faced challenges, it was nothing that their love couldn't overcome. *Boy Meets World* differed in that it focused on and was told from a kid's perspective. It is not an exaggeration to say that this show indoctrinated an entire generation, one lesson from Mr. Feeny at a time.

In *Boy Meets World*'s second season, with the class lines now drawn between the Matthewses and the Hunters—the givers of true charity and the deadbeats—the writers begin to play up Shawn's poverty and instability, in the process making the case that his family doesn't deserve to stay together. Shawn's central journey revolves around an identity crisis: Is he doomed forever to just be trailer trash? The focus shifts to crafting a new crucible for Shawn to be forged in. This means that he must lose his parents, who are holding him back.

To get there, Shawn's father appears onscreen for the first time—only to abandon him in the very same half hour of television. Chet Hunter, played by the blustering, Southern-accented Blake Clark, makes a surprise appearance in Mr. Turner's English classroom for career day, looking like a washed-up country star in a beige suit and a big gold belt buckle. During lunch, Chet waltzes into the cafeteria to break some bad news to Shawn: his mother, Virna, has up and left, driving away in their trailer. Looking back, the idea that a child should receive such life-altering news—Shawn has suddenly become motherless *and* homeless—in full view of his peers seems oddly cruel. That the scene is played for laughs seems even crueler, as though the writers don't believe that these characters are deserving of gravity. The message is that Chet is a joke of a father, which in turn makes Shawn a joke of a son.[4]

Chet sets off to find Virna, leaving Shawn with the Matthewses for what he promises will be just a few days. By the season finale, three weeks have passed, and Chet hasn't returned. Still, Shawn initially seems to be struggling less with his parents' absence than with the Matthewses' middle-class mores—no ice-cream sundaes for breakfast, no clipping toenails at the dinner table—as though being poor means that you were raised with no rules or manners. In the middle of the night, he gazes out Cory's window at a stray dog on the corner, envying his freedom. Soon he's out the window himself. Shawn's upbringing has made him an undomesticated outsider, uncomfortable in a "normal" family.[5]

It's a trope we see again and again in orphan stories, going all the way back to the 1800s. Shawn Hunter recalls Mark Twain's famous half orphan Huckleberry Finn, who resists efforts to be "sivilized" by the Widow Douglas, who takes him in because his mother is dead and his father is a drunk and a vagrant. In the opening chapter of *The Adventures of Huckleberry Finn*, he describes sitting by the window at the Widow Douglas's after a dreadful evening of being nagged for bad manners, looking out at the night: "The stars was shining, and the leaves rustled in the woods ever so mournful; and I heard an owl, away off, who-wooing about somebody that was dead, and a whippowill and a dog crying about somebody that was going to die."[6] Like Shawn, soon he's out the window. It's the start of Huck's true adventure, driven by an unstoppable Manifest Destiny–like urge to "light out for the territory."[7]

Huck can't stand being contained, but Shawn finds a middle ground. Mr. Turner—the cool young English teacher who rides a Harley-Davidson—offers Shawn a place to stay for as long as he needs. This solution affords Shawn the freedom he has grown accustomed to as a latchkey kid with parents who are permissive because they can't afford to pay attention to him, as well as the support of the Matthewses whenever he wants or needs it. Mr. Turner becomes his teacher-roommate, the kind of adult who doesn't mind if Shawn eats cold pizza for breakfast as long as he gets himself to school before the first bell.

It's worth noting that this arrangement is, at the least, surprising, especially because it involves a high school teacher who is a mandated reporter regarding suspected child maltreatment. Not even Mr. Feeny, now the high school principal, seems concerned with getting child protective services involved; he's more concerned that Turner is blurring the lines between "authority figure and chum."[8] That Virna and Chet's prolonged, indefinite absence—where one parent is MIA and the other is unreachable—does not result in any hotline calls makes no sense. Even more bizarre is that this state of affairs persists for an entire year in the world of the show and that, while Chet belatedly sends Turner legal guardianship paperwork to sign, Turner never commits.

In the real world, living without a legal guardian would have put Shawn in a state of limbo. Legal guardians, not random teachers in whose apartment one happens to crash, have the authority to make decisions for and about minors. While it's true that an adult can choose to care for a minor's basic needs—food, shelter, clothing—they are not *required* to do so in the same way parents and legal guardians are, meaning that Turner could have reneged at any time without repercussions. And so much of a minor's day-to-day life requires the signature of a guardian: from medical, dental, and psychological treatment, to enrollment in school and extracurricular activities, to something as simple as signing up for a library card. After my parents died, I had a heightened awareness of this with every form sent home from school for my "parents" to sign that my legal guardian, Aunt Alice, signed instead.

Given that *Boy Meets World* reinforced the primacy of the nuclear family at every turn, it makes sense that, soon enough, Chet would return to his fatherly duties. In season four, the writers back off the orphan tropes for a bit, giving Shawn his family back and allowing him and his parents to repair their relationships. It is here that they introduce Virna as an actual character. She appears on screen in just three episodes, which retcon her into a good wife and mother rather than a complete absence in Shawn's narrative. She is revealed to have sent Shawn a letter every day she was gone, telling him she loves him, absolving her of the sin of shirking the mothering obligations that undergird "True Womanhood." Virna's final act of domesticity is hosting Thanksgiving dinner for the Matthewses in an episode where their class differences are bizarrely drawn as akin to those of the Hutus and Tutsis in Rwanda.[9] (The episode, which aired two years after the Rwandan genocide, is perhaps the most ill-considered, whitest thirty minutes of 1990s television.) The overall effect is to show that the Hunters deserve to stay together as a family because they have started acting middle-class.

But as in the *Little Orphan Annie* comics, Shawn is orphaned over and over again for the purposes of creating tension and moving the plot forward. In the season five premiere, Chet once again abandons Shawn, turning him out of their trailer. Chet jumps at the opportunity for Shawn to move in with his newly revealed half brother, Jack, who is one year older and is starting college at nearby Pennbrook University. Chet doesn't reappear until midway through season six, when he materializes at Pennbrook, reconnects with his sons, and swiftly dies of a heart attack. Finally, Shawn becomes an actual orphan. When this episode aired, I was nine years old and could not imagine ever losing my own parents, though by that point the prostate cancer that would eventually kill my father was in remission, and my mother's lung cancer might have already been multiplying.

Boy Meets World's treatment of Shawn is bad writing in that it relies entirely on trope. That we buy into it anyway—that even now, when I watch the scene where Chet dies, I tear up—is a sign of how we've been wading in these stories for so long that we scarcely notice that we're underwater.

If Shawn Hunter is Huckleberry Finn for a 1990s sitcom audience, Ryan Atwood on *The O.C.* is Shawn Hunter for an early aughts teen drama audience. Like Shawn, Ryan is a hunky bad boy from the wrong side of the tracks—in this case, from Chino, in San Bernardino County, California, which the show portrays as a gritty city full of WT who adorn their lawns with broken-down pickups. Unlike Shawn, whose badness is contained to poor manners, class clowning, and an incident involving a cherry bomb and a mailbox, Ryan is portrayed as a bona fide juvenile delinquent from the start of the 2003 pilot. We open on Ryan (Ben McKenzie) and his older brother Trey approaching a dusty old Camaro in a dark alley festooned with graffiti that spells out "CHINO." Trey smashes in the driver's-side window with a crowbar, setting off a police chase. Clearly, their attempt at car theft does not succeed, and we quickly cut to Ryan in juvenile detention, meeting his court-appointed public defender, Sandy Cohen.

Sandy, played by Peter Gallagher and his bushy black eyebrows, immediately swoops in to play the role of surrogate father, just as Alan Matthews and Turner did for Shawn. Sandy is also a "Daddy" Warbucks of sorts—his wife Kirsten is a wealthy real estate development scion out of Newport Beach in the titular Orange County. It's the start of the same old nature-versus-nurture, rags-to-riches, fish-out-of-water story that we can't get enough of. Can Ryan transcend his roots? Sure, if he leaves Chino for Newport Beach. Cue the theme song, Phantom Planet's "California," its opening piano riff signaling a sunnier future.[10]

I never followed *The O.C.* when it was airing, not because I was above indulging in teen dramas when I was a teen myself but because I had dance class on Tuesday nights at 9:00 p.m. when it aired on FOX. Instead of tuning in to see if Ryan and Marissa Cooper (Mischa Barton) would finally get together, I was busy drilling time steps for my tap teacher. But I can see why it was so incredibly popular in the early aughts: we were all obsessed with rich California kids back then. A year after *The O.C.* premiered, we got its reality lookalike in the MTV show *Laguna Beach: The Real Orange County*, which followed eight hot teenagers as they shopped, surfed, partied, and slept together. For those of us who could only dream of affording spring break in Cabo like the kids on *Laguna Beach* did, watching Ryan Atwood infiltrate Newport Beach was like making our own entrée into that world.

But all the sparkle on *The O.C.*—diamonds on trophy wives' fingers, glistening infinity pools that look out on the ocean, the sun glinting off the rims on the teenagers' pimped-out rides—distracts from the fact that this is just another orphan-meets-the-rich plot, with the riches updated for the early 2000s. This one reminds me of *Wuthering Heights*: Ryan crashes into life at the Cohens' Newport Beach mansion in a manner that parallels Heathcliff's journey to living on the West Yorkshire moors.

A refresher: Emily Brontë's novel, published in 1847 but set largely in the late 1700s, concerns the haunted titular estate on the Yorkshire moors, owned by the Earnshaws, who are landed gentry—less rich than titled peers but richer than most everyone else. Life at Wuthering Heights is upended when Mr. Earnshaw ventures to Liverpool and finds a foundling boy "starving, houseless, and as good as dumb" on the streets. Despite the boy's "dirty, ragged, black-haired" appearance, Mr. Earnshaw immediately takes to him, brings him home, and names him "Heathcliff" after a son who didn't survive childhood.[11] The lady of the house expresses her disdain by immediately casting him as a racialized other and accusing her husband of having lost his mind.

True, Ryan's not a foundling—his parents are known. His father is in prison for armed robbery, and his mom, Dawn, is an alcoholic in an abusive relationship with another alcoholic. But Dawn swiftly kicks Ryan out of her run-down manufactured home. Soon enough, Sandy pulls up in his black BMW chariot to whisk Ryan away to his gated estate. Kirsten's reaction to Ryan's arrival replaces Mrs. Earnshaw's Victorian-era racism with modern pearl clutching. "He's not a stray puppy, Sandy! I knew it was only a matter of time before you started bringing home felons," she chides. "You're endangering our home. Did you even think of Seth?"—Seth being their nerdy son, who, like Ryan, is sixteen.[12]

Ryan floats through the pilot, giving himself over to the whims of the Cohens. What he thinks of his precarious situation is evidently beside the point—the writers barely give him any lines. He's a brooding, silent type in a wife beater, gray hoodie, and leather jacket. As the episode drones on, we watch as Ryan sullenly gets dressed up in a borrowed suit to attend a fashion show fund-raiser put on by Marissa, the Cohens' neighbor and the golden girl of Newport Beach. We watch as he sullenly climbs into the back of a yellow Jeep Wrangler to go to the beer-soaked afterparty at someone's parents' beach house, making eyes at Marissa, who's riding shotgun in her dumb boyfriend Luke's souped-up truck. He snaps out of it only for Marissa, who is already his object of forbidden desire, but she's called away immediately—they can't be together. Then we watch as Ryan sullenly brushes off stares, his jaw clenching, when it's revealed that he's an outsider ("Chino? Ew!" a girl whines). And we watch as his patience finally wears thin and he brawls on the beach with Luke. "Welcome to the O.C., bitch!" Luke yells as he kicks Ryan, who's writhing in the sand.

This class tension—and the reveal that the upper-class teens of Newport Beach are far more debauched and debased than Ryan, who's just a poor kid "dealt a bad hand"—is what *The O.C.* is really about. The circumstances of poverty, addiction, and abuse that led to Ryan's arrest and his abandonment by his family are not the focus here. They're merely the setup that allows for the writers to dig into the sexier material of revealing the hypocrisies and sins of the wealthy elite. Importing Ryan from Chino to Newport Beach allows for an outsider's perspective that shines a harsh light on everything these rich folks prefer to sweep under their plush rugs: their own precarious finances and crimes—Marissa's stockbroker father is in deep shit with the

Securities and Exchange Commission for embezzlement—and addiction, which applies to too many characters to name-check here.

Rich people behaving badly is one of the oldest stories in the book. It's the foundation of many an orphan tale, from essentially every Charles Dickens novel to *Wuthering Heights*. Brontë's Gothic novel is best remembered as a brooding, haunting, and haunted tale of doomed love between Heathcliff and his adoptive sister, Catherine Earnshaw. But their love is doomed in part due to greed—Catherine chooses to marry Heathcliff's foil, the heir to the neighboring estate, because, as she puts it, "he will be rich, and I shall like to be the greatest woman of the neighbourhood, and I shall be proud of having such a husband."[13]

Wuthering Heights can be read as a no-good-deed-goes-unpunished cautionary tale: Mr. Earnshaw's act of charity opens his family up to the figure who will destroy it. *The O.C.* functions in a similar way, as Ryan's arrival in Newport Beach sows discord. The Cohens argue among themselves about what to do with Ryan; the rich ladies-who-lunch who make up Kirsten's social circle gossip that he's a menace to the community. For his part, Ryan, like Shawn Hunter, tamps his feelings down until he explodes in anger, and in early episodes he's constantly in fisticuffs.

There is nothing new about *The O.C.*, but we'd rather tell ourselves this same old story about class tensions and hypocrisies than break new ground. *The O.C.* could have been a very different kind of show had it reflected even a sliver of reality, had it explored what foster care would actually have been like for a kid like Ryan in Southern California in the early 2000s. But the writers quickly dispensed with that option, with a representation of legal guardianship just as fantastical as that of *Boy Meets World*. By the series' fourth episode, set a matter of weeks after the events of the pilot, the Cohens have decided to assume legal guardianship of Ryan. Ryan needs to be in Newport Beach in order for the gears of *The O.C.* to grind on; any intervention that could pull him away must be summarily dispatched with.

We're not always satisfied to see orphan characters lose the family they had in order to get a second chance with a wealthier new family. In the biggest orphan show of the 1990s—the only one that featured honest-to-goodness orphans, whose parents were both dead—a rags-to-riches, nature-versus-nurture tale wouldn't have worked. That's because the family wasn't poor to begin with.

I'm talking about the teen drama *Party of Five*, which aired on FOX for six seasons from 1994 to 2000. It is impossible to write about orphans on television in the 1990s without considering *Party of Five*, which blended classic orphan tropes with the teen angst we came to love in the 1990s from shows like *My So-Called Life*, *Dawson's Creek*, and the very soap-y *Beverly Hills, 90210*. Christopher Keyser, who cocreated the show alongside Amy Lippman, remembered that the network's idea was "Don't tell the babysitter that Mom and Dad are dead!"[14] But Keyser and Lippman wanted to lean into the dark side of growing up too soon, and Lippman said that they hoped to flip "standard expectations about a family of orphans on its head."

The idea that *Party of Five* broke any new orphan ground is hilarious to me because it reinforces one of the oldest stories in the orphan book: the adventure plot. With its focus on a large family of orphans, *Party of Five* recalls the classic children's book series *The Boxcar Children*, which debuted in 1924 and is still publishing more than 150 books later, with new authors taking over for Gertrude Chandler Warner after her death in 1979. In the original version of the very first book, Henry, Jess, Violet, and Benny Cordyce, who range in age from thirteen to five, are orphaned after their drunk father drops dead from drinking. This happens on page two—might as well get the orphaning out of the way, I suppose. Their mother has already died of causes that are never revealed. That's because the books never focus on the children's loss, centering instead on their adventure of survival, self-reliance, and hard work.

The Cordyce orphans abandon their home in order to stay together and out of the reach of their rich steel-magnate grandfather ("Daddy" Warbucks, anyone?). They've never met their grandfather, but they fear he will treat them "cruelly" because he hadn't wanted their father to marry their mother. Soon they take refuge in an abandoned boxcar in a forest, which they make into a home replete with a bedroom on one side and a sitting room/dining room/kitchen/parlor on the other.[15] The youngest three children wash dishes they found at the dump in a makeshift washtub and decorate with a vase full of flowers, dutifully recreating acts of domesticity.[16] Henry, the oldest, finds work doing odd jobs at the home of a doctor, who has a cherry orchard. It all makes for a parable for American values of independence, stick-to-itiveness, and making ends meet that rivals the *Little Orphan Annie* comics.

When Warner, a first-grade teacher, rewrote and abridged the first book in 1942 to appeal to early readers, she sharpened the adventure plot by pulling back on the whole dead parents thing even further: here, both parents (now with the surname Alden instead of Cordyce) are dead from the get-go, and the circumstances of their deaths are a black hole that is never addressed.[17] In the books that follow, the children decide to move in with their grandfather, whom they discover is not the "cross" old man they feared him to be.[18] Their boxcar home is relegated to a playhouse in Grandfather Alden's backyard, and their adventures shift to solving mysteries. Conveniently, in a situation that mirrors the Annie comics, Grandfather Alden always seems to be off on business or out of town. This allows the orphans a similar degree of autonomy as they enjoyed when they were actually living in their boxcar, so they can go off and solve these mysteries, which concern everything from uranium mines to blackmail schemes to the theft of their boxcar.[19]

In *Party of Five*, the Salinger siblings, who are orphaned when their parents both die in a car accident six months before the pilot, are not sleuths. Instead, their adventures—like throwing wild parties in the San Francisco Victorian they've inherited—are scaled to fit into a 1990s teen drama. As in *The Boxcar Children*, we want to see the Salinger siblings stay together at all costs. It wouldn't be satisfying to have all of them enter the same foster home or even be adopted together, because the allure of the show is that there are no adults in charge. The tension that drives the show is not the grief of losing both parents so suddenly but the fact that the Salingers are caught between the glorious freedom of coming-of-age without a curfew and the burden of being responsible for their own upbringing.

They manage to avoid foster care or other adult supervision when their parents die because the oldest sibling, Charlie (Matthew Fox), is twenty-four—old enough on paper to be a legal guardian, even if he's so immature and ill-suited to the job that the others remind him that "a piece of paper doesn't make you a parent."[20] The next-oldest, Bailey (Scott Wolf), is only sixteen, but he takes over as the responsible one who balances the checkbook and takes charge when they have to hire a new nanny for Owen, the youngest, who is still an infant. In between are fifteen-year-old Julia (Neve

Campbell), the smart and sensitive one, and eleven-year-old Claudia (Lacey Chabert), a violin prodigy. Episodes in the first season revolve around typical teenage problems: Should I have sex? How do I find friends who respect me instead of just using my house for parties?

I missed out on *Party of Five* mostly because my parents themselves were not interested in watching teen dramas, and the show hopped around at the 9:00 p.m. timeslot on various weeknights, when they ruled the remote control and preferred to watch, say, *Seinfeld*. I never knew that *Party of Five* was an orphan show when it was airing; to me, it had a reputation as just another teen "problems" show. I tuned into *Party of Five* as an adult expressly to consider how it did—or didn't—jibe with the reality of contemporary American orphanhood. The show does get one thing right in my eyes. Unlike with Shawn Hunter on *Boy Meets World* and Ryan Atwood on *The O.C.*, it does actually make sense to me that the middle-class Salinger siblings were able to avoid foster care and stay together. After all, John and I did too.

That's because my family had the means to make other arrangements for us. My father visited a lawyer to make a will in late October 2002, ten months after my mom died. In that will, he appointed his sister Mary Ellen as "the Guardian of the person and property of any children of mine who have not attained the age of majority," with his sister Alice to act as guardian of the person if Mary Ellen should "fail or cease to act." This meant that when he died fifteen months later, John and I were not left in a legal limbo. If Dad hadn't named a legal guardian for us, a judge in Nassau County's Surrogate's Court, which handles the administration of deceased people's estates, would have named one for us, almost certainly choosing a relative and perhaps even the ones my father had chosen himself. Some states, like Pennsylvania and Maryland, even call these courts orphans' courts because historically they were concerned with protecting the material inheritances of children whose landowning fathers died.[21]

Even if our father hadn't had a will, John and I would have ended up in foster care only if no one in our lives had been suitable and willing to act as our legal guardian. Our lives were nowhere near that precarious. Children like me, with a certain degree of privilege afforded by class and race—even fictional children like the Aldens and the Salingers—still get to keep what remains of our families after our parents die. It's not as easy for charities and governments to exercise power over our lives and profit from doing so.

When it comes to the reality of *Party of Five*, it does seem implausible that Charlie would be named as legal guardian for all of his siblings, since when the show starts he is a barely employed college dropout who is bad with money. But unlike in *The Boxcar Children*, there is no kindly, rich grandfather here to step in to materially support, but lackadaisically supervise, the Salingers. Instead, they get financial support from their parents' estate—$15,000 every four months.[22] In the pilot, Charlie's suitability as a legal guardian and all of the kids' ability to parent themselves and manage money come into question. Charlie reveals that he was swindled out of $12,000 in a house-flipping deal gone wrong. The worst of their problems is not that their parents are dead but that they have to figure out how to stretch the money allotted for them to avoid further supervision. Going to the executor of the estate—some guy named Mr. Graham whose connection to the family is a mystery to viewers—isn't an option. "We've gotta seem in charge!" Bailey yells. "We've gotta make it seem like we can handle everything ourselves, like a normal family, or else they have an excuse to split us up." "They"—social workers?—are too scary to name.

The Salingers make it work—of course they do—and there's enough time left in the episode for Julia to both embark on a new romance with a bad boy and get broken up with, far sexier material than household budgeting. Other episodes in season one walk the same line of addressing questions viewers might have about how this whole orphans-taking-care-of-themselves thing works out alongside standard teen drama fare. Do the Salingers really not have other relatives? As a family tree assignment for Claudia reveals, there's only an uncle in France. Their grandparents are dead, save maybe their maternal grandfather, who walked out on the family when their mom was a kid, and Claudia's efforts to track him down lead to a dead end.[23] Are they really not on the radar of child protective services? Halfway through the season, the writers introduce a social worker named Mrs. Gideon who will never appear again, apparently convinced that the Salingers are doing just fine, despite the fact that when she makes a drop-in visit at 10:00 p.m. on a school night, Claudia is missing in action.[24]

On the one hand, yes, life goes on, even after your parents die—mine did. My parents' deaths were devastating, *and* I still had to go through my teen years after they died. On the other hand, the writers crammed the first season of *Party of Five* with what reads like a greatest hits of sensational teen dilemmas: Periods! Getting carded! Boyfriends! Sex, drugs, and drinking! Later seasons are no less over the top. A *Los Angeles Times* article about the series' ending in 2000 makes a macabre but apt declaration: "If you believe in karmic justice, hanging by a noose from a limb somewhere high atop the Salinger family tree is an ancestor who committed unspeakable horrors, forever condemning [the siblings] to make endless acts of attrition."

Party of Five struggled with Nielsen ratings at the beginning and end of its run, but it was a critical success. It's now remembered as an underrated teen drama, one that was especially good, as one writer for the *AV Club* argues in a retrospective, after it got its "orphan material mostly behind it."[25] It's a crass comment, but one that makes sense when we consider that the state of orphanhood in and of itself is not what we want to see on television. Instead, we want to treat being orphaned as a precipitating event, not look at what it really means to lose your parents.

We've gotten a little less afraid of representing foster care on television in the past decade. But in large part, the storylines have merely undergone the *Annie* remake treatment: instead of meaningfully grappling with what it would mean to accurately portray the experience of being in foster care, recent television shows have acted as though the major problem with earlier stabs at the narrative was that they were too white and heterosexual.

Take, for instance, the ABC Family drama *The Fosters*, which aired from 2013 to 2018 and was executive-produced by Jennifer Lopez. The series, conceived out of a desire to make a show that "reflected the modern American family," as though there is such a thing, follows a middle-class lesbian couple in a San Diego suburb—Stef Foster, a white police officer, and Lena Adams, a Black high school vice principal.[26] They have a teenage biological son (white) and teenage twins adopted from foster care (Latinx), and when the series starts, they are fostering a teenage girl (white) who has recently been released from juvenile detention. The pilot is full of drama: turns out the girl was in juvie for protecting herself against her abusive foster father, who is still abusing her little brother. Stef comes to the rescue, arresting the foster father at gunpoint. Of course, the Fosters will eventually adopt these kids too, as though the goal of foster care is not reunification but giving foster kids new middle-class families.

In an interview with *HuffPost*, cocreator Bradley Bredeweg noted that his perspective on foster care was shaped by a high school friend who was in the foster care system: "She was quite a broken girl. . . . Then she finally found a family that took her in and was paying close attention to her and giving her love. Over the next couple of years she really came in to her own. She learned to accept that love."[27] The idea that foster youth are fundamentally "broken," that they need to "learn to accept love," is offensive and damaging, and *The Fosters* spread it throughout its five-season run.

Then there's *the* family drama of recent memory, NBC's *This Is Us*, which ran from 2016 to 2022 and garnered a slew of accolades, including Emmy wins. The show follows the adult Pearson "triplets," Kate, Kevin, and Randall, through contemporary scenes and flashbacks. One of the original triplets was stillborn, but parents Jack (Milo Ventimiglia) and Rebecca (Mandy Moore) believed they should still have three children, so they adopted Randall (Sterling K. Brown), a Black baby abandoned as a foundling and born the same day as Kate and Kevin. We've already got an adopted-foundling plot, but wait, there's more—in the second season, Randall and his wife foster a Black teenage girl named Deja, who has been—get this—abused and neglected by other foster families. Deja's a troubled teen, but she eventually learns to accept the Pearsons' love and, ding ding ding, is adopted by them. These families may be more diverse, but the plot lines are *Boy Meets World* and *The O.C.* all over again.

Even the 2014 remake of *Annie*—the first race-switched treatment of the story—brought it up to the contemporary moment by changing mean Miss Hannigan's orphanage into mean Miss Hannigan's Harlem foster home. The film stars eleven-year-old Quvenzhané Wallis as Annie and Jamie Foxx as Will Stacks, a modern "Daddy" Warbucks. I literally screamed out loud recently while reading about how this fantasy infiltrated one child's mind so strongly that he ran away from home and landed himself and his siblings in foster care.

That story comes halfway through journalist Andrea Elliott's book *Invisible Child*, which traces the life of Dasani Coates, a girl who grew up in homeless shelters in New York City, her family frequently under the surveillance of child protective services. Dasani's youngest brother, Papa, was home alone in a dilapidated apartment in Staten Island one January afternoon when he watched the new *Annie* on a bootleg DVD.[28] Three days later, in eighteen-degree weather, he left home without a coat, wandering Staten Island's North Shore for hours until he was picked up by the police. He later told a child protective services worker, "I watched the movie *Annie* and I want to go to a foster home, too."[29] He got his wish—though only in part, for there are no "Daddy" Warbuckses or Will Stackses in real foster care.

Chapter Ten

THE BROKEN FOUNDATION
OF A BROKEN SYSTEM

While orphanages and the orphan train movement are far back enough in history for us to enjoy popular culture that paints silver linings onto their grim realities, America's foster care system represents ongoing misery so bleak that the only way to turn it into feel-good material is to largely sidestep it. Foster care is considered broken by just about everyone it touches—the children who are torn from their parents, the parents whose children are forcibly removed, the child protective services (CPS) workers who separate families, the foster parents who care for the children whose families are deemed "unfit," the caseworkers who monitor foster homes and children in the system, the lawyers who represent parents and children, and the family court judges who rule on which families get to reunify and which are forever legally dissolved.

Different stakeholders might give divergent and contradictory diagnoses for why foster care is broken. Maybe they see the system as too punitive toward families or not punitive enough. Maybe they're fed up with all the bureaucracy in a system that weaves together public oversight and private subcontracted agencies, or maybe they think individual players—judges, foster parents, caseworkers—have entirely too much sway and need more oversight. Maybe they think foster parents get too much money from federal and state governments to care for children in the system; maybe they think the system should cover more costs. Depending on whom you talk to, the system is either artificially bloated and overfunded or overburdened and underfunded. What most can agree on in our trauma-informed times is that simply entering the system harms children and that foster youth have worse outcomes in just about every aspect of life—physical and mental health, economic stability, educational attainment—than children who get to stay with their families.

If you have never experienced the system, you probably think of foster care as where children end up when their parents behave unspeakably. That's what popular culture about foster care hinges on. But this understanding is also fueled by the fact that foster care has, over the past several decades, become inextricably bound with our country's equally broken child-protection system. Together, these two interwoven systems make up the bulk of modern American child welfare. While children used to end up in orphanages because their poor parents placed them there, now almost all children in foster care enter the system involuntarily, due to the intervention of local CPS workers. Children most often enter the system because someone has made a maltreatment allegation against parents, accusing them of abuse (physical, sexual, emotional) or neglect—a loosely defined category that varies by state law—and a CPS worker deems the allegation credible upon investigation.

The fact is that most children do not end up in the foster care system because of the kind of maltreatment that scandalizes us. In 2022, the most recent year for which we have federal data, only 13 percent of the 186,602 children who entered foster care were removed from their families due to physical abuse.[1] Only 4 percent were removed due to sexual abuse. The most common reason for removal, by far, was neglect, which was associated with 62 percent of cases.[2] "Neglect" typically calls to mind purposeful deprivation, but intent does not factor into how states define it. The Children's Bureau—the federal agency proposed at the 1909 White House Conference on the Care of Dependent Children—explains that definitions of neglect generally include "the failure of a parent or other person with responsibility for the child to provide needed food, clothing, shelter, medical care, or supervision to the degree that the child's health, safety, and well-being are threatened with harm." Poverty makes it harder to keep children fed, clothed, housed, and cared for, and poverty is often seen as neglectful by CPS workers. Of course, children can suffer real harm due to neglect born out of poverty. But removing a child and punishing a parent is not the only way to address problems like hunger and unsafe housing. Parents who live below the poverty line are twenty-two times more likely to be subject to CPS surveillance.[3] And about 40 percent of children in foster care come from families eligible for "welfare"—more on that in a bit.[4]

During the 1909 White House Conference, child welfare advocates envisaged foster care as a safety net for families who could not remain intact "for urgent and compelling reasons." They expressly declared, "Surely poverty alone should not disrupt the home." But as was the case with orphanages and orphan trains, most children who end up in foster care in America *do* come from poor families, and the correlation between familial poverty and foster care involvement is not coincidental. Foster care began as an idealized answer to reforming our country's highly balkanized, privatized, institutional child welfare system, one that would allow children a substitute for family life while their real families got help for their non-poverty-related problems. By the end of the twentieth century, foster care's status as a cultural and societal bogeyman was well cemented. The system was broken.

The reality is that the foster care system has been broken from the start, just as the orphanages and orphan trains that came before were broken from the start. The child welfare experts who dreamed up foster care as a fix for families suffering for reasons other than poverty alone failed to understand that poverty is never "alone." The imagined future where poor families would be given sufficient relief to stay whole has never materialized, even after the federal government finally constructed a social welfare state in the 1930s and expanded it in the 1960s. Instead, over time, the welfare state that was meant to help poor children turned into an apparatus of family surveillance and punishment, one that would come to disproportionally split up poor families of color.

In the early 1900s, when foster care held promise as a Progressive solution for deinstitutionalizing "orphans," the federal government created the first agency devoted to child welfare: the Children's Bureau. The bureau had been unanimously proposed at the 1909 White House Conference, but it took eleven introductions of bills calling for its establishment before Congress finally passed one in January 1912; President William Howard Taft signed it into law in April of that year.

The federal government's first bureaucratic and financial foray into taking responsibility for the welfare of all American children—not just the Native children whose lives it had long been upending—thus came 136 years after our country's founding. But at its start, the Children's Bureau had limited power.[5] The initial budget was only $25,640, and only fifteen people were on staff.[6] And by design, the bureau was originally limited to research and reporting—not active policy or grant making to actually change conditions for children. The law that established the bureau called for it to "investigate and report upon all matters pertaining to the welfare of children and child life," especially "infant mortality, the birth rate, orphanages, juvenile courts, desertion, dangerous occupations, accidents and diseases of children, employment, and legislation affecting children in the several States and Territories."[7] Notably, foster care, which was still in its infancy at the time, was not on the list.

The bureau's small size, budget, and purchase on power seems related to the fact that it constituted a pink ghetto within the federal government. Women dominated the bureau's staff from its earliest years—Julia Lathrop, a former Hull-House resident, was chief from 1912 to 1921 and prioritized hiring fellow women.[8] But even with this leadership, the bureau was caught in the same bind as female-dominated social work: the struggle to prove that its work was indeed professional and not just an extension of maternal instinct.[9]

Under its second chief, Grace Abbott, another Hull-House alumna, the Children's Bureau began to study and report on foster care, providing guidance for the private and public organizations that oversaw foster placements. In 1923, the Children's Bureau published *Foster-Home Care for Dependent Children*, with chapters like "The Essentials of Placement in Free Family Homes" and "Special Problems Involved in Foster-Home Care," written by experts who primarily worked for private charities.[10] The publication also included a history of child placing, which was, in the 1920s, beginning to shift away from crowded orphanages and the haphazard indenture practices of orphan trains to a process that was, at least in theory, driven by the careful science of social casework.

While some experts and legislators were adamantly opposed to the public funding of private sectarian child welfare charities, just as orphanages had been primarily run by such charities, foster care placements were often overseen by them too. Public-private partnerships were unavoidable, since the charities that had long taken on the responsibilities of child welfare were reluctant to give up their power—and the state and local money they stood to make by continuing to care for vulnerable children. A Catholic bishop's outburst at an annual meeting of the National Conference of Catholic Charities in 1935 encapsulates this feeling of ownership: "The poor belong to us. We will not let them be taken from us!"[11] In 1923, even the Children's Aid Society (CAS), pioneer of the orphan trains, created a modern foster home department for local placements.[12] Given their larger investment in real estate, orphanages were slower to shift away from mass institutionalization—some, like the Orphan Asylum Society, first tried the "cottage system" of smaller, "homelike" units of children overseen by "house parents"—but within three decades, the vast majority of such charities would either transition to foster care or shutter.[13]

Even as the Children's Bureau aimed to establish professionalized child-placing standards, its ideals were in tension with on-the-ground realities, an issue that would plague foster care throughout the twentieth century. And it would be decades before the federal government would begin to fund foster care.

———

Modern foster care has a couple of progenitors. The "placing out" utilized by the CAS and the New York Foundling Hospital shared with foster care the practice of welcoming orphans and dependent children into private family homes. But whereas the CAS was essentially finding children jobs and the Foundling utilized indenture agreements in a sort of proto-adoption bid to grant "illegitimate" babies new families, foster care was meant to provide children with *temporary* family homes, without an exchange of labor or the dissolution of the legal ties of their biological families.

Foster care's closest ancestor was "boarding out," which might sound like a synonym for "placing out" but signals a meaningful difference. In "placing out," children went to "free" homes that received no payment to cover their care, with the caveat, of course, that the children were expected to earn their keep via labor—working on farms and as housekeepers. "Boarding" homes, on the other hand, received payments, typically from the children's parents themselves, and the children did not have to work. In the mid- to late 1800s, as organizations like the CAS "placed out" children, families also made informal arrangements to board children; the practice persisted well into the twentieth century.[14] Many poor and immigrant women made livings running their own boarding homes, sometimes placing classified ads announcing their services in local newspapers.[15] Parents sometimes ran their own ads, looking for boarding homes for young children they could not manage to care for, perhaps due to a mother's death or a father's abandonment.

Boarding had long been the dominion of poor women whose only employable skills were mothering and homemaking or who could not work outside the home because they had their own young children to care for. They were not licensed or trained and functioned independently with no oversight from public or private child welfare agencies. This informal system was mutually beneficial for both poor women who needed extra income and poor families in temporary moments of crisis. A boarding home was a solution that allowed parents to avoid the strict rules of orphanages or the permanent separation of an orphan train and that spared children—often very young children—from both institutionalization and being put to work.

When child welfare professionals began to agitate for a shift from institutions to foster care, they envisaged a boarding system rather than a free home system, because free homes were associated both with child labor, which by the twentieth century the middle and upper classes had deemed unacceptable, and with abuse—Mary Ellen Wilson had lived in a "free" indenture home.[16] At the turn of the century, some child welfare institutions, notably the Foundling, already had "boarding out" departments. The Foundling paid poor women to nurse and care for babies before they were old enough to be sent west via train. In *How the Other Half Lives*, Jacob Riis wrote that the Foundling "pays the rent of hundreds of poor families" by employing women as nurse "mothers."[17]

It might seem natural that women who had already been boarding children in their homes would make for ready-built foster mothers. Many wrote to the Children's Bureau over the years wanting to take in children in exchange for board payments, wrongly assuming that the federal government had anything to do with the selection of foster parents (it never has).[18] But child welfare professionals were uncomfortable with employing these women as foster parents: they were too poor and wanted the boarding payments too much.

Boarding payments have always been artificially low by design.[19] As public and private child welfare agencies gradually began to shift toward foster care in the 1920s and child welfare professionals began to transform child placement into a carefully supervised science, they set low boarding rates. On the one hand, experts believed that it was necessary to pay *something* toward the cost of caring for dependent children—they understood they couldn't rely on charity alone and that "free" homes were bound to expect children to work, a practice they now viewed as abusive. But they were also concerned with making the profit motive too attractive. This was in part due to the recent and scandalous history of "baby farms"—sorts of daycares where desperate unwed and poor working mothers paid to leave their infants.[20] The farms were operated by profit-driven women who presided over often squalid and overcrowded conditions that could prove deadly for babies.[21] But the low payments also stemmed from a queasiness about paying women to care for children and the belief they should be motivated first and foremost by maternal instinct. As historian Catherine E. Rymph argues in *Raising Government Children*, the gap between what it actually costs to take care of a child and what private and public agencies have historically paid foster families exposes "the hidden role of women's unpaid care work in sustaining American public welfare provision." Rymph focuses on women because, from the start, the child welfare system has assumed that women—mothers—would be doing the work of caring for dependent children. In other words, female social workers, themselves discounted as merely acting on maternal feeling, further discounted what it took to raise foster children.

Even though experts focused on foster *mothers*, a foster father needed to be in the picture. In the 1920s, child welfare professionals believed that the women best suited to the underpaid care work of foster parenting were middle-class and married. As the Children's Bureau's *Foster-Home Care for Dependent Children* advised, a caseworker seeking to recruit acceptable foster parents could "prevent much waste of time and money which is needed for investigation, by selecting approved sections and neighborhoods and desirable families," advocating a sort of redlining for foster homes.[22] Another chapter equates poverty and single parenthood with abnormality, advising that foster homes should not be "wrecked by disease or destitution. . . . [T]he child [should not] be removed from one abnormal situation merely to be injected into another. His stay under the supervision of the agency should be in a home that is intact and has normal relationships."[23] A normal relationship was, of course, synonymous with marriage.

———

Even as they wrung their hands over the careful selection of the right kind of foster mother, child welfare professionals in the early twentieth century still hoped to keep poor families together. As the first resolution of the 1909 White House Conference attested, "home life" was sacrosanct as "the highest and finest product of civilization." Even children with poor single mothers should not be deprived of family life. But the resolution injected the same ideas about who is "deserving" that have always haunted conversations about poverty in America: "Children of parents of worthy character, suffering from temporary misfortune, and children of reasonably efficient and deserving mothers who are without the support of the normal breadwinner, should, as a rule, be kept with their parents."[24] By "mothers who are without the support of the normal breadwinner," the conference-goers really meant widows.[25]

The conference's first adopted resolution called not just for "deserving" single mothers to keep their children home with them, as opposed to their being sent to orphanages or foster care, but for the women to receive sufficient monetary aid "to maintain suitable homes for the rearing of children."[26] The resolution on home care specified that the aid for single mothers/widows should come "preferably in the form of private charity, rather than of public relief." Many attendees represented private, religious charities, and they wanted to keep public funds flowing to their institutions; at the same time, even those opposed to the public subsidization of private charity were all too aware of taxpayers' continuing distaste for "outdoor relief."

But states that paid attention to the 1909 White House Conference didn't leave the administration of monetary aid up to private charities. By 1920, thanks primarily to the lobbying of women's voluntary associations, forty states had passed laws for publicly funded "mothers' pensions."[27] The same kind of middle- and upper-class women who had worked to establish orphanages and societies for the prevention of cruelty to children (SPCCs) in the nineteenth century were at the forefront of the mothers' pension movement. One prominent supporter argued that "the mother of young children [does] better service to the community and one more worthy of pecuniary remuneration when she stays at home and minds her children than when she goes out charing and leaves them to the chances of the street or to the care of a neighbor."[28] The argument that women could best serve their communities—and their nation—by raising the next generation of productive citizens appealed to the same impulses that drove the movements against child labor and child abuse in the late nineteenth century. Childhood was precious, and so, too, was motherhood; the woman's proper domain was serving her family at home, even if her husband had died or deserted her.

The relief offered by state-funded mothers' pensions was purposefully limited to certain kinds of women. The earliest laws specified that the aid was meant for widows with children. In some states, women who had been deserted by their husbands or whose husbands were disabled were also eligible. If you were an unwed or divorced mother, you were likely not "deserving" enough to receive aid to keep your children at home. By 1931, when every state except Georgia and South Carolina had enacted mothers' pension laws, only three states specifically extended aid to unmarried mothers.[29] Even if states allowed mothers of "illegitimate" children funds to keep them at home, the actual local administration of aid was even more limited in practice—in 1931, only *fifty-five* mothers' pension recipients in the entire United States were unwed.[30] Eighty percent of the 93,600 families receiving aid from mothers' pensions in 1931 were headed by widows.[31] And mothers' pensions were almost exclusively for white women—in 1931, only 3 percent of recipients were Black.[32] Most Black recipients lived in either California or Ohio, and only *two* Black women in the *entire* South received mothers' pension benefits.[33]

The gap yawned between the number of women who were in theory eligible for state mothers' pensions and the number of women who were actually receiving aid—in the 1920s, a Children's Bureau study estimated that fewer than one-third of women who should be receiving grants got the money in reality.[34] In order to receive aid, women not only had to fit into certain categories but had to be deemed "worthy" and "deserving" by local public charity administrators who processed their applications. In order to pass muster, they had to adhere to moral and behavioral standards, like teetotaling and avoiding live-in boyfriends, and put up with caseworkers' surveillance of their housekeeping, parenting, and budgeting.[35] Immigrant women were penalized for speaking their native languages at home and were sometimes compelled to apply for citizenship in order to receive aid.[36] In this way, caseworkers replicated the xenophobia and inappropriate application of white middle-class standards that plagued the amateur "friendly visitor" model of SPCCs just a few decades earlier. While states were not actively splitting up "unfit" families in large numbers at this time—through the 1950s, most children ended up in foster care because their parents had placed them there—the social control that public charity administrators and social workers exerted over mothers who sought relief foreshadowed the policing that poor families would face a few decades later.[37]

Even if single women did make it through the application and supervision gauntlet, they received very little money to help keep their children at home. In 1931, the median monthly mothers' pension grant was $21.78—the equivalent of $418.74 today.[38] In the Deep South, where the local funding of mothers' pensions was the worst, the average monthly aid, in states that offered any, ranged from $4 to $15.[39] Even the best-funded state, Massachusetts, only gave mothers an average of $69.31 a month, or $1,361.49 today.[40] A woman with one child receiving such a pension in 2024 would fall well below the federal poverty line.[41]

Most women receiving mothers' pensions still had to engage in part-time wage work that often took them outside the home at a time when subsidized daycare was nonexistent and daycare in general was stigmatized. States typically prohibited recipients from full-time employment.[42] A Children's Bureau study of mothers' pensions noted that the "shortcomings of the grants" created "injuries to home life brought about by the lack of a few dollars a week or month that nullified the benefits derived from the public money expended for the family."[43] In other words, poor single mothers faced a double-bind that would remain constant for welfare recipients in the decades to come. In order to receive benefits to keep their children at home, they needed to pass muster with officials who judged them for working at "undesirable" low-wage occupations like cleaning houses or sewing piecework when they should be focusing all their attention on their children.[44] And any benefits they did receive weren't enough to support full-time stay-at-home motherhood "for the proper care and protection of the children," as the Children's Bureau put it.[45] This meant that poor mothers struggled to meet middle-class parenting expectations, and their children might have suffered from hunger, insufficient supervision, and unstable housing conditions. States might have professed to want to take care of children when they passed mothers' pension laws, but they seemed to care more about judging those children's mothers.

The mothers' pension movement spread across the states just before America entered into the Roaring Twenties. While we now remember the decade as a time of decadent, freewheeling optimism following World War I, only those at the top of the industrial economy—the "Daddy" Warbuckses of the country—were fiscally secure. Rural agricultural workers and low-wage workers suffered under antifarmer and antilabor policies. Meanwhile, the fiscally conservative federal government rolled back the Progressive era's expansion of the regulatory state and commitments to addressing the inequalities laid bare during the Gilded Age, leaving the country's poor even more vulnerable.

As stock market speculation ran rampant, President Calvin Coolidge endorsed laissez-faire economics. Coolidge allowed his secretary of commerce, Herbert Hoover, to disinvest in the regulatory state, and his secretary of the treasury, Andrew Mellon, to lead the charge in reducing taxes and federal spending. Seven months after Coolidge left office, the stock market that his policies had stoked crashed.[46] President Hoover reacted with calls for "rugged individualism" that would later earn him excoriation in the *Annie* musical (even as *Annie* itself rests on an individualist message).

By the time Franklin D. Roosevelt took office in 1933, a quarter of the workforce was unemployed, affecting some thirty million families.[47] More people than ever were relying on private charity and public welfare. By 1935, more than seven million children were in families receiving emergency federal relief.[48] (Only about 230,000 children, meanwhile, were benefiting from mothers' pension payments.)[49] As the US Congress's Committee on Economic Security noted in a 1935 report supporting what would become the Social Security Act, for "most of the children on relief lists . . . nothing is wrong with their environment but their parents' lack of money to give them opportunities which are taken for granted in more fortunate homes."[50]

Meanwhile, more children than ever before were placed in institutions and foster care. In total, about 487 out of every 100,000 people under the age of twenty-one in the United States were receiving such care.[51] In New York, the number surged to about 1,078 per 100,000. Not only did the number of orphanages in operation reach its pinnacle in the 1930s, but per the 1933 census, 140,352 children were warehoused in them, up from about 122,000 a decade earlier.[52] Meanwhile, 102,577 children were in foster care in 1933, up from about 73,000 in 1923. Of course, the census would have missed all the children who were still living in unlicensed boarding homes, which were still common at the time. Orphanages still primarily served white children, and white children vastly outnumbered children of color in foster homes, which required racial matching—more than 93 percent of children in institutions were white, and about 90 percent of children in foster homes were white.

Enter FDR's New Deal, which, as Annie sings in the musical, heralded that "tomorrow's at hand." After the First New Deal's efforts at stabilizing the banking system passed, the Second New Deal seemed poised to revolutionize child welfare by creating, for the first time in America's 159 years, a social welfare state. Thanks to the provisions of the 1935 Social Security Act, child welfare experts believed that poverty would finally decrease, and thus parents' need to leave children in orphanages and foster care in times of crisis would drop dramatically. But while the Social Security Act built a safety net comprised of old-age social insurance (the benefits we now call Social Security), unemployment compensation, and a federalization of mothers' pensions known formally as Aid for Dependent Children (ADC) but colloquially as "welfare," its holes gaped.

The Social Security Act's protections assumed a vision of the nuclear family headed by a male breadwinner that left out wide swaths of America. Not only did the Social Security Act rest on the idea that families were best protected when men's work was protected, but it discriminated against people of color, especially Black people. While Black men had the highest unemployment rates during the Depression, they were also more likely to work at jobs excluded from unemployment insurance and retirement benefits, namely agricultural work.[53] Domestic workers, large proportions of whom were Black women, were also excluded. The decision to exclude Black people from the protections of the Social Security Act was purposeful. In total, 65 percent of Black people were ineligible for Social Security Act benefits; for Black women in particular, 90 percent were ineligible.[54] It wouldn't be until the 1950s that Congress repealed the exclusions under pressure from the National Association for the Advancement of Colored People.

Meanwhile, ADC reenacted the same limitations that hampered state mothers' pensions. Technically, the act defined a "dependent child" as "a child under the age of sixteen who has been deprived of parental support or care by reason of the death, continued absence from the home, or physical or mental incapacity of a parent" who was living with a family member. But while this definition might seem to include not just orphans and the children of widows but the children of deserted mothers, unwed single mothers, and disabled parents, each state set its own eligibility metrics. This allowed local aid administrators to pass judgment on and socially control mothers much in the way that mothers' pensions had.

Indeed, states and local officials had power in determining who could benefit from ADC because the program was constructed as a federal-state partnership—the federal government provided matching grants amounting to one-quarter of the total cost of administering ADC programs developed by states.[55] Southern congressmen had pushed for state and local control of ADC benefits in order to preserve economies that relied on Black labor.[56] As Laura Briggs argues in *Taking Children: A History of American Terror,* "The push coming from the federal government to end discrimination against African Americans in welfare was a problem for the South, because the region had counted on Black women's labor in the fields and in other people's homes for centuries."[57] From the 1940s to the early 1960s in the South, state eligibility criteria were written specifically to exclude Black mothers.[58] In 1943, Louisiana even enacted a policy that denied ADC benefits to women during cotton-picking season.[59]

With all these restrictions, ADC did not reach all the woman-headed households that needed help caring for their children. By 1939, the number of children receiving aid was 657,000, but up to two million children might have been eligible.[60] As had long been the case, only some children were seen as "deserving" of aid and care because of how society judged their mothers. Even at a time when the federal government was offering its most generous social welfare, Black children and the children of unwed mothers were kept in poverty because of racism and patriarchal morals.

When the Social Security Act was first amended in 1939, the emphasis on male breadwinners only deepened. The amendment expanded the insurance benefits for covered workers to include not just retired (male) workers themselves but their spouses and minor children.[61] The new insurance also included survivor's benefits to be paid to the families of workers who died before reaching retirement age. My brother and I received these benefits until we each reached eighteen, and although they increased after my father—our family's primary breadwinner—died, the monthly amount was less than $1,000 for each of us.

My father himself had also received survivor's benefits—his father, Jack, died of a heart attack in 1962 at age thirty-six, leaving behind my grandma Mary and five children. Jack and Mary were both born and raised in Brooklyn—he in an Irish American family in Prospect Heights, she in an Italian immigrant family in Flatbush—and attended Boys' High School and Girls' Commercial High School, respectively. Shortly after they graduated, America entered World War II. Jack was drafted into the navy and served as a second-class hospital apprentice in the Pacific, while Mary contributed to the war effort by splitting mica, a heat-resistant mineral used in military equipment from planes to radios. Though they had lived and gone to school within a two-mile radius of one another, Jack and Mary's paths didn't cross until after the war. In 1952, they married and settled in the top-floor apartment of Mary's parents' house, where they started their family. When Jack died, my dad, Robert, their oldest child, was just shy of turning ten; his youngest sibling, my aunt Nancy, had just turned four. Grandma didn't talk much about her grief, but one afternoon after my dad died, she told me about her husband's death. The night before, she brought him a drink as he sat in his favorite armchair in their living room. The next morning, he was still in that armchair, not moving.

Years later, Grandma said that her first thought upon losing her husband was "Will I have to put my children in foster care?" She was lucky never to get close to that devastation. Though she was left to raise five young children alone, she had the support of her family—and, crucially, material support. Jack had worked as a field auditor for Traveler's Insurance and had a $6,000 life insurance policy, equivalent to about $60,000 today. Supplementing the life insurance were Social Security survivors' benefits, which didn't amount to much. In those days, the maximum benefit for a widowed mother and all surviving children together was $254 a month, about $2,600 today.[62] My father and his sisters also received benefits from the Veterans Benefits Administration, but my aunt Joan remembers these as "minuscule, under $100 a month probably."

Mary had been a dressmaker and part of the International Ladies' Garment Workers Union before she had children, and she took in sewing work to support her family after her husband's death, since the government benefits they received were scarcely enough. She eventually got a higher-paying job as a check clearer at Irving Trust, later acquired by the Bank of New York. In this way, Mary was able to put all five of her children through Catholic school. Her daughters were beautifully outfitted in matching dresses and coats that she sewed herself. Even though Mary might have been considered eligible for ADC, my aunt Joan told me that she never would have applied because it would have been shameful for her—she was a very proud woman. At any rate, the survivor's benefits my father's family received, though meager, were almost certainly higher than what they would have gotten under ADC.

My grandma's divergent attitudes toward survivor's benefits and ADC might seem arbitrary, but the Social Security Act baked a meaningful distinction into the two types of aid. While survivor's benefits are a form of social insurance, ADC was a form of public assistance. As historian Michael B. Katz explains in his landmark work on American welfare, *In the Shadow of the Poorhouse*, social insurance is an entitlement with benefits that "cross class lines," whose recipients are distinguished "from the irregularly employed or otherwise dependent poor who [remain] outside the labor force."[63] Since my grandfather had been gainfully employed and had paid income tax, his surviving family was *entitled* to benefits. Public assistance, meanwhile, is means-tested—you are only eligible if you are (very) poor. People who receive "welfare" like ADC "carry the historic stigma of the unworthy poor, and, as a consequence, they are treated meanly," Katz writes. "Their benefits, which do not lift them out of poverty, remain far below those paid by social security."[64] As a white widow, my grandma was certainly "worthy"; her half-orphan children were too. It's not surprising, then, that she would have opted for survivor's benefits instead of ADC.

At a 1960 conference, the director of New York State's Bureau of Public Assistance, Margaret Barnard, noted this preference in a speech that emphasized how attitudes had shifted drastically from the mothers' pension push in the early 1900s. "Most of the socially acceptable mothers of dependent children have moved over to insurance coverage, and we have remaining on public assistance those who are divorced, separated, deserted, or unmarried, with the fathers not supporting," Barnard said. "We wind up with an ADC case load filled with all the social and economic problems that the community wishes to push under the rug. Because of this community disapproval, workers and clients alike are under great pressure."[65] By "socially acceptable mothers of dependent children," Barnard clearly meant only widows—that much had not changed in fifty years. But whereas public assistance in the form of mothers' pensions was once reserved for worthy white widows, the federal descendant of that aid was by then stigmatized and associated with unworthy mothers. This new stigma was tainted with racism—as more Black women moved to northern states during the Great Migration and joined the ADC rolls, welfare began to lose its public popularity.[66] By 1961, 48 percent of welfare recipients were Black, up from 14 percent in 1937.[67] Meanwhile, the problems that the "community wishes to push under the rug"—unwed parenthood and divorce chief among them—would fuel foster care.

By mid-century, it should have been clear to child welfare experts that ADC and the other protections of the Social Security Act were not enough to prevent the breakup of families due to poverty. In 1950, while the population of children in both foster care and orphanages had fallen significantly from its 1933 high, and while the number of children in foster homes had finally edged out the number of children institutionalized, some 193,000 children were still "dependent" and reliant on out-of-home care, and the vast majority of them came from poor families.[68] Instead, experts clung to the theory that individual faults—not societal failures—were what tore families apart. A few key factors contributed to their willful misunderstanding.

First, in the 1940s and 1950s, the social work profession had zeroed in on individual treatment via casework, influenced both by the spread of Freudian theories in the field and a retreat from the focus on collective social reform that had dominated during the crisis of the Great Depression.[69] As John Ehrenreich notes in his history of social work, the profession has always swung back and forth between these two poles. On the one hand, in times of upheaval and crisis, like the Progressive era and the Great Depression, social workers have understood "human misery in terms of the social environment," Ehrenreich writes, necessitating systemic reforms and advocacy.[70] But after World War II, America was in a period that Ehrenreich writes was "characterized by the repression and decline of social movements" and "a retreat into political apathy and acquiescence."[71] Without a loud, front-and-center movement pointing out societal inequality, it was easier for social workers to buy into a more psychological and psychiatric approach to their profession, one that assumed "individual character flaws" were at the heart of clients' problems.[72]

It wasn't just that social movements had lost their power in the postwar period—the country was also amid a spate of prosperity and a baby boom that fueled a specific vision of the American family. The perfect 1950s nuclear family was white and middle-class, with a breadwinning father, stay-at-home mother, and 2.5 children, all living in a suburban single-family home. My mother's family—the Dascoles—fit this image when they moved to Long Island from Williamsburg, Brooklyn, in 1956. My mom, Amelia, the youngest of three children, was four years old at the time. Her parents replaced their 1920s row house with a 1947 Cape Cod in West Hempstead—the same house I would later grow up in. Papa Dascole served in the army during World War II and was probably able to afford the move thanks to the GI Bill, which provided government-backed fixed-rate mortgages and fueled white flight to the postwar sprawl of Long Island.

Plenty of American families did not meet this ideal. For one, even before his father died, my father's family, living in a multigenerational home in Brooklyn, would have stood outside the glorification of the small (white) nuclear family that sitcoms like *The Adventures of Ozzie and Harriet* and *Leave It to Beaver* promoted. As Stephanie Coontz writes in *The Way We Never Were*, her brilliant takedown of nostalgic myths about the American family, these shows put forth a vision of family life that was both "a new invention" and "a historical fluke," one that would not last and never reached the poor and many people of color.[73]

In the 1940s and 1950s, social workers and other child welfare experts blamed social ills and poverty on divorce and unwed motherhood. These two issues topped the list of supposed "family pathologies" that they believed fueled foster care, along with mental illness (usually attributed to "psychotic" mothers).[74] The overwhelming assumption was that New Deal programs and postwar prosperity had lifted all but the most abnormal families out of poverty and that mothers in particular who stood outside the newly middle-class glorification of marriage and the nuclear family were individually to blame for their problems.

Through this lens, foster care took on a new purpose—instead of just providing poor and orphaned children with temporary family homes, it needed to rehabilitate families that were damaged by pathology. Foster care is still meant to play this role in the lives of families—but it has never lived up to this ideal. Until the 1960s, foster care was poorly funded and poorly staffed, especially outside major cities. While Title V of the Social Security Act provided grants to states for "child welfare services," that money could not be used to fund foster care maintenance payments—the boarding payments that went to foster parents themselves.[75] The federal government was reluctant to fund foster care in part because so many foster care placement agencies were run by the same private, sectarian charities that had run orphanages. Instead, states were to use the money to establish—but not deliver—public services "for the protection and care of homeless, dependent, and neglected children and children in danger of becoming delinquent."

In the absence of federal funding for foster care, local agencies couldn't afford adequate and appropriately trained staff, both in terms of foster parents and caseworkers. Even in the early 1960s, only half of all caseworkers had professional training, and through the 1950s, only half of all American counties had even one full-time child welfare caseworker.[76] As was the case in the 1920s, though child welfare experts believed that the women best suited to be foster mothers were middle-class and married, agencies were never able to recruit and train enough such women; instead, they were perpetually deal-ing with shortages of suitable homes and had to lower their standards to find foster parents who would accept their low board payments.

Further undermining the foster care system's ability to actually pro-vide "therapeutic" services for families forced to rely on it was the rhetoric organizations used to recruit foster parents. For instance, during World War II, child welfare professionals and organizations promoted foster parenting as a patriotic war job and foster children as war orphans, despite the fact that the Children's Bureau estimated that only about sixty thousand chil-dren lost their fathers to military service during World War II.[77] During the war, most children in foster care were there due to poverty and related issues, not because their parents had died. Thinking of these children as orphans both evoked sympathy for them and rendered their parents nonentities. If we conflate foster children with orphans, then only the children—not their parents—need help. How could foster care possibly rehabilitate a "patholog-ical" family if it entailed first removing the children from that family and then pretending that they were parentless? And how could it do so if the system offered no social services to help "pathological" families reunify?[78] In this sense, foster care functioned not all that differently than the orphanages of the nineteenth century—both were essentially way stations where families could park their children in times of crisis, but they could not expect any other help to alleviate the underlying causes of their crisis.

Through mid-century, foster care was still predominantly "voluntary," but the choices that many parents made when they ceded their children to the system were, as in the orphanage era, scarcely choices. I think about my grandma Mary and her fear of having to place my father and his sisters in fos-ter care after her husband died in the early 1960s. She was only thirty-seven years old herself, and she woke up one morning with her life utterly and irreparably changed—she was now a widow, the single mother of five young children, and she didn't have a job. If she had gone to a public or private social services agency for assistance at the time, and its agents had strongly urged her to place her children in foster care, she might not have felt like she had much of a choice to do otherwise.

At the same time, young women who got pregnant out of wedlock were subject to the forcible removal of their babies under a private system that worked parallel to—but barely interacted with—foster care. The postwar gospel of the nuclear family had strengthened the taboo against unwed pregnancy and also fed a desire for infant adoption among middle- and upper-class married couples who could not conceive children of their own.[79] From 1946 to 1972, the year before *Roe v. Wade* legalized abortion nationwide, the number of unwed mothers increased from 125,200 to 403,200.[80] Just as in the late 1800s, this increase in unwed pregnancies sparked the establishment of private charities that disappeared the evidence of the supposed sins by coercing young women to give birth and give up their babies in secret. The Foundling had St. Ann's Maternity Hospital—and later St. Mary's Shelter for Pregnant Women; by 1965 other private and religious groups had opened more than two hundred such maternity homes across the United States.[81]

Rather than placing these children out on baby trains, maternity homes coerced mothers to relinquish them for private adoption, which had by mid-century become a highly specialized industry that sought to erase any evidence that adoptees were, well, adopted. Notably, while some babies born in maternity homes were initially placed in foster care, they were only meant to stay there for a few months so that social workers could assess their suitability for adoption.[82] In almost all cases, foster parents were not thought of as suitable adoptive parents, largely because agencies considered them to be drawn from an inferior (and lower-class) pool—a viewpoint at odds with their high standards for potential foster homes.[83]

Private maternity homes were almost exclusively for white women, and until the 1960s foster care services were similarly exclusionary. Black children in particular were left out of the system, in part because agencies would only place children with foster families of the same race, and they struggled to recruit sufficient Black foster families. This issue stemmed from racist and classist housing, employment, and economic standards for foster parents that Black people struggled to meet, as well as the realities of a still-segregated country—in the South in particular, child welfare services for Black children were essentially nonexistent.[84] In the early 1960s, as the proportion of Black children in foster care began to increase, researchers believed they were entering care for issues common "among white foster placement cases several decades ago," like poverty.[85] But financial need was still driving children into foster care across races—experts simply lacked the data to wake them up to this fact.

Indeed, the biggest issue driving the swing toward attributing problems to individuals rather than society was the fact that even supposed experts in child welfare poorly understood the population they were serving. This is because until the late 1950s, they relied on little more than anecdotes and suppositions to guide their work, rather than systematic analysis of the families relying on foster care. It took an infuriating fifty years after foster care was first proposed as the solution to child welfare's ills for the first large-scale study of the system to be released. By then, approximately a quarter million children were in foster care.[86]

Given the remit of the Children's Bureau, which was originally established to "investigate and report upon all matters pertaining to the welfare of children," one might imagine that it was responsible for this study. But while the bureau had continued to issue advice, as it had with its 1923 publication on foster care, that advice was not based on research into what was actually happening with foster care on the ground.[87] Well into the 1950s, the bureau barely studied foster care at all—it couldn't even furnish numbers about how many children were in foster care in each state.[88] Instead, the Child Welfare League of America, a private charitable organization founded in 1920 as a voluntary coalition of public and private child welfare agencies, had taken the lead.[89] The resulting 1959 book, *Children in Need of Parents*, a 462-page tome by Henry S. Maas, a social work professor, and Richard E. Engler, a sociologist, finally made clear that children were still entering foster care for reasons of poverty alone.[90]

Their study examined the foster care populations of nine representative communities across the United States, ranging from rural areas to large cities, with the assistance of employees of the foster care agencies and family courts in each community.[91] *Children in Need of Parents* found that a quarter of children in these communities had entered foster care not because of their parents' individual faults but because of financial hardship or the illness or death of a parent—little had changed since the orphanage and orphan train eras. In areas with low ADC grants, the proportion of children entering the system primarily because of poverty, illness, or death was higher.[92] Katherine Oettinger, the Children's Bureau chief, reacted to *Children in Need of Parents* by ruing that "much foster placement was still associated with poor parental health, low income, unemployment, and inadequate housing."[93] She found it upsetting that ADC and the rest of the new social safety net remained insufficient to keep families whole and that poverty was still driving children into foster care.

Shortly after the publication of *Children in Need of Parents* helped wake the child welfare community up to the fact that the Social Security Act had not had the impact on foster care that they had long believed it had, the act underwent a reform that would cement the relationship between "welfare" and foster care and create the punitive system of surveillance that we have today.

In July 1962, a few months after my grandpa Martin died, Congress passed the Public Welfare Amendments to the Social Security Act, which transformed ADC into Aid to Families with Dependent Children (AFDC).[94] Along with the name change, the federal government increased its matching funds to participating states and allowed AFDC to cover some of the costs of children in foster care. For the first time, the federal government would fund payments for out-of-home care of dependent children, more than a hundred years after the explosion of orphanages across the country.

On first blush, it might seem beneficial that foster care would finally be federally funded—by supplementing state and local money for foster care services, agencies could finally hire appropriate staff, pay foster parents better board payments, and offer rehabilitative services to parents separated from their children. But by coupling foster care with AFDC, the government inextricably linked child welfare with much-stigmatized public assistance and thus with poverty. Even as child welfare experts were disappointed that children were still entering foster care due to poverty—and not the "family pathologies" they believed the system should address—the federal government cemented the relationship between poverty and family separation and made it seem as though only poor parents required rehabilitation. It even literalized this: in order to be eligible for AFDC-funded foster care, a child needed to be involuntarily removed from its birth family by court order.[95] In other words, AFDC marked the beginning of a foster care system that was in large part driven by the forcible removal of children from their poor parents.

The higher federal matching rates for foster care through AFDC—as high as 85 percent by the late 1960s—as opposed to other child welfare services, which averaged about 10 percent, also encouraged caseworkers to place more children receiving AFDC in foster care rather than provide their families with other forms of assistance to stay whole.[96] This trend was only compounded in 1967, when a rule change enabled AFDC-funded foster care to apply not just to children whose families were already receiving AFDC but to children who should have been considered *eligible* for the benefits prior to their removal.[97] By the early 1970s, AFDC subsidized the board payments of a quarter of all children in publicly funded foster care.[98] By 2000, that proportion had increased to more than *half* of all children in foster care.[99] This means that poor children were increasingly being shunted into foster care instead of receiving other kinds of support that might have helped their parents keep them safely at home.

AFDC came to include funding children in foster care in the first place just after the implementation of a federal rule that had good intentions but a terrible outcome. Arthur Flemming, secretary of the Department of Health, Education, and Welfare, which was subsequently replaced by the Departments of Health and Human Services and Education, created the so-called Flemming Rule in response to racist "suitable home" laws passed by Louisiana in 1960 that included immediate termination of ADC benefits if a mother lived with a "man in the house" and if a mother had given birth out of wedlock.[100] These "suitable home" acts were passed during a special legislative session in Louisiana when Governor Jimmie Davis proposed a series of racist bills, which were deemed a "segregation package."[101] One bill sought to legally exclude Black women from delivering their babies at charity hospitals, another to send women to prison for conceiving a child out of wedlock.[102] While those bills didn't pass, the "suitable home" laws did, and they essentially segregated ADC. Following the Louisiana laws' passage, more than twenty-nine thousand Black women and children were purged from the ADC rolls; an estimated 98 percent of the families cut off from benefits were Black.[103]

Mississippi had in fact pioneered "suitable home" laws that targeted Black women five years earlier, and Arkansas, Georgia, Texas, Virginia, and Michigan passed similar legislation.[104] As was the case in Louisiana, these "suitable home" laws were passed by legislatures in a bid to claw back poor Black women's access to ADC as part of the "massive resistance" that Virginia senator Harry Byrd called for to prevent integration after *Brown v.*

Board of Education of Topeka.[105] The difference in Louisiana was that Black mothers responded with fervent activism that ultimately led the American Civil Liberties Union to bring their case to the Department of Health, Education, and Welfare, which was responsible for certifying state ADC plans.[106] In January 1961, though the Social Security commissioner declared Louisiana's ADC plan legal, Flemming was unhappy with the outcome and issued his own rule the same day.[107] The Flemming Rule required that if states were to remove families from ADC by simply declaring their homes "unsuitable," they then needed to remove the children from those "unsuitable" homes and pay for them to be placed in foster homes. Flemming's intention was to lessen the arbitrary removal of families from the ADC rolls, assuming that states would prefer to continue to pay for the less-expensive ADC benefits rather than assume the burden of bankrolling a swelling foster-care population.

In practice, the Flemming Rule created the grounds on which caseworkers nationwide could investigate the homes of mothers applying for AFDC, deem them "unsuitable," deny them benefits, and remove their children to federally subsidized foster care. This situation hearkens back to the logic of the Black Codes that allowed for the children of "unfit" parents to be functionally re-enslaved by their white masters. While the rule might have been created in response to a law that disproportionally affected Black families, it would in fact lay the groundwork for a foster care system that disproportionally tears apart Black families.

Chapter Eleven

POLICING POOR BLACK AND NATIVE FAMILIES

When New York City's Administration for Children's Services (ACS), the local child protective services (CPS) agency, removed Joyce McMillan's two daughters from her custody in 1999, it wasn't because caseworkers had found her home "unsuitable" after she applied for welfare or because they believed she was abusing her girls. McMillan, a Black single mother, had a stable life before ACS barged into it. She was working at a bank, had her own car, and was providing her daughters—Courtnie, who was about to turn nine, and Kaylah, who was a newborn—with everything needed to keep them safe.[1] McMillan's family supported her—in fact, since she had recently given birth to Kaylah, she was staying with her mother in Brooklyn for extra help.[2] And unlike many Black families, no one in McMillan's had ever interacted with CPS. She had only thought about the system through the lens of her family's longtime neighbor in East Flatbush, Brooklyn, who worked for the Bureau of Child Welfare, a predecessor to ACS. When McMillan was growing up in the 1960s and 1970s, her neighbor would babysit her in the summer, and she'd sometimes make stops to check in with families or speak with colleagues. But McMillan didn't know much about the nature of her neighbor's work. "She didn't talk about safety for children, she didn't talk about making sure they were OK, she didn't talk about taking them out of their home," McMillan told me. "I had no idea."

Her experience with ACS began when someone called a child maltreatment prevention hotline alleging that she was using drugs. McMillan still doesn't know the exact nature of the allegations against her or who made the call, since such reports are anonymous.[3] When ACS workers showed up at her door to investigate, McMillan complied. She didn't know that it was within her rights to ask the investigators to obtain a court order to enter her home, interview and examine her children, and compel her to take a drug test. In fact, CPS workers across the country rely on the fact that parents accused of maltreatment don't know their rights—since these are not criminal investigations, in most states, CPS investigators aren't required to read parents a Miranda-style warning and routinely conduct investigations without court orders.[4]

After McMillan's urine sample came back positive for using an illicit substance, ACS obtained an order from a family court judge to immediately remove her daughters from her care, without first making any efforts to keep her family together.[5] As is the case nationwide, ACS didn't need to prove to the judge beyond a reasonable doubt that McMillan was neglecting or abusing her daughters in order to remove them—it merely needed to convince the judge that the girls were more likely than not in danger, a highly subjective call. "It's like when you play Monopoly and go straight to jail, some cases are just straight to separation," McMillan told me. Courtnie went to live with her father and grandmother in New Jersey, but they didn't have the capacity to take Kaylah, who was only three months old at the time.[6] The baby was placed in foster care in Brooklyn, with her case overseen by St. Vincent's, a Catholic charity founded in 1869 to serve homeless working boys—a Catholic counterpart to the Children's Aid Society's Newsboys' Lodging House.[7] Now known as HeartShare St. Vincent's Services, the organization shifted its focus to foster care in the 1980s.

At the time that ACS tore her family apart, McMillan was only using drugs recreationally and said that her daughters were not in imminent danger because of her substance use.[8] After all, as McMillan often argues, "a drug test is not a parenting test."[9] If she were a white middle-class mother living in Park Slope and had used drugs on a few nights out while her children were being babysat, McMillan likely wouldn't have attracted ACS scrutiny. And ACS didn't need to immediately separate McMillan's family—caseworkers could have recommended instead that she undergo drug treatment in a program that would have allowed her to continue living with and caring for her daughters. But, as McMillan explained, cases "are only straight to separation when people look like me."

After her daughters were removed from her care, McMillan's recreational drug use morphed into an addiction.[10] Her family support vanished. "Everyone was angry with me," McMillan told me. Meanwhile, the case plan that ACS required her to complete to move toward reunification with her baby was a "check-the-box situation," McMillan said. It was not tailored to her needs; nor did it meaningfully help her reunify with her daughters. In fact, McMillan was sent to a mother-and-baby program, but ACS wouldn't release Kaylah to attend with her, a situation she calls "torture in and of itself." McMillan ended up with a drug-related arrest and spent eight months incarcerated on Rikers Island. When she told me this part of her story, she took a deep breath and said, "They don't help, Kristen. They send your life into a tailspin."

A family like McMillan's would likely not have come into contact with a child welfare agency in the 1950s. There would have been no impetus for government caseworkers to knock on her door and demand to examine her cupboards, her housekeeping, and her children's bodies, no impetus to demand that she undergo a drug test. A mother like McMillan, who was not on "welfare," who was not actively seeking out the help of social services, and who was not accused of physically harming her children, would be unlikely to get on the radar of a caseworker and would not have to worry about having her children removed via court order and placed in foster care.

All that started to change in the early 1960s. Alongside the development of Aid to Families with Dependent Children (AFDC) funding for foster care and the passage of the Flemming Rule—which together created incentives for the involuntary removal of children from "unsuitable" homes—came a moral panic over the "rediscovery" of child abuse and a push for widespread reporting of suspicions of maltreatment. Together, these forces would swell the foster care population dramatically and lead to racial disproportionality in the system. Foster care would transition from a primarily voluntary service for poor white families to a coerced intervention into which Black and Indigenous children were increasingly being shunted.

At the same time, a consensus developed that in order to protect children's welfare, parents needed to be punished for their failures. It was no accident that our country's foster care system would start to entangle Black and Indigenous families at disproportionate rates just as it became synonymous with government-sponsored surveillance and investigations of parental wrongdoing. To borrow a phrase from journalist Adam Serwer, the cruelty is the point. I say this because tearing apart families and punishing parents does not keep children safe—it leaves them worse off by every measure. In the meantime, the foster care industrial complex rakes in government money, and poor families stay poor.

———

In 1962, the same year that Aid for Dependent Children (ADC) turned into AFDC, the *Journal of the American Medical Association* published "The Battered-Child Syndrome." Written by University of Colorado pediatrician C. Henry Kempe and four of his colleagues, the article was based on radiologists' prior studies of children's broken bones, as well as a new survey of seventy-one American hospitals and seventy-seven district attorneys regarding children's injuries. Kempe proposed the titular syndrome as "a clinical condition in young children who have received serious physical abuse, generally from a parent or foster parent"—though it would live on in the popular imagination as primarily concerning parents as perpetrators.

Kempe proposed that physicians consider diagnosing battered-child syndrome "in any child exhibiting evidence of fracture of any bone, subdural hematoma, failure to thrive, soft tissue swellings or skin bruising, in any child who dies suddenly, or where the degree and type of injury is at variance with the history given."[11] It's worth noting that this guidance lumps together bruises and death and that one in three of us will break a bone in childhood.[12]

But "The Battered-Child Syndrome" posited not only that physicians ought to be suspicious about the provenance of children's injuries but that the incidence of caretakers purposefully physically harming their children "has been a particularly common problem in our hospitals"—though the numbers cited didn't bear out this claim.[13] By modern standards of peer review, the article is shockingly scant on details. There is no information about survey methodology, and the incidence rate of reported syndrome cases is not contextualized as a proportion of the child population at large. Nevertheless, in an accompanying editorial in the same issue, *JAMA*—which remains among the most respected medical journals in the country—hyped that while the data were incomplete, the syndrome would "likely . . . be found to be a more frequent cause of death than such well recognized and thoroughly studied diseases as leukemia."[14]

Though "The Battered-Child Syndrome" didn't center on the story of a particular child, it captivated the media—and the public—just as Mary Ellen Wilson's plight had almost one hundred years earlier. The article would become the inciting incident for the "rediscovery" of child abuse. Kempe argued that "to the informed physician, the bones tell a story the child is too young or too frightened to tell."[15] The story Kempe was telling was one America wanted to hear. Shortly after the *JAMA* issue's publication, *Time* magazine ran an article spreading word of battered-child syndrome far beyond Kempe's intended audience of physicians.[16] The *Time* article opened with a moral-panic-inducing lede: "To many doctors, the incident is becoming distressingly familiar. A child, usually under three, is brought to the office with multiple fractures—often including a fractured skull. The parents express appropriate concern, report that the baby fell out of bed, or tumbled down the stairs, or was injured by a playmate. But X rays and experience lead the doctor to a different conclusion: the child has been beaten by his parents. He is suffering from what last week's A.M.A. *Journal* calls 'the battered-child syndrome.'" By emphasizing the devious behavior of parents who play up "appropriate concern" to physicians while having secretly fractured their toddlers' skulls, the *Time* article immediately puts the focus on the perpetrators' psychology, a lead it takes from Kempe's *JAMA* article itself, which spends more column inches opining on the "psychiatric aspects" that drive caretakers to physically abuse children than on how battered children present clinically.

Off the bat, Kempe acknowledges that "psychiatric knowledge pertaining to the problem of the battered child is meager, and the literature on the subject is almost nonexistent."[17] Nevertheless he goes on to assert that the abusers are often reported to be "psychopathic or sociopathic characters" who exhibit "alcoholism, sexual promiscuity, unstable marriages, and minor criminal activities"—the same sorts of "pathologies" that child welfare experts believed necessitated foster care at mid-century.[18] And though Kempe admits that "people with good education and stable financial and social background" also beat children, they usually have "a defect in character structure."[19] In other words, individual faults, not societal faults, are to blame for child abuse. In fact, Kempe's article does not consider socioeconomic risk factors like poverty or unstable housing at all.

A few months later, an article in the *Saturday Evening Post* similarly highlighted parents' mental illness as the culprit in its headline: "Parents Who Beat Children: A Tragic Increase in Cases of Child Abuse Is Prompting a Hunt for Ways to Detect Sick Adults Who Commit Such Crimes."[20] And *Newsweek* actually scooped the *JAMA* article itself by two months, with an April 1962 article that mentioned Kempe's then ongoing survey and also—you guessed it—focused on the character faults of parents.[21] The *Newsweek* article, which featured a photograph of a small child's naked, bruised back, ran under the headline "When They're Angry . . . ," a snippet of a quote from an anonymous Los Angeles social worker who suggested that abusive parents "act like children who break their dolls."[22]

Newsweek also quoted the chief of the Children's Bureau, Katherine Oettinger, who said that the bureau had been "receiving an increasing number of reports from pediatricians and hospitals about physical abuse of children by their parents" over the past three years. In fact, throughout the 1960s and 1970s, there was no reliable evidence to prove the assertion that caretakers were physically abusing children more often than at any prior point in history—they weren't.[23] Later, it would become clear that while tens of thousands of American children *do* suffer from physical abuse each year, our perception of this issue has long been out of proportion with reality.

Nevertheless, the Children's Bureau turned its attention to combating a seeming rise in child abuse cases. In a 1963 publication titled *The Abused Child*, the bureau presented model state legislation on requirements for the mandatory reporting of physical abuse.[24] The bureau recommended requiring physicians to report physical child abuse, since they were "in an optimum position to perform reasonable, preliminary judgments" about how a child's injuries had actually been inflicted.[25] To make an allegation, a physician need only to have "reasonable cause to suspect that physical injury was inflicted by a parent or other person responsible for the care of the child"—suspicion, but not proof, in other words.[26] The proposed legislation would indemnify reporters against liability if they acted in good faith and stipulated that physicians who didn't make a report when they suspected child abuse could be charged with a misdemeanor.[27]

The bureau also suggested that allegations be received by the "appropriate police authority" in the jurisdiction, which could either investigate them itself or refer the duty to a "voluntary or public social agency"—pivoting the perceived role of caseworker from benevolent helper to antagonistic detective. Following an investigation, a case plan could include temporary foster care or even the termination of parental rights, rendering the child a legal orphan who could be placed for adoption.[28] Notably, the Children's Bureau's model statute did not dictate exactly what law enforcement *should* do after receiving a report of child abuse. The focus of the model legislation was solely on the *reporting* of abuse—not what should be done with those reports. Casting reporting as an end in itself would be prescient. It spurred a deluge of largely unfounded anonymous child maltreatment accusations that have continued to overburden our country's child welfare systems.

In the wake of the publications of Kempe's article and *The Abused Child*, state legislatures acted swiftly to pass their own mandated reporting laws based on the Children's Bureau's model; by 1967, all fifty states had done so.[29] Lawmakers weren't just following the bureau's advice blindly—they were also acting in response to the media-fueled panic over the battered-child syndrome, which cemented the concept that heinous physical abuse of children by their psychologically damaged parents was omnipresent, on the rise, and hiding in plain sight.[30] By 1970, a false estimate that as many as four million American children were being physically abused by their parents per year had lodged itself in the public imagination.[31] (The researcher responsible for publishing this statistic would later argue that it was "meaningless," as it was based on a public opinion survey that asked a sample of Americans about cases of child abuse they knew about.)[32] Not until 1981 would the federal government release actual data from its first National Study of the Incidence and Severity of Child Abuse and Neglect, which indicated that

212,400 American children were maltreated in a year—"maltreatment" is a category inclusive of neglect, not just physical abuse.[33] Sociologist Duncan Lindsey would argue in his landmark 1994 book *The Welfare of Children* that during this period, child abuse emerged as the "red herring" of child welfare—a "highly charged issue that draws attention away from the real and more difficult problem," namely, poverty.[34]

Given the popular overinflated estimate of how many children were being physically abused, it's not surprising that while the Children's Bureau had suggested that only physicians need be mandated reporters, states like Nebraska, Tennessee, and Utah put the onus on *all* adults who suspected child abuse.[35] The more people on the lookout for defenseless battered children who might be too young to speak about what havoc their parents were wreaking on them, the better. By the late 1970s, twenty states had passed similar universal mandated reporting laws.[36] But, as Lindsey argued, universalized and increased reporting of child abuse did not help solve the problem: "The irony is that the more effort, attention, and resources we devote to the problem, the less we seem to achieve."[37] Nevertheless, politicians, the media, and the public saw the flood of child maltreatment reports in and of themselves as evidence of the success of the laws, even if children were not made any safer by the increased awareness of abuse and surveillance and punishment of their parents.[38]

The explosion of child maltreatment reports, founded and not, can be traced back to how our definition of what constitutes "abuse" expanded and blurred in the 1970s. The "rediscovery" of child abuse had been precipitated by an article written for physicians about actual physical injuries. Even if pediatricians made reports based on unfounded suspicions about injuries that had benign causes, the children themselves still would have been suffering from real broken bones or bruises. In other words, actual harm of some form, visible to the eyes or through X-rays, would have precipitated a report. The Children's Bureau's model mandatory reporting statute kept this focus on the physical, defining child abuse as "serious physical injury or injuries inflicted upon [the child] other than by accidental means by a parent or other person responsible for [the child's] care."[39]

Quickly, though, the definition of abuse—and the public's conception of it—expanded far beyond the physical, making reported suspicions of abuse, well, suspect. Nebraska's universal mandatory reporting law, for instance, defined abuse as "knowingly, intentionally, or negligently causing or permitting a minor child . . . to be: (a) placed in a situation that may endanger [the child's] life or health; (b) tortured, cruelly confined, or cruelly punished; (c) deprived of necessary food, clothing, shelter, or care; or (d) left unattended in a motor vehicle, if such minor child is six years of age or younger."[40] This expanded definition matches the modern lumping together of abuse and neglect under the mantle of "maltreatment," and it would soon become the norm rather than the exception. Under this law my own mother would have been guilty of child abuse every time she left my brother and me in our locked station wagon while she ran into our local mom-and-pop market—something she did probably once a month. And the inclusion of the language "deprived of necessary food, clothing, shelter, or care" effectively renders poverty as child abuse.

In 1974, Congress passed the Child Abuse Prevention and Treatment Act (CAPTA), cementing the blurred lines between physical abuse and neglect, ratcheting up mandatory reporting, and spurring racial disproportionality within the foster care system. While each state could write its own laws, CAPTA set a definition of "child abuse and neglect" as "the physical or mental injury, sexual abuse, negligent treatment, or maltreatment of a child under the age of eighteen by a person who is responsible for the child's welfare under circumstances which indicate that the child's health or welfare is harmed or threatened thereby."[41] States needed to adhere to this extraordinarily vague and broad definition—and to have laws requiring the mandatory reporting of child abuse *and* neglect in place—in order to qualify for federal funding of "programs and projects designed to prevent, identify, and treat child abuse and neglect."[42]

During congressional hearings over CAPTA in 1973, the bill's primary sponsor, Senator Walter Mondale, a Democrat from Minnesota, presented child abuse as omnipresent in American society, saying, "You may go into some of the finest communities from an economic standpoint and find child abuse as you would in the ghettos of this country. . . . This is not a poverty problem; it is a national problem."[43] Mondale made this assertion despite the fact that it was already abundantly clear to researchers that poverty is indeed correlated with increased incidence of child abuse. This is to say not that poverty makes parents uniquely evil but that the constant struggle to meet material needs increases stress, family tensions, and overwhelm, making it more likely that parents will lash out at their children.[44] And given the higher rates of poverty among people of color, abuse was also more common in minority families. Child abuse researcher David Gil testified about the higher rate of child abuse in poor and minority families during the CAPTA hearings, but Mondale pushed back, forcing Gil to acknowledge that abuse also happens in middle-class families.[45] Gil also emphasized that children are publicly abused and neglected "by society collectively" via the "malnutrition and at times starvation of expectant mothers and children, inadequate medical care of mothers, children, and whole families, substandard housing and other aspects of life in poverty-stricken neighborhoods," among other issues that "tend to seriously inhibit normal and healthy human growth and development."[46] This societal responsibility for the maltreatment of children was not enshrined in CAPTA.

Instead, Mondale was eager to downplay the links between poverty and child abuse. He proposed CAPTA during the presidency of Richard Nixon, who had vetoed the 1971 Comprehensive Child Development Act, which Mondale had cosponsored. Among other initiatives, the Comprehensive Child Development Act would have created federally subsidized universal day care (yes, we almost had universal child care more than fifty years ago).[47] The bill was controversial among conservatives, who likened it to a plan to "Sovietize our youth."[48] In his veto message, Nixon argued that the bill had "family-weakening implications."[49] This echoed the talking points of conservative family values groups who lobbied against the legislation, with slogans like "Whose Children? Yours or the State's?"—an argument I find especially rich as the lack of affordable child care continues to drive neglect accusations that lead to foster care, a system that actually renders children wards of the state.[50] But the bill also failed because of the unpopularity of President Lyndon B. Johnson's War on Poverty, which was already receiving backlash as the country settled into another period of fetishizing personal responsibility.[51]

In the aftermath of the Comprehensive Child Development Act veto, Mondale was politically motivated to disentangle child abuse, his new focus, from poverty and racial inequality, despite evidence that they were strongly linked. Mondale sought to portray child abuse as driven by psychological problems—the same focus on individual faults that has always prevailed in American child welfare. Rather than implement poverty-alleviation programs that would actually make children safer and improve their development, CAPTA cemented the tendency to blame and punish parents for society's failures.

During the CAPTA hearings, Gil tried to explain to lawmakers not only that child abuse was tied to poverty but that poor people were subject to more scrutiny in every aspect of their lives. "Everything they do or fail to do is immediately reported and considered a major issue, whereas the upper and middle classes get away with a variety of questionable acts and behaviors," Gil testified.[52] This increased surveillance of the poor—especially of Black families—was bound to get worse with the passage of CAPTA, which enshrined neglect as on equal footing with abuse in its requirements for mandatory reporting laws. As is the case with abuse, neglect is strongly correlated with poverty, and poor Black families are especially vulnerable to accusations of neglect. Most child welfare researchers call this increased scrutiny of the poor an "unintended consequence" of CAPTA. Others have argued that these consequences should have been easy to anticipate and that they functioned as a means of extending social control over poor Black families.[53]

CAPTA may have given states funding for the prevention, identification, and treatment of child abuse and neglect, but in practice state agencies turned nearly all their energy toward investigating child maltreatment reports. This is due in no small part to the explosion of such reports that accompanied the law's passage, continuing the moral panic over physical abuse. In 1967, there were about 10,000 reports of child maltreatment; in 1977, there were 800,000; by 1987, there would be 2.1 million.[54] Increased reporting did not lead to increased funding or staffing of child welfare agencies, and in the process, child welfare morphed into child protection. Concurrently, the foster care population exploded, as foster care became the primary form of "treatment" for families that received indicated reports of maltreatment. In 1961, the year before AFDC made federal money available for foster care, there were approximately 244,500 children in foster care.[55] By the late 1970s, that number would exceed half a million.[56] Over the same period, the foster care population grew disproportionately Black and Indigenous, but the federal government would only take action to reduce the removal of one of those group's children.

When it comes to the entanglement of Native American families in the modern child welfare system, the consequences were certainly intentional, just as they had been in the boarding school era. A few years before the moral panic over child abuse exploded, the Bureau of Indian Affairs (BIA)—the same federal agency that had been responsible for boarding schools like the Carlisle Indian Industrial School—embarked on a mission to place Native children in white adoptive families, not because they were suffering from increased rates of abuse but because they were poor. In 1958, the BIA banded together with the Children's Bureau and the nonprofit Child Welfare League of America (CWLA) to found the Indian Adoption Project (IAP).[57] Just as federal Indian boarding schools had once been positioned as an answer to the "Indian Problem," forcibly placing Native children in foster care and in adoptions was positioned as a new answer to a new version of the "Indian Problem": government dependence.[58] That this dependence was itself a foreseeable outcome of hundreds of years of federal policies toward Native peoples was beside the point.

The BIA sought a new method of removing Native children from their families and tribes amid a renewed push for assimilation and cultural genocide, this time in the form of "termination" policies that sought to end federal recognition of—and federal aid to—tribes.[59] (If "termination" sounds violent, consider that the original phrasing employed the term "liquidation" until policy makers realized the Nazis had used it.)[60] In the 1950s, Congress passed legislation that terminated the official recognition of 109 tribes, about half of the tribes the federal government had agreements with.[61]

Once a tribe was terminated, the federal government would cease trusteeship over the tribe's reservation, eliminating all of the public services that the BIA had once provided. When it came to child welfare, this crucially meant the suspension of operations at the remaining boarding schools on reservations, transferring responsibility for educating Native children to the states.[62] Life at these schools was regimented at best and brutal at worst for students. Still, some extremely poor Native families had come to rely on the schools as a safety net for getting their children housed, clothed, and fed, much in the way poor white families had used orphanages in the nineteenth century.[63] Many poor Native children who had been attending the boarding schools were forcibly placed in foster care, which cost less per child per year than the schools had.[64]

Native mothers were put in this bind because they were systematically denied "welfare," especially by Western states home to reservations—Nevada was so loath to pay ADC benefits to Native women that it had no ADC program at all through the late 1950s.[65] When Native women did apply for ADC and later AFDC, they opened up their homes to the scrutiny of state welfare workers. These mostly white, middle-class workers judged Native mothers by white, middle-class standards, holding the nuclear family as an ideal—an extremely poor fit for tribal child-rearing practices, which emphasized extended kinship networks looking after children. The Flemming Rule mandating state provision of alternatives to "unsuitable" homes would thus prove disastrous for Native families, too, throwing more Native children into foster care.

Two other federal Indian policies further opened up Native families to the vagaries of state welfare systems. In 1953, Congress passed Public Law 280, which gave Alaska, California, Minnesota, Nebraska, Oregon, and Wisconsin criminal jurisdiction over reservations, without consulting tribes.[66] Crucially, the law allowed state child welfare systems to further encroach on the lives of Native families living on reservations.[67] Concurrently, the BIA undertook Operation Relocation, a campaign that pushed for Indians to leave their reservations and move to cities for supposedly better employment opportunities. The BIA would cover the costs of moving and the first month's rent. Congress attempted to sweeten the deal—and respond to criticisms that employment prospects were much exaggerated—in 1956 by passing the Indian Relocation Act, which provided vocational training programs for Natives who moved to cities.[68] More than thirty-five thousand Native Americans took the bait from 1952 through the early 1960s.[69] In the process, the federal government was able to shirk its duties toward Indians who had left reservations: if they needed public assistance in their new urban homes, state and local governments would have to foot the bill.[70] Through a combination of termination, Public Law 280, and relocation, Native families were newly exposed to states' child welfare systems.

Native Americans were especially vulnerable to the incursions of child welfare workers because many *did* need public assistance at mid-century. As had been the case with Black families, Native Americans did not enjoy the same postwar ascension to the middle class that many white families experienced. In fact, Native Americans were even worse off. They had the highest rates of unemployment, low life expectancy (forty-four years compared to seventy years for whites), and high rates of infant mortality.[71] Even those who participated in Operation Relocation fared poorly—they experienced continued unemployment, and any jobs they could find paid low wages.[72] Meanwhile, in the wake of termination and the shuttering of boarding schools, states resisted taking responsibility for the welfare needs of Native families.[73]

The federal government had in effect created a "dependency" problem, first via failed assimilation policies that robbed Natives of their ancestral ways of sustaining themselves and traumatized their children and then via termination policies that further eroded tribal cultures and launched ill-prepared Natives into job markets designed to exclude them. Hypocritically, the government put the blame on individuals and sought an individualist solution. The BIA proposed the Indian Adoption Project to shift the burden of providing for dependent Native children from federal and state governments to adoptive families—what historian Margaret Jacobs calls "the ultimate private sector." The IAP would be the ultimate manner of assimilating Native children and shirking responsibilities toward their families. Between 1958 and 1967, when the project ceased, almost four hundred Native children were adopted by white families—a scale that is noteworthy given that racial matching was considered to be an inviolable aspect of a "successful" adoption at the time.[74] Even after the IAP officially ended, the CWLA adopted out hundreds more Native children into white families throughout the late 1960s and 1970s, under a new program designed to promote the adoption of "hard-to-place" children (read: minorities).[75]

Though it focused on permanently severing Native children's relationships with their families and tribes, the IAP was also intimately related to the growing number of Native children in foster care. In an article for the CWLA introducing the IAP, Arnold Lyslo, the white man who directed the program, argued that it was needed in part because so many Native children were languishing in foster care. He wrote, "The Bureau of Indian Affairs has long been concerned about the reports from their welfare staff that many children who might have been firmly established in secure homes at an early age through adoption have been passed from family to family on a reservation, or have spent years at public expense in Federal boarding schools or in foster care."[76] The BIA evidently did not consider supporting these children's families to help keep them in their own "secure homes." Lyslo further argued that the children had "never had the security of family life to promote their development and assure their future."[77] As Jacobs writes, this framing ignores that the BIA itself had been responsible for removing children and institutionalizing them in boarding schools—"instead, officials deflected blame to rest upon Indian families themselves."[78] It also ignores the fact that after the BIA closed boarding schools, desperate parents who had relied on them as a means of child care frequently lost their children to state foster care.

Once Native children were removed to foster care via meddling state welfare workers who found their homes "unsuitable" or determined their parents were maltreating them, the courts could terminate their parents' rights, making them available for adoption into white families. As Jacobs notes, in the 1950s, even before the dawn of the IAP, "state officials imagined the adoption of Indian children in state care as the ultimate solution to their budgetary concerns," as it allowed them to unload the costs of caring for dependent Native children onto private families.[79] The BIA similarly thought of adoption as a cost-saving measure. In 1958, the head of the BIA's Welfare Branch argued that the IAP "could in future years reduce the expenditures of the Bureau for foster home care since we are now paying for care for a number of children for whom adoption should be possible."[80] The project ultimately *did* make more Native children in foster care free for adoption by discouraging BIA welfare workers from taking active measures to reunify poor families once they had been separated.[81]

But the IAP was not just fueled by making children from foster care "adoptable." It also sought to create a supply of adoptable Native infants straight from birth. In order to do so, Lyslo and other IAP workers needed to convince unwed Native mothers to relinquish their babies. While unmarried pregnant white women during this period were often sent to maternity homes by their families out of shame, Indigenous communities did not brand "illegitimate" children with the same stigma and often absorbed them into large kinship networks.[82] The IAP worked to stigmatize unwed motherhood in Native communities by applying assimilationist logic, arguing that Native families had to embrace the nuclear family model of middle-class whites.[83] Under Lyslo's direction, BIA social workers and other social services providers promoted adoption to unwed pregnant Native women who sought welfare assistance, often using coercive methods to encourage them to relinquish their newborns.[84]

Together, IAP and its successor program orchestrated close to one thousand adoptions of Native children. While this number may sound small, it represents hundreds of Native women who forever had their children stolen from them under a social engineering experiment designed by the federal government, as well as hundreds of children who lost contact with their families and Indigenous identities. Whereas federal Indian boarding schools separated families temporarily, adoption irreparably severed the legal ties between Native children and their parents and tribes. And these programs were not alone in permanently separating Native families—more than twelve thousand more Native children were placed for adoption between 1961 and 1976 by agencies acting independently of the BIA and CWLA projects.[85]

Altogether, the number of Native children removed from their families via adoption or foster care was shocking. In the late 1960s, research by the Association on American Indian Affairs (AAIA) determined that between 25 and 35 percent of all Native children had been placed in foster or adoptive homes or institutions, 90 percent of them with non-Natives.[86] The AAIA also found massive disproportionality in foster care populations in several states. In Montana, for instance, thirteen times as many Native children were in foster care as non-Native children.[87]

In 1968, the Devil's Lake Sioux Tribal Council responded to child welfare workers' systemic removal of children from their reservation despite the North Dakota Supreme Court's ruling that tribal courts had jurisdiction over their children. They passed a bold resolution that prohibited county officials from removing children from their reservation.[88] The county punished the tribe by ceasing welfare payments, which actually came from the BIA, not state coffers.[89] In the following years, more Sioux and Lakota nations in North Dakota passed similar tribal council resolutions.[90]

At a 1968 press conference for international reporters, the AAIA's executive director, William Byler, stated, "The Devil's Lake Sioux people and American Indian tribes have been unjustly deprived of their lands and their livelihood, and now they are being dispossessed of their children."[91] He emphasized that "county welfare workers frequently evaluate[d] the suitability of an Indian child's home on the basis of economic or social standards unrelated to the child's physical or emotional well-being"—these children were being removed for reasons of poverty alone, in other words—"and Indian children [were] removed from the custody of their parents or Indian foster family for placement in non-Indian homes without sufficient cause and without due process of law."

By the mid-1970s, further Native activism led to congressional hearings over the alarming rates of Native child removal.[92] By then the federal government's stance toward Native Americans had changed—the government was now supporting tribal self-determination. The time was right for a federal reckoning with how our country had continued to break apart Native families and tribes.

In 1978, Congress passed the Indian Child Welfare Act (ICWA), now considered a gold standard in the field of child welfare. While proposing the bill, the chairman of the Senate Select Committee on Indian Affairs, Senator James Abourezk of South Dakota, highlighted that at least a quarter of Native children had been removed "against the best interest of families and Indian communities" and that poverty did not make Indian parents "unfit."[93] Abourezk called out unchecked "abusive child removal practices, the lack of viable, practical rehabilitation and prevention programs for Indian families facing severe problems, and a practice of ignoring the all-important demands of Indian tribes to have a say in how their children and families are dealt with" as necessitating the interventions of ICWA.[94] He even used the phrase *cultural genocide* to describe how the federal government had, up until that point, "chosen to allow these agencies to strike at the heart of Indian communities by literally stealing Indian children."[95]

During the congressional hearings, Native peoples argued that Native nations—not state and county welfare agencies, not the BIA—had sovereignty over their children. ICWA enshrined this sovereignty. It also established minimum federal standards for the removal of Native children from their families and their placement in foster and adoptive homes. The law decrees that tribes have exclusive jurisdiction over child custody proceedings—including foster care placement, the termination of parental rights, and adoptive placements—for Native children who live on reservations, as well as for Native children who don't live on reservations but whose parents petition for tribal court jurisdiction.[96] Crucially, ICWA also stipulates that if a Native child is placed for adoption under state law, preference must be given first to the child's extended family, second to members of the child's tribe, and third to other Indian families. The same stipulation holds for foster care placements.

In the 1970s, the Black community also faced losing increasing numbers of their children to foster care. But unlike Native Americans, they could not point to sovereignty and jurisdiction as rationales for stemming the tide of child removal. In 1977, Black children made up only about 11 percent of the total child population but about 25 percent of the foster care population, a proportion that would only become more skewed throughout the twentieth century.[97] By 1999, the year Joyce McMillan's daughters were removed, Black children made up about 16 percent of the total child population but 38 percent of the foster care population.[98] White children, meanwhile, were vastly underrepresented, making up about 78 percent of the total child population but only 35 percent of the foster care population.[99] In fact, McMillan's experience of losing her daughters to foster care in the late 1990s was shockingly common for Black New Yorkers—one in twenty-two Black children in New York City were in foster care at the time.[100] That rate exceeds the 1890 height of orphanages in New York City, when one in thirty-five children was institutionalized.

This skewed racial representation marked a dramatic reversal from more than a century and a half of history, when orphanages, orphan trains, and foster care were almost exclusively for white children. The system was increasingly Black. "Spend a day at dependency court in any major city and you will see the unmistakable color of the child welfare system," Dorothy Roberts writes in her 2002 book *Shattered Bonds*. "If you came with no preconceptions about the purpose of the child welfare system, you would have to conclude that it is an institution designed to monitor, regulate, and punish poor Black families."[101] With *Shattered Bonds*, which was as revolutionary to the field as Andrew Billingsley and Jeanne M. Giovannoni's *Children of the Storm* had been thirty years earlier, Roberts was among the first to draw attention to the problem of racial disproportionality in foster care, making a trenchant argument that racism itself is to blame. As Roberts sees it, it's not just that Black families are more likely to be poor and that poor families are more likely to be reported for child maltreatment and investigated by CPS, to have CPS "indicate" the report, and to lose their children to foster care.[102] It's that bias colors every step of a Black family's CPS case, just as it does for Native American families.

First off, though, as David Gil acknowledged during his testimony at the CAPTA hearings in the early 1970s, poor families in general are much more likely to be reported to CPS.[103] This is partially because of the blurred lines between neglect and poverty and partially because of the nature of mandated reporting itself. Nowadays about 70 percent of calls to CPS hotlines come from mandated reporters, a category that has expanded since the 1960s in ways that have widened the web of surveillance over poor families.[104] State laws commonly dictate that not just doctors but all health-care workers, teachers and school administrators, day-care providers, law enforcement personnel, social services workers, and mental health providers must report suspicions of child maltreatment. Some states, like Texas and New Jersey, have embraced universal mandated reporting and make all adults reporters.[105] Mandated reporters who flout the law are typically subject to misdemeanor charges; in some states, like Pennsylvania, withholding a report can constitute a felony. I have been a mandated reporter myself while teaching creative writing to teenagers in a summer program in New York City. I needed to undergo a federal background check and attend trainings about extremely vague warning signs of abuse and neglect, including a child always seeming sleepy—which every single one of my students was at 9:00 a.m. each morning.

This expansion of who is responsible for the surveillance of families has led to an explosion of child maltreatment reports. In 2022, CPS agencies across the country received more than four million referrals alleging maltreatment of more than 7.5 million children.[106] Researchers now estimate that one in three children will be subject to CPS investigation before reaching age eighteen. For Black children, that statistic is even higher—more than half of all Black children will be exposed to CPS.[107]

It's important to note that most child maltreatment reports are unfounded. In 2022, only 49.5 percent of maltreatment allegations were screened in for further investigation, meaning almost half were bogus or didn't contain enough information to warrant CPS involvement. Of the more than three million alleged maltreatment cases investigated by CPS workers, only 558,899 children were considered "victims."[108] In other words, only about 7 percent of the children who were reported as being maltreated in 2022 were actually found to be abused or neglected. And the vast majority of those children experienced neglect, not abuse: 74.3 percent were neglected, while only 17 percent were physically abused, and about 10 percent were sexually abused.[109]

Meanwhile, increased reporting is not actually associated with increased identification of children suffering from abuse. After Pennsylvania lawmakers expanded the population of mandated reporters and the definition of abuse in the aftermath of the Penn State child sexual abuse scandal in 2012, the state hotline was inundated with unfounded maltreatment allegations that overburdened the system. The flood of reports made it harder for CPS investigators to weed through and find children who were actually being grievously abused; in fact, more children in Pennsylvania died due to maltreatment after the state focused on increasing reports. Nor did the expanded reporting identify more cases of child sexual abuse, despite an increased number of allegations and investigations.[110]

While it is true that children and families of all classes interact with mandated reporters on a regular basis, poor families encounter them more often due to increased involvement with welfare bureaucracy workers, public housing workers, and the police. Each stressful trip to a public benefits office with children in tow invites scrutiny of one's parenting. And mandated reporters tend to be more suspicious of poor people. For instance, a pediatrician in private practice who has seen a middle-class girl since birth isn't likely to view a bruise on her arm as evidence of abuse—I am sure my parents were never worried about our beloved Dr. Blinderman calling a CPS hotline for any of my childhood injuries. A doctor working in the emergency room of a publicly funded hospital that a poor family is using in lieu of primary care might view a similar bruise through different eyes—that doctor has no ongoing relationship with the parents or child and a legal duty to report suspicions.

But when it comes to the relationship between poverty, race, and foster care, Roberts argues that increased scrutiny over poor families isn't applied equally across races. She points out that Hispanic families are also more likely to be poor but, in the early 2000s, were placed in foster care at a rate that matched their percentage of the total child population.[111] (Hispanic children are actually underrepresented in foster care nationwide, though in twenty states they make up a larger proportion of the foster care population than the child population.[112] Asian children, meanwhile, have always been underrepresented in foster care—they currently make up only 1 percent of the foster care population but almost 6 percent of the total child population.)[113] So it's not just poverty that increases a Black family's likelihood of having their children removed to foster care.

Instead, racial bias begins at the point when someone picks up the phone to make a call to a child maltreatment hotline.[114] This increased scrutiny is of a piece with the racist stereotypes that govern the public's perception of Black parenting in general and Black motherhood in particular—stereotypes that took on new dimensions in the 1960s and 1970s, in the aftermath of the Flemming Rule, as mandated reporting laws spread and backlash to the civil rights movement and the War on Poverty grew. In fact, these stereotypes gained credence in the highest halls of government. In 1965, Daniel Patrick Moynihan, then the assistant secretary of labor under President Johnson, released "The Negro Family: The Case of National Action," which vilified Black motherhood and claimed it was responsible for the "deterioration of the Negro family" and "a startling increase in welfare dependency."[115] For Moynihan, the problem wasn't just that Black single motherhood was associated with dependency due to social inequalities; it was that families led by Black mothers were a "disturbed group" representing a "tangle of pathology" who would suffer a "cycle of poverty and deprivation." Moynihan even linked the expansion of AFDC—which had begun as a fairly popular program to help keep (primarily white) children at home with their single mothers—to the "disintegration of the Negro family structure over the past generation in the United States." The apotheosis of this stigmatization came in 1976, when Ronald Reagan raised the specter of the "welfare queen"—a lazy Black woman who bilks the government of AFDC benefits she shouldn't receive—during his successful presidential campaign.

Racial bias in reports to CPS is followed by racial bias in which reports get investigated and substantiated and which children end up in foster care.[116] While only 12 percent of all American children will ever be the subject of a substantiated case of maltreatment following a CPS investigation, 20 percent of Black children—one in five—will.[117] When it comes to foster care, only 6 percent of all American children will ever experience it, while 10 percent of Black children will.[118] And once Black children are removed to foster care, they spend more time separated from their families and are less likely to reunify.[119]

In 1977, the foster care population hit what was then an all-time high of 503,000 children.[120] Between fiscal years 1971 and 1979, states and the federal government went from spending $70 million on AFDC foster care to almost $400 million.[121] The mushrooming of the system led the head of New York City's mayoral task force on child abuse and neglect to decry foster care as a "dumping ground for children" in a 1978 hearing. He called for more investment in keeping families together—yet another pendulum swing in opinion on how to best care for dependent children—citing that foster care was funded at a rate one hundred times higher than preventative services.[122] The funding disparity resulted from the fact that when Congress amended the Social Security Act in 1962 to create AFDC foster care as an uncapped matching grant, it left other child welfare services, including preventative services, as a capped block grant.[123] Clearly, unchecked government spending on foster care had fueled this mess.

Beyond the expense and the sense that children were being dumped in foster care, child welfare advocates knew, even in the 1970s, that mandated reporting and the foster care system had failed at keeping children safe and healthy. Policing and punishing poor parents—especially Black and Native parents—was at odds with protecting the welfare of children, but it was the policy that the federal government funded. Researchers bemoaned that children were "languishing" in foster care for years on end and that they suffered psychologically from a lack of "permanency," or a permanent plan for their futures, either via reunifying with their parents or being adopted.[124]

By the end of the 1970s, it was clear that children were also being mal-treated in foster care.[125] In New York City, a city council investigation of Special Services for Children—then the city's public agency overseeing foster care—found that children in foster care died at a rate three times the national average.[126] Thirty-three children in foster care died that year, including one who was murdered.[127] The city council's report also indicated that the private agencies the city subcontracted to deliver foster care took an average of one week to notify the city that a child in foster care had died and nine days to report maltreatment.[128] City CPS workers were then slow to investigate.[129] The majority of children in foster care in the city were removed from their birth parents due to poverty and parental drug use. As physician and histo-rian Mical Raz puts it in her book *Abusive Policies*, "Foster care placement involved taking children from suboptimal homes that could have benefited from further support and placing them in homes where there was a greater danger of physical abuse and death."[130]

In 1980, Congress responded to the foster care crisis by passing the Adop-tion Assistance and Child Welfare Act (AACWA), which was signed into law by President Jimmy Carter.[131] Its name alone makes clear that, in part, the law positioned adoption as the solution to the problems of foster care. AACWA made provisions for federal money to defray the costs of adopting children from foster care who received or were eligible for AFDC payments when they were removed from their parents, as well as children with "special needs"—a category that included not just "medical conditions or physical, mental, or emotional handicaps" but factors like "ethnic background, age, or membership in a minority or sibling group" that would make a child harder to place in adoption.

And, of course, in order to be adoptable in the first place, a child had to be a legal orphan—the parents' rights must have been terminated. This means that the child's parents either had to have voluntarily signed away their rights, or—as was becoming common for the first time in history—a CPS agency had to have initiated termination of parental rights (TPR) pro-ceedings before a family court judge.[132] In other words, in order to lessen the burden on the foster care system, Congress was promoting creation of more orphans, an ironic twist for a child welfare system that had begun in the nineteenth-century due in part to the plight of parentless children.

But AACWA was not solely focused on achieving permanency for children in foster care via TPR and adoption. It created new prevention and reunification requirements to further decrease the foster care population. AACWA replaced the AFDC foster care program with the Title IV-E Foster Care Program, which remains the mechanism for federal funding of foster care.[133] The switch to Title IV-E, named after the corresponding amended section of the Social Security Act, was meant to pair foster care with other child welfare services, including prevention services, which were funded under the same program. In order to receive Title IV-E funding for a child in foster care, the state would first be required to use "reasonable efforts" to prevent removing the child from the home in the first place. The state also needed to use "reasonable efforts" to reunify a child with their family.

The AACWA "reasonable efforts" provision was an attempt to pair prevention and rehabilitation services addressing individual parents' "pathologies"—rather than actual poverty-prevention services—with child welfare. It once again assumed that in order to keep children safe, the state needed to address parents' faults rather than the socioeconomic issues that more often than not underlay why they had come to the attention of CPS in the first place. "Reasonable efforts" remains the standard that states must meet, but states can and do define these efforts in vague, broad ways. Typically "reasonable efforts" constitute both making available services like individual and family therapy, parenting classes, and substance use treatment programs, which are the bread and butter of case plans for parents caught in the CPS web, and requiring caseworkers to make safety checks and home visits to surveil parents as they complete their case plans.[134] Parents might have to attend therapy or a substance use program in order to prevent CPS from removing their children to foster care or to reunify with their children after removal. But parents whose children are removed because of inadequate and unsafe housing need material help to afford a safe place for their family to live, not therapy and parenting classes. CPS cannot offer them that kind of help. Instead, in 2022, almost twenty thousand children entered foster care at least in part due to housing issues, and state and federal governments paid foster parents to take care of them.[135]

As was McMillan's experience, case plans are typically not tailored to a parent's actual needs, not least because they are doled out by caseworkers who tend to be overworked, burnt out, and undertrained. Up to 40 percent of caseworkers leave their jobs each year, representing a sky-high turnover rate.[136] Most states do not require CPS workers to be licensed social workers; in some states, like Texas, a CPS worker needs only a high school diploma, limited college credits, and relevant work experience.[137] This situation would have horrified the social workers who worked to professionalize their field and make casework a "science" in the early twentieth century.

Meanwhile, a case plan that constitutes "reasonable efforts" might itself be so onerous that it actually makes it harder for parents to reunify with their children. Imagine being a poor parent with an hourly minimum-wage job that determines your shifts on a weekly basis. Imagine that you've been forcibly separated from your children because you couldn't afford a babysitter or find anyone to watch your kids while you went to work. Imagine that you need to keep that job to prove your suitability to the CPS worker in charge of your case plan while somehow also attending parenting classes, therapy, family court dates, and supervised visits with your children. Such a case plan does nothing to address your fundamental problem, and yet it's what federal funding dictates. In the meantime, the subcontracted agencies that provide parenting classes and therapy make government money off your nightmare.

When Congress held the hearings that led to AACWA, they didn't reconsider two of the fundamental flaws that had led to the foster care crisis they were trying to solve—the flawed logic of individual faults leading to maltreatment and the blurring of neglect and abuse that underlie CAPTA. As Raz writes, "There was no political will to argue that not all undesirable behavior toward children was in fact abuse, or that not all situations of suboptimal parenting required reporting and investigation."[138] Politicians and the public were simply too attached—and remain too attached—to the idea that increased awareness and reporting of child abuse was an unqualified good that led to children being "saved" from their willfully abusive and neglectful parents. That CPS workers had little to offer such children besides traumatic investigations and removals from their families, and that these families were mostly suffering from societally induced poverty and racism, were not palatable facts.

Between 1977 and 1982, the foster care population fell by more than half, from 503,000 to 244,300.[139] AACWA—and more likely the tumult over the foster care crisis that led to it—fueled the decline.[140] But given the continuing conflation of poverty with neglect and neglect with abuse, the ever-rising numbers of reports to CPS alleging maltreatment, and the ineffectiveness of "reasonable efforts" at family preservation and reunification, it's not surprising that the foster care population ticked back upward over the course of the 1980s and 1990s. By 1990, 400,000 children were in foster care; by 1999, there were 567,000—a number that exceeded the panic-inducing population of twenty years earlier.[141]

A major contributor to the swelling of the foster care population—and to racial disproportionality within it—was the war on drugs in the 1980s and 1990s. A moral panic developed over Black women who used crack cocaine during their pregnancies, producing so-called crack babies. The panic had its roots in racist perceptions of Black drug users, who were more likely to use cheap crack cocaine, versus white drug users, who were more likely to use expensive powder cocaine. In 1986, Congress passed the Anti–Drug Abuse Act, which set massively disproportionate minimum sentencing requirements for distribution of crack cocaine and powder cocaine—distributing just five grams of crack dictated a five-year minimum sentence, whereas distributing five hundred grams of powder cocaine carried the same sentence.[142] This 100:1 disparity led to higher federal sentences for Black people, despite the fact that Black and white people used drugs at similar rates and that crack cocaine and powder cocaine had identical effects on users.[143]

Similarly, Black women, especially poor Black women, were more likely to be tested for drugs while pregnant and to be reported for prenatal substance abuse, even though there was no evidence that Black women had significantly higher rates of prenatal drug usage.[144] The overall result was that Black women were being punished for prenatal drug use with child removal via the family court system rather than being charged with criminal offenses. As Roberts writes, media portrayals of pregnant Black women who used crack contributed to the idea that they were "unfit" mothers who deserved to lose custody. "News stories reported that the chemical properties of crack destroyed 'maternal instinct,' making women who smoked the drug incapable of nurturing their children," Roberts writes. "A public health crisis that affected all communities became yet another example of Black mothers' depravity that justified harsh state intervention."[145]

Decades later, it would become clear that the "crack baby" moral panic was just that and that fetuses exposed to crack or powder cocaine in utero did not experience major long-term effects on their brain development.[146] We now know that fetal cocaine exposure is less damaging than alcohol exposure and about the same as tobacco exposure.[147] Nevertheless, media coverage of a supposed "crack baby epidemic" fueled punitive treatment of mothers who tested positive for the drug during pregnancy—testing that was more likely to occur at public hospitals and ensnare Black women.[148] Beginning in the 1980s, states passed laws that categorized prenatal drug use as child maltreatment, classifying the fetus as a child and spurring both criminal prosecutions and child removals at birth.[149] Congress doubled down on punishing prenatal drug use in 2003, when it passed an amendment to CAPTA that required health-care workers to notify CPS of babies who test positive for illegal drugs at birth.[150]

Meanwhile, the federal government continued to punish poor parents and walked back what few commitments it had made to preserve and reunify families, further growing foster care. AFDC, already unpopular in the 1970s as it was accessed by more Black mothers, grew only more stigmatized in the Reagan-dominated 1980s. In 1994, neoliberal conservative congressman Newt Gingrich proposed eliminating AFDC and reestablishing orphanages to care for the children of welfare recipients.[151] Gingrich's rosy ideas about orphanages had clearly been shaped by pop culture, not history—he even suggested that First Lady Hillary Clinton, who called his proposal "absurd," watch the 1938 Spencer Tracy and Mickey Rooney movie *Boys Town*, in which a priest starts a home for indigent boys reminiscent of the Children's Aid Society's Newsboys' Lodging House. Gingrich's proposal was outrageous and proved that the politicians making child welfare laws are swayed by the stories we tell ourselves about orphans.

President Bill Clinton blocked Gingrich's orphanage proposal, but in 1996 he signed the bipartisan Personal Responsibility and Work Opportunity Reconciliation Act into law, making good on his campaign promise to "end welfare as we know it."[152] Welfare reform equaled eliminating AFDC. The law's name alone makes clear how the country's attitude toward means-tested welfare for "deserving" poor mothers had soured in the sixty plus years since the New Deal. ADC had been envisioned as a program that would allow poor (white) single mothers to stay at home with their children, obviating the need for orphanages and reserving foster care for "pathological" cases. The idea was that these women would not need to work. By 1996, though, a public steeped in decades of personal-responsibility-centered bootstrapping rhetoric dictated that it was no longer possible for mothers both be "deserving" and unemployed. That the prototypical mother receiving AFDC benefits had by then morphed into a Black welfare queen in the public's mind was no accident. Nor did it really matter that the actual intended recipients of welfare aid were the children, who were always "deserving." "Public assistance to poor families and programs dealing with neglected children are two sides of the same coin," Roberts points out. "Yet Americans' compassion toward poor children has always existed in tension with the impulse to blame their parents. . . . Racism has consistently led to a resolution of this tension that refuses adequate social support for families and hurts Black families the most."[153]

As limited as AFDC was, the program that replaced it, Temporary Assistance for Needy Families (TANF), is wholly inadequate.[154] TANF cash-assistance benefits are time limited and, for at least half of recipients, predicated on parents participating in "work activities" for twenty to thirty hours a week. The federal government only allows parents to receive TANF for five years in an entire lifetime; some states have imposed even shorter eligibility windows. Even when families do meet all the hurdles to access TANF, the benefits still leave them living well below the federal poverty line. This is especially true for families headed by Black single mothers.

Even though welfare reform eliminated AFDC, it didn't eliminate the ties between AFDC and the funding of foster care. Title IV-E funding eligibility remains tied to whether a family would have been eligible for AFDC, not TANF, which is much more restricted.[155] The cost of foster care under Title IV-E has continued to balloon, even as the government has battened down the hatches on welfare. In 2022, the federal government spent more than $4.8 billion on Title IV-E foster care. That actually marks a decrease over the preceding four years, when Title IV-E foster care costs topped $5 billion.[156] In comparison, the government spent only $64 million on prevention services in 2022. The federal government has continued to monetarily incentivize splitting up poor children and their parents instead of spending money on services like housing, child care, and cash assistance that might actually keep families together and make children safer.

Children from "welfare" families have always been overrepresented in foster care. Economic researchers attribute 15 percent of the growth of the foster care population from 1985 to 2000 to reductions in both AFDC and TANF cash assistance, which states have continually restricted.[157] A 2022 study of the relationship among state-level TANF policies, CPS involvement, and foster care placement between 2004 and 2016 found that if states had eased TANF restrictions like work requirements and time limits, about twenty-nine thousand fewer children would have entered foster care during the study period.[158] Even though TANF benefits are laughably low, they still prevent foster care placement. Giving parents even a little bit more cash assistance might actually save the federal government money, given how much it spends on Title IV-E foster care.

———

At the same time as the federal government "ended welfare as we know it" and made poor families even poorer, it made reunification harder for parents whose children had been removed. In 1997, President Clinton signed the Adoption and Safe Families Act (ASFA) into law in an effort to yet again increase permanency for children in foster care by rendering them legal orphans. The law not only provided further financial incentives for the adoption of children whose parents' rights had been terminated but created a new ticking time bomb that parents were up against if they wanted to reunify with their children. The law, which remains on the books, requires that states initiate TPR proceedings against parents whose children have been in foster care for fifteen out of the past twenty-two months. This clock starts as soon as children are forcibly removed from their families.

The only exceptions are if the child is in "kinship care," being cared for by a relative under the supervision and at the discretion of the state; if the state agency has a "compelling reason" that TPR would "not be in the best interests of the child"; or if the state has failed to make "reasonable efforts" to provide parents the services they need to reunify in that period.[159] But the law also absolves states of making "reasonable efforts" at prevention and reunification in a slew of circumstances, including some that seem reasonable, such as in cases where the child has been subjected to torture, chronic abuse, and sexual abuse. But states can also move straight to TPR if a parent has previously involuntarily lost their rights to a sibling of the child in question—a situation that can punish parents who have previously been accused of neglect and have struggled to work their case plans in the past.[160]

The fifteen-month time crunch infuses already onerous case plans with new anxiety over the looming threat of TPR. This timeline is also an especially poor fit for parents with substance use disorders. Not only does addiction, which tends to be chronic and relapsing, often take longer than fifteen months to address, but our country lacks both sufficient treatment facilities and successful treatment methods to help parents stay consistently sober.[161] In fact, at the same time that Congress passed ASFA, it rejected proposals to expand drug-treatment services for CPS-involved families.[162] Considering the ASFA timeline and McMillan's experience of plunging into addiction after her daughters were removed, she is very lucky not to have had her case go to TPR.

Congress passed ASFA amid yet another moral panic over child welfare. This time politicians were convinced that the family-preservation methods barely supported by AACWA had failed and that children were suffering both from "foster care drift"—a concept first introduced in Henry S. Maas and Richard Engler's 1959 work *Children in Need of Parents*—and at the hands of their abusive parents. There was once again public outcry that children were languishing in foster care for years, drifting from placement to placement, but since AACWA had mandated "reasonable efforts" at reunification, the blame no longer fell on the system itself but on parents who couldn't get their acts together.

Meanwhile, the bill's bipartisan sponsors alluded to media coverage of horrific child abuse deaths attributed to family-preservation practices. Just as politicians make policy decisions about child welfare based on pop culture myths, à la Gingrich and *Boys Town*, they are also swayed by news media narratives. And just as it had with the battered-child syndrome, the media had made it seem as though parents and family caregivers who had been known to CPS were routinely murdering their children. "Every one of us in this body can turn to and refer to headlines in their papers . . . headlines telling us the very worst can happen," said Representative Barbara Kenneally, a Democrat from

Connecticut, during the hearings that led to ASFA.[163] Senator John Chafee, a Republican from Rhode Island who had coauthored the bill, alluded to the then recent beating death of a nine-year-old girl in New York as Clinton signed the bill: "We cannot bring Sabrina Green back to life, but we can take action to prevent such deaths in the future."[164] In January 1996, *Newsday*—the Long Island newspaper that my parents subscribed to—even ran an opinion article about a Brooklyn girl's death under the headline "Family Preservation—It Can Kill."[165] The article, which claimed that "extremist family-preservation pressure groups" attack adoptive families in ways that "chillingly mirror the hate speech of racists and anti-Semites," ran with an illustration of a family portrait featuring a little girl with a black eye and a bandage over one cheek. That such deaths were extremely rare was not discussed.

Congress bought into the idea that speeding up TPR and adoption was the best path to permanency for children in foster care. TPR also promotes the sense that parents must lose their legal relationships with their children—and often their literal relationships, since it eliminates parents' protected rights to ever see or communicate with their children again—in order for children to have their "best interests" met. ASFA's push for TPR renders a child's parents nonentities who must be discarded in order for the child to get a new, better family. In this way, pop culture representations of foster care do get one thing right.

But despite the logic of plenary adoption, which eliminates the relationship with a child's family of origin and wholly replaces it with a new family, down to amending the child's birth certificate to state they were born to their adoptive parents, there are other options for permanency, even for children who can't reunify with their parents in extreme cases. After my parents died, I was not only a literal orphan but a legal orphan. When executing my father's will and his plans for my brother and me, Nassau County's Surrogate's Court set up not an adoption but a legal guardianship. I did not have to have my birth certificate amended to pretend that I was born to my aunts. I did not have to have my parents erased.

When it comes to TPR, Black children and Native American children are the most likely to become legal orphans after being separated from their families

223

by the child welfare system—in fact, Native children are 2.7 times as likely to have their parents' rights terminated as white children, and Black children are 1.7 times as likely.[166] And while ASFA has met its goal of increasing adoptions from foster care, far from all of the children whose cases go to TPR become adopted. Since the passage of ASFA, only about half of the more than two million children whose parents' rights were terminated have been adopted.[167] There are currently more than a hundred thousand children in foster care awaiting adoption. In 2022, children in foster care whose parents' legal rights had been terminated and whose case goal was adoption had already been waiting an average of nineteen months for a new family.[168] Each year, about twenty thousand teens and young adults "age out" of foster care without ever achieving permanency via reunification or adoption.[169]

This is despite the massive financial incentives that ASFA created to spur adoptions, which go far beyond the assistance programs of AACWA that provide subsidies to individual families. (Those incentives have been costly for the federal government—in 2022, it shelled out more than $3.7 billion on Title IV-E adoption assistance.)[170] ASFA provides states with bonus payments for increasing their rates of adoption from foster care. For each child adopted above a baseline rate, states receive $4,000; "special needs" children net states $6,000 each.[171] Since 1998, the federal government has paid more than $942 million in adoption incentives to states.[172] While Supreme Court Justice Samuel Alito cited a need for a "domestic supply of infants" available for adoption in his opinion striking down *Roe v. Wade*, Americans who are looking to adopt a child are much less interested in opening their homes to older children and teens, children of color, children who are part of sibling groups looking to be adopted together, and children with disabilities—precisely the "waiting child" population.[173]

Even if a child in foster care whose parents' rights have been terminated does manage to be adopted into a new family, the results are not guaranteed to be the romanticized scenes of domesticity promoted on shows like *The Fosters* and *This Is Us*. Sixto Cancel, who is Black, experienced an adoption nightmare after being adopted from foster care at age nine.[174] Cancel first entered foster care in Bridgeport, Connecticut, as an eleven-month-old baby in the early 1990s. He was removed from the care of his single mother due to her drug addiction and poverty. When he was six, he briefly got to reunify with his mother—and his seven siblings—but he reentered foster care within a year. Cancel told me that while he does believe that "removal possibly needed to happen at one point" due to his mother's addiction, he also feels "there could have been more opportunities where she would have gotten the proper support to be able to actually keep us." Cancel remembers bouncing between about seven different foster homes during his time in care, and in all that time, he was only ever placed with one of his siblings for a few months. His siblings were mostly dispersed among different foster homes. One of his younger brothers lived in a restrictive and abusive group home for five years—the sort of institutional setting that Progressives railed against in the early twentieth century when they promoted mothers' pensions and foster care.[175] In 2022, 9 percent of children in the foster care system—about thirty-four thousand—lived in a group home or institution.[176]

When Cancel was nine, he was adopted by a white woman. "It was a very racist and abusive adoption," he told me. His adoptive mother regularly called him the N-word and "faggot."[177] He wasn't allowed to touch the refrigerator. When I asked him why he thought the woman who fostered and adopted him was able to do so and maintain custody despite the abuse she perpetrated, he told me, "Because the system believed her—she's a white female—versus me." Cancel was only able to get out of the adoption system—and back into the foster care—at age fifteen, after he taped a recorder to his chest to gather evidence of the abuse.[178] He needed to go to this extreme to get CPS investigators to believe that his white adoptive mother was abusing him. They hadn't even listened to Cancel's school and other trusted adults who had made calls alleging maltreatment. Cancel had been couch surfing on and off for two years at that point, because his adoptive mother would lock him out of the house. Once back in the system, he went into yet another foster home. He'd eventually age out.

Cancel's experience is harrowing and evidence that the state-sponsored foster care system does not do enough to vet and monitor the caretakers it entrusts vulnerable children with, even as it removes those children from homes it deems "unsafe." Children continue to be abused in foster care—rates of physical and sexual abuse are two to four times higher in foster care and group homes than in the general population.[179] When it comes to adoption from foster care, we have no data about maltreatment—or even how many adoptions are dissolved, like Cancel's was—because the government does not closely monitor or study this population. The assumption is that every adoption is a happy one.

In March 2018, this illusion was shattered for the American public by an especially gruesome and heartbreaking case. A white lesbian couple drove their SUV off a cliff in California, killing themselves and their six adopted Black children. Jennifer and Sarah Hart had adopted these children from foster care, welcoming them into what had seemed like a happy, loving family. In reality, as journalist Roxanna Asgarian reveals in her groundbreaking 2023 book *We Were Once a Family*, the pair abused and neglected the children for years, evading CPS in several states.

The media focused mostly on the couple's motives and backgrounds, overlooking what Asgarian calls "major questions about the child welfare system's role in the deaths."[180] *We Were Once a Family* fills in this crucial gap by tracing how two Texas sibling groups—first Markis, Hannah, and Abigail, then Devonte, Jeremiah, and Ciera—came to be removed from their families and adopted by the Harts. While the abuse and eventual murders of these children might seem an aberration of the child welfare system, this was in fact a case in which the system worked exactly as designed. As Asgarian reconstructs how the children came to be adopted by the Harts, she methodically lays out how it was no accident that while the birth families were subjected to intense scrutiny by caseworkers and judges, the Harts received "glowing reports" and had their adoption of Devonte, Jeremiah, and Ciera fast-tracked—even though the children's aunt was simultaneously trying to adopt them and even though the Harts had already been accused of abusing Hannah.[181] Asgarian notes that "many people, both inside and outside the child welfare system, held a common assumption: that these six Black children must be better off with the white women who adopted them, that whatever issues they were having as a family must have been an improvement for the children over the poor conditions of their early childhood homes."[182] That presumption proved fatally wrong.

I once believed that the state would only intervene in the lives of families if children were being physically or sexually abused or willfully neglected—and that, contrary to cases like those of the Harts, CPS would actually identify and save all children suffering from grievous maltreatment. These are the kinds of stories that have always made the news—in this way, the moral panic of the battered-child syndrome era lives on.

When I was a junior in high school, I saw Nixzmary Brown on the news for weeks. Nixzmary was a seven-year-old Puerto Rican and Pakistani American girl from Bedford-Stuyvesant, Brooklyn, with wavy brown hair parted down the center and almond-shaped brown eyes.[183] Her stepfather, who had recently lost his job as a security guard, beat her to death over utterly normal childhood behaviors: taking a snack from the fridge without permission, jamming his printer with toys.[184] She was emaciated when she died, and her body bore signs of prolonged physical abuse. If only New York's Administration for Children's Services had intervened more meaningfully—caseworkers had looked into the family but made huge missteps in responding to allegations of abuse and neglect—Nixzmary might still be alive, I thought back then.

I didn't know that ACS itself had been developed about a decade earlier after the killing of another little girl, Elisa Izquierdo. In pictures, Elisa, who was Puerto Rican and Cuban American, wears her curly brown hair in pigtails or pulled back into a ponytail with a big scrunchie.[185] She has an upturned button nose and pierced ears. Elisa and I were both born in 1989; she was six when her mother, who was addicted to crack cocaine and a victim of domestic abuse, fatally beat her in their apartment on Manhattan's Lower East Side.[186] Like Nixzmary, Elisa had been abused repeatedly. Her family's problems were long known to authorities across a wide range of city agencies, including the Child Welfare Administration.[187] After Elisa's killing, Mayor Rudy Giuliani ordered the creation of ACS, calling it the city's first public agency entirely devoted to child welfare.[188] The new ACS was meant to focus primarily on protecting children rather than keeping families together. Protecting children meant punishing individual parents for their failures. But ACS failed Nixzmary a decade later, and the parallels between the two cases are horrific: both Elisa and Nixzmary were victims of long-term physical abuse that evaded CPS intervention; both died of brain hemorrhages. Both girls have New York State laws meant to curb and harshly punish child abuse named after them.[189]

America's interwoven foster care and child-protective systems are meant to prevent and punish child abuse, but each year a small number of children like Elisa and Nixzmary still die as a result of abuse and neglect. The federal government estimates that approximately 1,990 children died as a result of maltreatment in 2022.[190] Physical abuse was cited in only 677 of these deaths.[191] Parents were the perpetrators of 1,280, or 81.8 percent, of 2022's child maltreatment fatalities. A small number of children died of abuse or neglect in foster care too; foster parents were responsible for six deaths.[192]

Of course, even one child's death because of parental abuse is a tragedy. But the very fact that children continue to die of abuse in the United States proves that our child welfare system has failed. Our country has long been in a cycle of tragedy, scandal, and panic when it comes to CPS: a child dies of abuse, we lay the blame on the cracks in the child welfare system that the family fell through, and there is a public outcry for more CPS surveillance, more reporting of child maltreatment, and harsher punishments for the perpetrators. In fact, Elisa's death was the subject of that 1996 *Newsday* op-ed about the harms of family preservation.

So far, panicked measures to fill the cracks of CPS have not been enough to keep children safe. If such reforms worked, Nixzmary would have been removed from her mother and stepfather and placed in foster care. If reforms worked, ACS would have intervened and saved four-year-old Jayce Eubanks, seven-year-old Julissia Batties, and four-year-old Aisyn Emerson-Gonzalez, all New York City children who were fatally beaten in their homes in 2021.[193]

In the meantime, CPS continues to subject millions of families a year to surveillance, despite the fact that more than 80 percent of children subject to CPS investigations are not found to have been maltreated. In other words, as sociologist Kelley Fong writes, "the state is investigating a large and growing share of parents who—according to the investigating agency itself—do not pose a clear and present danger to their children."[194] That's because despite politicians' rhetoric, our child welfare system does not function primarily to keep children safe. Its purpose is punishing and socially controlling poor parents. Many activists and scholars argue that it's most accurate to refer to it as a "family-policing system."[195] I agree with them now.

Chapter Twelve

No Separation Between Church and State

In March 2018, the *Philadelphia Inquirer* broke a foster care discrimination story that the Department of Human Services (DHS), which oversees the city's family-policing system, had been clueless about.[1] Two private, religious foster care agencies that the city had contracted with for more than twenty years were refusing to work with same-sex couples who wanted to become foster parents. The agencies, Catholic Social Services (CSS) and the Protestant evangelical Bethany Christian Services, had yearly contracts with the city that together totaled $3 million in taxpayer money.

In discriminating against LGBTQ+ people, both agencies were in violation of Philadelphia's Fair Practices Ordinance, which is included in all city contracts and prohibits discrimination against protected classes (including on the basis of sexual orientation) in the areas of employment, public accommodations (including the deployment of city services, like foster care), and housing.[2] The agencies also violated their foster care contract with the city, which includes a clause that states, in part, "Provider shall not reject a child or family including, but not limited to . . . prospective foster or adoptive parents, for Services based upon . . . their . . . sexual orientation."[3]

Within three years, the fight between Philadelphia's right to assert its own regulations over its taxpayer-funded foster care program and religious charities' right to exercise their beliefs by discriminating against LGBTQ+ people would result in a Supreme Court decision. It would be just the latest case in the tug-of-war between religious charities, which see their role in foster care as historically sanctioned and biblically supported, and the governmental entities that now fund and oversee child welfare—one that would yet again test whether church and state are truly separate in America.

Philadelphia has a byzantine privatized foster care system.[4] It is this privatization that got the city into a battle with Bethany and CSS in the first place. In other locales, you can become certified as a foster parent through a city or county agency that oversees child welfare. Meanwhile, Philadelphia's DHS completely contracts out the recruitment, screening, training, and licensing of foster parents to private foster care agencies, like Bethany and CSS. These agencies, in turn, are overseen by private community umbrella agencies (CUAs), which provide daily case management for foster families and children in foster care. Two of the four current CUAs are either outwardly Christian or have a Christian history.[5] Bethanna, the CUA for the region of Philadelphia where I live, stylizes its *t* as a crucifix. The city's DHS, meanwhile, is in charge of conducting child maltreatment investigations—and thus removing children from their families.

Philadelphia's foster care privatization effort, euphemistically called Improving Outcomes for Children (IOC), is the result of DHS's own gross failings and a familiar cycle of scandal, panic, and reform. The city implemented IOC in 2012, in large part in response to the case of a Black teenager named Danieal Kelly, who starved to death in her own home despite DHS supervision.[6] Fourteen-year-old Danieal had cerebral palsy and was bedridden; when she died during a heatwave in August 2006, she was covered in gaping bedsores and weighed only forty-two pounds. She was one of nine siblings. Sixteen people—including Danieal's parents, DHS case workers and social workers, and staff from the private contractor hired to assist Danieal's parents—were convicted of charges stemming from Danieal's death. In 2007, Pennsylvania downgraded Philadelphia's DHS to a provisional license—essentially putting the agency on probation—in part because

DHS was deficient in investigating maltreatment reports, like those filed in Danieal's case.[7]

When first implemented in 2012 after recommendations by experts who reviewed Danieal's case, IOC was meant to be a top-to-bottom reform of Philadelphia's child welfare system that would disentangle who exactly is accountable for the children in its care, emphasize neighborhood-based care and oversight, speed up reunifications, and reduce the use of institutional group homes.[8] But in 2016, the state yet again gave Philadelphia's DHS a provisional license, this time citing falsified visit reports, disorganized case documentation, and a regular practice of having new foster children sleep in agency offices because caseworkers couldn't find them placements fast enough. The secretary of Pennsylvania's DHS blamed these failings on a "troubled transition" to the new IOC system, which evidently had not yet improved outcomes for children.[9]

Given this level of dysfunction, it is not surprising that in 2018 DHS was unaware that Bethany and CSS were boldly flouting the city's antidiscrimination law. *Philadelphia Inquirer* journalist Julia Terruso unveiled the agencies' misconduct after hearing from Megan Paszko, who had tried to become a foster parent in the city.[10] Paszko and her wife were determined to navigate Philadelphia's labyrinth of acronyms in order to care for foster children in need. After sending out applications to different agencies, the couple waited months before finally hearing back from Bethany, which invited them to an orientation. But when they walked into the meeting, Paszko said, "The trainer approached us, and she was really nice, but she told us, 'I just want to be upfront. This organization has never placed a child with a same-sex couple.'"[11]

Paszko reached out to the *Inquirer* in March 2018 because Terruso had just written a story about the city's desperate need for more foster parents—DHS was calling on about three hundred more families to take up the task of caring for children that the department had removed from their biological families.[12] DHS had been spreading the word through phone banks and public service announcements, noting that new foster parents would be resources for some 250 children who were being held in group homes because there weren't enough foster care beds.

Paszko and her wife felt that they were such a family, but Bethany decided that their status as a same-sex couple made them ineligible—this, despite the fact that a foster parent recruiter for Bethany had told Terruso, "We'll get 200 requests a month from DHS and we'll be able to place maybe 10 of them." A spokesperson for Bethany later confirmed that they declined to work with LGBTQ+ couples because evangelical Christianity teaches that same-sex relationships are sinful.

Bethany, founded in Michigan in 1944, casts its mission as closing "the gap between the way God sees people and the way the world sees people."[13] The idea of "the gap" itself comes from scripture, which evangelical Protestants believe is literally true and treat as instruction for their lives here on earth, the good news that they must spread. In the Old Testament book of Ezekiel, the prophet speaks for God, noting the sins of the nation of Israel, stating, "I looked for someone among them who would build up the wall and stand before me in the gap on behalf of the land so I would not have to destroy it, but I found no one."[14] On its website, Bethany notes that the organization's "guiding star" is "to demonstrate the love and compassion of Jesus Christ by protecting and enhancing the lives of children and families through quality social services." In explaining why LGBTQ+ couples could not help Bethany further this mission, a spokesperson told Terruso, "This has been our practice throughout our nearly 75 years of operation and is based on our adherence to what we believe to be foundational Biblical principles."

While Bethany was the only agency that turned Paszko and her wife down, Terruso's reporting revealed that CSS was operating with the same discriminatory practices. The charity arm of the Archdiocese of Philadelphia, CSS ambitiously traces its history in the city back to the yellow fever epidemic of 1797, when Catholic laypeople cared for children orphaned by the disease and opened the city's first orphanages.[15] The organization believes it is drawing on centuries of Catholic experience of taking responsibility for poor children and orphans—the same oversight that blossomed in the 1800s as a means of protecting the Catholic faith. In reality, CSS has only existed as a distinct organization in Philadelphia since 1917, when it formed under the name Catholic Children's Bureau (it became Catholic Social Services in 1964).[16] As is the case with other branches of Catholic Charities USA, which operates nationwide, CSS's purview has always included care for orphaned and neglected children.[17] Its mission is "to serve the most vulnerable and at-risk members of our society"; its website claims, "We change lives with faith-filled compassion." Again, that compassion does not extend to LGBTQ+ couples. A spokesman for the archdiocese told Terruso that "Catholic Social Services is, at its core, an institution founded on faith-based principles. The Catholic Church does not endorse same-sex unions, based upon deeply held religious beliefs and principles."

When DHS finally got wind of the fact that Bethany and CSS were refusing to certify LGBTQ+ couples as foster parents, it froze the agencies' foster care contracts and launched a Human Relations Commission investigation within days.[18] Bethany soon changed its policy on same-sex couples in Philadelphia in order to comply with the city's Fair Practices Ordinance and resume its contract.[19] Later that year, Bethany also granted permission for branches nationwide to work with LGBTQ+ families if state and local contracts called for it; by 2020, the organization was working with same-sex couples in twelve states, though it did not advertise these new inclusive practices. Still, this marked a quiet sea change for Bethany, which is one of the largest adoption and foster care agencies in the country and the largest Protestant one, with eighty locations across twenty-seven states. In 2019, it facilitated 3,406 foster placements and 1,123 adoptions. In March 2021, Bethany formally extended the policy change nationwide, announcing that it would work with LGBTQ+ couples everywhere it operates. In relaying the new policy to Bethany staff, president and chief executive Chris Palusky wrote, "We will now offer services with the love and compassion of Jesus to the many types of families who exist in our world today."[20]

Meanwhile, CSS dug in its heels, suing Philadelphia in May 2018.[21] The suit, filed on behalf of CSS and three Catholic foster parents who worked with the organization, alleged that the city was discriminating against CSS because of its religious beliefs. A lawyer for CSS told the *Inquirer*, "The city is refusing to place children with parents just because those parents choose to work with Catholic Social Services." That CSS was in this position because it refused to work with members of the LGBTQ+ community to place foster children in their homes was apparently beside the point. CSS further claimed that no LGBTQ+ couple had ever asked to become certified through its agency.[22] And it's not like CSS was discriminating against LGBTQ+ youth—it accepted placements of such children from the city. So did Bethany at the time that it was refusing to work with LGBTQ+ foster parents.

That religious agencies were openly condemning same-sex couples but over-seeing the care of LGBTQ+ youth raised alarm bells for advocacy groups around the country. Attorney Currey Cook, head of Lambda Legal's Youth in Out-of-Home Care Project, told the *Inquirer*, "LGBT youth who have faced so much isolation, stigma, prejudice in the system are left wonder-ing, 'What's going to happen if I come out, and I'm being served by par-ents or an agency that basically says trans parents, LGBT people, aren't good parents?'"[23]

The fact that LGBTQ+ youth are overrepresented in the foster care sys-tem makes this mismatch all the more concerning. A 2019 study in the med-ical journal *Pediatrics* found that 30.4 percent of foster youth ages ten to eighteen in California self-reported an LGBTQ+ identity, compared to only 11.2 percent of youth in a nationally representative sample. Similar statis-tics hold across the country.[24] In a 2021 study of foster youth in Cuyahoga County, Ohio, 32 percent of participating youth between the ages of twelve and twenty-one self-identified as LGBTQ+.[25] A 2020 New York City survey found the highest proportion of LGBTQ+ foster youth—34.1 percent, or more than one in three—among foster youth aged thirteen to twenty.[26] As is the case with foster youth at large, the New York study found that LGBTQ+ foster youth are less likely to be white, meaning that these marginalized youth are disproportionally represented intersectionally, by both their race and their sexuality and/or gender.

One reason LGBTQ+ youth are overrepresented in foster care is rejection by their biological families, who might force them to move out or maltreat them because of their sexual orientations, their gender identities, or both. The 2020 New York City study found that 23.3 percent of LGBTQ+ foster youth reported having at some point been homeless after being kicked out of their homes or running away. Once they enter foster care, they are at risk for the same rejection, harassment, and abuse that they may have experienced at home. In New York City, LGBTQ+ youth were more likely to be placed in group homes or residential treatment centers—intensive, restrictive insti-tutions meant for children with behavioral, psychological, or substance use problems. The same was true in the 2021 Cuyahoga County study. Children are often placed in residential treatment centers under flimsy rationales—a study by the federal Department of Health and Human Services found that more than 40 percent of children in institutions didn't have a clinical reason to be there—and the centers, which are staffed by poorly paid and poorly trained workers, are rife with abuse.[27]

Perversely, in Texas, parents' *acceptance* of their children's gender identities can make them vulnerable to removal by child protective services (CPS). In February 2022, amid a moral panic about transgender youth, Governor Greg Abbott directed the state's Department of Family Protective Services (DFPS) to investigate parents who provide gender-affirming care to their trans children.[28] Governor Abbott's order was based on Attorney General Ken Paxton's nonbinding legal opinion that "a number of so-called 'sex change' procedures constitute child abuse under existing Texas law."[29] Lambda Legal and the American Civil Liberties Union (ACLU) filed lawsuits challenging the ordered DFPS investigations on behalf of affected families, which are ongoing but have resulted in a temporary injunction blocking the state from investigating families who are members of PFLAG, an advocacy group.[30] Texas's attempt to use CPS surveillance against gender-affirming families may represent a particularly brazen form of social control, but it demonstrates how definitions of child maltreatment have always been malleable and politically constructed.

The harassment of LGBTQ+ youth in the foster care system is unfortunately nothing new. Matt Hartman was once a gay foster youth who needed someone he could talk to freely about his problems at home.[31] Instead, in the mid-2000s, when he was about fourteen, he was met with religious homophobia—not from a foster parent or from a private religious foster care agency but from his court-ordered therapist, who brought her Christian religion into her practice. This was a therapist that Los Angeles County's Department of Children and Family Services (DCFS)—one of the largest CPS agencies in the United States—paid for.[32] At the time, the DCFS budget was about $1.6 billion, with funding from federal, state, and local sources.[33]

By the time Matt met his homophobic therapist, he had already spent his entire conscious life in foster care. When Matt, an only child, was first taken away from his parents in the Antelope Valley of Los Angeles County, he was only about a year old. Matt was removed because his mother has schizophrenia and both of his parents had drug and alcohol use disorders. Even as a baby, he lived with two different foster families in the span of a few months. He stayed in his second placement for almost a year. "My [second] foster mother was a school bus driver named Mrs. Green, and that was what I had to call her—Mrs. Green, at like two years old," Matt said.[34]

Soon, Matt's maternal grandfather, whom I'll call Jake, became certified as a kinship foster carer and took him in. Kinship care requirements vary by state, but in general child welfare agencies require family members to meet the same licensing requirements as strangers—including passing criminal and child abuse background checks and meeting income and housing requirements—in order to receive stipend payments to support the care of the child.[35] Jake was then in his early sixties and had retired years before, after closing his jewelry business in Santa Monica; he lived alone near LAX.

After Matt had been at his grandfather's for about six months, his father regained custody. The arrangement would be short-lived, due to his father's continued issues with alcohol and drugs, and Matt was sent to live with his grandfather again. Besides a few months-long stints with other relatives, including two aunts who "just decided they couldn't take care of me," Matt would stay at his grandfather's house until he moved into the dorms at the University of California, Los Angeles (UCLA), at seventeen.

This may sound like an informal arrangement—lots of children are raised by their grandparents, after all. I was myself for a short period. But in Matt's case, because DCFS removed him from his parents when he was a baby and the state took legal custody of him, he was in state-supervised foster kinship care for his entire childhood. Caseworkers made regular supervisory visits to Jake's home, and every six months Matt and Jake reported to family court.

Matt was court-ordered to go to therapy, and DCFS sent him to an organization it contracted with, Pacific Asian Counseling Services. Though located in the neighborhood he lived in, the counseling center wasn't a great match for Matt to begin with. Matt is white—not the target demographic of the agency, which advertises itself as tailored to "immigrant Asian Pacific Islander populations."[36] Making matters worse, Matt told me, "a lot of [the therapists] had no experience with children's welfare cases at all, or expertise in it, or necessarily interest in it."[37]

That all was bearable, but when Matt was in ninth grade, his longtime therapist at Pacific Asian Counseling Services moved out of the country. DCFS assigned him a new therapist at the counseling center, who quickly informed him that she practiced Christ-centered therapy. This meant, essentially, that she spent their sessions talking about "how you have to have a belief in Christ, and how her belief in Christ was at [the center of] everything she does, and Christ heals everything," Matt told me. Government funding paid for this woman to evangelize to Matt, who was not raised in any religion but was ethnically and culturally Jewish. That a child welfare agency in one of the least religious regions of the United States was contracting with an organization that employs Christ-centered therapists to work with foster youth speaks to the overwhelming pervasiveness of religion in the system.

"It was nothing like outright horrible, other than the fact that, you know, she told me that being gay isn't OK," Matt said with a laugh. "I only saw her a few times before I refused to go." In a sense, Matt was lucky that he was able to evade further sessions with this Christian therapist and that she didn't try conversion therapy on him, as is disturbingly the case for some LGBTQ+ foster youth, according to Children's Rights, an advocacy nonprofit that branched off from the ACLU.[38]

Matt could have used the outlet of therapy to process the instability of living with his grandfather. Matt told me that Jake "was constantly threatening to call DCFS to send [him] to a foster home" for little things, like not keeping his room as clean as Jake preferred. "My grandfather had a lot of issues with anger . . . and was taking a lot of it out on me," Matt told me. "And not just emotional [abuse], but sometimes physical too. And I just did not have any type of feeling that I was safe to voice anything that was happening. I remember that the few times that I did, it would always be pointed back to me."

When Matt was in tenth grade, the situation at his grandfather's house devolved further, and he experienced a second strike of homophobia in the foster care system. Multiple times a week, Matt said, Jake was "threatening to send me to foster homes, throwing shoes at me, hitting me." After Matt's high school called DCFS to report Jake, a social worker came out to investigate.

She told him that she could remove him from Jake's house but added, "There is a fifty-fifty chance that you might end up somewhere worse than here, so if you want to take the risk, you can," Matt said. The social worker—a county employee—also told Matt that he should stay in the closet for a few years. Matt wouldn't come out to his grandfather until he was an adult and living on his own.

A few months later, Matt was tired of feeling like he had no control over his life because he was a foster youth. He learned that he could take California's high school equivalency exam and did so at age fifteen in a bid to exercise agency and achieve a modicum of independence from the system. Upon passing, he immediately enrolled in Santa Monica Community College. "I knew that if I didn't [go to college] I would be stuck in a similar situation to my parents or my family, and I never wanted that," Matt said. "My whole childhood, I felt like I was waiting for the time that I would be able to do things on my own accord and not be stuck in all of these outside pressures that were constantly making things even more difficult for me." After two years, Matt transferred to UCLA and completed his degree in history early, right after his nineteenth birthday. He wrote his senior thesis on the history of stigma in the American foster care system.

Being a college graduate makes Matt exceptional among former foster youth. Only about half graduate high school, and college numbers are worse: only about 4 percent obtain a four-year degree.[39] For the approximately twenty thousand foster youth who "age out" of the system each year, like Matt did, as many as one in five instantly experience homelessness; as many as half experience homelessness within eighteen months.[40] Researchers estimate that these statistics are even worse for LGBTQ+ former foster youth.[41]

Matt's experience emphasizes that casual homophobia pervades the child welfare system at all levels, from the contractors the federal government funds, but does not subject to sufficient oversight, to the CPS caseworkers who are responsible for the safety and well-being of youth in the system. The lack of acceptance that he dealt with in the system made him feel even less secure in a childhood that was marked by feeling that he was at the mercy of people who did not have his best interests at heart.

Emi Nietfeld, who is bisexual, experienced extreme insecurity due to a gross failure of the foster care system. She became homeless as a teenager in the mid-2000s after she had already been expelled from her evangelical foster parents' home, in part due to homophobia.

Emi's troubles began in in 2002, when she was in the fifth grade and her biological parents divorced after her father came out as trans. Her mother won full custody, hiding evidence of her hoarding in the upstairs apartment of her Minneapolis duplex during the home visit. As Emi writes in her 2022 memoir *Acceptance*, the duplex soon became uninhabitable, "full of trash and rustling with mice," with no hot water in the winter.[42] Emi's other parent disappeared from her life.

Authorities always appeared to side with her mother. "She was white and well spoken, with a house, a college degree, and full custody of me," Emi writes.[43] At medical appointments, her pediatrician "seemed unfazed" by a series of illnesses and injuries caused by the condition of the duplex but listened to her mother, who lobbied for Emi to be diagnosed with and over-medicated for conditions she didn't actually have.[44] This provided an early lesson in how the system overlooks abuse and neglect in white families while overemphasizing the maltreatment risks of Black families.

In her early teens, Emi turned to self-harm to cope, and after a suicide attempt, a psychiatrist finally reported her case to the county. But, she writes, "there was no maltreatment investigation; instead, I was assigned to a special social worker who handled troubled teenage girls sick enough to be their own problems."[45] This would be the start of years in which Emi—and not her mother—was blamed as the source of her struggles, a theme that she smartly hammers home in *Acceptance* in order to illustrate the ways in which the American fetish with personal responsibility poisons us. When Emi was hospitalized for an eating disorder, her new psychiatrist told her she could choose to be sick or well, as though it were possible to recover through will alone.

When it came time for Emi to be discharged from the hospital, her case-worker initially recommended that she be voluntarily placed in a therapeutic foster home—a home where foster parents have undergone specialized training to care for children with significant behavioral, mental, or physical needs and where foster parents are paid higher stipends.[46] Emi's health-care team and caseworker understood that her mother's mental illness was causing

Emi's distress, but they still deferred to her parental rights and did not forcibly remove Emi due to a maltreatment allegation. But Emi didn't go to a foster home then—her mother voluntarily signed her into a residential treatment center, under the suggestion of her caseworker. She later found out this was because the caseworker couldn't find a foster home that had an open bed and was qualified to take her in.[47]

In 2022, 8 percent of children who entered foster care were placed there because of their own behavioral problems.[48] It's not clear how many of these children ultimately ended up in residential treatment centers, but social worker Ilena Robbins told me that when she was a caseworker at a New York residential treatment center run by Children's Village in the early 2010s, about 70 percent of her caseload had been voluntarily placed there.[49] The population was also almost entirely Black and brown. "Kids get caught up in the child welfare system because other systems aren't properly funded," Robbins said. "If their parents had access to respite, or a better educational placement, or if they could have afforded child-care support or better housing, I think a lot of those kids could have stayed home."

In Emi's case, the system was unwilling to intervene to address her mother's mental illness, which made her home uninhabitable. The system did not attempt to place her with a family member, even though she later found out that her older half brother would have been happy to take her in. "All of the elements were there to make the connections with family," Emi told me. "My brother lives across the street from my old high school." Still, the caseworker never approached him about undergoing the training to provide kinship foster care for Emi. Instead, she spent months in a locked unit of a residential treatment center where staff demanded that the teens accept fault for their circumstances to cure their suffering.

"I've wondered throughout the years if the reason I was discharged when I was didn't have to do with progress, but because they found a home," Emi told me. The home her caseworker found was with an evangelical Christian couple whom she calls the Parkers, in a distant suburb of Minneapolis. While she had set up her weekly visits with her mother on Sunday mornings specifically to avoid having to attend church with them, her mom would often arrive so late that she was forced to attend service with the Parkers. She told me she believes they got involved in fostering because of their Christian beliefs. "It was a lot of, 'We were called to do this,' and then when I met up with them later, they told me 'God brought you into our lives for such and such a reason,'" she said.

While Emi had grown up religious and while church life was everywhere in Minnesota, she and the Parkers were bound to clash culturally. First of all, Emi was fixated on getting into an Ivy League university as a form of escape from her circumstances, and the Parkers didn't understand her drive. But their blinkered, prudish, homophobic worldview led to the most tension. They accused Emi of "printing out pornography" when she was making flashcards of works like Michelangelo's *David* to study for her art history class.[50] A final blowup came about nine months into Emi's stay, toward the end of her sophomore year of high school, when she asked her foster father to pick her up from school after a meeting of the Gay-Straight Alliance and revealed her sexuality. The Parkers told Emi she had to leave their home after her last Advanced Placement exam, even though she still had two weeks left at school after that.

Emi had kept her sexuality under wraps for all that time on purpose. "It was a burden that I was feeling that I didn't necessarily know how to articulate at the time," she told me. The Parkers had always wanted Emi to open up to them. "In these conversations that we ended up having with my therapist or my social worker, it was always like, 'What's wrong with you that you don't want to open up?' And then it's like, okay, well, when I do tell you something relatively basic about my identity, it causes a huge problem. And then shortly after, I have to leave your house."

Luckily, Emi had lined up an escape plan—she was going to photography camp at the prestigious Interlochen Center for the Arts. She parlayed her camp experience into a merit scholarship for boarding school at Interlochen that fall. But when winter and summer breaks rolled around, Emi was left with an impossible situation—return to her mother's uninhabitable house or be functionally homeless, cobbling together a string of camps and couch-surfing stints. Emi chose the latter the summer she was sixteen and working on college applications, but when plans to stay with friends fell apart, she had to live out of her car and stay at a homeless shelter. Foster care was not an option anymore because the system had allowed her mother to sign her out voluntarily. Even if it had been an option, her caseworker would have had just as much difficulty finding her a place to stay as the first time around. The same family-policing system that is all too eager to intervene in the lives of poor Black and Native families allowed this white, bisexual teen-age girl to slip through its cracks.

Emi eventually graduated from Harvard College, but as she writes in *Acceptance*, "All the other lives that could have been mine—lost to incarcera-tion, addiction, lethal violence—were supposed to make my success shine in bright relief. Yet these alternative fates weighed on me. . . . It did not console me that I had worked hard: in hindsight, my adolescence felt like buying every lottery ticket I could afford."[51] In a way, coming out to the Parkers was like buying a lottery ticket, one that was bound to end up in a disrupted placement. "I think I would feel very differently about it if I had then been sent to another residential treatment center, or I had to change schools," Emi told me. "I would have been absolutely devastated—that could have had a big trajectory on my future."

The homophobia that Matt and Emi experienced in the foster care system represents a microcosm of a bigger battle over religious beliefs and LGBTQ+ rights in the foster care world. That battle formed the backdrop of *Fulton v. City of Philadelphia.*

In July 2018, US District Court for the Eastern District of Pennsylvania judge Petrese B. Tucker—a Bill Clinton–era appointee—denied CSS's dis-crimination claim against Philadelphia. In her decision, she wrote, "In the context of foster care and adoption, DHS and Philadelphia have a legitimate interest in ensuring that the pool of foster parents and resource caregivers is as diverse and broad as the children in need of foster parents and resource caregivers." In other words, LGBTQ+ youth—who experience so much hardship in the foster care system—deserve the possibility of being placed with LGBTQ+ couples. Judge Tucker also cited the "factual precedent" that other local branches of Catholic Charities USA had shut down their agencies because they didn't want to work with LGBTQ+ families.[52]

CSS immediately appealed, taking the case to the Court of Appeals for the Third Circuit. In April 2019, it lost that federal appeal when a three-judge panel affirmed the lower court's ruling. In June 2019, Sharonell Fulton, one of the Catholic foster parents who worked with CSS, played the last card the CSS had in its hand. She was the lead complainant in a petition filed with the Supreme Court, along with fellow Catholic foster parent Toni Lynn Simms-Busch and CSS itself, asking for a judicial review of the Third Circuit's ruling.[53] That former CSS foster parents filed suit speaks to how religious hegemony over the system has trickled down to individual foster parents, who believe that they deserve the right to practice their religion while taking physical custody of children in the government's care. In February 2020, the Supreme Court granted the petition, agreeing to hear the case.[54]

The *Fulton* case was expected to set a precedent as to whether nondiscrimination laws are constitutional—whether they violate the First Amendment right to free exercise of religion. During oral arguments before the court in November 2020, Lori Windham, a lawyer from the Becket Fund for Religious Liberty who was representing CSS and its copetitioners, essentially posited that providing foster care—a government-funded and -supervised service—was a tenet of Catholicism. "The City has no compelling reason for excluding Catholic Social Services, which has exercised its faith by serving at-risk children in Philadelphia for two centuries," Windham said, repeating the stretched truth that the agency itself had been operating since the late eighteenth century. She said that Philadelphia lacked standing because "the City is trying to regulate an area that has historically been an area of religious practice." Later, she elaborated on this argument that foster care is a religious practice, again repeating the dubious two-hundred-year claim not once but twice: "Here, the City is reaching out and telling a private religious ministry which has been doing this work for two centuries how to run its internal affairs and trying to coerce it to make statements that are contrary to its religious beliefs as a condition of continuing to participate in the religious exercise that they have carried out in Philadelphia for two centuries."[55] Such coercion was against the constitutional right to practice religion freely, Windham said, arguing that "the Free Exercise Clause is at the heart of our pluralistic society, and it protects the Petitioners' vital work for the Philadelphia community."

In this sense, the *Fulton* case was just the latest iteration in a long reckoning with the original sin of our country's child welfare system: the fact that we allowed religious charities to fulfill the needs of orphans and other vulnerable children essentially from America's founding and have struggled to assert government control over child welfare ever since. Because religious charities, not the government, established orphanages and orphan trains in the nineteenth century, it is not surprising that when the tides of child welfare finally turned to foster care in the mid-twentieth century, the same religious charities continued their dominant involvement in the field. Nor is it surprising that those same religious charities would fight to stay in control even as federal, state, and local governments finally started taking responsibility for the fates of dependent children by subsidizing, litigating, and overseeing their care. In belatedly getting involved in child welfare, the state entered a minefield created by its own abdication of responsibility. Governments at every level became involved in religion in a way that was forbidden by the establishment clause of the First Amendment, in that they were sponsoring certain religions by paying for children to be cared for—and inculcated by—religious groups.

Fulton v. City of Philadelphia may have been the first case involving religious charities' involvement in foster care to make it to the Supreme Court, but it had predecessors in the legal field—most notably, a 1970s case that got to the heart of the establishment clause conundrum. That case, known first as *Wilder v. Sugarman* and later as *Wilder v. Bernstein*, confronted the same argument that Lori Windham would weave on behalf of CSS almost fifty years later: that foster care and religious practice were so intertwined as to be inseparable.

In 1973, the New York Civil Liberties Union (NYCLU) filed a class action lawsuit against the city's Human Resources Administration and private foster care agencies on behalf of Black, Protestant children who had been removed from their biological families in the city.[56] The suit alleged that New York City's entire foster care system was unconstitutional because 90 percent of all foster beds were controlled by Catholic and Jewish charities who could choose to only work with children of their own "kind" among the city's foster care population.[57] The charities' right to religious matching of their foster care wards was originally dictated by New York's 1875 Children's Law—passed during the panic over children in almshouses—and reaffirmed by a 1921 amendment to the New York Constitution.[58] This meant that Black children—whom the city automatically assumed to be Protestant—were routinely turned down by Catholic and Jewish charities, even though they already comprised more than half of the city's foster children in the 1970s.[59] Those charities received between 70 and 95 percent of their budgets from federal and state taxpayer funding.

The NYCLU argued that this arrangement violated both the First Amendment's establishment and free exercise clauses and the Fourteenth Amendment's equal protection and due process clauses. The *Wilder* suit took as its lead complainant a Black teenage girl named Shirley Wilder, who was placed in a detention center for juvenile delinquents not because she had committed a crime but because no foster care agency would offer her a home.[60]

The NYCLU took on *Wilder* in order to set a precedent. It was a test case, designed like *Roe v. Wade* to go all the way to the Supreme Court, that sought to stop the city from funding child-care agencies that discriminated on the basis of religion or race and to prohibit its child welfare agencies from referring children for placement based on their religion or race.

But the case faltered against the power of religion in the United States from the start. The city's religious charities were up in arms over a challenge to their dominance in the foster care system. The lede of a 1975 *New York Times* article on the suit emphasizes not the actual harm done to Black children that gave rise to the case to begin with but the perceived "threat" to religious hegemony: "A little-noticed lawsuit called Wilder v. Sugarman is forcing some of the city's Roman Catholic, Jewish and Protestant leaders and their lawyers into a series of intense negotiations to combat what they see as a direct threat to the traditional role of religious groups in caring for children who are neglected, unwanted and abandoned."[61] Later the article notes, "For many Catholics, religious supervision of homeless children is a means of transmitting values to the young, the kind of standards that Catholics see as vital to breaking the cycle of broken families and dependence." Essentially, they said the quiet part out loud: that a primary purpose of child welfare was keeping Catholic children Catholic, as had been the case since the nineteenth century.

Marcia Lowry, the NYCLU lawyer who filed the suit, found hostility even in the courtroom—federal district court judge Harold Tyler's mother-in-law was on the board of one of the defendant agencies.[62] Judge Tyler recommended that the sides settle. He later said, "This is a fascinating case, but not one you love as a judge. You have all these nice people—do-gooders—on the boards of all these religious organizations who were very upset."[63] It seemed that the priority was maintaining the power of the religious charities, not considering the fates of Black children shunted away from suitable care.

The case met with judicial delays so dramatic that it never actually made it to trial. Instead, Lowry eventually acquiesced to a settlement, since such an agreement would be more likely to actually effect change in the system. Lowry herself had come to realize, as journalist Nina Bernstein writes in *The Lost Children of Wilder*, that while there was "no way, except in violation of the Constitution, that the city could fulfill a government obligation (child placement) by financing agencies whose mission was religious," it was equally true that "no judge was going to come to the same conclusion, since that would mean dismantling the foster-care system."[64] The entire system was predicated on the participation of the same religious charities that had begun caring for orphans in the nineteenth century, and they not only wielded immense power but felt entitled by their faith to lucrative city contracts—the same kind of entitlement we would later see in *Fulton v. City of Philadelphia*.

A final settlement wasn't reached until December 1986, thirteen years after the NYCLU initially filed suit. The plaintiffs won the stipulations that children entering foster care in New York City would be placed on a rational "first come, first served" basis, which would resolve the equal protection issues, and that religious matching would only occur at the request of children's biological families. The establishment clause issues were wholly abandoned. But the consent decree that resulted from the settlement was never implemented: the city dragged its feet, arguing that by the early 1990s the decree was already obsolete because, due to poverty, the war on drugs, and AIDS, the foster care population had exploded and was mostly made up of Black children. Racial disproportionality, driven by the Flemming Rule, the Child Abuse Prevention and Treatment Act, and the underlying racism and classism of the system, became an excuse to ignore the religious hegemony at the heart of child welfare.

The *Wilder* consent decree was finally dissolved in 1999, after Lowry settled a different case, *Marisol A. v. Giuliani*, which brought in an independent panel of national experts to advise New York City's Administration for Children's Services on system reform over a period of two years. Only two years of oversight after twenty-six years of legal fighting. Shirley Wilder herself died of AIDS at just thirty-nine, a few days before a judge approved *Marisol A. v. Giuliani.* "Being in foster care shouldn't mean that you grow up to die alone," Lowry said at the settlement hearing.[65]

The question at the heart of the *Wilder* case—whether the dominance of religious charities in foster care constituted a violation of the separation of church and state—has still not been officially considered in our country. Instead, we continue to allow religious charity—and its underlying motive of inculcating orphans—to take the place of social welfare policies in the United States and to subject our neediest children to the whims of religious charities that receive federal and state funding to carry out their missions. Fifty years later, those charities have only gotten bolder in their sense of entitlement to government money and power over vulnerable children's lives. That entitlement is now in direct tension with the rights of LGBTQ+ youth in the system and the LGBTQ+ adults who wish to be foster parents.

In June 2021, seven months after *Fulton v. City of Philadelphia* was argued before the Supreme Court, the justices issued their ruling. The decision was unanimous—and devastating for supporters of LGBTQ+ rights, as the court found that Philadelphia's foster care contract violated the free exercise clause of the First Amendment.

The ruling, though, did not set the clear precedent that religious rights groups were hoping for. The Supreme Court's decision was narrow: it found that Philadelphia's foster care agency contract was unconstitutional because it "burdened CSS's religious exercise" *and* because it did not "satisfy the threshold requirement of being neutral and generally applicable." Because the city's policy contained "a mechanism for individualized exemptions" to the rule that agencies cannot reject foster parents due to their sexual orientation—exemptions that Philadelphia said it had never granted—"it invite[d] the government to consider the particular reasons for a person's conduct." In other words, it was not a blanket regulation, and therefore Philadelphia was wrong in not granting CSS a "religious hardship" exemption.[66]

The paper-thin ruling, then, didn't really have anything to say about whether antidiscrimination laws could hold up against religious rights. It seemed that Philadelphia might have prevailed if its foster care contract hadn't included the exemption clause, and in fact, after the ruling, the city rewrote the contract to remove the clause.[67] The city also chose to settle with CSS, reaching a resolution in October 2021 stipulating that it would renew CSS's foster care contract, write in an exemption to the Fair Practices Ordinance's regulations about nondiscrimination against LGBTQ+ people, and pay CSS's $1.95 million legal bill. For 2022, CSS's foster care contract with Philadelphia was for $350,000.

Some of the Supreme Court justices *did* want to radically change constitutional law in *Fulton v. City of Philadelphia*. In a concurring (but irritated) decision, Justice Samuel Alito, joined by Justices Clarence Thomas and Neil Gorsuch, wrote, "This decision might as well be written on the dissolving paper sold in magic shops," predicting that Philadelphia would simply get rid of its foster care contract exemption clause. If Justices Alito, Thomas, and Gorsuch had their way, they would have used *Fulton* to overturn the 1990 *Employment Division v. Smith* ruling, which found that "general and neutrally applicable" laws—like Philadelphia's new exemption-free foster care contract—cannot be challenged on the grounds that they violate First Amendment rights.

———

In the end, as Justice Alito complained, *Fulton* resolved very little. It is only a matter of time before the central tensions in the case come to a head elsewhere. Maybe then *Smith* will be overturned. Maybe then the religious charities that have always dominated child welfare in the United States will have even more power.

It's difficult to imagine that the issue that once animated the *Wilder* case—the fact that religious charities' involvement in foster care violates the establishment clause—will ever again reach the courts. When I spoke to Matt Hartman about the prevalence of religious organizations in child welfare, he agreed. "I just think it's one of the areas where separation between church and state is the most blatantly not existing," Matt said. "And it's interesting that people continue to uphold it in the way they do. I think that a lot of people who aren't religious just accept it as a thing, or feel like these organizations that are religious organizations are doing more good than harm."

And it's not just that government funding of religion happens at an organizational level that bothers Matt. It's the fact that individuals who work within the child welfare system use the system to exercise their religion. "The counseling organization that I was contracted to, it wasn't necessarily a Christian counseling agency," Matt said. "It was just that they had hired a therapist that very much was [Christian]."

Even more common is Emi Nietfeld's experience of being placed in a home with a couple who were fostering as a means of exercising their religion. Evangelical zeal for foster care is nothing new and fits neatly into the broader history of the outsize role that Christians have always played in child welfare. Evangelicals are galvanized to care for children in foster care under the ideals of "orphan care." They apply the label "orphan" not just to children whose parents have died but to children who are "vulnerable" (read: poor). The defining scriptural passage of the orphan care movement is James 1:27: "Religion that God our Father accepts as pure and faultless is this: to look after orphans and widows in their distress and to keep oneself from being polluted by the world."

In his book *Growing God's Family*, sociologist Samuel L. Perry traces the current iteration of evangelical "orphan care" to the early 2000s.[68] In 2004, evangelical leaders like Rick Warren (founder of megachurch Saddleback, one of the largest in the country), James Dobson (founder of Focus on the Family), and Dennis Rainey (president of FamilyLife, a subsidiary of Campus Crusade for Christ)—along with the heads of Bethany and other Christian foster care and adoption agencies—met to establish the Christian Alliance for Orphans (CAFO). Perry calls CAFO "the central organizing hub of the contemporary evangelical orphan care movement." It partners with churches around the country to establish foster care and adoption ministries. Each year CAFO hosts "summits" with more than a hundred workshops and sponsorship booths that cost up to $30,000.[69]

At first groups like CAFO were mostly focused on international adoption of "orphans"—often meaning children who had poor parents who did not fully understand the permanent nature of American adoption—from countries like Guatemala, Ethiopia, and Haiti. In her 2013 book *The Child*

Catchers: Rescue, Trafficking, and the New Gospel of Adoption, investigative journalist Kathryn Joyce explains that in the early aughts, evangelical churches "had begun to view adoption as a perfect storm of a cause: a way for conservative churches to get involved in poverty and social justice issues that they had ceded years before to liberal denominations . . . and, more quietly, as a window for evangelizing."[70] She tracks how evangelical pastors cited an overblown "orphan crisis" to rally their congregants to pursue adoption. For example, Elizabeth Styffe, director of Saddleback's Global Orphan Care Initiative, referenced a grossly exaggerated number of adoptable "orphans": "There are 163 million orphans [globally], but there are two billion people who call themselves Christians. If you do the math, this is doable in our generation."[71]

Even as evangelicals pushed an end to the "orphan crisis," international adoption was drying up. Inadequate regulation, corruption, and trafficking born of Western demand for adoptable children plagued many countries' systems and led them to curtail or outright ban the practice. Guatemala suspended international adoptions in 2008, Ethiopia in 2018.[72] According to the US State Department's Bureau of Consular Affairs, international adoptions in the twenty-first century peaked in 2004—the year of CAFO's founding—when 22,987 children were adopted into the United States. They have since fallen precipitously—in 2022, only 1,517 children were adopted internationally into the United States.[73]

When I spoke with Joyce about what has changed in the orphan care movement since the publication of *The Child Catchers*, she noted a shift in how evangelicals talked about orphan care in 2017, when she was invited to a CAFO summit for a "civil disagreement" panel. "There was more of a focus on promoting in-country alternatives to international adoption," Joyce said. It seemed to her that some in the movement had reached the conclusion that "if you really want to help widows and orphans . . . it made more sense to do so by keeping them together by helping families that were poor, rather than just helping the kids."

The same ethos of family preservation has not entirely carried over to domestic foster care. While some evangelical foster parents promote family reunification as the goal of foster care, their reasoning tends to be rooted in what they believe to be God's vision of the family, and they do not seek to stop children from being removed in the first place. A prominent evangelical foster momfluencer, Jamie Finn, aka Instagram's @fosterthefamilyblog, once posted an image of a baby's tiny striped-sock feet cradled in her lap with a message that explains she is pro-reunification because of her "foundational conviction that God created the family and that He longs for it to be restored."[74] While Finn believes that God longs for the family to be restored, she does not seem to feel that the family-policing system shouldn't split up families—she believes that evangelical foster parents play a crucial role in "standing in the gap" for families riven by the sins of neglect and abuse. Finn's caption was an excerpt from her book *Foster the Family: Encouragement, Hope, and Practical Help for the Christian Foster Parent*, which Christian publisher Baker Books released in 2022. Finn went on a twenty-one-city tour to support it, stopping at churches and Christian conferences across the country.[75]

When Matt and I spoke about how evangelical foster parents like Finn take up space on social media, he told me, "I think their ability to even exist in that way stems from the bigger picture issue of how dominant religion is in child welfare in general, and continues to be. . . . The system already allows them to [evangelize], and has encouraged doing it in many cases for a long time." Until we reckon with the power our country has yielded to religion in child welfare, we will continue to violate children's rights and the separation between church and state.

Conclusion

IMAGINING A BETTER WORLD
FOR CHILDREN AND FAMILIES

I n the past few years, whenever I told people about this book project, they wanted to tell me about the orphan stories they had grown up loving. Would I be writing about *A Series of Unfortunate Events*, the books written under the pseudonym Lemony Snicket? (No, because the series is basically a rehash of *The Boxcar Children*, but creepier.) What about *Anne of Green Gables* or *The Secret Garden*? (Those are Canadian and British, respectively, and I was only focusing on American cultural products, which is why I also sidelined Harry Potter.)[1] Had I thought about all the half-orphan or pseudo-orphan stories, from *Rebecca of Sunnybrook Farm* through to the many versions of Sabrina Spellman's story? (Huckleberry Finn would have to do.)

That it would have been impossible for me to touch on each and every seminal American orphan narrative proves just how much we are attached to spinning fictions about this most vulnerable childhood experience. Even in a culture that has spent the last several years reckoning with questions of visibility and whose stories are told, our appetite for orphan characters whose experiences in no way mesh with reality cannot be sated.

In the book world alone, since my own deal was announced in early 2022, more than fifty more titles with orphan protagonists have sold to mainstream publishers.[2] Allow me a few sample descriptions:

- A historical novel for adults in which "a newly orphaned girl must protect her sick little brothers, and when the authorities send the boys to an unknown orphan asylum, she feels she's lost everything apart from a secret weapon—a promise from Eleanor Roosevelt, the most famous woman in America."[3] (*Annie* meets *Orphan Train*)
- A chapter book "about the adventures of two unlucky orphans who leap off of a train rather than be split up into separate foster homes and find themselves in an increasingly madcap series of mishaps."[4] (The *Orphan Train Adventures* series set in contemporary foster care)
- A middle-grade fantasy that "follows an orphaned girl who is sent to a mysterious island—home not only to a school for extraordinary teens, but also a sanctuary for endangered species—where she confronts a menacing deputy headmaster, a group of mean girls, and shocking family secrets."[5] (Geri Halliwell-Horner's take on Harry Potter. *Et tu*, Ginger Spice?)

Orphan stories new and old reinforce the central myth that America's policies toward dependent children have always been based on: individualism. Individual children call upon their grit and resilience to save themselves. Individual adults intervene, either with cruelty or love. If biological parents are still in the picture, we blame them for their individual faults. All the while, we never question the underlying structures that make these children vulnerable. The supremacy of the systems that govern their lives, from orphanages to foster care, are such a given that even in fiction, we often can't see a way to challenge them.

Our favorite orphan stories also conveniently obscure the political forces that demand we focus on fixing individual faults and saving individual "deserving" children in the first place. From the start, child welfare in this country has been driven by a fear and hatred of the poor and by moral panics acted out on the most vulnerable and least enfranchised members of our society. Classism's close cousin, racism, has always colored our determinations of which children and families are "deserving." And religious groups' entitlement to protect their own—and proselytize—has always shaped and distorted our child welfare systems' goals, from orphanages to orphan trains to foster care. Instead of focusing primarily on the well-being of children and their families, we have allowed these systems to be avenues for exerting religious power, for enacting cultural genocide, for furthering racial segregation and white supremacy, for socially controlling immigrants and the poor, and for policing and punishing Black people.

Experts and advocates have known that the system has failed at its goals of keeping children safe and repairing families since at least the 1970s, but the public remains attached to—and placated by—myths spread by popular culture, which seep into media coverage of actual child welfare cases and influence politicians' viewpoints. We want to believe that all it takes to save a child from grievous harm is for one person to step up and intervene by calling a hotline or becoming a foster parent or caseworker. The vast majority of children and families in the crosshairs of child protective services (CPS) need material support that the system cannot provide them with, but that's not the kind of story we want to hear.

We need to stop telling ourselves the same old stories about orphans, and we need to wake up from our historical amnesia. Most of all, though, we need to finally attempt true societal reform, and we need to do so urgently, because the family-policing system continues to wreck children's and parents' lives.

While foster care's racial disproportionality has become less egregious since the late 1990s, when New York City's Administration for Children's Services (ACS) removed Joyce McMillan's daughters, Black children remain overrepresented and white children underrepresented. In 2022, Black children made up 23 percent of the foster care population but only about 15 percent of the total child population; white children comprised 43 percent of the foster care population but about 70 percent of the total child population.[6] As Dorothy Roberts writes in her 2022 book *Torn Apart*, in which she returns to the subject of racism in the child welfare system twenty years after the publication of *Shattered Bonds*, racial disparity in foster care has continued despite increased awareness of the issue. "Since I wrote *Shattered Bonds*, 'racial disproportionality' has become a buzzword in child welfare research and policy making," Roberts writes. "State child welfare departments and nonprofit organizations alike have launched projects across the nation to reduce the foster care population, along with its racial disparities. Despite numerous reforms, the family-policing system has not changed its punitive ideology or racist impact."[7] The very foundation of the modern system perpetuates racism.

Even our awareness of the system's disparities and their root causes has proven flimsy and provisional. Recently, the Indian Child Welfare Act (ICWA), the gold standard law that protects tribal sovereignty and attempts to actively preserve and reunify Native families, faced an existential threat—a Supreme Court case that challenged its constitutionality. It's true that ICWA did not eliminate the problem of Indigenous disproportionality in the foster care population. Native children still make up a larger slice of the nationwide foster care population than their representation in the child population: 2 percent versus 1 percent.[8] In some states with large Native populations, the proportions are dramatically out of whack—in South Dakota, for instance, Indigenous children make up 12 percent of the child population but 53 percent of the foster care population. Nationwide, one in nine Native American children will enter foster care during childhood.[9] The National Indian Child Welfare Association chalks up the high rates of Indigenous children placed in foster care to a combination of systemic bias in the child-protective system and continually high rates of poverty in the American Indian and Alaska Native populations.[10] Nevertheless, ICWA remains a crucial means of protecting Native families and tribes after centuries of American policies that sought to eliminate and assimilate them.

The case that challenged ICWA, *Haaland v. Brackeen*, on its face concerned the adoption of a single Native child, but it had much larger implications. Brought on behalf of an evangelical couple who felt a religious calling to foster and adopt, the case sought to portray tribal belonging as a racial, not national, category, opening up grounds to claim that ICWA promoted unconstitutional racial discrimination.[11] As journalist Rebecca Nagle, a citizen of the Cherokee Nation, explains on the documentary podcast *This Land*, the case against ICWA was a "trojan horse" designed by far-right groups with deep pockets seeking to delegitimize tribal sovereignty.[12] In June 2023, the Supreme Court upheld ICWA's constitutionality in a 7–2 ruling, with Justices Samuel Alito and Clarence Thomas dissenting. That ICWA faced such a challenge less than fifty years after its author argued it was necessary to rectify cultural genocide reflects America's short historical attention span.

———

Even in the face of continued racial disparities and our reluctance to learn from the past, we are amid a major shift in mainstream attention to the realities of the family-policing system.[13] Most media coverage of child welfare has been sensational, tracing all the way back to Mary Ellen Wilson's case in the late nineteenth century. While reporting on children who die due to maltreatment remains lurid, mainstream publications have in recent years begun to meaningfully inform the public about the capriciousness and irrationality of the system. In 2017, a *New York Times* article titled "Foster Care as Punishment: The New Reality of 'Jane Crow'" brought widespread attention to what reporters Stephanie Clifford and Jessica Silver-Greenberg note is a long-standing issue in New York City: "the power of Children's Services to take children from their parents on the grounds that the child's safety is at risk, even with scant evidence."[14] The article cited lawyers defending the predominantly poor Black and Hispanic women whose children were removed because of "the criminalization of their parenting choices"—choices that would not lead to similar scrutiny if white mothers made them—lawyers who call the practice "Jane Crow." The article provides a rare sympathetic portrayal of the parents whose children are removed by CPS, who have all too often been characterized as monsters willfully harming their children rather than as people making choices constrained by their socioeconomic realities.

More groundbreaking reporting came in 2021, when NPR and The Marshall Project launched an investigative series called "The Hidden Bill for Foster Care."[15] The series began by uncovering the shockingly widespread practice of state agencies essentially stealing the Social Security Insurance (SSI) benefits of children in foster care—the exact benefits that my brother and I, and my father and aunts before us, once received. The investigation found that about 10 percent of children in foster care were entitled to SSI benefits, either due to parental death or their own physical or mental disabilities, and that state foster care agencies were garnishing millions of dollars of these benefits per year to pay for their care, despite the fact that foster care is itself government funded.

NPR later revealed that states don't just steal children's SSI benefits to pay for foster care—they charge parents for it too.[16] One story illuminated the fact that agencies in every state ask biological parents to reimburse some of the costs of foster care in the form of "child support," to the tune of up to $1,000 a month. These bills "almost exclusively" target "the poorest families," and "when parents get billed, children spend added time in foster care and the extra debt follows families for years, making it hard for them to climb out of poverty." Even more perversely, "the government raises little money, or even loses money, when it tries to collect." This practice represents a double punishment—first, the forcible removal of one's children; second, a bill to pay for their care—and rests on the foundational logic of the "undeserving" poor.[17] NPR's reporting highlighted that it is neglect and poverty, and not abuse, that ensnare most families in foster care.

A 2022–2023 investigative series from ProPublica and NBC News has even further exposed what Duncan Lindsey once referred to as "the red herring" of child abuse in the system. The series, "Overpolicing Parents: How America's CPS Dragnet Ensnares Families," includes articles with provocative and damning headlines like "Mandatory Reporting Was Supposed to Stop Severe Child Abuse. It Punishes Poor Families Instead" and "In Child Welfare Cases, Most of Your Constitutional Rights Don't Apply"—topics I have highlighted in this book.

Perhaps the biggest breakthrough in media coverage of the system's harms came in December 2022, when *CBS Sunday Morning*, the flagship news show that reaches nearly 5.5 million viewers, featured a twelve-minute segment titled "When the System Fails, Families May Pay the Ultimate Price."[18] The segment told the story of Vanessa Peoples, a Black nursing student and mother of two in Colorado who was hogtied by police during a CPS investigation. CPS entered Peoples's life after her toddler son momentarily wandered off at a family picnic. Roberts tells the same story toward the beginning of *Torn Apart*. She appears in the *CBS Sunday Morning* segment, offering context and analysis for Peoples's experience and spreading word to Americans drinking their coffee that the child welfare system ought to be called the family-policing system.

Shifting the narrative around child welfare and raising awareness of the harms the system perpetuates—as I am attempting to do with this book—remains a crucial first step in garnering the political will to enact policy changes. After all, it was storytelling that drove major revisions of the system in the past, from Charles Loring Brace's classist and xenophobic propaganda to Sister Mary Irene Fitzgibbon's referencing of headlines of infanticide, from the *Delineator*'s Child-Rescue Campaign to the parade of articles about parents battering their children, from Newt Gingrich's outrageous faith in *Boys Town* to the stories of Elisa Izquierdo and Nixzmary Brown. Telling the real story of orphanhood in America is the first step toward creating change.

Our country's child welfare policies remain woefully unaligned with the realities on the ground. While the federal government's most recent legislative reform of the system—2018's Family First Prevention Services Act (FFPSA)—might seem to be heading in the right direction, it leaves a punitive and coercive vision of CPS in place. The act attempts to increase the number of children who can remain at home with their families by uncapping federal funding for preventative programs like mental health treatment, substance use programs, and parenting classes. But in order for a family to receive these services, they must be facing imminent risk of child removal to foster care—in other words, they must already find themselves under the surveillance of a CPS investigation.[19] Taking part in preventative programs is not voluntary for parents under CPS supervision; it's either accept these "supports" or lose your children to foster care. And while FFPSA attempts to forefront prevention, it leaves in place the Child Abuse Prevention and Treatment Act and the Adoption and Safe Families Act—laws that promote the forcible removal of children and termination of parental rights.

In the meantime, millions of Americans continue to suffer as a result of spending time in foster care. Beyond the abysmal statistics about education and homelessness, former foster youth are at higher risk of poor physical and mental health and substance use problems as adults. According to ground-breaking research into adverse childhood experiences (ACEs), toxic stress experienced in childhood impacts adult health.[20] ACEs comprise ten catego-ries of traumatic childhood events; for each category you've experienced, you get one point. The higher your ACE score, the worse your risk for negative outcomes, including higher "risks of injury, sexually transmitted infections, maternal and child health problems . . . involvement in sex trafficking, and a wide range of chronic diseases and leading causes of death, such as cancer, diabetes, heart disease, and suicide," per the Centers for Disease Control and Prevention. Being placed in foster care is, in and of itself, an ACE. My ACE score is one, because my parents died. More than half of former foster youth are estimated to have an ACE score of three or four.[21] Beyond these increased health risks, former foster youth are also more likely to live in poverty, strug-gle to maintain employment, and be incarcerated, either in the juvenile jus-tice system or as adults.[22]

The system that creates these outcomes, meanwhile, has only grown more expensive. In 2020, the most recent year for which there are data, state and local child welfare agencies spent $31.4 billion of state, local, and federal funding.[23] Almost half of that money went toward foster care. Even with FFPSA in place, states spent less of their funding on prevention services (14 percent) than on CPS investigations themselves (18 percent).[24] Local foster care agencies—including many religious ones, like Bethany Christian Ser-vices and Catholic Charities USA—as well as subcontractors that provide therapy (like Matt Hartman's "Christ-centered" therapist), parenting classes, substance use treatments, and other services, are prime beneficiaries of this funding. These organizations profit under a system that splits up poor chil-dren and their families.

While journalists are raising awareness of the realities of the child welfare system, and while policy making lags, nonprofit organizations on the ground are making a difference in the lives of families currently torn apart while fighting to reform the system at large. In fact, after Joyce McMillan lost cus-tody of her daughters, the organizations that *did* help were not ones that ACS connected her with and paid for but nonprofits. After she was released from Rikers, McMillan was able to move into a two-bedroom apartment thanks to the Women's Prison Association (WPA), a nonprofit founded in 1845 as the nation's first organization for systems-involved women's rights. Her apartment was in Sarah Powell Huntington House, a shelter on 10th Street and Avenue B in Manhattan that WPA opened in 1994 specifically to serve formerly incarcerated mothers so that they can reunify with their families.[25]

Around the same time, McMillan was appointed a new lawyer to represent her in her ACS family court case: Lauren Shapiro, of Brooklyn Legal Services, which provides free civil defense for low-income Brooklynites.[26] Shapiro stepped in to hold the system accountable when Kaylah's foster mother was sabotaging McMillan's mandated weekly visits by bringing the baby as much as forty-five minutes late to a two-hour visit. She also vigorously objected in family court when ACS was refusing to return Kaylah to McMillan simply because she had not completed a drug treatment program, even though she had maintained sobriety on her own and had fifteen straight months of negative toxicology on court-ordered drug tests to prove it.

Ultimately, it took McMillan two and a half years to regain custody of Kaylah.[27] Her ex-husband returned Courtnie to her care much sooner, without family court intervention, since she was never technically in foster care. Both girls joined McMillan at her new apartment in Huntington House while she pieced her life back together.

For both parents and children, access to quality legal representation in family court can hugely impact chances at reunification. But while a person's right to a lawyer is guaranteed regardless of ability to pay in criminal cases, the same right does not always apply to civil cases like the ones CPS brings. Currently, all states give parents in child maltreatment cases *some* civil right to counsel, but that right is only categorical—without qualification—in thirty-eight states.[28] For children, the right is only categorical in sixteen states. Pennsylvania, where I live, offers parents a categorical right to council, but the right is qualified for children.

Kathleen Creamer, the managing attorney of the Family Advocacy Unit of Community Legal Services (CLS) in Philadelphia, told me that "anecdotally, termination of parental rights is really rare in our practice, even though Philly [Department of Human Services (DHS)] terminates at a very aggressive clip."[29] Right away, a CLS lawyer like Creamer will advocate for conditions that help reunification, like placing removed children with kin rather than strangers and increasing visitation so families can see one another more than the mandated once every two weeks. CLS also litigates whether DHS made reasonable efforts to prevent removal in the first place or even has enough evidence to prove its maltreatment case. "Often we're litigating to have the entire case dismissed," Creamer told me.

When a case does continue, CLS will advocate for a case plan that actually fits the facts as DHS lays them out. "If you are one of those ten percent of families in Philadelphia who were separated from their children due to housing, do you need a parenting class to get your child back?" Creamer asked. "Is lack of adequate housing a sign of inadequate parenting that you need, like, to sit at a class for sixteen weeks? . . . We're often fighting against those kinds of onerous reunification requirements."

Beyond the courtroom, CLS employs a holistic, interdisciplinary defense model that pairs parents not just with a lawyer but with a social worker and a peer advocate, a model Creamer has been promoting at the national level through her work with the American Bar Association. "Our clients are persistently deprived of voice and choice," Creamer told me. "We're constantly trying to put that voice and choice back in their court as much as we can."

Children in the foster care system are especially lacking in voice and choice. But organizations like New York City's Lawyers for Children, which provides representation and advocacy for children in foster care and other family court proceedings, push to actually represent children's wishes. Like CLS, Lawyers for Children utilizes a holistic model, pairing children with lawyers and social workers. Ilena Robbins, the social worker who once worked at a residential treatment center in New York City, is now a senior staff social worker at Lawyers for Children. While nationwide children in foster care might be paired with a guardian ad litem (a volunteer lawyer) or a court-appointed special advocate (a plain old volunteer) who represents their "best interests" in court, Lawyers for Children advocates for what children actually want. That might not be the same as what adults determine to be in their best interests. "When you're a child in foster care, everyone is telling you what to do," Robbins told me. "It's really important for our clients to feel like they have someone who's advocating only for them, not for what the judge wants, not for what the agency wants, not for what mom wants, not for what dad wants, not for what their sibling wants if it's something different. I think it's really empowering for kids to know that someone is speaking for them." Most kids, Robbins told me, want to go home. "Kids often know what's going to work for them, what's going to be best for them. Not always, but often. And not being able to express that is really damaging to them."

The former foster youth I spoke to have all beat the odds in that they have college degrees, stable employment, and support systems. Their relative stability enables them to raise their voices now. Still, they all expressed some version of being damaged by not being listened to while in foster care. Sixto Cancel, who had to record evidence of his adoptive mother's abuse for case-workers to believe him, has now dedicated his career to transforming the child welfare system by utilizing the perspectives of people with lived experience. His organization, Think of Us, conducts research and partners with government agencies like the Children's Bureau, lawmakers, and advocacy groups to implement solutions at the federal, state, and local levels.[30] Think of Us has compiled reports on youths' lived experience in institutional placements and on aging out of the system.[31] The organization's current focus is on promoting kinship care, an avenue that Cancel didn't even know was available to him as a foster youth.

In a 2021 op-ed for the *New York Times*, Cancel wrote about finding out at a family reunion in his late twenties that he had four aunts and uncles on his father's side who were foster and adoptive parents.[32] Growing up, Cancel hadn't known his father, who died before they could meet in person; nor had Cancel known these aunts and uncles existed. But still, they were family; still, they would have been able to care for him. One aunt had even been fostering for longer than Cancel had been alive. "I pulled out my phone and searched the distance between my aunt's home and where I grew up: 58 miles," he writes. "That's how close I'd been to family members who would have taken me in, who I would have loved to have lived with. But the system never thought to find my family." Instead, he aged out of the system at twenty-three.

Kinship care operates under the surveillance of CPS, and children who are placed with kin, like Matt Hartman was, are still subject to caseworker visits, court dates, and mandated services. But kinship care preserves familial and cultural ties, is better for children's behavioral and mental health, and gives them better chances at permanency.[33] Rates of kinship placement have improved in recent years—now, more than one-third of children in foster care are placed with family members or "fictive kin" like family friends.[34] But it has been historically deprioritized and underfunded. Kinship carers face cumbersome licensing requirements that can take months to complete, often while children wait in a stranger's foster home.[35]

Think of Us hopes to keep families together by first aiming to prevent unnecessary removals in cases of neglect. They are researching the problems driving removals and pushing to create prevention services that actually match those needs, beyond the mental health, substance use, and parenting classes the government will pay for. But for the children who do enter foster care, the organization wants to "make kinship care the norm in the country," Cancel told me. They are currently partnering with advocacy organizations like Children's Rights and the National Indian Child Welfare Association in an effort to establish standards for child welfare agencies to follow to increase the uptake of kinship care.[36]

Think of Us's goal of making kinship care the norm nudged closer to becoming a reality in September 2023, when President Joe Biden's administration announced a package of new Department of Health and Human Services (HHS) regulations and proposals.[37] The first regulation—which was immediately implemented—aims to support foster care by allowing states to simplify the process kin need to undergo to care for children in the system and by requiring that states pay kinship carers the same stipends as other foster parents. The rule "creates some opportunity to disregard the income, transportation, literacy issues, and the some of the room size requirements" that can render kin ineligible to foster, according to Rebecca Jones Gaston, commissioner of the Administration on Children, Youth and Families.[38]

Another announced HHS regulation, this one still a proposal, would allow the use of federal funding for legal representation for families with CPS involvement whose cases have not yet occasioned the removal of children from the home. "Families facing eviction, utility shutoffs, or benefit terminations deserve concrete legal help rather than unnecessary child welfare intervention," Creamer told *The Imprint*, a publication focused on child welfare. She said the proposed rule reflects "the value of offering families legal representation that is holistic and tailored to their actual and diverse legal needs." States wouldn't need to extend this legal representation, but if they did, they would get 50 percent matching funds from Title IV-E and would potentially strengthen family preservation.

The final proposed regulation would require state child welfare agencies to "implement specific processes and requirements" that "ensure that LGBTQI+ children in their care are placed in foster homes where they will be protected from mistreatment related to their sexual orientation or gender identity, where their caregivers have received special training on how to meet their needs, and where they can access the services they need to thrive."[39] While this rule might seem on its face to ban religious homophobia, HHS would not actually require that every foster care agency provide safe placements for LGBTQ+ youth—instead, states would need to have enough safe placements "in totality," across agencies. In other words, agencies like Philadelphia's Catholic Social Services that prohibit LGBTQ+ foster parents can continue to provide care without violating the rule.

———

While the work that nonprofit organizations like CLS and Think of Us do is crucial to support individual families and push for systemic changes like the new HHS regulations, these reforms leave in place a system that was founded on flawed logic. Since the boom of orphanages in the mid-nineteenth century, the solutions that we have applied in the child welfare system have been predicated on a misunderstanding of the problem. The problem that most families face has always been desperate poverty, which we as Americans are loath to view as societally determined. Instead, we have been all too eager to buy into alternative conceptions of what creates childhood dependency—conceptions driven by cultural anxieties and moral panics, from the anti-immigrant "vicious" gemmules that Charles Loring Brace hawked to the idea that parents who abuse their children do so because they are "psychopathic or sociopathic characters." Our fictions have served to cement these misconceptions.

When I first started writing this book, I believed that reforms would be sufficient to address the foster care system's racial disproportionality and religious hegemony. I believed that foster care was necessary to keep children safe. The more I learned, the more I realized that even for the minority of children who do enter foster care because of abuse, the system does not keep them safe—it traumatizes them. I began to question if a system that presupposes that parents need to be punished could ever succeed at the goal of "improving the lives of children and families," as the Children's Bureau aims to do.[40] Most of all, I started feeling that CPS and foster care were designed specifically to intervene in the lives of poor families, especially poor Black and Native families. I had to confront the fact that there is no way that my brother and I would have ever ended up in foster care, even in some alternate reality where my parents had lived and been abusive. There is no way that my father and his sisters would have ended up in foster care. Being white and middle-class didn't protect us from death and grief, but it did protect our family from being torn apart by the state.

I am far from the first person to confront the history and reality of the child welfare system and undergo this transformation in thinking. In *Torn Apart*, Roberts writes about how, in the twenty years since the publication of *Shattered Bonds*, she came to believe not only that the system is impervious to reforms but that it needs to be abolished and replaced "with a radically reimagined way of caring for families and keeping children safe."[41] She reached this perspective after participating in a variety of "efforts to improve foster care, address its racial disparities, and reduce its population," including nearly a decade spent on a task force in Washington State.[42] "No doubt some of the reforms I participated in helped raise awareness of the racism and harm in America's child welfare system," Roberts writes. "None rendered a significant blow to the system's fundamental design."

Like Roberts, I have come to believe that actual societal reform goes hand in hand with the abolition of the family-policing system. I have been influenced not only by books like *Torn Apart* but by impacted parents like Joyce McMillan, who became involved in advocacy work about a decade ago after realizing that what happened to her family was part of a larger pattern of ACS intrusion into the lives of Black families. McMillan now heads her own organization, Just Making a Change for Families (JMAC), which calls for abolition of the system and works toward that goal via storytelling that contravenes dominant narratives, as well as through legislative advocacy and programming for impacted parents. In 2020, JMAC plastered New York City with posters that read, "They separate children at the border of Harlem too #AbolishACSNYC."[43] The posters challenged New Yorkers to confront the destruction of families happening right under their noses.

That same year, JMAC's legislative advocacy group led a successful campaign to challenge New York's Statewide Central Register (SCR), a sort of civil version of a criminal registry that adults with indicated reports of child abuse or neglect get listed on. Being on the SCR limits employment opportunities—hirers at any job where you interact with children might search the registry—and punishes parents long after their cases are closed. The new legislation, which went into effect in 2022, raises the standard of evidence to list someone on the SCR and seals records after eight years instead of up to twenty-eight years.[44] JMAC is currently promoting New York State bills that would require CPS workers to inform parents of their rights with a Miranda-style warning, eliminate anonymous maltreatment reporting and replace it with confidential reporting that collects callers' names and contact information, and require informed consent for testing pregnant people and babies for drugs.[45] While these might seem like mere reforms, they in fact represent abolitionist steps that would shrink the power, reach, and legitimacy of the family-policing system.[46]

I have also been moved by the work of Rise, founded in New York City in 2005 as a magazine that showcases the voices of parents harmed by the family-policing system. In addition to publishing the magazine, Rise trains parent-leaders for community organizing, hosts peer support groups, and advocates for abolition. Rise's executive director, Jeanette Vega, a Puerto Rican mother impacted by the system, told me, "At Rise, we are all parents impacted and we are fighting for a just system that supports our families' well-being, and we are creating the support networks we want and need in our own communities. We are developing a better future for our children."[47] Those supports include advocating and organizing for universal child care without ACS oversight, replacing mandated reporting with support and access to community resources, and investing in community-led mental health programs.[48]

In other words, like prison abolitionists, child welfare abolitionists have a vision not just of dismantling but of imagining and building societal systems of support that actually address families' needs instead of punishing and separating them. Alan Dettlaff, a social work professor who once worked as a CPS abuse investigator in Fort Worth, Texas, told me, "The idea of a world without the police and prisons and child welfare is difficult for people to wrap their heads around. Most people, I think, also misunderstand abolition and only focus on the *ending* parts and not the *building up* parts, which abolition is really paying much more attention to."[49] In 2020, Dettlaff, along with others at the University of Houston, cofounded the upEND Movement, an abolitionist organization that argues, "We can't reform a punishment system. We must imagine and invest in care and healing."[50] Like JMAC and Rise, upEND combines research, storytelling, and grassroots advocacy, but from an academic standpoint, challenging what Dettlaff calls social work's "myth of benevolence" and its underlying white saviorism.

Within the academic field of social work, while there is growing engagement with abolitionist ideas, they are not wholeheartedly embraced. In fact, in late 2022, Dettlaff was removed from his position as dean of the University of Houston's Graduate College of Social Work in part due to his abolitionist stance, which had ironically drawn students to the school in the first place.[51] He remains on the faculty, and upEND remains headquartered at the university, where it hosted an October 2023 conference called "How We endUP," bringing together academics, activists, researchers, and policy makers to "envision a world where families are liberated from the unjust clutches of family policing."[52]

Abolition envisions a world in which families are lifted out of poverty via universal basic income and guaranteed housing.[53] A world where families have access to universal medical and child care, as well as mutual aid and peer networks, and where they no longer need to worry about being reported to CPS. A world where families and communities are empowered to intervene when abuse and harm occurs. The fact is that we already have a world where family policing doesn't exist—the white middle- and upper-class suburbs like the one I grew up in on Long Island. It's one that all children and families deserve.

America's modern foster care system—entwined mandated reporting and court-ordered family separation—has only existed for about fifty years. Orphanages and orphan trains operated for much longer, and those systems were abolished. A historical perspective allows us to understand that this system is not inevitable, is not set in stone, is not necessary. Our fictions may not help us envision a better world, but waking up to the facts can.

ACKNOWLEDGMENTS

Many people and institutions supported and influenced me in the years I worked on this book—and well before I ever thought I would write a book about orphans. While this list is by no means exhaustive, I wish to especially thank the following:

This book would not exist in your hands without my steadfast agent, Jamie Carr, my acquiring editor, Hillary Brenhouse, and my editor, Anu Roy-Chaudhury. Jamie's feedback, advocacy, and encouragement have buoyed me throughout this entire process. Hillary saw what this book could be and set me down that path. Anu stepped in at a crucial moment with a clear understanding of where I was going and the editorial guidance to get me there. Thank you for being my dream team.

Thank you to my fact-checker, Richard Beck, for shoring up the accuracy of my research, reporting, and assertions—and to Bold Type and Type Media Center for including fact-checking in my contract, a rarity in publishing. Thank you to my copyeditor, Jen Kelland, and to Annie Chatham and Olivia Loperfido for shepherding this book through production. Thank you to Chin-Yee Lai and Ann Kirchner for my gorgeous cover. Thank you to my publicist Brooke Parsons and marketer Brieana Garcia, as well as to Liz Wetzel, for introducing this book to the wider world. Thank you to Brettne Bloom and DJ Kim at The Book Group.

A version of Chapter 5 originally appeared as an essay in *Lapham's Quarterly* titled "Novel Transport." Thank you to Jaime Fuller for commissioning me to write for the pop culture period piece series and to Jaime and Sarah

Fan for your edits. The passages in Chapter 12 about evangelical zeal for foster care originally appeared in different form in an essay for *The Baffler* titled "Wards of God." Jess Bergman shaped that piece and many others with me over the years—thank you for your attention as an editor and for your friendship.

Librarians and archivists provided me with crucial access to the materials that form the foundations of this book. Thank you to everyone at the Patricia D. Klingenstein Library at the New-York Historical Society and especially to Gina Modero, Crystal Toscano, and Jill Reichenbach. Thank you to Blair Williams at the Cumberland County Historical Society. Librarians at the University of Pennsylvania helped me seamlessly access many, many books; Sarah Heim at the Kislak Center was especially helpful in my early research on *Little Orphan Annie.*

Many people with personal experience with child protective services and foster care shared their stories with me and helped me understand the inner workings of the system. Thank you to Sixto Cancel, Kathleen Creamer, Alan Dettlaff, Matt Hartman, Rosalie Knecht, Joyce McMillan, Emi Nietfeld, Ilena Robbins, and Jeanette Vega.

Thank you to other writers on the child welfare beat, especially Kathryn Joyce and Roxanna Asgarian. Thank you to the scholars whose books on orphanages, orphan trains, and foster care shaped my thinking, especially Andrew Billingsley and Jeanne Giovannoni, Matthew Crenson, Timothy Hacsi, Stephen O'Connor, Dorothy Roberts, and Catherine Rymph.

I wrote portions of this book during a residency at Yaddo and revised it during a residency at the Virginia Center for the Creative Arts. Both residencies provided me with the time and space to think clearly and deeply and nourished me with excellent food and thoughtful community; I am forever thankful for the time I spent there.

My time studying at the Columbia University School of the Arts and at the University of Pennsylvania shaped the writer I am today. At Columbia, I especially benefited from workshops and seminars with Phillip Lopate, Brenda Wineapple, Margo Jefferson, and Leslie Jamison. I first wrote about why I hated being called an orphan in a short assignment for Lis Harris's "Family Matters" seminar. Thank you to these professors, and to my classmates, especially Sophie Unterman and Kristi D. Osorio. At Penn, Paul

Hendrickson helped me begin to write about my parents and their lives and deaths, and Anthony DeCurtis showed me that writing about popular culture is serious enough to be the subject of multiple Ivy League courses.

I am forever indebted to the Kelly Writers House, my home sweet heart, and to Jamie-Lee Josselyn, fearless leader of the Dead Parents Society and dearest friend. Thank you to Blue Stoop for a new community when I moved back to Philly.

My friends kept me sane while I wrote this book. Thank you forever to Katie Stoll, who has been with me through everything and gets it all. Thank you to Sarah Arkebauer, Marshall Bright, Maureen Devenny, and Emma McClafferty, the Bar Keeper's Friends. Let's eat shrimp to celebrate.

Thank you to everyone in the Martin family, especially my brother, John, and my aunts Mary Ellen Martin, Joan Martin, and Nancy Brady, for their unending support and love. I miss you and love you, Mom, Dad, Grandma Martin, Nanny, Aunt Alice, and Uncle Joe. Thank you to my generous and sweet mother-in-law, Gloria Ritacco-Stewart. Thank you to Bruce Stewart and the Bisignanos.

Thank you to Penny Loafer for requiring walks that clear my head, to Suzy Creamcheese for demanding that we sit in the sun, to Kiwi Cat for acting as a (very) large paperweight, and to Dougie Jones for purring behind me as I wrote.

To my husband, Robby Ritacco—I especially could not have written this book without you. Thank you for listening to me rant about child welfare and agreeing that none of it's good. Thank you for proofreading almost everything I write, for constantly refilling my water glass, and for loving me and caring for me and grounding me all these years.

WORKS CITED

Asgarian, Roxanna. *We Were Once a Family: A Story of Love, Death, and Child Removal in America*. New York: Farrar, Straus and Giroux, 2023.

Bernstein, Nina. *The Lost Children of Wilder: The Epic Struggle to Change Foster Care*. New York: Pantheon, 2001.

Billingsley, Andrew, and Jeanne M. Giovannoni. *Children of the Storm: Black Children and American Child Welfare*. New York: Harcourt, Brace, Jovanovich, 1972.

Bland, Sidney R. "Shaping the Life of the New Woman: The Crusading Years of the 'Delineator.'" *American Periodicals* 19, no. 2 (2009): 165–188.

Brace, Charles Loring. *The Dangerous Classes of New York, and Twenty Years' Work Among Them*. New York: Wynkoop & Hallenback, 1872.

Briggs, Laura. *Somebody's Children: The Politics of Transracial and Transnational Adoption*. Durham, NC: Duke University Press, 2012.

Briggs, Laura. *Taking Children: A History of American Terror*. Oakland: University of California Press, 2021.

Brown, Dorothy M., and Elizabeth McKeown. *The Poor Belong to Us: Catholic Charities and American Welfare*. Cambridge, MA: Harvard University Press, 1997.

Coontz, Stephanie. *The Way We Never Were: American Families and the Nostalgia Trap, Revised and Updated Edition*. New York: Basic Books, 2016.

Costin, Lela B. "Unraveling the Mary Ellen Legend: Origins of the 'Cruelty' Movement." *Social Service Review* 65, no. 2 (June 1991): 203–223.

Creagh, Dianne. "The Baby Trains: Catholic Foster Care and Western Migration, 1873–1929." *Journal of Social History* 46, no. 1 (fall 2012): 197–218.

Crenson, Matthew. *Building the Invisible Orphanage: A Prehistory of the American Welfare System.* Cambridge, MA: Harvard University Press, 2001.

Dettlaff, Alan. *Confronting the Racist Legacy of the American Child Welfare System: The Case for Abolition.* Oxford: Oxford University Press, 2023.

Du Bois, W. E. B. *The Negro American Family.* Atlanta: Atlanta University Press, 1908.

Ehrenreich, John. *The Altruistic Imagination: A History of Social Work and Social Policy in the United States.* Ithaca, NY: Cornell University Press, 2014.

Elliott, Andrea. *Invisible Child: Poverty, Survival, and Hope in an American City.* New York: Random House, 2022.

Fear-Segal, Jacqueline, and Susan D. Rose, eds. *Carlisle Indian Industrial School: Indigenous Histories, Memories, and Reclamation.* Lincoln: University of Nebraska Press, 2016.

Firor Scott, Anne. *Natural Allies: Women's Associations in American History.* Champaign: University of Illinois Press, 1992.

Fitzgerald, Maureen. "The Perils of 'Passion and Poverty': Women Religious and the Care of Single Women in New York City, 1845–1890." *U.S. Catholic Historian* 10, no. 1/2 (1991/1992): 45–58.

Fong, Kelley. *Investigating Families: Motherhood in the Shadow of Child Protective Services.* Princeton, NJ: Princeton University Press, 2023.

Glaser, Gabrielle. *American Baby: A Mother, a Child, and the Shadow History of Adoption.* New York: Viking, 2021.

Gordon, Linda. *Heroes of Their Own Lives: The Politics and History of Family Violence.* New York: Viking, 1988.

Graham, Janet, and Edward Gray, dir. *American Experience: The Orphan Trains*. PBS: 1995. DVD.

Gray, Harold. *The Complete Little Orphan Annie*. Vol. 1. San Diego, CA: IDW Publishing, 2008.

Gray, Harold. *The Complete Little Orphan Annie*. Vol. 2. San Diego, CA: IDW Publishing, 2009.

Gray, Harold. *The Complete Little Orphan Annie*. Vol. 3. San Diego, CA: IDW Publishing, 2009.

Hacsi, Timothy. *Second Home: Orphan Asylums and Poor Families in America*. Cambridge, MA: Harvard University Press, 1997.

Hainze, Emily. "Rescued Children and Unfit Mothers: Dreiser's Social Work in the *Delineator*'s Child-Rescue Campaign." *American Literature* 89, no. 1 (March 2017).

Herman, Ellen. *Kinship by Design: A History of Adoption in the Modern United States*. Chicago: University of Chicago Press, 2008.

Holt, Marilyn Irvin. *The Orphan Trains: Placing Out in America*. Lincoln: University of Nebraska Press, 1994.

Jacobs, Margaret D. *A Generation Removed: The Fostering and Adoption of Native Children in the Postwar World*. Lincoln: University of Nebraska Press, 2014.

Jambor, Harold. "Theodore Dreiser, the 'Delineator' Magazine, and Dependent Children: A Background Note on the Calling of the 1909 White House Conference." *Social Service Review* 32, no. 1 (1958): 33–40.

Johnson, Mary Ellen, ed. *Orphan Train Riders: Their Own Stories*. Vol. 1. Baltimore: Otter Bay Books, 1992.

Johnson, Mary Ellen, ed. *Orphan Train Riders: Their Own Stories*. Vol. 2. Little Rock: Orphan Train Heritage Society of America, 1993.

Johnson, Mary Ellen, ed. *Orphan Train Riders: Their Own Stories*. Vol. 3. Little Rock: Orphan Train Heritage Society of America, 1995.

Johnson, Mary Ellen, ed. *Orphan Train Riders: Their Own Stories*. Vol. 4. Little Rock: Orphan Train Heritage Society of America, 1997.

Jones-Rogers, Stephanie. *They Were Her Property: White Women as Slave Owners in the American South*. New Haven, CT: Yale University Press, 2019.

Joyce, Kathryn. *The Child Catchers: Rescue, Trafficking, and the New Gospel of Adoption*. New York: PublicAffairs, 2013.

Katz, Michael B. *In the Shadow of the Poorhouse: A Social History of Welfare in America, Tenth Anniversary Edition*. New York: Basic Books, 1996.

Kempe, C. Henry, Frederic N. Silverman, Brandt F. Steele, William Droegemueller, and Henry K. Silver. "The Battered-Child Syndrome." *Journal of the American Medical Association* 181, no. 1 (July 1962): 17–24.

Kenneally, Christine. *Ghosts of the Orphanage: A Story of Mysterious Deaths, a Conspiracy of Silence, and a Search for Justice*. New York: PublicAffairs, 2023.

Kidd, Thomas S. *George Whitefield: America's Spiritual Founding Father*. New Haven: Yale University Press, 2014.

Kline, Christina Baker. *Orphan Train*. New York: William Morrow, 2013.

Krupat, Arnold. "I Talk White Nicely: The 1890 Letters of Returned Students from Carlisle." In *Boarding School Voices: Carlisle Indian School Students Speak*. Lincoln: University of Nebraska Press, 2021.

Lindsey, Duncan. *The Welfare of Children*. 2nd ed. Oxford: Oxford University Press, 2003.

Lynch, Gordon. *Remembering Child Migration: Faith, Nation-Building, and the Wounds of Charity*. New York: Bloomsbury Academic, 2015.

Maas, Henry, and Richard Engler. *Children in Need of Parents*. New York: Columbia University Press, 1959.

Magnuson, James, and Dorothea G. Petrie. *Orphan Train*. New York: Dial Press, 1978.

Maraniss, David. *Path Lit by Lightning: The Life of Jim Thorpe*. New York: Simon & Schuster, 2022.

Miller, Julie. *Abandoned: Foundlings in Nineteenth-Century New York City*. New York: New York University Press, 2008.

Myers, John E. B. *Child Protection in America: Past, Present, and Future*. Oxford: Oxford University Press, 2006.

Newland, Bryan. "Federal Indian Boarding School Initiative Investigative Report." Washington, DC: US Department of the Interior, Office of the Secretary, 2022.

Nietfeld, Emi. *Acceptance*. New York: Penguin Press, 2022.

Nixon, Joan Lowery. *The Orphan Train Adventures: A Family Apart*. New York: Bantam Doubleday Dell Books for Young Readers, 1987.

Nixon, Joan Lowery. *The Orphan Train Adventures: Caught in the Act*. New York: Bantam Doubleday Dell Books for Young Readers, 1988.

O'Connor, Stephen. *Orphan Trains: The Story of Charles Loring Brace and the Children He Saved and Failed*. Chicago: University of Chicago Press, 2004.

Orphan Train Heritage Society of America. *Orphan Train Riders: Their Own Stories*. Vol. 5. Little Rock: Orphan Train Heritage Society of America, 1999.

Orphan Train Heritage Society of America. *Orphan Train Riders: Their Own Stories*. Vol. 6. Little Rock: Orphan Train Heritage Society of America, 2007.

Pelton, Leroy. *For Reasons of Poverty: A Critical Analysis of the Child Welfare System of the United States*. New York: Praeger, 1998.

Perry, Samuel L. *Growing God's Family: The Global Orphan Care Movement and the Limits of Evangelical Activism*. New York: New York University Press, 2017.

Pope, Andrew. "Making Motherhood a Felony: African American Women's Welfare Rights Activism in New Orleans and the End of Suitable Home Laws, 1959–1962," *Journal of American History* 105, no. 2 (September 2018): 291–310.

Pratt, Richard Henry. *Battlefield and Classroom: Four Decades with the American Indian, 1867–1904*. Norman: University of Oklahoma Press, 2003.

Proceedings of the Conference on the Care of Dependent Children Held at Washington, D.C., January 25, 26, 1909. Washington, DC: Government Printing Office: 1909.

Raz, Mical. *Abusive Policies: How the American Child Welfare System Lost Its Way.* Chapel Hill, NC: University of North Carolina Press, 2020.

Riis, Jacob. *How the Other Half Lives: Studies Among the Tenements of New York.* New York: Charles Scribner's Sons, 1914.

Roberts, Dorothy. *Shattered Bonds: The Color of Child Welfare.* New York: Basic Books, 2002.

Roberts, Dorothy. *Torn Apart: How the Child Welfare System Destroys Black Families—and How Abolition Can Build a Safer World.* New York: Basic Books, 2022.

Rymph, Catherine E. *Raising Government Children: A History of Foster Care and the American Welfare State.* Chapel Hill, NC: University of North Carolina Press, 2017.

Seraile, William. *Angels of Mercy: White Women and the History of the Colored Orphan Asylum.* New York: Empire State Editions, 2011.

Skocpol, Theda. *Protecting Soldiers and Mothers: The Political Origins of Social Policy in the United States.* Cambridge, MA: Harvard University Press, 1995.

Theimer, Kate. *Walking Tour of the Grounds of the Carlisle Indian Industrial School.* Carlisle, PA: Cumberland County Historical Society, 2022.

Trafzer, Charles E., Jean A. Keller, and Lorene Sisquoc, eds. *Boarding School Blues: Revisiting American Indian Educational Experiences.* Lincoln, NE: Bison Books, 2006.

Trammell, Rebecca S. "Orphan Train Myths and Legal Reality." *Modern American* 5, no. 2 (fall 2009), 3–13.

Tripp, Valerie. *Changes for Samantha: A Winter Story.* Middleton, WI: Pleasant Company, 1988.

Vidal, Gore. *Imperial America: Reflections on the United States of Amnesia.* New York: Nation Books, 2004.

Warner, Gertrude Chandler. *The Box-Car Children: The Original 1924 Edition*. Mineola, NY: Dover, 2020.

Warner, Gertrude Chandler. *The Boxcar Children, Book 1*. Chicago: Albert Whitman & Company, 1942.

Warner, Gertrude Chandler. *The Boxcar Children, Book 105: The Mystery of the Orphan Train*. Chicago: Albert Whitman & Company: 2005.

Warren, Andrea. *We Rode the Orphan Trains*. Boston: Houghton Mifflin Company, 2001.

Welter, Barbara. "The Cult of True Womanhood: 1820–1860." *American Quarterly* 18, no. 2, pt. 1 (summer 1966): 151–174.

Williams, Heather Andrea. *Help Me to Find My People: The African American Search for Family Lost in Slavery*. Chapel Hill, NC: University of North Carolina Press, 2012.

Woolford, Andrew. *This Benevolent Experiment: Indigenous Boarding Schools, Genocide, and Redress in Canada and the United States*. Lincoln: University of Nebraska Press, 2015.

Zelizer, Viviana. *Pricing the Priceless Child: The Changing Social Value of Children*. Princeton, NJ: Princeton University Press, 1994.

NOTES

Introduction: Americans Love Orphans

1. "Survey of Income and Program Participation (SIPP)," US Census Bureau, last modified February 12, 2024, https://www.census.gov/programs-surveys/sipp.html.

2. Zachary Scherer, "When Do We Lose Our Parents?," US Census Bureau, May 6, 2019, https://www.census.gov/library/stories/2019/05/when-do-we-lose-our-parents.html.

3. "Losing Our Parents: Recent Statistics on Parent Mortality and Change During the Coronavirus (COVID-19) Pandemic," US Census Bureau, last modified February 1, 2024, https://www.census.gov/library/visualizations/interactive/losing-our-parents.html.

4. "POP1 Child Population: Number of Children (in Millions) Ages 0–17 in the United States by Age, 1950–2022 and Projected 2023–2050," Federal Interagency Forum on Child and Family Statistics, accessed April 11, 2024, https://www.childstats.gov/americaschildren/tables/pop1.asp.

5. "Orphan Statistics Explained," Schuster Institute for Investigative Journalism, Brandeis University, last modified February 23, 2011, https://web.archive.org/web/20230123145633/https://www.brandeis.edu/investigate/adoption/orphan-statistics.html.

6. Crenson, 335n25.

7. "History," National Orphan Train Complex, accessed April 11, 2024, https://orphantraindepot.org/history.

8. "The AFCARS Report: Preliminary FY 2022 Estimates as of May 9, 2023—No. 30," US Department of Health and Human Services, Children's Bureau, March 13, 2024, https://www.acf.hhs.gov/sites/default/files/documents/cb/afcars-report-30.pdf, 1.

9. "The AFCARS Report: Preliminary Estimates," 3.

10. Fong, 2.

11. "The AFCARS Report: Preliminary Estimates," 2; "POP3 Race and Hispanic Origin Composition: Percentage of U.S. Children Ages 0–17 by Race and Hispanic Origin, 1980–2022 and Projected 2023–2050," Federal Interagency Forum on Child and Family Statistics, accessed April 11, 2024, https://www.childstats.gov/americaschildren/tables/pop3.asp.

Chapter One: It's the Hard-Knock Life

1. Walter Kerr, "Nothing's Comic About Annie," *New York Times*, September 5, 1976, https://www.nytimes.com/1976/09/05/archives/stage-view-nothings-comic-about-annie.html.

2. Richard Keys Rein, "Freckles and Charm," *People*, July 12, 1982, https://people.com/archive/cover-story-freckles-and-charm-vol-18-no-2.

3. It would later run in the *Chicago Tribune* and other Tribune-owned publications.

4. Jeet Heer, "Jeet Heer on the Complex Origins of Little Orphan Annie," *Literary Hub*, August 3, 2020, https://lithub.com/jeet-heer-on-the-complex-origins-of-little-orphan-annie.

5. "'Little Orphant Annie' (1918) with Colleen Moore," video posted to YouTube by Silent Hall of Fame, October 31, 2021, https://www.youtube.com/watch?v=sduwxYTUPB4.

6. "James Whitcomb Riley," Academy of American Poets, accessed April 11, 2024, https://poets.org/poet/james-whitcomb-riley.

7. "'Raggedy Man' and 'Little Orphant Annie,'" Lilly Library, Indiana University, accessed April 11, 2024, https://wayback.archive-it.org/219/20061219000603/http://www.iub.edu/~liblilly/riley/exhibit.htm.

8. Sadie Stein, "Gobble-uns," *Paris Review*, October 7, 2014, https://www.theparisreview.org/blog/2014/10/07/gobble-uns.

9. Heer, "Jeet Heer on the Complex Origins of Little Orphan Annie."

10. August 29, 1924, strip, in Gray, 1:43.

11. Strip intended for August 30, 1924, in Gray, 1:32.

12. October 23, 1924, strip, in Gray, 1:58.

13. January 5, 1925, strip, in Gray, 1:80.

14. Tom Spurgeon, "CR Holiday Interview #2: Jeet Heer on Little Orphan Annie," *Comics Reporter*, December 23, 2008, https://www.comicsreporter.com/index.php/cr_holiday_interview_2_jeet_heer_on_little_orphan_annie.

15. Heer, "Jeet Heer on the Complex Origins of Little Orphan Annie."

16. Jeet Heer, "Harold Gray and the Limits of Conservative Anti-racism," *Comics Journal*, July 7, 2014, https://www.tcj.com/harold-gray-and-the-limits-of-conservative-anti-racism.

17. Brian Cronin, "When Daddy Warbucks Celebrated the Death of Franklin Delano Roosevelt," *CBR*, February 10, 2019, https://www.cbr.com/annie-daddy-warbucks-roosevelt-death-celebration.

18. Richard Sandomir, "Martin Charnin, Who Brought 'Annie' to the Stage, Dies at 84," *New York Times*, July 8, 2017, https://www.nytimes.com/2019/07/08/theater/martin-charnin-who-helped-create-annie-dies-at-84.html; Richard F. Shepard, "Leapin' Lizards! It's Orphan Annie," *New York Times*, March 24, 1977, https://www.nytimes.com/1977/03/24/archives/leapin-lizards-its-orphan-annie.html.

19. November 22, 1924, strip, in Gray, 1:68.

20. Thomas Meehan, "On Making Little Orphan Annie Sing and Dance," *New York Times*, April 17, 1977, https://www.nytimes.com/1977/04/17/archives/on-making-little-orphan-annie-sing-and-dance-making-orphan-annie.html.

21. Robert McG. Thomas Jr., "'Annie' Sweeps 7 Tonys; 'Shadow Box' Named Top Play," *New York Times*, June 6, 1977, https://www.nytimes.com/1977/06/06/archives/annie-sweeps-7 -tonys-shadow-box-named-top-play-dorothy-loudon-julie.html.

22. A. H. Weiler, "$9.5 Million for Filming 'Annie,'" *New York Times*, December 30, 1977, https://www.nytimes.com/1977/12/30/archives/95-million-for-filming-annie.html.

23. Noel Murray, "'Annie Live!' Review: The Sun, as Always, Came Out," *New York Times*, December 3, 2021, https://www.nytimes.com/2021/12/03/arts/television/annie-live -review.html.

24. "The Hidden U.S. COVID-19 Pandemic: Orphaned Children—More Than 140,000 U.S. Children Lost a Primary or Secondary Caregiver Due to the COVID-19 Pandemic," Centers for Disease Control and Prevention, last modified October 7, 2021, https://archive.cdc .gov/#/details?url=https://www.cdc.gov/media/releases/2021/p1007-covid-19-orphaned-chil dren.html.

Chapter Two: Indoctrinating Poor Children

1. Heer, "Jeet Heer on the Complex Origins of Little Orphan Annie."

2. Judy Klemesrud, "Seven Splendid Reasons Why 'Annie' Is a Smash," *New York Times*, May 1, 1977, https://www.nytimes.com/1977/05/01/archives/seven-splendid-reasons-why -annie-is-a-smash-seven-reasons-why.html.

3. Hacsi, 11.

4. Zelizer, 59.

5. Hacsi, 17.

6. Hacsi, 18; Kidd, 101.

7. Kidd, 110; "George Whitefield," Penn & Slavery Project, accessed April 11, 2024, https://pennandslaveryproject.org/exhibits/show/campus/earlycampus/georgewhitefield.

8. "Major American Epidemics of Yellow Fever (1793–1905)," American Experience, WGBH Educational Foundation, accessed April 11, 2024, https://www.pbs.org/wgbh/american experience/features/fever-major-american-epidemics-of-yellow-fever.

9. Holly Caldwell, "Orphanages and Orphans," Encyclopedia of Greater Philadelphia, accessed April 11, 2024, https://philadelphiaencyclopedia.org/essays/orphanages-and-orphans; "Washington Square," National Parks Service, last updated February 7, 2024, https://www .nps.gov/inde/learn/historyculture/places-washingtonsquare.htm.

10. Dana Robinson and Ann Battenfield, "The Worst Outbreaks in U.S. History," *Healthline*, last modified May 10, 2023, https://www.healthline.com/health/worst-disease -outbreaks-history#cholera; "Cholera Epidemics in the 19th Century," Curiosity Collections, Harvard Library, accessed April 11, 2024, https://curiosity.lib.harvard.edu/contagion/feature /cholera-epidemics-in-the-19th-century.

11. Hacsi, 24.

12. "Eleventh Census—Volume 3 (Part I & Part II). Report on Crime, Pauperism, and Benevolence in the United States: Inmates of Benevolent Institutions," US Census Bureau, 1895, https://www2.census.gov/library/publications/decennial/1890/volume-3/1890a_v3p1 -04.pdf.

13. "Eleventh Census," 366.

14. Kenneally, 57; Crenson, 17n25.

15. Katz, 4–5.

16. Katz, 5–6.

17. "Total and Foreign-born Population New York City, 1790–2000*," New York Department of City Planning, Population Division, accessed April 11, 2024, https://www1 .nyc.gov/assets/planning/download/pdf/data-maps/nyc-population/historical-population /1790-2000_nyc_total_foreign_birth.pdf.

18. Hacsi, 19, 53.

19. Crenson, 37–38.

20. Hacsi, 17.

21. Zelizer, 3.

22. Hacsi, 52–53.

23. Hacsi, 19.

24. Firor Scott, 12.

25. Isabella Graham, *The Power of Faith, Exemplified in the Life and Writings of the Late Mrs. Isabella Graham*, July 12, 2005, https://www.gutenberg.org/files/16276/16276-h /16276-h.htm.

26. "History," Graham Windham, accessed April 11, 2024, https://www.graham-windham .org/about-us/history.

27. "Home," Eliza's Story, accessed April 11, 2024, elizasstory.org.

28. "Our History," Sisters of Charity of New York, accessed April 11, 2024, https://scny .org/about-us/our-history.

29. Michael Barga, "The Sisters of Charity of New York," VCU Libraries Social Welfare History Project, 2013, https://socialwelfare.library.vcu.edu/programs/child-welfarechild-labor /the-sisters-of-charity-of-new-york.

30. "A Short History of the Sisters of Charity," Emmitsburg Area Historical Society, accessed April 11, 2024, http://www.emmitsburg.net/archive_list/articles/history/stories /sisters_of_charity.htm.

31. Hacsi, 89–91.

32. Brown and McKeown, 3; Hacsi, 55–56.

33. Crenson, 42–43.

34. Hacsi, 53.

35. Based on Hacsi, chap. 5.

36. Based on Hacsi, chap. 6.

37. Hacsi, 131.

38. Hacsi, 94.

39. Hacsi, 106.

40. Katz, 14–15.

41. Katz, 17.

42. Katz, x.

43. Katz, 3.

44. Katz, 17–18, 41–43.

45. Katz, 23.

46. Katz, 29.

47. Katz, 25–26.

48. Katz, 30.

49. Quoted in Crenson, 46–47.

50. Crenson, 3.

51. Hon. Wm. P. Letchworth, "Removal of Children from Almshouses in the State of New York (1894)," VCU Libraries Social Welfare History Project, accessed April 11, 2024, https://socialwelfare.library.vcu.edu/programs/child-welfarechild-labor/removal-children -almshouses-state-new-york-1894.

52. Crenson, 49.

53. Crenson, 50.

Chapter Three: Black Children, White Property; Black Orphans, White Saviors

1. Hilary Lewis, "NBC Finds Its Annie for Upcoming Live Musical," *Hollywood Reporter*, August 24, 2001, https://www.hollywoodreporter.com/tv/tv-news/nbc-annie-live-musical -celina-smith-1235002117.

2. Daniel D'Addario, "'Annie Live!' Is a Spirited, Likable Reprieve from Hard Times: TV Review," *Variety*, December 2, 2021, https://variety.com/2021/tv/reviews/annie-live -review-1235125225.

3. Billingsley and Giovannoni, 23.

4. Billingsley and Giovannoni, 24.

5. Roberts, *Torn Apart*, 88.

6. Title of chap. 4, in Roberts, *Torn Apart*, 85.

7. Briggs, *Taking Children*, 19–20; Roberts, *Torn Apart*, 90.

8. Briggs, *Taking Children*, 20.

9. Briggs, *Taking Children*, 45.

10. Du Bois, 21.

11. Anne C. Bailey, "They Sold Human Beings Here," *New York Times Magazine*, February 12, 2020. https://www.nytimes.com/interactive/2020/02/12/magazine/1619-project -slave-auction-sites.html.

12. Williams, 25.

13. Williams, 23–24.

14. Williams, 23–24.

15. Williams, 24.

16. Williams, 25.

17. It is this kind of history that far-right Republicans are writing out of American children's education. In Texas in 2021, Governor Greg Abbott signed into law a so-called critical race theory ban that, among other provisions, bars social studies teachers at K-12 schools from teaching concepts that might cause students to "feel discomfort, guilt, anguish, or any other form of psychological distress" because of their "race or sex." This law essentially makes it illegal to make white children think about racism, let alone slavery. See Isabella Zou and Jason Kao, "Texas Teachers Say GOP's New Social Studies Law Will Hinder How an Entire Generation Understands Race, History, and

Current Events," *Texas Tribune*, August 3, 2021, https://www.texastribune.org/2021/08/03
/texas-critical-race-theory-social-studies-teachers.

18. Briggs, *Taking Children*, 15.

19. Briggs, *Taking Children*, 6.

20. Briggs, *Taking Children*, 7–8.

21. "Uncle Tom's Cabin, 1852," Granger Historical Picture Archive, accessed April 11,
2024, https://www.granger.com/results.asp?image=0037771.

22. Roberts, *Torn Apart*, 97.

23. "Religion and the Founding of the American Republic," Library of Congress,
accessed May 1, 2024, https://www.loc.gov/exhibits/religion/rel01-2.html.

24. "Germantown Quaker Petition Against Slavery," National Park Service, accessed
May 1, 2024, https://www.nps.gov/articles/quakerpetition.htm.

25. "Germantown Friends' Protest Against Slavery 1688. [Facsimile]," Library of Congress, accessed June 4, 2024, https://www.loc.gov/resource/rbpe.14000200/?st=text.

26. Seraile, 2–3.

27. "Association for the Care of Colored Orphans Records," TriCollege Libraries Digital Collections, accessed April 11, 2024, https://digitalcollections.tricolib.brynmawr.edu
/collections/association-care-colored-orphans-records.

28. "The Fifth Annual Report of the Association for the Care of Colored Orphans," Tri-
College Libraries Digital Collections, accessed May 1, 2024, https://digitalcollections.tricolib
.brynmawr.edu/object/sc211636.

29. "The Fifth Annual Report of the Association for the Care of Colored Orphans," 6.

30. Seraile, 8; Billingsley and Giovannoni, 26–27; *From Cherry Street to Green Pastures:
A History of the Colored Orphan Asylum at Riverdale on Hudson*, Association for the Benefit of
Colored Orphans Records, MS 24, The New-York Historical Society, Records of the Association for the Benefit of Colored Orphans, Series X: Centennial Booklet, 1936, https://digital
collections.nyhistory.org/islandora/object/islandora%3A131345#page/2/mode/1up.

31. *From Cherry Street to Green Pastures*, 3.

32. Seraile, 8–9.

33. "Race and Antebellum New York City: The New York Manumission Society,"
Examination Days: Thee New York African Free School Collection, New-York Historical Society, accessed April 11, 2024, https://www.nyhistory.org/web/africanfreeschool/history/manu
mission-society.html.

34. Seraile, 5.

35. Seraile, 11.

36. Seraile, 15–16.

37. Seraile, 16; Billingsley and Giovannoni, 27.

38. Cited in Seraile, 18.

39. Billingsley and Giovannoni, 30.

40. Seraile, 6; "M-002 Astor, John Jacob (Correspondence)," St. Louis Mercantile
Library, accessed April 11, 2024, http://www.umsl.edu/mercantile/collections/mercantile
-library-special-collections/special_collections/slma-002.html.

41. Nathan Tempey, "NYC Doesn't Fly Confederate Flags, but It's Still a Shrine to Slave-owners and Slave Profiteers," *Gothamist*, June 6, 2015, https://gothamist.com/news/nyc-doesnt-fly-confederate-flags-but-its-still-a-shrine-to-slaveowners-slave-profiteers.

42. Seraile, 63.

43. Seraile, 6; "Slave Market," Mapping the African American Past, accessed April 11, 2024, https://maap.columbia.edu/place/22.html; Seraile, 4.

44. Seraile, 4.

45. Seraile, 19.

46. Billingsley and Giovannoni, 28–29.

47. Seraile, 31; "Colored Orphan Asylum," Mapping the African American Past, accessed April 11, 2024, https://maap.columbia.edu/place/35.html.

48. "An Act for Enrolling and Calling Out the National Forces, and for Other Purposes," Congressional Record, 37th Cong., 3d. Sess., Ch. 74, 75, March 3, 1863, https://glc.yale.edu/act-enrolling-and-calling-out-national-forces.

49. Seraile, 65.

50. Seraile, 69; Leslie M. Harris, *In the Shadow of Slavery: African Americans in New York City, 1626–1863* (Chicago: University of Chicago Press, 2003), 279–288.

51. David W. Dunlop, "Remembering a Vile Civil War Act, on Fifth Avenue," *New York Times*, February 18, 2016, https://www.nytimes.com/2016/02/18/nyregion/remembering-a-vile-civil-war-act-on-fifth-avenue.html.

52. Seraile, 70.

53. "Vol. 3, Minutes of the July 25, 1863 Board Meeting," Records of the Association for the Benefit of Colored Orphans, 1836–1972 (bulk 1850–1936), Series I: Minutes of Board Meetings, 1836–1936, The New-York Historical Society, https://cdm16694.contentdm.oclc.org/digital/collection/p15052coll5/id/32205.

54. "Blackwell's Island (Roosevelt Island), New York City," National Park Service, accessed April 11, 2024, https://www.nps.gov/places/blackwell-s-island-new-york-city.htm; Seraile, 70–71.

55. "The Colored Orphan's Asylum," *New York Times*, August 1, 1863, https://www.nytimes.com/1863/08/01/archives/the-colored-orphan-asylum.html.

56. "Hamilton Grange," National Park Service, accessed April 11, 2024, https://www.nps.gov/hagr/index.htm.

57. Billingsley and Giovannoni, 52–53.

58. Jones-Rogers, 187.

59. Roberts, *Torn Apart*, 97–98; "On This Day: Nov 22, 1865, Mississippi Authorizes 'Sale' of Black Orphans to White 'Masters or Mistresses,'" A History of Racial Injustice, Equal Justice Initiative, accessed April 11, 2024, https://calendar.eji.org/racial-injustice/nov/22.

60. "The Freedmen's Bureau," African American Heritage, National Archives, last modified October 28, 2021, https://www.archives.gov/research/african-americans/freedmens-bureau.

61. Jones-Rogers, 188; Roberts, *Torn Apart*, 96.

62. Jones-Rogers, 188.

Chapter Four: The Dawn of Child Abuse and the Progressive Campaign to Save Children

1. "The Mission of Humanity," *New York Times*, April 11, 1874, https://timesmachine.nytimes.com/timesmachine/1874/04/11/79069541.pdf; Costin, 207; "Mary Ellen Wilson," American Humane Association, accessed April 12, 2024, https://web.archive.org/web/20110519134618/http://www.americanhmane.org/about-us/who-we-are/history/mary-ellen-wilson.html; "Mr. Bergh Enlarging His Sphere of Usefulness," *New York Times*, April 10, 1874, https://timesmachine.nytimes.com/timesmachine/1874/04/10/79069479.pdf.

2. "Mr. Bergh Enlarging His Sphere of Usefulness."

3. "The Story of Mary Ellen," American Humane Association, accessed April 12, 2024, https://web.archive.org/web/20110514072857/http://www.americanhumane.org/about-us/who-we-are/history/story-of-mary-ellen.html.

4. "The Story of Mary Ellen."

5. Costin, 207.

6. Costin, 205.

7. Costin, 206.

8. Costin, 207.

9. "Mary Ellen Wilson. Mrs. Connolly, the Guardian, Found Guilty, and Sentenced to One Year's Imprisonment at Hard Labor," *New York Times*, April 28, 1874, https://timesmachine.nytimes.com/timesmachine/1874/04/28/79072965.pdf.

10. Costin, 209; "The Story of Mary Ellen."

11. Costin, 207; search of the *New York Times* archives.

12. "Mary Ellen Wilson. Further Testimony in the Case—Two Indictments Found Against Mrs. Connolly by the Grand Jury," *New York Times*, April 14, 1874, https://timesmachine.nytimes.com/timesmachine/1874/04/14/79070043.pdf.

13. Aaron O'Neill, "Child Mortality Rate (Under Five Years Old) in the United States, from 1800 to 2020*," Statista, February 2, 2024, https://www.statista.com/statistics/1041693/united-states-all-time-child-mortality-rate.

14. Gordon, 33.

15. Costin, 209.

16. "Our Founder's Legacy," St. Christopher's, accessed April 12, 2024, https://mystchristophers.org/about-us/our-founder-her-legacy/our-founder-her-legacy.html.

17. "Waifs and Strays," *New York Times*, April 11, 1874, https://timesmachine.nytimes.com/timesmachine/1874/04/11/79069606.pdf.

18. Myers, 35–36; Pelton, 11.

19. Hacsi, 106.

20. "The New York Society for the Prevention of Cruelty to Children, 125th Anniversary, 1875–2000," nyspcc.org, accessed May 2, 2024, https://nyspcc.org/wp-content/uploads/2021/01/booklet.pdf, 7.

21. The organization still exists and is a 501 (c)(3) nonprofit but no longer serves a policing function.

22. "The New York Society for the Prevention of Cruelty to Children," 8.

23. "The New York Society for the Prevention of Cruelty to Children," 9.

24. "The New York Society for the Prevention of Cruelty to Children," 8–9.

25. Costin, 219.

26. Quoted in Costin, 218.

27. Ehrenreich, 20–21.

28. Ehrenreich, 22.

29. Costin, 205.

30. Costin, 215.

31. "About Us," Massachusetts Society for the Prevention of Cruelty, accessed April 12, 2024, https://www.mspcc.org/about.

32. Gordon, 33.

33. Gordon, 35.

34. Gordon, 37.

35. Gordon, 48.

36. "1860–1900: The Friendly Visitor," Global Institute of Social Work, accessed April 12, 2024, https://www.thegisw.org/copy-of-charity-organization-societ; Marian C. Putnam, "Friendly Visiting," Presentation at the Annual Meeting of the National Conference of Charities and Correction, 1887, accessed April 12, 2024, https://socialwelfare.library.vcu.edu/eras/civil-war-reconstruction/friendly-visitors-1887.

37. Myers, 38.

38. Gordon, 46–47.

39. Ehrenreich, 24.

40. Ehrenreich, 25.

41. Ehrenreich, 26–27.

42. Ehrenreich, 28.

43. Ehrenreich, 29.

44. Ehrenreich, 36–37.

45. Ehrenreich, 34.

46. John E. Hansan, "Charity Organization Societies (1877–1893)," Social Welfare History Project, accessed April 12, 2024, https://socialwelfare.library.vcu.edu/eras/civil-war-reconstruction/charity-organization-societies-1877-1893.

47. Ehrenreich, 62.

48. "About Jane Addams and Hull-House Settlement," Jane Addams Hull-House Museum, accessed April 12, 2024, https://www.hullhousemuseum.org/about-jane-addams.

49. Ehrenreich, 62.

50. "About Jane Addams and Hull-House Settlement."

51. Cathy Moran Ajo, "Questions About Settlements? Ask Jane!," Jane Addams Papers Project, Ramapo College, July 12, 2016, https://janeaddams.ramapo.edu/2016/07/questions-about-settlements-ask-jane.

52. Quoted in Angie C. Kennedy, "Eugenics, 'Degenerate Girls,' and Social Workers During the Progressive Era," *Affilia: Journal of Women and Social Work* 23, no. 1 (February 2008): 29, https://journals-sagepub-com.proxy.library.upenn.edu/doi/10.1177/08861099073 10473.

53. Stacy Lynn, "Jane Addams, Ida B. Wells, and Racial Injustice in America," Jane Addams Papers Project, Ramapo College, August 22, 2018, https://janeaddams.ramapo .edu/2018/08/jane-addams-ida-b-wells-and-racial-injustice-in-america.

54. "About Jane Addams and Hull-House Settlement"; "About Jane Addams Hull-House Museum," Jane Addams Hull-House Museum, accessed April 12, 2024, https://www .hullhousemuseum.org/about-us.

55. "Get to Know JPA," Juvenile Protective Association, accessed April 12, 2024, https://www.jpachicago.org/about.

56. Crenson, 19.

57. "James E. West Chief Scout Executive," Order of the Arrow, Boy Scouts of America, accessed April 12, 2024, https://oa-bsa.org/history/james-e-west-chief-scout-executive; Crenson, 7–8.

58. Crenson, 7.

59. "Our History: James E. West Chief Scout Executive," Order of the Arrow, Boy Scouts of America, accessed April 12, 2024, https://oa-bsa.org/history/james-e-west -chief-scout-executive.

60. Crenson, 7–8.

61. Crenson, 9.

62. Jambor, 35.

63. "The Delineator Child-Rescue Campaign," *The Delineator* 70, no. 5 (November 1907): 715, https://babel.hathitrust.org/cgi/pt?id=mdp.39015080400750&view=1up&seq =71&q1=child-rescue.

64. Quoted in Crenson, 10.

65. "The Delineator Child-Rescue Campaign," 716.

66. Quoted in Crenson, 10.

67. "The Delineator Child-Rescue Campaign: The First Anniversary of a Notable Movement to Find Good Homes for the Dependent Children of America," *The Delineator* 72, no. 4 (October 1908): 575, https://babel.hathitrust.org/cgi/pt?id=mdp.39015080400776&seq=114.

68. All examples are from *The Delineator* 72, no. 5 (November 1908), https://babel .hathitrust.org/cgi/pt?id=mdp.39015080400768&view=1up&seq=5.

69. Crenson, 10.

70. "The Delineator Child-Rescue Campaign," 718.

71. Crenson, 10.

72. *Proceedings of the Conference on the Care of Dependent Children*, 18.

73. *Proceedings of the Conference on the Care of Dependent Children*, 17.

74. *Proceedings of the Conference on the Care of Dependent Children*, 32; Crenson 33.

75. *Proceedings of the Conference on the Care of Dependent Children*, 27.

76. *Proceedings of the Conference on the Care of Dependent Children*, 26.

77. "Folks, Holmer," Social Welfare History Project, accessed April 14, 2024, https:// socialwelfare.library.vcu.edu/people/folks-homer-4.

78. Deduced via a search of the text of the *Proceedings of the Conference on the Care of Dependent Children*. Bergh and Gerry were not invited, and "Society for the Prevention of Cruelty" does not appear in the invitation list.

79. *Proceedings of the Conference on the Care of Dependent Children*, 5.

80. *Proceedings of the Conference on the Care of Dependent Children*, 5–6.

81. *Proceedings of the Conference on the Care of Dependent Children*, 10.

82. *Proceedings of the Conference on the Care of Dependent Children*, 11.

83. *Proceedings of the Conference on the Care of Dependent Children*, 11–12.

84. *Proceedings of the Conference on the Care of Dependent Children*, 14.

85. Kenneally, 294.

Chapter Five: Make Something of Yourself in the West

1. A search of "orphan train" on Goodreads on October 9, 2023, pulled up 457 results, many of them self-published; "History," National Orphan Train Complex, accessed April 11, 2024, https://orphantraindepot.org/history.

2. O'Connor, xix.

3. Nixon, *The Orphan Train Adventures: A Family Apart*.

4. Magnuson and Petrie, 41.

5. Magnuson and Petrie, 22.

6. Magnuson and Petrie, 22.

7. Magnuson and Petrie, 54.

8. Magnuson and Petrie, 42.

9. Magnuson and Petrie, 80–81.

10. Brace, n.p.

11. Magnuson and Petrie, 60, 158.

12. Nixon, *The Orphan Train Adventures: A Family Apart*, 48.

13. Nixon, *The Orphan Train Adventures: A Family Apart*, 152.

14. Based on a search of the Publishers Marketplace archive of best-seller lists. Kline's *Orphan Train* was number one on the *New York Times* paperback fiction list for the weeks of March 16, 23, and 30, 2014, and April 6, 2014.

15. Kline, 23.

16. Kline, 110.

17. Kline, prologue (unpaginated).

Chapter Six: Train Cars Full of "Dangerous" Children

1. Records of the Children's Aid Society, The New-York Historical Society, Series X1.2, Box 46, Folder 4: Emigration/Placing-Out Program, Correspondence Received, 1860.

2. Records of the Children's Aid Society, The New-York Historical Society, Series X1.2, Box 46, Folder 6: Emigration/Placing-Out Program, Correspondence Received, 1861 February.

3. Records of the Children's Aid Society, The New-York Historical Society, Series X1.2, Box 46, Folder 8: Emigration/Placing-Out Program, Correspondence Received, 1861 April.

4. Records of the Children's Aid Society, The New-York Historical Society, Series III.1, Box 1023, Vol. 17, Annual Reports, 1856–1866, inclusive; 1861 annual report, 5.

5. "Life in Mid-19th Century Five Points," American Social History Project, accessed April 14, 2024, https://shec.ashp.cuny.edu/exhibits/show/life-in-five-points.

6. Charles Dickens, *American Notes for General Circulation* (London: Chapman Hall, 1913), https://www.gutenberg.org/files/675/675-h/675-h.htm.

7. O'Connor, 17.

8. O'Connor, 17.

9. O'Connor, 18.

10. O'Connor, 26.

11. O'Connor, 48.

12. O'Connor, 38.

13. Brace, n.p.

14. Brace, n.p.

15. Brace, n.p.

16. Brace, n.p.

17. Records of the Children's Aid Society, The New-York Historical Society, Series III.1, Box 1023, Vol. 16, Annual Reports, 1854–1855, inclusive; First Annual Report 1854, 3–4.

18. Brown and McKeown, 17; Brace, n.p.

19. Brace, n.p.

20. O'Connor, 107.

21. I constructed this sketch with background primarily from Stephen O'Connor's *Orphan Trains*, Marilyn Irvin Holt's *The Orphan Trains*, and Andrea Warren's *We Rode the Orphan Trains*.

22. "Jackson County Federal, Holton, Kansas, Thursday January 6, 1887," National Orphan Train Complex, accessed April 14, 2024, https://orphantraindepot.org/1-jackson-county -federal-holton-ks-th-6-jan-1887.

23. Holt, 62.

24. Lynch, 20–21.

25. Trammell, 4; O'Connor, 154, 173.

26. O'Connor, 96.

27. Cited in O'Connor, 253–254.

28. Records of the Children's Aid Society, The New-York Historical Society, Series V.2, Box 23, Folder 6: Clara Comstock, placing-out agent, memoir/address to CAS staff, and Helen Baxter's introductory remarks.

29. Herman, 307n17.

30. Johnson, 2:305; other details in this paragraph are from Johnson, 2:306, 308.

31. Johnson, 2:341–343.

32. Johnson, 2:341–342.

33. Quoted in Warren, 14. She also speaks in the 1995 PBS documentary *American Experience: The Orphan Trains*, directed by Janet Graham and Edward Gray.

34. Johnson, 1:213–219.

35. Johnson, 1:215.

36. O'Connor, 307–308.

Chapter Seven: Catholic Remedies for "Fallen Women" and Foundlings

1. "Who We Are: Making History Together," New York Foundling, accessed April 14, 2024, https://www.nyfoundling.org/who-we-are/history.

2. The Sisters of Charity of Mount St. Vincent, *The New York Foundling Hospital: Its Foundress and Its Place in the Community* (New York: Sisters of Charity of Mount St. Vincent, 1944), 12; Records of the New York Foundling Hospital, MS 347, The New-York Historical Society, Series IX, Box 57, Folder 2, Histories, 1917–1939, inclusive; undated history, 2.

3. Records of the New York Foundling Hospital, MS 347, The New-York Historical Society, Series II, Box 80, Vol. 15: Biennial Reports, 1870–1883, inclusive; first annual report opening letter.

4. Records of the New York Foundling Hospital, MS 347, The New-York Historical Society, Series IX, Box 57, Folder 2, Histories, 1917–1939, inclusive; undated history, 2.

5. The organization's original full name includes "of the Sisters of Charity in the City of New York."

6. Records of the New York Foundling Hospital, MS 347, The New-York Historical Society, Series II, Box 80, Vol. 15: Biennial Reports, 1870–1883; 1873 report, 9.

7. Ibid., 12.

8. Ibid., 10.

9. "Who We Are: Making History Together."

10. Creagh, 203.

11. Creagh, 203.

12. Records of the New York Foundling Hospital, MS 347, The New-York Historical Society, Series IV.30, Box 35, Folder 2: "Orphan Train"—Application and Indenture forms, 1909 and undated.

13. Creagh, 198; Herman, 126.

14. Dianne Creagh, "Faith in Fostering: Catholic Adoption and Boarding-Out in Depression-Era New York," *American Catholic Studies* 122, no. 1 (2011): 9; Miller, 3–4 (there were actually two Protestant foundling asylums: Infant's Home and the New York Infant Asylum).

15. Lemn Sissay, "Superman Was a Foundling," Foundling Museum, accessed April 14, 2024, https://foundlingmuseum.org.uk/event/superman-was-a-foundling.

16. Dana Goldstein, "Drop Box for Babies: Conservatives Promote a Way to Give Up Newborns Anonymously," *New York Times*, August 6, 2022, updated June 22, 2023, https://www.nytimes.com/2022/08/06/us/roe-safe-haven-laws-newborns.html.

17. During oral arguments in the *Dobbs* case in December 2021, Justice Amy Coney Barrett—a Donald Trump appointee and a conservative Catholic who adopted two children from Haiti—asked why safe haven laws don't "take care" of the "problem" of "the consequences of parenting and the obligations of motherhood that flow from pregnancy." This line of thinking creates a false equivalency between abortion and adoption, since the assumption is that babies surrendered would be available for adoption. From this viewpoint, being forced to endure pregnancy and its attendant risks does not matter. In the same oral arguments, Barrett referred to the decision as coming down to "the state requiring the woman to [be pregnant] 15, 16 weeks more and then terminate parental rights at the conclusion." (See "Thomas E. Dobbs, State Health Officer of the Mississippi Department of Health, et al. v. Jackson Women's Health Organization, et al.," Supreme Court of the United States, December 21, 2021, https://www.supremecourt.gov/oral_arguments/argument_transcripts/2021/19-1392_bq7d.pdf, 56–57.)

18. Goldstein, "Drop Box for Babies"; Luterman, "What Are Safe Haven Laws."

19. Research has proven that the vast majority of women who are denied abortions go on to raise the children they carry to term. See the Turnaway Study: "Adoption Decision Making Among Women Seeking Abortion," ANSIRH, March 1, 2017, https://www.ansirh.org/research/publication/adoption-decision-making-among-women-seeking-abortion.

20. Maria Laurino, "The Right's New Post-*Dobbs* Panacea: The Baby Safe Deposit Box," *New Republic*, June 29, 2023, https://newrepublic.com/article/173399/post-dobbs-panacea-baby-safe-deposit-box.

21. Miller, 227.

22. Miller, 14.

23. Miller, 18, 135–136; Laurino, "The Right's New Post-*Dobbs* Panacea."

24. Miller, 16–18.

25. Miller, 99, 101.

26. Miller, 99–103.

27. Miller, 17.

28. Miller, 41.

29. *Second Annual Report of the Metropolitan Board of Health of the State of New York* (New York: Union Printing House, 1867), 94, https://www.google.com/books/edition/Annual_report_of_the_Metropolitan_Board/pEToaUWG9gIC?hl=en&gbpv=1.

30. Even if they were taken in by institutions like the Foundling, infant mortality rates were appalling. An 1874 medical report from the Foundling notes that of the 1,125 babies taken in from October 1872 to October 1873, more than half—or 599—died. The babies died of a variety of ailments and diseases, ranging from intestinal issues to syphilis to "marasmus," or undernourishment. The physician who wrote the report noted that in the following year, when record-keeping was less precise, mortality rates were worsened by epidemics of diphtheria and measles. (See Records of the New York Foundling Hospital, MS 347, The New-York Historical Society, Series II, Box 80, Vol. 15: Biennial/Annual Reports, 1870–1884, inclusive.)

31. Miller, 5.

32. See Records of the New York Foundling Hospital, MS 347, The New-York Historical Society, Series IX, Box 57, Folder 1: Histories, 1869–1899, inclusive; typewritten copy of Sister Theresa Vincent's diary.

33. Records of the New York Foundling Hospital, MS 347, The New-York Historical Society, Series II, Box 80, Vol. 15: Biennial Reports, 1870–1883, inclusive; 1882 report, 8; Series IX, Box 57, Folder 2: Histories, 1917–1939, inclusive.

34. Brown and McKeown, 20.

35. Records of the New York Foundling Hospital, MS 347, The New-York Historical Society, Series II, Box 80, Vol. 15: Biennial Reports, 1870–1883, inclusive; 1882 report, 8–10.

36. Ibid., 8–9.

37. Holt, 15.

38. Welter, 152–153.

39. Welter, 171.

40. Miller, 10.

41. Records of the New York Foundling Hospital, MS 347, The New-York Historical Society, Series II, Box 80, Vol. 15: Biennial Reports, 1870–1883, inclusive; 1879–1881 report.

42. Rheann Kelly, Christina Kovats, and Natalie Medley, "What About the 'Lost Children' (and Mothers) of America?," The Marshall Project, March 11, 2017, https://www.themarshall project.org/2017/11/03/what-about-the-lost-children-and-mothers-of-america.

43. Ed O'Laughlin, "These Women Survived Ireland's Magdalene Laundries. They're Ready to Talk," New York Times, June 6, 2018, https://www.nytimes.com/2018/06/06/world /europe/magdalene-laundry-reunion-ireland.html.

44. Ed O'Laughlin, "A Blot on Ireland's Past, Facing Demolition," New York Times, January 15, 2018, https://www.nytimes.com/2018/01/15/world/europe/magdalene-laundries -ireland.html.

45. O'Laughlin, "These Women Survived Ireland's Magdalene Laundries."

46. Fintan O'Toole, "The Sisters of No Mercy," The Guardian, February 15, 2003, https://www.theguardian.com/film/2003/feb/16/features.review1; Carol Ryan, "Irish Church's Forgotten Victims Take Case to U.N.," New York Times, May 25, 2011, https://www.nytimes .com/2011/05/25/world/europe/25iht-abuse25.html. In the early 1990s, after the Sisters of Our Lady of Charity of Refuge sold their laundry to a developer, a mass grave with 155 bodies was discovered on the property. In 2011, an advocacy group called Justice for Magdalenes lobbied the United Nations Committee Against Torture to rebuke Ireland for its collusion in the human rights abuses that the laundries committed. Ireland responded with a 2013 state investigation that found "significant" state responsibility for the enslavement at the laundries, resulting in a formal apology from the Irish president and some financial reparations for survivors. (Harry McDonald, "Magdalene Laundries: Ireland Accepts State Guilt in Scandal," The Guardian, February 5, 2013, https://www.theguardian.com/world/2013/feb/05/magda lene-laundries-ireland-state-guilt; Michael Brennan, "Tearful Kenney Says Sorry to the Magdalene Women," Irish Independent, February 19, 2013, https://www.independent.ie/irishnews /tearful-kenny-says-sorry-to-the-magdalene-women-29082107.html.)

47. Kelly, Kovats, and Medley; Michelle Jones and Lori Record, "Magdalene Laundries: The First Prisons for Women in the United States," Journal of the Indiana Academy of the Social Sciences 17 (2014), https://drive.google.com/file/d/0B0WaPggKV2mkWXZXY0JEUS1HQWc /view?resourcekey=0-PG6Rypr1SgYCKVcBEpaBiQ.

48. Miller, 134; Fitzgerald, 45–58.

49. Brown and McKeown, 2.

50. Brown and McKeown, 17.

51. Brown and McKeown, 3, 15.

52. Miller, 62–65. Notably, the Foundling refused to take in the wet nurses' own children. See Records of the New York Foundling Hospital, MS 347, The New-York Historical Society, Series II, Box 80, Vol. 15: Biennial Reports, 1870–1883, inclusive; 1876 report, 12.

53. Records of the New York Foundling Hospital, MS 347, The New-York Historical Society, Series II, Box 80, Vol. 15: Biennial Reports, 1870–1883, inclusive; 1882 report.

54. Approximately 30,000 children, per O'Connor, xvii.

55. Creagh, 204.

56. Creagh, 204–205.

57. Holt, 110–113; Creagh, 206.

58. Records of the New York Foundling Hospital, MS 347, The New-York Historical Society, Series IV.30, Box 34, Folder 6: Orphan Train, Arizona Incident—Correspondence Photocopies, 1904 June 18–1914 June 29, Agent Swayne's report; Folder 8: Orphan Train, Arizona Incident—Newspaper Clippings (folder 1 of 2), 1904 October 4–1905 January 22; Herman, 126–127; Creagh, 206.

59. Records of the New York Foundling Hospital, MS 347, The New-York Historical Society, Series IV.30, Box 34, Folder 6: Orphan Train, Arizona Incident—Correspondence Photocopies, 1904 June 18–1914 June 29, Agent Swayne's report.

60. Records of the New York Foundling Hospital, MS 347, The New-York Historical Society, Series IV.30, Box 34, Folder 8: Orphan Train, Arizona Incident—Newspaper Clippings (folder 1 of 2), 1904 October 4–1905 January 22.

61. Ibid.

62. *New York Foundling Hospital v. Gatti*, 203 U.S. 429 (1906), https://caselaw.findlaw.com/us-supreme-court/203/429.html.

63. Records of the New York Foundling Hospital, MS 347, The New-York Historical Society, Series II, Box 80, Vol. 15: Biennial Reports, 1870–1883, inclusive; report 1879–1881.

64. Records of the New York Foundling Hospital, MS 347, The New-York Historical Society, Series II, Box 80, Vol. 17: Biennial/Annual Reports, 1870–1884, inclusive; report 1892–1893.

65. Records of the New York Foundling Hospital, MS 347, The New-York Historical Society, Series IV.30, Box 35, Folder 6: "Orphan Train"—Miscellaneous Correspondence and Other Materials, Circa 1984–1995, Helen Macior request form.

66. Records of the New York Foundling Hospital, MS 347, The New-York Historical Society, Series IV.30, Box 35, Folder 6: "Orphan Train"—Miscellaneous Correspondence and Other Materials, Circa 1984–1995, Marguerite Thomson request form.

67. O'Connor, 224–225.

68. Records of the New York Foundling Hospital, MS 347, The New-York Historical Society, Series III, Box 13, Folder 17: Correspondence with State Board of Charities, and Related Documents, 1893–1922, inclusive; 1900 letter to secretary of state charities board.

69. Records of the New York Foundling Hospital, MS 347, The New-York Historical Society, Series III, Box 13, Folder 20: Correspondence—Chief Examiner of Accounts of Institutions to Comptroller Edward Grout Arguing for Foundling Records' Secrecy—copy, 1903 April 20.

70. "Wants to Know His Parents," *New York Times*, July 6, 1900, https://timesmachine.nytimes.com/timesmachine/1900/07/06/102604958.pdf.

71. "Two Sisters Shot in Foundling Asylum," *New York Times*, July 18, 1902, https://timesmachine.nytimes.com/timesmachine/1902/07/18/117979960.pdf.

72. "Birth Certificates," New York State Department of Health, accessed April 14, 2024, https://www.health.ny.gov/vital_records/birth.htm.

73. Trammell, 7.

74. Michael Fitzgerald, "Adoption Secrecy Has Ended for Thousands Since New York Unsealed Birth Records," *The Imprint*, February 17, 2017, https://imprintnews.org/adoption

/adoption-new-york-unsealed-birth-certificates/51893; Assembly Bill A5954, New York State Senate, https://www.nysenate.gov/legislation/bills/2019/A5494.

75. "NY Foundling Hospital—Notes Left with Children," New-York Historical Society Flickr, uploaded September 29, 2010, https://www.flickr.com/photos/n-yhs/5035989331/in /album-72157624935511447.

76. Ibid.

77. "NY Foundling Hospital—Notes Left with Children," New-York Historical Society Flickr, uploaded September 27, 2010, https://www.flickr.com/photos/n-yhs/5030373674/in /album-72157625045984970.

78. O'Connor, 174.

79. Records of the New York Foundling Hospital, MS 347, The New-York Historical Society, Series IV.30, Box 35, Folder 5: "Orphan Train"—Correspondence from Former "Riders" to Sister Marie de Lourdes Walsh, 1968 February–August, Mary Carl Hesser Kingdon letter.

80. Ibid.

81. Records of the New York Foundling Hospital, MS 347, The New-York Historical Society, Series IV.30, Box 35, Folder 3: "Orphan Train"—Nebraska Reunion, 1962 April 1— Correspondence, Clippings, Photographic Prints, Other Materials, Circa 1962 March–1963 April.

82. Records of the New York Foundling Hospital, MS 347, The New-York Historical Society, Series IV.30, Box 35, Folder 5: "Orphan Train"—Correspondence from Former "Riders" to Sister Marie de Lourdes Walsh, 1968 February–August, Mary Carl Hesser Kingdon letter.

83. Records of the New York Foundling Hospital, MS 347, The New-York Historical Society, Series IV.30, Box 35, Folder 3: "Orphan Train"—Nebraska Reunion, 1962 April 1— Correspondence, Clippings, Photographic Prints, Other Materials, Circa 1962 March–1963 April, clipping from *Catholic News*.

84. Records of the New York Foundling Hospital, MS 347, The New-York Historical Society, Series IV.30, Box 35, Folder 8: "Orphan Train" Reunion—Correspondence, Photographic Prints, Memos, Other Materials, 1994–1995, inclusive; letter from Helen Macior.

85. Records of the New York Foundling Hospital, MS 347, The New-York Historical Society, Series IV.30, Box 35, Folder 7: Correspondence from Former "Riders" to Sister Marilda Joseph (Includes Photographic Prints), Circa 1994 September–1995 August; letter from Alice Bernard.

86. "Mother and Child Program," New York Foundling, accessed April 14, 2024, https:// www.nyfoundling.org/what-we-do/our-programs/child-welfare/mother-and-child-program.

87. Robert D. McFadden, "Developer Buys 3d Avenue Site from Hospital," *New York Times*, October 22, 1985, https://www.nytimes.com/1985/10/22/nyregion/developer -buys-3d-avenue-site-from-hospital.html.

Chapter Eight: Forced Assimilation by Transcontinental Railroad

1. "Historic Carlisle Barracks," US Army War College, accessed April 14, 2024, https://www.armywarcollege.edu/history.cfm.

2. Theimer, 16.

3. "Visitors Access to Carlisle Barracks," US Army War College, accessed April 14, 2024, https://www.armywarcollege.edu/directions.cfm.

4. Theimer, 16.

5. Theimer, 16.

6. Newland, 27; Fear-Segal and Rose, 6.

7. "List of Federal Indian Boarding Schools as of April 1, 2022," US Department of the Interior, Bureau of Indian Affairs, https://www.bia.gov/sites/default/files/dup/inline-files/appendix_a_b_school_listing_profiles_508.pdf, 58.

8. Newland, 6.

9. "Richard Henry Pratt," Historical Marker Database, last updated February 7, 2023, https://www.hmdb.org/m.asp?m=122821.

10. "'Kill the Indian in Him, and Save the Man': R. H. Pratt on the Education of Native Americans," Carlisle Indian School Digital Resource Center, accessed May 1, 2024, https://carlisleindian.dickinson.edu/teach/kill-indian-him-and-save-man-r-h-pratt-education-native-americans.

11. Newland, 51.

12. Newland, 53.

13. For historians who use this term, see Fear-Segal and Rose, 4, 15; Woolford, 21–45 (esp. 26); for activists, see "US Indian Boarding School History," National Native American Boarding School Healing Coalition, accessed April 14, 2024, https://boardingschoolhealing.org/education/us-indian-boarding-school-history. Note that some Native activists believe that the Indian boarding schools were part of a genocide, full stop.

14. "Secretary Deb Haaland," US Department of the Interior, accessed April 14, 2024, https://www.doi.gov/secretary-deb-haaland; Deb Haaland, "My Grandparents Were Stolen from Their Families as Children. We Must Learn About This History," *Washington Post*, June 11, 2021, www.washingtonpost.com/opinions/2021/06/11/deb-haaland-indigenous-boarding-schools; "Secretary Haaland Announces Federal Indian Boarding School Initiative," US Department of the Interior, last updated February 15, 2023, https://www.doi.gov/pressreleases/secretary-haaland-announces-federal-indian-boarding-school-initiative; Ian Austen, "How Thousands of Indigenous Children Vanished in Canada," *New York Times*, last updated March 28, 2002, https://www.nytimes.com/2021/06/07/world/canada/mass-graves-residential-schools.html.

15. Deb Haaland, "Federal Indian Boarding School Initiative," June 22, 2021, https://www.doi.gov/sites/doi.gov/files/secint-memo-esb46-01914-federal-indian-boarding-school-truth-initiative-2021-06-22-final508-1.pdf.

16. "War of 1812," National Parks Service, accessed April 15, 2024, https://www.nps.gov/subjects/warof1812/indigenous-peoples.htm.

17. Kathryn Braund, "Losing Ground: The Wages of War in Indian Country," National Parks Service, last updated August 14, 2017, https://www.nps.gov/articles/losing-ground.htm.

18. Mark Hirsch, "1871: The End of Indian Treaty-Making," *American Indian Magazine*, summer/fall 2014, https://www.americanindianmagazine.org/story/1871-end-indian-treaty-making. Note that some treaties predated the founding of the United States and were negotiated with Britain.

19. "The 'Indian Problem,'" Smithsonian National Museum of the American Indian, March 3, 2015, https://www.si.edu/object/indian-problem%3Ayt_if-BOZgWZPE.

20. Claudio Saunt, "The Invasion of America," *Aeon*, January 7, 2015, https://aeon.co/essays/how-were-1-5-billion-acres-of-land-so-rapidly-stolen.

21. "200 Years of Bureau of Indian Affairs History," US Department of the Interior, Bureau of Indian Affairs, accessed April 15, 2024, https://www.bia.gov/bia/history.

22. Ken Drexler, "Indian Removal Act: Primary Documents in American History," Library of Congress, last updated May 14, 2019, https://guides.loc.gov/indian-removal-act; Chapter 148, Statutes at Large, 21st Congress, 1st Session, 1830, in *A Century of Lawmaking for a New Nation: U.S. Congressional Documents and Debates, 1774–1875*, https://memory.loc.gov/cgi-bin/ampage?collId=llsl&fileName=004/llsl004.db.

23. "Preludes to the Trail of Tears," National Parks Service, last updated September 5, 2021, https://www.nps.gov/articles/000/preludes-trail-of-tears.htm.

24. "Trail of Tears: A Brief History," National Parks Service, last updated August 3, 2023, https://www.nps.gov/trte/learn/historyculture/index.htm.

25. Fear-Segal and Rose, 7.

26. Special Subcommittee on Indian Education, "Indian Education: A National Tragedy—a National Challenge" (Washington, DC: US Government Printing Office, 1969), 142, https://files.eric.ed.gov/fulltext/ED034625.pdf.

27. Quoted in Newland, 21.

28. Newland, 59–61.

29. Carlisle Indian School Collection, Cumberland County Historical Society, PI 4-2-1, The Laundry, Grades I, II, III, Normal Department, Teacher Miss Hawk, 1907–1908; PI 4-10-4, The Tailor Shop, Grade VII, Beginning, Room X, Teacher Miss Scalps, IIS 1907–1908; PI 4-6-1, Emily Mitchell, Penobscot, Age 15, Third Grade, The Village BlackSmith.

30. Claudio Saunt, "Invasion of America: How the United States Took Over an Eighth of the World," ArcGIS Web Application, accessed April 15, 2024, https://usg.maps.arcgis.com/apps/webappviewer/index.html?id=eb6ca76e008543a89349ff2517db47e6.

31. "Homestead Act (1862)," National Archives, last updated June 7, 2022, https://www.archives.gov/milestone-documents/homestead-act.

32. "Homesteading by the Numbers," National Parks Service, last updated August 8, 2021, https://www.nps.gov/home/learn/historyculture/bynumbers.htm.

33. "Land Tenure History," Indian Land Tenure Foundation, accessed April 14, 2024, https://iltf.org/land-issues/history.

34. Trammell, 6.

35. Trammell, 6.

36. Newland, 60–61.

37. Theimer, 39.

38. Richard Henry Pratt, "Request to Recruit 50 Ute Students," Carlisle Indian School Digital Resource Center, July 22, 1880, https://carlisleindian.dickinson.edu/documents /request-recruit-50-ute-students; Richard Henry Pratt, "Request to Recruit Students with a Female Assistant," Carlisle Indian School Digital Resource Center, October 17, 1880, https:// carlisleindian.dickinson.edu/documents/request-recruit-students-female-assistant.

39. Fear-Segal and Rose, 5; Alfred J. Standing, "A. J. Standing's Report from His Trip to Indian Territory," Carlisle Indian School Digital Resource Center, April 5, 1880, https://carlisle indian.dickinson.edu/documents/j-standings-report-his-trip-indian-territory.

40. Zach Levitt et al., "War Against the Children," *New York Times*, August 30, 2023, https://www.nytimes.com/interactive/2023/08/30/us/native-american-boarding-schools.html.

41. William H. H. Llewellyn, "Severe Measures to Be Taken to Recruit Apache Girls for Carlisle," Carlisle Indian School Digital Resource Center, September 8, 1884, https://carlisle indian.dickinson.edu/documents/severe-measures-be-taken-recruit-apache-girls-carlisle.

42. Fear-Segal and Rose, 5.

43. Newland, 1.

44. Theimer, 12–13.

45. Theimer, 13–14.

46. Theimer, 15.

47. Barb Landis, "Pratt, Ft. Marion Prisoners and Hampton," Carlisle Indian School History, Cumberland County Historical Society, accessed April 15, 2024, https://carlisleindian .historicalsociety.com/history-of-the-carlisle-indian-school.

48. Landis, "Pratt, Ft. Marion Prisoners and Hampton."

49. F. Hilton Crowe, "Indian Prisoner Students at Fort Marion," *Regional Review*, December 1940, https://www.nps.gov/parkhistory/online_books/regional_review/vol5-6c.htm.

50. Fear-Segal and Rose, 7; Landis, "Pratt, Ft. Marion Prisoners and Hampton."

51. Pratt, 218; quoted in Fear-Segal and Rose, 7.

52. Pratt, 217.

53. "List of Federal Indian Boarding Schools as of April 1, 2022"; Newland, 6.

54. Fear-Segal and Rose, 6.

55. Quoted in Fear-Segal and Rose, 6.

56. Trafzer, Keller, and Sisquoc, 17–18.

57. Trafzer, Keller, and Sisquoc, 14; Theimer, 13.

58. Theimer, 13–14.

59. "Luther Standing Bear (1879)," in *America: A Narrative History*, W. W. Norton & Company: StudySpace, accessed April 15, 2024, https://wwnorton.com/college/history /america7_brief/content/multimedia/ch19/research_01d.htm.

60. "Luther Standing Bear (1879)."

61. Kenny Cooper, "'We Just Want to Be Welcomed Back': The Lenape Seek a Return Home," WHYY, July 30, 2021, https://whyy.org/articles/we-just-want-to-be-welcomed -back-the-lenape-seek-a-return-home.

62. "Susquehannock Indians," Occom Circle, Dartmouth Libraries, accessed April 15, 2024, https://collections.dartmouth.edu/occom/html/ctx/orgography/org0162.ocp.html.

63. Fear-Segal and Rose, 5.

64. Carlisle Indian School Collection, Cumberland County Historical Society, PI 1-2, Letter from Richard Henry Pratt to the Honorable William E. Miller, Secretary of the Hamilton Library Association, February 11, 1908.

65. Ibid.

66. Fear-Segal and Rose, 9; Richard Henry Pratt, "General Outline of Trip to Chicago for World's Fair," Carlisle Indian School Digital Resource Center, September 25, 1893, https://carlisleindian.dickinson.edu/documents/general-outline-trip-chicago-worlds-fair.

67. Fear-Segal and Rose, 8–9.

68. My personal photo of the Carlisle Indian Industrial School (1879–1918) Collection exhibit at the Cumberland County Historical Society Museum.

69. "Four Pueblo Children from Zuni, New Mexico, c.1880," Carlisle Indian School Digital Resource Center, accessed April 15, 2024, https://carlisleindian.dickinson.edu/index.php/images/four-pueblo-children-zuni-new-mexico-c1880.

70. Virginia More Roediger, *Ceremonial Costumes of the Pueblo Indians: Their Evolution, Fabrication, and Significance in the Prayer Drama* (Berkeley: University of California Press, 1991), 17.

71. "Frank Cushing, Taylor Ealy, Mary Ealy, and Jennie Hammaker [version 1], c.1880," Carlisle Indian School Digital Resource Center, accessed April 15, 2024, https://carlisleindian.dickinson.edu/index.php/images/frank-cushing-taylor-ealy-mary-ealy-and-jennie-hammaker-version-1-c1880.

72. "Request to Repatriate of Frank Cushing's Body to Zuni," September 30–October 18, 1881, Carlisle Indian School Digital Resource Center, accessed April 15, 2024, https://carlisleindian.dickinson.edu/index.php/documents/request-repatriate-frank-cushings-body-zuni; "Excerpt from Annual Report of the Commissioner of Indian Affairs, 1881," Carlisle Indian School Digital Resource Center, accessed April 15, 2024, https://carlisleindian.dickinson.edu/sites/default/files/docs-publications/BIA-Annual-Report_1881_Narrative_OCR.pdf, 184.

73. Newland, 56; Theimer, 12.

74. Theimer, 12.

75. "Taylor Ealy Student Information Card," Carlisle Indian School Digital Resource Center, accessed April 15, 2024, https://carlisleindian.dickinson.edu/index.php/student_files/taylor-ealy-student-information-card.

76. Richard Henry Pratt, "Report on the Death of Taylor Ealy," Carlisle Indian School Digital Resource Center, July 13, 1883, https://carlisleindian.dickinson.edu/sites/default/files/docs-documents/NARA_RG75_91_b0145_12683.pdf.

77. Jeff Gammage, "Rosebud Sioux Teens, Now Young Adults, Return to Claim Relatives' Remains from Carlisle Indian School Cemetery," *Philadelphia Inquirer*, July 18, 2021, https://www.inquirer.com/news/rosebud-sioux-carlisle-indian-school-repatriation-boarding-school-army-cemetery-20210717.html; "CIS Cemetery Information," Carlisle Indian School Digital Resource Center, accessed April 15, 2024, https://carlisleindian.dickinson.edu/cemetery-information/resources.

78. "Carlisle Barracks Main Post Cemetery," Office of Army Cemeteries, accessed April 15, 2024, https://armycemeteries.army.mil/Cemeteries/Carlisle-Barracks-Main-Post-Cemetery.

79. "CIS Cemetery Information"; "Carlisle Barracks Main Post Cemetery,"

80. "Plenty Living Bear (Plenty Horses) Student File," Carlisle Indian School Digital Resource Center, accessed April 15, 2024, https://carlisleindian.dickinson.edu/student_files/plenty-living-bear-plenty-horses-student-file.

81. Fear-Segal and Rose, 2–3.

82. David J. Wishart, ed., "Wounded Knee Massacre," Encyclopedia of the Great Plains, accessed April 15, 2024, http://plainshumanities.unl.edu/encyclopedia/doc/egp.war.056.

83. Quoted in Fear-Segal and Rose, 3.

84. "Julia Powlas Student Information Card," Carlisle Indian School Digital Resource Center, accessed April 15, 2024, https://carlisleindian.dickinson.edu/student_files/julia-powlas-student-information-card; David J. Wishart, ed., "Indian Agents," Encyclopedia of the Great Plains, accessed April 15, 2024, http://plainshumanities.unl.edu/encyclopedia/doc/egp.pg.032.xml.

85. Krupat, 9–10.

86. Pratt, xxiii.

87. "William Little Elk Student Information Card," Carlisle Indian School Digital Resource Center, accessed April 15, 2024, https://carlisleindian.dickinson.edu/student_files/william-little-elk-student-information-card-0; Krupat, 34.

88. "Age-Based Divisions: Football," Pop Warner Little Scholars, accessed April 15, 2024, https://www.popwarner.com/Default.aspx?tabid=2676344.

89. Theimer, 50.

90. Maraniss, 32–33.

91. Maraniss, 31–33.

92. Maraniss, 20, 59.

93. "Jim Thorpe Student File," Carlisle Indian School Digital Resource Center, accessed April 15, 2024, https://carlisleindian.dickinson.edu/student_files/jim-thorpe-student-file.

94. David Maraniss, "The Damaging Myth of Pop Warner as Jim Thorpe's Savior," *Washington Post*, August 8, 2022, washingtonpost.com/sports/olympics/2022/08/08/jim-thorpe-book-pop-warner.

95. Barbara Landis, "The Origin of Lacrosse at Carlisle Indian School," Gardner Digital Library, accessed April 15, 2024, https://gardnerlibrary.org/encylopedia/origin-lacrosse-carlisle-indian-school.

96. James Ring Adams, "The Jim Thorpe Backlash: The Olympic Medals Debacle and the Demise of Carlisle," *American Indian Magazine*, summer 2012, https://www.americanindianmagazine.org/story/jim-thorpe-backlash-olympic-medals-debacle-and-demise-carlisle.

97. Maraniss, "The Damaging Myth of Pop Warner as Jim Thorpe's Savior."

98. Adams, "The Jim Thorpe Backlash."

99. David Wallace Adams, "More Than a Game: The Carlisle Indians Take to the Gridiron," *Western Historical Quarterly* 32, no. 1 (spring 2001): 45.

100. Adams, "The Jim Thorpe Backlash."

101. Adams, "The Jim Thorpe Backlash."

102. Fear-Segal and Rose, 10.

103. "History," US Department of the Interior, Bureau of Indian Education, accessed April 15, 2024, https://www.bie.edu/topic-page/bureau-indian-education.

104. "Kill the Indian, Save the Man: An Introduction to the History of Boarding Schools," National Native American Boarding School Healing Coalition, accessed April 15, 2024, https://boardingschoolhealing.org/kill-the-indian-save-the-man-an-introduction -to-the-history-of-boarding-schools.

105. Newland, 54.

106. Newland, 58.

107. Newland, 56.

108. Newland, 88.

109. Newland, 89–90.

110. Newland, 89.

111. Newland, 89.

Chapter Nine: All in the Family

1. David Trainer, dir., "Wrong Side of the Tracks," season 2, episode 19 of *Boy Meets World*, airing February 24, 1995, on ABC.

2. David Trainer, dir., "Santa's Little Helper," season 1, episode 10 of *Boy Meets World*, airing December 10, 1993, on ABC.

3. John Tracy, dir., "Pilot," season 1, episode 1 of *Boy Meets World*, airing September 24, 1993, on ABC.

4. David Trainer, dir., "Career Day," season 2, episode 22 of *Boy Meets World*, airing May 12, 1995, on ABC.

5. David Trainer, dir., "Home," season 2, episode 23 of *Boy Meets World*, airing May 19, 1995, on ABC.

6. Mark Twain, *Adventures of Huckleberry Finn* (New York: W. W. Norton & Company, 1999), 16.

7. Twain, *Adventures of Huckleberry Finn*, 296.

8. David Trainer, dir., "Career Day," season 2, episode 22 of *Boy Meets World*, airing May 12, 1995, on ABC.

9. Jeff McCracken, dir., "Turkey Day," season 4, episode 10 of *Boy Meets World*, airing November 22, 1996, on ABC.

10. Doug Liman, dir., "Premiere," season 1, episode 1 of *The O.C.*, airing August 5, 2003, on FOX.

11. Emily Brontë, *Wuthering Heights* (New York: Bantam Classic, 1981), 32.

12. Liman, "Premiere."

13. Brontë, *Wuthering Heights*, 71.

14. Jennifer Vineyard, "'Everybody Wants to Live': An Oral History of *Party of Five*'s First Season," *Vulture*, September 3, 2014, https://www.vulture.com/2014/09/party-of-five -oral-history-1994-1995-week.html.

15. Warner, *The Box-Car Children: The Original 1924 Edition*, 36.

16. Warner, *The Box-Car Children: The Original 1924 Edition*, 44, 47.

17. "Connecticut: Home to the Boxcar Children Mysteries—Who Knew?," Connecticut History, accessed April 15, 2024, https://connecticuthistory.org/connecticut-home -to-the-boxcar-children-mysteries-who-knew; Marah Eakin, "What the Hell Happened to the

Boxcar Children's Parents?," *AV Club*, July 9, 2015, https://www.avclub.com/what-the-hell
-happened-to-the-boxcar-children-s-parents-1798281636.

18. Warner, *The Boxcar Children, Book 1*, 136.

19. "The Boxcar Children Mystery Series," Penguin Random House, accessed April 15,
2024, https://www.penguinrandomhouse.com/series/LCP/the-boxcar-children-mysteries.

20. Richard Pearce, dir., "Pilot," season 1, episode 1, of *Party of Five*, airing September
12, 1994, on Fox.

21. "The History of the Orphans' Court in Maryland," Maryland Courts, accessed April
15, 2024, https://mdcourts.gov/orphanscourt/history; Neal G. Wiley, "A Brief History of
Pennsylvania's Orphans' Court," *Pennsylvania Bar Association Quarterly*, July 2019, https://ncp
j.files.wordpress.com/2019/10/wiley-a-brief-history-of-the-pennsylvania-orphans-court.pdf.

22. Pearce, "Pilot."

23. Richard Pearce, dir., "Homework," season 1, episode 2 of *Party of Five*, airing September 19, 1994, on FOX.

24. Peter O'Fallon, dir., "Private Lives," season 1, episode 11 of *Party of Five*, airing
November 21, 1994, on FOX.

25. Emily St. James, *"Party of Five* Is the Great Forgotten Drama of the '90s," *AV
Club*, July 22, 2013, https://www.avclub.com/party-of-five-is-the-great-forgotten-drama-of
-the-90s-1798239377.

26. Rich Valenza, "Bradley Bredeweg, Executive Producer, Discusses ABC Family's
'The Fosters,'" *HuffPost*, January 10, 2014, https://www.huffpost.com/entry/bradley-bredeweg
-the-fosters_n_4569014.

27. Valenza, "Bradley Bredeweg."

28. Elliott, 266.

29. Elliott, 267.

Chapter Ten: The Broken Foundation of a Broken System

1. "The AFCARS Report: Preliminary Estimates," 3.

2. Note that the reasons for removal are not mutually exclusive, and percentages total
more than 100 percent.

3. "Family Poverty Is Not Neglect," United Family Advocates, accessed April 15, 2024,
https://www.unitedfamilyadvocates.org/family-poverty-is-not-neglect.

4. John Sciamanna, "Less Than 2 in 5 Children Now Covered by Federal Foster Care
Funding," Child Welfare League of America, accessed April 15, 2024, https://www.cwla.org
/less-than-2-in-5-children-now-covered-by-federal-foster-care-funding.

5. Rymph, 31.

6. Youth and Families Administration on Children, the Children's Bureau, Administra-
tion for Children and Families, US Department of Health and Human Services, *The Children's
Bureau Legacy: Ensuring the Right to Childhood* (Washington, DC: US Government Printing
Office, 2013).

7. Youth and Families Administration on Children, *The Children's Bureau Legacy*, 22.

8. Youth and Families Administration on Children, *The Children's Bureau Legacy*, 15,
50; Rymph, 32. In fact, a man would not be appointed as chief of the Children's Bureau until

1968; the first five chiefs were women. See "The Children's Bureau's Tradition of Leadership," Administration for Children and Families, December 11, 2013, https://www.acf.hhs.gov /archive/blog/2013/12/childrens-bureaus-tradition-leadership.

9. Rymph, 32.

10. Youth and Families Administration on Children, *The Children's Bureau Legacy*, 54; Children's Bureau, *Foster-Home Care for Dependent Children* (Washington, DC: US Government Printing Office, 1929), https://www.mchlibrary.org/history/chbu/20577.PDF.

11. Brown and McKeown, 193.

12. "Children's Aid Society Records," New-York Historical Society, accessed April 15, 2024, https://findingaids.library.nyu.edu/nyhs/ms111_childrens_aid_society.

13. "History," Graham Windham, accessed April 15, 2024, https://www.graham-windham .org/about-us/history.

14. Rymph, 23.

15. Rymph, 25, 49.

16. Rymph, 23–24.

17. Riis, 190.

18. Rymph, 49.

19. Rymph, 24.

20. Rymph, 24; Herman, 32.

21. Herman, 32–34.

22. US Children's Bureau, *Foster-Home Care for Dependent Children*, 38.

23. US Children's Bureau, *Foster-Home Care for Dependent Children*, 61.

24. *Proceedings of the Conference on the Care of Dependent Children*, 9.

25. *Proceedings of the Conference on the Care of Dependent Children*, 41.

26. *Proceedings of the Conference on the Care of Dependent Children*, 9.

27. Skocpol, chap. 8; Crenson, 17.

28. Cited in Skocpol, 477.

29. Skocpol, 457, 467.

30. Skocpol, 467.

31. Skocpol, 466–467.

32. Skocpol, 471.

33. Briggs, *Taking Children*, 31.

34. Skocpol, 472.

35. Skocpol, 468.

36. Skocpol, 469.

37. Rymph, 45.

38. Skocpol, 472.

39. Skocpol, 474.

40. Skocpol, 474; CPI Inflation Calculator, https://data.bls.gov/cgi-bin/cpicalc.pl (calculated for the period between January 1931 and March 2024).

41. "HHS Poverty Guidelines for 2024," Office of the Assistant Secretary for Planning and Evaluation, January 17, 2024, https://aspe.hhs.gov/topics/poverty-economic-mobility /poverty-guidelines.

42. Skocpol, 476.

43. Skocpol, 476.

44. Skocpol, 476.

45. Skocpol, 476.

46. David Greenberg, "Calvin Coolidge: Impact and Legacy," Miller Center, University of Virginia, accessed April 15, 2024, https://millercenter.org/president/coolidge/impact-and-legacy.

47. "The Great Depression, 1929–1933—CCEA: Impact on the Workers," *Bitesize*, *BBC*, accessed April 15, 2024, https://www.bbc.co.uk/bitesize/guides/zxy3k2p/revision/4; Rymph, 53.

48. US House of Representatives, Committee on Ways and Means, *Economic Security Act Hearings* (Washington, DC: US Government Printing Office, 1935), 47, https://www.ssa.gov/history/pdf/hr35report2.pdf.

49. Rymph, 46.

50. US House of Representatives, *Economic Security Act Hearings*, 47.

51. Bureau of the Census, *Children Under Institutional Care and in Foster Homes, 1933* (Washington, DC: US Government Printing Office, 1935), 8.

52. Bureau of the Census, *Children Under Institutional Care and in Foster Homes, 1933*, 4; Bureau of the Census, *Children Under Institutional Care, 1923* (Washington, DC: US Government Printing Office, 1927), 14.

53. Katz, 252; Ife Floyd et al., "TANF Policies Reflect Racist Legacy of Cash Assistance," Center on Budget and Policy Priorities, August 4, 2021, https://www.cbpp.org/research/income-security/tanf-policies-reflect-racist-legacy-of-cash-assistance#_ftnref25; "Charles H. Houston and the New Deal Exclusion," SSI/SSDI Outreach, Access, and Recovery, January 2022, https://soarworks.samhsa.gov/article/charles-h-houston-and-the-new-deal-exclusion.

54. "Charles H. Houston and the New Deal Exclusion"; Floyd et al., "TANF Policies Reflect Racist Legacy of Cash Assistance."

55. "Title IV—Grants to States for Aid to Dependent Children Appropriation," Social Security Act of 1935, accessed April 15, 2024, https://www.ssa.gov/history/35act.html#TITLE%20IV.

56. Floyd et al., "TANF Policies Reflect Racist Legacy of Cash Assistance."

57. Briggs, *Taking Children*, 31.

58. Rymph, 60–61; "'Suitable Home' Requirements in Many States Denied ADC Access, Especially in the South," Center on Budget and Policy Priorities, accessed April 15, 2024, https://www.cbpp.org/suitable-home-requirements-in-many-states-denied-adc-access-especially-in-south; Linda Gordan and Felice Batlan, "The Legal History of the Aid to Dependent Children Program," Social Welfare History Project, 2011, https://socialwelfare.library.vcu.edu/public-welfare/aid-to-dependent-children-the-legal-history.

59. Floyd et al., "TANF Policies Reflect Racist Legacy of Cash Assistance."

60. Jane Hoey, "Aid to Families with Dependent Children," *Annals of the American Academy of Political and Social Science* 202, no. 1 (March 1939): 71, 74, https://doi-org.proxy.library.upenn.edu/10.1177/000271623920200109open_in_newPublisher.

61. "1939 Amendments," Social Security Administration, accessed April 15, 2024, https://www.ssa.gov/history/1939amends.html.

62. US House of Representatives, Committee on Ways and Means, *Social Security Amendments of 1960* (Washington, DC: US Government Printing Office, 1960), 4, https://www.ssa.gov/history/pdf/Downey%20PDFs/Social%20Security%20Act%20of%20 1960%20Vol%201.pdf. (Note that there is nothing in the 1961 amendments about children's benefits. My grandpa died in March 1962, months before the next big amendments.)

63. Katz, ix, 187.

64. Katz, x.

65. J. L. Roach, "Public-Welfare and the ADC Program in New-York State," *Child Welfare* 39, no. 8 (1960): 15.

66. Dettlaff, 57.

67. Pope, 292.

68. Bernadine Barr, "Spare Children, 1900–1945: Inmates of Orphanages as Subjects of Research in Medicine and in the Social Sciences in America" (PhD diss., Stanford University, 1992), 32, figure 2.2, https://pages.uoregon.edu/adoption/archive/Barrstats.htm; Rymph, 131.

69. Rymph, 102.

70. Ehrenreich, 10.

71. Ehrenreich, 13.

72. Ehrenreich, 10.

73. Coontz, 28, xvii.

74. Rymph, 115, 116.

75. "Title V—Grants to States for Maternal and Child Welfare," Social Security Act of 1935, Social Security Administration, accessed April 15, 2024, https://www.ssa.gov/history /35act.html#TITLE%20V; Rymph 62–64.

76. Rymph, 161.

77. Rymph, 81.

78. Rymph, 159.

79. Glaser, 6–7.

80. Glaser, 54.

81. "Who We Are: Making History Together"; Glaser, 55.

82. Glaser, 81–82.

83. Herman, 72–74; Rymph 95–96.

84. Rymph, 126–130.

85. Rymph, 131.

86. Maas and Engler,1.

87. See Children's Bureau Collection, Maternal and Child Health Library, Georgetown University, accessed April 15, 2024, https://www.mchlibrary.org/collections/childrens-bureau.php.

88. Rymph, 92.

89. "Our Story," Child Welfare League of America, accessed April 15, 2024, https://www .cwla.org/history; "About the Child Welfare League of America," Child Welfare League of America, accessed April 15, 2024, https://www.cwla.org/about-us.

90. Rymph, 159–161.

91. Maas and Engler, 3.

92. Rymph, 160.

93. Rymph, 131.

94. US Congress, "Public Welfare Amendments of 1962," GovInfo, https://www.gov info.gov/content/pkg/STATUTE-76/pdf/STATUTE-76-Pg172.pdf.

95. Rymph, 168.

96. Rymph, 167.

97. Rymph, 167.

98. Rymph, 168.

99. Sciamanna, "Less Than 2 in 5 Children Now Covered by Federal Foster Care Funding."

100. "The 'Suitable-Home' Requirement," *Social Service Review* 35, no. 2 (June 1961): 203–206.

101. Dettlaff, 59; Pope, 291–310.

102. Pope, 291.

103. Pope, 291–292.

104. Pope, 292.

105. Pope, 292; "Massive Resistance," Virginia Museum of History and Culture, accessed April 15, 2024, https://virginiahistory.org/learn/civil-rights-movement-virginia/massive -resistance.

106. Pope, 303–304.

107. Pope, 305.

Chapter Eleven: Policing Poor Black and Native Families

1. Information on Joyce McMillan's experience with ACS comes from my own interview with Joyce on July 11, 2023, as well as the following sources: Diane L. Redleaf, "Meet Joyce McMillan: Making Connections at the Intersections of Child Welfare and Criminal Justice Reform Advocacy for Families," Family Defense Consulting, May 15, 2018, https://www.family defenseconsulting.com/features/https/wwwfamilydefenseconsultingcom/features; Roxana Saberi and Lisa Semel, "In NY, Black Families More Likely to Be Split by Foster Care System," *Al Jazeera America News*, June 25, 2015, http://america.aljazeera.com/articles/2015 /6/25/new-york-foster-care-system-racial-disparity.html.

2. My interview with Joyce McMillan, July 11, 2023.

3. My interview with Joyce McMillan, July 11, 2023.

4. Eli Hager, "NYC Child Welfare Agency Says It Supports 'Miranda Warning' Bill for Parents. But It's Quietly Lobbying to Weaken It," *ProPublica*, June 5, 2023, https://www.pro publica.org/article/new-york-families-child welfare-miranda-warning; Fong, 98–100.

5. Redleaf, "Meet Joyce McMillan."

6. My interview with Joyce McMillan, July 11, 2023.

7. "Our History," HeartShare St. Vincent's Services, accessed April 15, 2024, https:// hsvsnyc.org/who-we-are/our-history.

8. Redleaf, "Meet Joyce McMillan."

9. Olivia Hampton, "'Deluged' Child Welfare Systems Struggle to Protect Kids amid Calls for Reform," NPR, November 20, 2023, https://www.npr.org/2023/11/30/1211781955 /deluged-child-welfare-systems-struggle-to-protect-kids-amid-calls-for-reform.

10. My interview with Joyce McMillan, July 11, 2023.

11. Kempe, 105.

12. Mayo Clinic, "Childhood Fractures May Indicate Bone-Density Problems," *Science-Daily*, January 7, 2014, https://www.sciencedaily.com/releases/2014/01/140107170602.htm.

13. Kempe, 105.

14. JAMA Editors, "The Battered-Child Syndrome," *Journal of the American Medical Association* 181, no. 1 (July 1962): 130.

15. Kempe, 106.

16. Raz, 3; "Medicine: Battered Child Syndrome," *Time*, July 20, 1962.

17. Kempe, 106.

18. Kempe, 106.

19. Kempe, 106.

20. "Parents Who Beat Children: A Tragic Increase in Cases of Child Abuse Is Prompting a Hunt for Ways to Detect Sick Adults Who Commit Such Crimes," *Saturday Evening Post*, October 6, 1962, 30–35.

21. Ian Hacking, "The Making and Molding of Child Abuse," *Critical Inquiry* 17, no. 2 (1991): 266–267.

22. "When They're Angry," *Newsweek*, April 16, 1962.

23. US Senate, Committee on Labor and Public Welfare, *Child Abuse and Prevention Act, 1973, Hearings Before the Subcommittee on Children and Youth* (Washington, DC: Government Printing Office, 1973), 16, https://files.eric.ed.gov/fulltext/ED081507.pdf.

24. US Children's Bureau, *The Abused Child: Principles and Suggested Language for Legislation on Reporting of the Physically Abused Child* (Washington, DC: Government Printing Office, 1963), https://babel.hathitrust.org/cgi/pt?id=purl.32754078884032&seq=1.

25. US Children's Bureau, *The Abused Child*, 6.

26. US Children's Bureau, *The Abused Child*, 6.

27. US Children's Bureau, *The Abused Child*, 12–13.

28. US Children's Bureau, *The Abused Child*, 4.

29. Leonard G. Brown III and Kevin Gallagher, "Mandatory Reporting of Abuse: A Historical Perspective on the Evolution of States' Current Mandatory Reporting Laws with a Review of the Laws in the Commonwealth of Pennsylvania," *Tolle Lege* 59, no. 6 (2017): 39, https://digitalcommons.law.villanova.edu/cgi/viewcontent.cgi?article=3262&context=vlr.

30. Brown and Gallagher, "Mandatory Reporting of Abuse," 39–40.

31. Raz, 4.

32. US Senate, *Child Abuse and Prevention Act, 1973*, 18.

33. National Center on Child Abuse and Neglect, *Study Findings: National Study of the Incidence and Severity of Child Abuse and Neglect* (Washington, DC: N.p., 1981), https://cw library.childwelfare.gov/permalink/01CWIG_INST/10a03se/alma991001246839707651.

34. Lindsey, 177.

35. Brown and Gallagher, "Mandatory Reporting of Abuse," 40–41.

36. Brown and Gallagher, "Mandatory Reporting of Abuse," 42.

37. Lindsey, 178.

38. Raz, 6.

39. US Children's Bureau, *The Abused Child*, 11.

40. Brown and Gallagher, "Mandatory Reporting of Abuse," 41.

41. Child Abuse Prevention and Treatment Act, Pub. L. No. 93-247, https://www.govinfo.gov/content/pkg/STATUTE-88/pdf/STATUTE-88-Pg4.pdf#page=1, 5.

42. Child Abuse Prevention and Treatment Act, 6, 5.

43. Raz, 10–11; US Senate, *Child Abuse and Prevention Act, 1973*, 17.

44. Roberts, *Shattered Bonds*, 31; Fong, 5.

45. Raz, 12.

46. US Senate, *Child Abuse and Prevention Act, 1973*, 14.

47. Raz, 13.

48. Olivia B. Waxman, "The U.S. Almost Had Universal Childcare 50 Years Ago. The Same Attacks Might Kill It Today," *Time*, December 9, 2021, https://time.com/6125667/universal-childcare-history-nixon-veto.

49. Richard Nixon, "Veto Message—Economic Opportunity Amendments of 1971," US Senate, https://www.senate.gov/legislative/vetoes/messages/NixonR/S2007-Sdoc-92-48.pdf.

50. Waxman, "The U.S. Almost Had Universal Childcare 50 Years Ago."

51. Raz, 13.

52. US Senate, *Child Abuse and Prevention Act, 1973*, 18.

53. Dettlaff, 76–77.

54. Fong, 8.

55. Pelton, 6.

56. "A Child Welfare Timeline," National Coalition for Child Protection Reform, accessed April 16, 2024, https://nccpr.org/a-child welfare-timeline; Leroy H. Pelton, "Not for Poverty Alone: Foster Care Population Trends in the Twentieth Century," *Journal of Sociology & Social Welfare* 14, no. 2 (1987), 9, https://scholarworks.wmich.edu/cgi/viewcontent.cgi?article=1809&context=jssw; Pelton, 6.

57. "Indian Adoption Project," Adoption History Project, accessed April 16, 2024, https://pages.uoregon.edu/adoption/topics/IAP.html.

58. Jacobs, xxvii.

59. Jacobs, 8.

60. Briggs, *Somebody's Children*, 71.

61. Jacobs, 8.

62. Jacobs, 12–13.

63. Jacobs, 12.

64. Jacobs, 16.

65. Briggs, *Somebody's Children*, 70.

66. "Tribal Crime and Justice: Public Law 289," National Institute of Justice, May 19, 2008, https://nij.ojp.gov/topics/articles/tribal-crime-and-justice-public-law-280.

67. Briggs, *Somebody's Children*, 72.

68. Max Nesterak, "Uprooted: The 1950s Plan to Erase Indian Country," *American Public Media Reports*, November 1, 2019, https://www.apmreports.org/episode/2019/11/01/uprooted-the-1950s-plan-to-erase-indian-country.

69. Jacobs, 9.

70. Jacobs, 9.

71. Nesterak, "Uprooted"; Jacobs, 7.

72. "Indian American Urban Relocation," National Archives, last modified March 3, 2003, https://www.archives.gov/education/lessons/indian-relocation.html.

73. Jacobs, 15.

74. "Indian Adoption Project"; Jacobs, 20.

75. Jacobs, 20.

76. Arnold Lyslo, "The Indian Adoption Project," *Child Welfare* 40, no. 5 (May 1961): 4.

77. Lyslo, "The Indian Adoption Project."

78. Jacobs, 20.

79. Jacobs, 17.

80. Jacobs, 19.

81. Jacobs, 22.

82. Jacobs, 24.

83. Jacobs, 26.

84. Jacobs, 25–28.

85. Roberts, *Torn Apart*, 105.

86. Christie Renick, "The Nation's First Family Separation Policy," *The Imprint*, October 9, 2018, https://imprintnews.org/childwelfare-2/nations-first-family-separation-policy-indian-childwelfare-act/32431.

87. Raz, 78.

88. Briggs, *Taking Children*, 62–63.

89. Briggs, *Taking Children*, 63.

90. Briggs, *Taking Children*, 64.

91. Briggs, *Taking Children*, 66.

92. Briggs, *Taking Children*, 71.

93. US Senate, *Hearing Before the United States Senate Select Committee on Indian Affairs on S. 1214* (Washington, DC: Government Printing Office, 1977), http://www.narf.org/nill/documents/icwa/federal/lh/hear080477/hear080477.pdf, 1.

94. US Senate, *Hearing Before the United States Senate Select Committee on Indian Affairs on S. 1214*, 1–2.

95. US Senate, *Hearing Before the United States Senate Select Committee on Indian Affairs on S. 1214*, 2.

96. Indian Child Welfare Act of 1987, Pub. L. No. 95-608, https://www.govinfo.gov/content/pkg/STATUTE-92/pdf/STATUTE-92-Pg3069.pdf.

97. Raz, 79.

98. "The AFCARS Report: Preliminary Estimates," 2; "POP3 Race and Hispanic Origin Composition; "The AFCARS Report: Final Estimates for FY 1998 through FY 2002," US

Department of Health and Human Services, Children's Bureau, October 2006, https://www
.acf.hhs.gov/sites/default/files/documents/cb/afcarsreport12.pdf.

99. "The AFCARS Report: Final Estimates."

100. Meanwhile, the rate for white children was 1 in 385. See Roberts, *Shattered Bonds*, 9.

101. Roberts, *Shattered Bonds*, 6.

102. Roberts, *Shattered Bonds*, 45, 27.

103. US Children's Bureau, "Separating Poverty from Neglect in Child Welfare,"
Child Welfare Information Gateway, February 2023, https://www.childwelfare.gov/pubPDFs
/bulletins-povertyneglect.pdf, 2–3.

104. "Child Maltreatment 2022," US Department of Health and Human Services,
Children's Bureau, January 29, 2024, https://www.acf.hhs.gov/sites/default/files/documents
/cb/cm2022.pdf.

105. Roxanna Asgarian, "The Case for Child Welfare Abolition," *In These Times*, October
3, 2023, https://inthesetimes.com/article/child welfare-abolition-cps-reform-family-separation.

106. "Child Maltreatment 2022," x.

107. Fong, 2; Hyunil Kim et al., "Lifetime Prevalence of Investigating Child Maltreatment Among US Children," *American Journal of Public Health* 102, no. 2 (February 2017),
https://www.ncbi.nlm.nih.gov/pmc/articles/PMC5227926.

108. "Child Maltreatment 2022," x, ii. Note that the total number of referrals alleging
maltreatment concerned 7.53 million children.

109. "Child Maltreatment 2022," ii. Note that percentages don't add up to 100 because
a child can be both abused and neglected.

110. Mike Hixenbaugh, Suzy Khimm, and Agnel Philip, "Mandatory Reporting
Was Supposed to Stop Severe Child Abuse. It Punishes Poor Families Instead," *ProPublica*,
October 12, 2022, https://www.propublica.org/article/mandatory-reporting-strains-systems
-punishes-poor-families.

111. Roberts, *Shattered Bonds*, 48.

112. Roberts, *Torn Apart*, 39.

113. "The AFCARS Report: Preliminary Estimates," 2; "POP3 Race and Hispanic Origin Composition."

114. US Children's Bureau, "Child Welfare Practice to Address Racial Disproportionality and Disparity," Child Information Gateway, April 2021, https://www.childwelfare.gov
/pubPDFs/racial_disproportionality.pdf, 3.

115. Daniel Geary, "The Moynihan Report: An Annotated Edition," *The Atlantic*,
September 14, 2015, https://www.theatlantic.com/politics/archive/2015/09/the-moynihan
-report-an-annotated-edition/404632.

116. US Children's Bureau, "Child Welfare Practice to Address Racial Disproportionality and Disparity," 3.

117. Youngmin Yi, Frank R. Edwards, and Christopher Wildeman, "Cumulative Prevalence of Confirmed Maltreatment and Foster Care Placement for US Children by Race/Eth-
nicity, 2011–2016," *American Journal of Public Health* 110, no. 5 (May 2020), https://www
.ncbi.nlm.nih.gov/pmc/articles/PMC7144424.

118. Yi, Frank, and Wildeman, "Cumulative Prevalence of Confirmed Maltreatment and Foster Care Placement for US Children by Race/Ethnicity, 2011–2016."

119. US Children's Bureau, "Child Welfare Practice to Address Racial Disproportionality and Disparity," 3.

120. Pelton, 6.

121. Raz, 86.

122. Peter Kihss, "Foster Care Program Is Called 'A Dumping Ground for Children,'" *New York Times*, January 13, 1978, https://www.nytimes.com/1978/01/13/archives/foster care-program-is-called-a-dumping-ground-for-children.html.

123. US Children's Bureau, "Separating Poverty from Neglect in Child Welfare," 4.

124. Raz, 83; see Joseph Goldstein, Anna Freund, and Albert J. Solnit, *Beyond the Best Interests of the Child* (New York: Free Press, 1984).

125. Raz, 83.

126. Raz, 84.

127. Raz, 84.

128. Clyde Haberman, "City Foster-Care Unit Cited for Failures in Abuse Cases," *New York Times*, April 24, 1982, https://www.nytimes.com/1982/04/24/nyregion/city-foster-care -unit-cited-for-failures-in-abuse-cases.html.

129. Haberman, "City Foster-Care Unit Cited for Failures in Abuse Cases."

130. Raz, 84.

131. Adoption Assistance and Child Welfare Act of 1980, Pub. L. No. 96-272, https:// www.congress.gov/96/statute/STATUTE-94/STATUTE-94-Pg500.pdf.

132. Rymph, 185.

133. "Title IV-E Foster Care," US Department of Health and Human Services, Children's Bureau, last modified May 10, 2023, https://www.acf.hhs.gov/cb/grant-funding/title -iv-e-foster-care.

134. US Children's Bureau, "Reasonable Efforts to Preserve or Reunify Families and Achieve Permanency for Children," Child Welfare Information Gateway, September 2019, https://www.childwelfare.gov/pubpdfs/reunify.pdf, 2.

135. "The AFCARS Report: Preliminary Estimates," 3.

136. "Hot Topic: Strengthen and Build Welfare Workforce," 2022 Legislative Agenda, Child Welfare League of America, https://www.cwla.org/wp-content/uploads/2022 /04/2022HotTopicWorkforce.pdf.

137. "What Is a CPI Investigator Specialist?," Texas Department of Family and Protective Services, accessed April 16, 2024, https://www.dfps.texas.gov/Jobs/CPS/cpi_investigator _specialist.asp.

138. Raz, 87.

139. Pelton, 6. Note that there is a methodological difference between these two counts.

140. Raz, 88.

141. Raz, 88; "The AFCARS Report: Final Estimates."

142. Deborah J. Vagins and Jesselyn McCurdy, "Cracks in the System: Twenty Years of Unjust Federal Crack Cocaine Laws," American Civil Liberties Union, October 2006, https:// www.aclu.org/documents/cracks-system-20-years-unjust-federal-crack-cocaine-law, i.

143. Vagins and McCurdy, "Cracks in the System," 7.

144. Roberts, *Shattered Bonds*, 50–51.

145. Roberts, *Shattered Bonds*, 63.

146. Susan Okie, "The Epidemic That Wasn't," *New York Times*, January 27, 2009, https://www.nytimes.com/2009/01/27/health/27coca.html.

147. Okie, "The Epidemic That Wasn't."

148. Roberts, *Torn Apart*, 2.

149. Raz, 111.

150. Raz, 112.

151. "Are Orphanages Better for Kids Than Welfare?," *Baltimore Sun*, November 27, 1994, https://www.baltimoresun.com/news/bs-xpm-1994-11-27-1994331010-story.html; "The Fight over Orphanages," *Newsweek*, last updated March 13, 2010, https://www.newsweek.com /fight-over-orphanages-181934; "Hillary Clinton Says Orphanage Idea Is 'Absurd,'" *Chicago Tribune*, last updated August 9, 2021, https://www.chicagotribune.com/news/ct-xpm-1994 -11-30-9412010070-story.html.

152. "The Personal Responsibility and Work Opportunity Reconciliation Act of 1996," Office of the Assistant Secretary for Planning and Evaluation, August 31, 1996, https://aspe.hhs .gov/reports/personal-responsibility-work-opportunity-reconciliation-act-1996.

153. Roberts, *Shattered Bonds*, 173.

154. One key difference is that whereas AFDC was funded by uncapped federal matching to states, TANF is funded by fixed block grants to states. Instead of growing with inflation and population needs, the federal TANF block grants have been funded at a fixed budget of $16.5 billion since 1996. And states can use their TANF block grants not just to provide families with monthly cash assistance but to fund programs that promote job preparation, marriage, and unwed pregnancy prevention. See "Policy Basics: Temporary Assistance for Needy Families," Center on Budget and Policy Priorities, last updated March 1, 2022, https://www cbpp.org/research/income-security/temporary-assistance-for-needy-families.

155. "Title IV-E—Federal Payments for Foster Care and Adoption Assistance," State Justice Institute, accessed April 16, 2024, https://fundingtoolkit.sji.gov/title-iv-e-federal -payments-for-foster-care-and-adoption-assistance.

156. "Title IV-E Programs—Total Costs Federal Financial Participation (FFP) Claims by FY Reported," US Department of Health and Human Services, Children's Bureau, https://www .acf.hhs.gov/sites/default/files/documents/cb/fy-2022-title-iv-e-five-year-summary.xlsx.

157. Donna K. Ginther and Michelle Johnson-Motoyama, "Associations Between State TANF Policies, Child Protective Services Involvement, and Foster Care Placement," *Health Affairs* 41, no. 12 (December 2022): footnote on 10, https://www.healthaffairs.org /doi/10.1377/hlthaff.2022.00743.

158. Ginther and Johnson-Motoyama, "Associations Between State TANF Policies, Child Protective Services Involvement, and Foster Care Placement."

159. Adoption and Safe Families Act of 1997, Pub. L. No. 105-89, https://www.congress .gov/105/plaws/publ89/PLAW-105publ89.pdf, 4.

160. Adoption and Safe Families Act of 1997, 3–4.

161. Roberts, *Shattered Bonds*, 138.

162. Roberts, *Shattered Bonds*, 138.

163. Roberts, *Shattered Bonds*, 108.

164. Roberts, *Shattered Bonds*, 108.

165. Michael Quinn, "'Family Preservation'—It Can Kill," *Newsday*, January 11, 1996, A33.

166. Christopher Wildeman, Frank R. Edwards, and Sara Wakefield, "The Cumulative Prevalence of Termination of Parental Rights for U.S. Children," *Child Maltreatment* 25, no. 1 (February 2020): 32–42.

167. Martin Guggenheim, "Let's Root Out Racism in Child Welfare, Too," *The Imprint*, June 15, 2020, https://imprintnews.org/child welfare-2/lets-root-out-racism-child welfare-too/44327; Asgarian, 35.

168. "The AFCARS Report: Preliminary Estimates," 5.

169. "About the Children," Adopt US Kids, accessed April 16, 2024, https://www.adoptuskids.org/meet-the-children/children-in-foster-care/about-the-children.

170. "Title IV-E Programs—Total Costs Federal Financial Participation (FFP) Claims by FY Reported."

171. Adoption and Safe Families Act of 1997.

172. "Adoption and Legal Guardianship Incentive Payment Program—Earning History by State: FY 1998–FY 2022," US Department of Health and Human Services, Children's Bureau, updated October 2023, https://www.acf.hhs.gov/sites/default/files/documents/cb/algipp-earning-history-by-state.pdf.

173. "About the Children."

174. My interview with Sixto Cancel, August 2023.

175. Sixto Cancel, "I Will Never Forget That I Could Have Lived with People Who Loved Me," *New York Times*, September 16, 2021, https://www.nytimes.com/2021/09/16/opinion/foster-care-children-us.html.

176. "The AFCARS Report: Preliminary Estimates," 2.

177. Sixto Cancel, "Reimagining the Future for Foster Youth," *HuffPost*, last updated June 9, 2013, https://www.huffpost.com/entry/reimagining-the-future-fo_b_3039060.

178. Manoush Zomorordi, "How Placing Kids with Family Can Radically Change the Way Foster Care Works in the US," *TED Radio Hour*, NPR, June 20, 2023, https://www.npr.org/transcripts/1185025494; Sixto Cancel, "A Foster Care System Where Every Child Has a Loving Home," TED2023, April 2023, https://www.ted.com/talks/sixto_cancel_a_foster_care_system_where_every_child_has_a_loving_home.

179. Dettlaff, 109.

180. Asgarian, xii.

181. Asgarian, 97.

182. Asgarian, 221.

183. Annie Correal, "Covering a Notorious Crime in Spanish: Fascination, and a Different Angle," *New York Times*, March 8, 2008, https://www.nytimes.com/2008/03/08/nyregion/08nixzmary.html.

184. Correal, "Covering a Notorious Crime in Spanish."

185. Marc Peyser, "The Death of Little Elisa," *Newsweek*, last updated March 13, 2020, https://www.newsweek.com/death-little-elisa-180258.

186. Lizette Alvarez, "A Mother's Tale: Drugs, Despair, and Violence," *New York Times*, November 27, 1995, https://www.nytimes.com/1995/11/27/nyregion/mothers-tale -drugs-despair-violence-life-mired-urban-ills-ends-daughter-s-death.html.

187. Lizette Alvarez, "Report in Wake of Girl's Death Finds Failures in Child Agency," *New York Times*, April 9, 1996, https://www.nytimes.com/1996/04/09/nyregion/report-in -wake-of-girl-s-death-finds-failures-in-child-agency.html.

188. "Elisa's Law," NYC Children's Services, accessed April 16, 2024, https://web .archive.org/web/20130409194706/http://www.nyc.gov/html/acs/html/about/elisaslaw.shtml.

189. "Gov. Paterson Signs Nixmary's Law," *New York Daily News*, last updated January 11, 2019, https://www.nydailynews.com/news/gov-paterson-signs-nixzmary-law-article-1.381561.

190. "Child Maltreatment 2022," ii.

191. "Child Maltreatment 2022," 55.

192. "Child Maltreatment 2022," 61.

193. Andy Newman, Ashley Southall, and Chelsia Rose Marcius, "These Children Were Beaten to Death. Could They Have Been Saved?," *New York Times*, October 26, 2021, https://www .nytimes.com/2021/10/26/nyregion/child-abuse-reports-deaths-nyc.html.

194. Fong, 14.

195. See Roberts, *Torn Apart*, 24; upEND Movement, https://upendmovement.org.

Chapter Twelve: No Separation Between Church and State

1. Julia Terruso, "Two Foster Agencies in Philly Won't Place Kids with LGBTQ People," *Philadelphia Inquirer*, March 13, 2018, https://www.inquirer.com/philly/news/foster-adoption -lgbtq-gay-same-sex-philly-bethany-archdiocese-20180313.html.

2. "The Philadelphia Code and Home Rule Charter," American Legal Publishing, March 19, 2024, https://codelibrary.amlegal.com/codes/philadelphia/latest/philadelphia_pa /0-0-0-195759.

3. "Syllabus: Fulton et al. v. City of Philadelphia, Pennsylvania, et al.," Supreme Court of the United States, June 17, 2021, 7, https://www.supremecourt.gov/opinions/20pdf/19-123 _g3bi.pdf.

4. "Parent to Parent: A Guide to Navigating Philadelphia's Child Welfare System," Community Legal Services of Philadelphia, April 2019, https://clsphila.org/wp-content /uploads/2019/04/Part-1-DHS-Investigations-and-CUA-Services_0.pdf.

5. At the time of this writing, the four CUAs were Asociación Puertorriqueños en Marcha, Bethanna, Catholic Community Services (CSS), and NET Community Care. For information on Bethanna's Christian focus, see https://bethanna.org/about.

6. Carolyn Davis, "DHS Change Will Emphasize Private Oversight," *Philadelphia Inquirer*, August 7, 2012, https://www.inquirer.com/philly/news/homepage/20120807_DHS _change_will_emphasize_private_oversight.html; John Sullivan et al., "Girl Wasted Away Under DHS Care," *Philadelphia Inquirer*, July 31, 2008, https://www.inquirer.com/philly /news/special_packages/inquirer/child_welfare/Girl_wasted_away_under_DHS_care.html.

7. John Sullivan, "Pa. Gives DHS Only Provisional License," *Philadelphia Inquirer*, July 11, 2017, https://www.inquirer.com/philly/health/20070711_Pa__gives_DHS_only_provisional _license.html.

8. Miriam Hill and Carolyn Davis, "DHS Overhauls Structure to Set Clear Lines of Accountability," *Philadelphia Inquirer*, September 15, 2011, https://www.inquirer.com/philly /health/20110915_DHS_overhauls_structure_to_set_clear_lines_of_accountability.html.

9. Julia Terruso, "Pa. Downgrades City DHS License, Citing Shortcomings," *Philadelphia Inquirer*, May 16, 2016, https://www.inquirer.com/philly/news/politics/20160517_Pa __downgrades_DHS_s_license__citing_shortcomings.html.

10. Julia Terruso (@JuliaTerruso), "After writing about the need for more foster families in Philly, I heard from a same-sex couple who was turned away because of their sexual orientation . . . ," Twitter, March 13, 2018, https://twitter.com/JuliaTerruso /status/973551132055363584?s=20.

11. Terruso, "Two Foster Agencies in Philly Won't Place Kids with LGBTQ People."

12. Julia Terruso, "Philly Puts Out 'Urgent' Call—300 Families Needed for Fostering," *Philadelphia Inquirer*, March 8, 2018, https://www.inquirer.com/philly/news/foster-parents -dhs-philly-child welfare-adoptions-20180308.html.

13. "Family Changes Everything," Bethany Christian Services, accessed April 16, 2024, https://bethany.org/about-us.

14. "What Does It Mean to Stand in the Gap (Ezekiel 22:30)?," Got Questions Ministries, last updated September 14, 2022, https://www.gotquestions.org/stand-in-the-gap.html.

15. "About," Catholic Social Services Philadelphia, accessed April 16, 2024, https://css philadelphia.org/about.

16. "A History of Foster Care in Philadelphia," Free to Foster, accessed April 16, 2024, https://s3.amazonaws.com/becketnewsite/A-History-of-Foster-Care-in-Philadelphia.pdf. This resource was created by Free to Foster, a propaganda website in support of the CSS in the *Fulton v. City of Philadelphia* case. See Free to Foster, https://web.archive.org/web/20220314023712 /https://freetofoster.com.

17. "Mission," Catholic Charities USA, accessed April 16, 2024, https://www.catholic charitiesusa.org/about-us/mission.

18. Julia Terruso, "City Halts Foster Care Intakes at Two Agencies That Discriminate Against LGBTQ People," *Philadelphia Inquirer*, March 15, 2018, https://www.inquirer.com/philly/news /city-council-lgbtq-discrimination-foster-adopt-child-welfare-hearings-20180315.html.

19. Julia Terruso, "City Resumes Foster-Care Work with Bethany Christian Services After It Agrees to Work with Same-Sex Couples," *Philadelphia Inquirer*, June 28, 2018, https://www .inquirer.com/philly/news/foster-care-lgbt-bethany-christian-services-same-sex-philly-lawsuit -catholic-social-services-20180628.html.

20. Ruth Graham, "Major Evangelical Adoption Agency Will Now Serve Gay Parents Nationwide," *New York Times*, March 1, 2021, https://www.nytimes.com/2021/03/01/us /bethany-adoption-agency-lgbtq.html.

21. Julie Shaw and Jeremy Roebuck, "Catholic Social Services, Foster Parents Sue City, DHS," *Philadelphia Inquirer*, May 18, 2018, https://www.inquirer.com/philly/news/catholic -social-services-lawsuit-city-dhs-foster-children-20180518.html.

22. Julia Terruso, "The Supreme Court Has Decided on a Case Involving Philadelphia and Religious Rights. Here's What You Need to Know," *Philadelphia Inquirer*, last updated June 17, 2018, https://www.inquirer.com/news/fulton-vs-philadelphia-decision-supreme-court-2021 0608.html.

23. Terruso, "Two Foster Agencies in Philly Won't Place Kids with LGBTQ People."

24. Laura Baams, Bianca D. M. Wilson, and Stephen T. Russell, "LGBTQ Youth in Unstable Housing and Foster Care," *Pediatrics* 143, no. 3 (March 1, 2019), https://publications .aap.org/pediatrics/article-abstract/143/3/e20174211/76787/LGBTQ-Youth-in-Unstable -Housing-and-Foster-Care.

25. "The Cuyahoga Youth Count: A Report on LGBTQ+ Youth Experience in Foster Care, 2021," Institute for Innovation and Implementation at University of Maryland's School of Social Work, https://theinstitute.umaryland.edu/media/ssw/institute/Cuyahoga-Youth-Count.6.8.1.pdf, 6.

26. Theo G. M. Sandfort, "Experiences and Well-Being of Sexual and Gender Diverse Youth in Foster Care in New York City: Disproportionality and Disparities," New York City Administration for Children's Services, 2020, https://www1.nyc.gov/assets/acs/pdf /about/2020/WellBeingStudyLGBTQ.pdf, 5.

27. Sarah Fathallah and Sarah Sullivan, "Away from Home: Youth Experiences of Institutional Placements in Foster Care," Think of Us, July 2021, https://assets.website-files .com/60a6942819ce8053cefd0947/60f6b1eba474362514093f96_Away%20From%20 Home%20-%20Report.pdf, 9.

28. Eleanor Klibanoff, "Texas Resumes Investigations into Parents of Trans Children, Families' Lawyers Confirm," *Texas Tribune*, May 20, 2022, https://www.texastribune .org/2022/05/20/trans-texas-child-abuse-investigations.

29. Greg Abbott, letter to Jaime Masters, Commissioner of the Texas Department of Family and Protective Services, February 22, 2022, https://gov.texas.gov/uploads/files /press/O-MastersJaime202202221358.pdf.

30. Brian Klosterboer, "Texas' Attempt to Tear Parents and Trans Youth Apart, One Year Later," American Civil Liberties Union, February 23, 2023, https://www.aclu.org/news/lgbtq -rights/texas-attempt-to-tear-parents-and-trans-youth-apart-one-year-later; Eleanor Klibanoff, "Texas' Child Welfare Agency Blocked from Investigating Many More Parents of Trans Teens," *Texas Tribune*, September 16, 2022, https://www.texastribune.org/2022/09/16/texas -trans-teens-investigation-child-abuse.

31. My interview with Matt Hartman, December 20, 2021.

32. "Who We Are," Los Angeles County Department of Children and Family Services," accessed April 16, 2024, https://dcfs.lacounty.gov/about/who-we-are.

33. "The County of Los Angeles Annual Report 2007–2008," LACounty.gov, accessed April 16, 2024, http://file.lacounty.gov/SDSInter/lac/1037084_AnnlRpt07-08.pdf, 35.

34. My interview with Matt Hartman, December 20, 2021.

35. US Children's Bureau, "Kinship Care and the Child Welfare System," Child Welfare Information Gateway, May 2022, https://cwig-prod-prod-drupal-s3fs-us-east-1.s3.amazonaws .com/public/documents/f_kinshi.pdf?VersionId=hsjh.qpq9B8VsKJ6tqTX5CKkvRJ802Kp.

36. "About Us," Pacific Asian Counseling Services, accessed April 16, 2024, https://pacsla .org/overview.

37. My interview with Matt Hartman, December 20, 2021.

38. "LGBTQ+ Rights," Children's Rights, accessed April 16, 2024, https://www.children srights.org/lgbtq-2.

39. "Higher Education for Foster Youth," National Foster Youth Institute, accessed June 4, 2024, https://nfyi.org/issues/higher-education.

40. "Aging Out of Foster Care," National Foster Youth Institute, accessed April 16, 2024, https://nfyi.org/51-useful-aging-out-of-foster-care-statistics-social-race-media; Shalita O'Neale, "Foster Care and Homelessness," *Foster Focus Magazine*, August 2015, https://www.fosterfocusmag.com/articles/foster-care-and-homelessness.

41. Nicholas Forge et al., "LGBTQ Youth Face Greater Risk of Homelessness as They Age Out of Foster Care," Urban Institute, April 3, 2019, https://housingmatters.urban.org/research-summary/lgbtq-youth-face-greater-risk-homelessness-they-age-out-foster-care.

42. Nietfeld, 13.

43. Nietfeld, 14.

44. Nietfeld, 16.

45. Nietfeld, 18.

46. US Children's Bureau, "Treatment Foster Care," Child Welfare Information Gateway, accessed April 16, 2024, https://web.archive.org/web/20230207030034/https://www.childwelfare.gov/topics/outofhome/foster-care/treat-foster.

47. My interview with Emi Nietfeld, June 13, 2023.

48. "The AFCARS Report: Preliminary Estimates," 3.

49. My interview with Ilena Robbins, June 7, 2023.

50. Nietfeld, 71.

51. Nietfeld, 348.

52. Julia Terruso, "Judge Denies Catholic Social Services Discrimination Claim in Foster Care Case," *Philadelphia Inquirer*, July 13, 2018, https://www.inquirer.com/philly/news/foster-care-philadelphia-dhs-same-sex-couples-catholic-social-services-lawsuit-20180713.html.

53. Sharonell Fulton et al., petitioners, Petition for a Writ of Certiorari, Supreme Court of the United States, accessed April 16, 2024, https://www.supremecourt.gov/DocketPDF/19/19-123/108931/20190722174037071_Cert%20Petition%20FINAL.pdf.

54. A similar suit to *Fulton v. City of Philadelphia* that was filed in Texas in 2019, with major implications for how the federal government operates in the foster care system. The state had joined the Catholic Archdiocese of Galveston Houston in filing suit against the Department of Health and Human Services (HHS), the cabinet branch that now houses the Administration for Children and Families and the Children's Bureau, which oversees foster care. The Texas suit challenged a rule adopted in the last days of the Barack Obama presidency that prohibited federal taxpayer-funded foster care, adoption, and other social services agencies from discriminating on the basis of gender identity, sexual orientation, or religion. Texas and the archdiocese wanted to be able to turn down LGBTQ+ foster and adoptive parents-to-be. They were acting on precedent, as HHS had granted a waiver to South Carolina in January 2019, after the state had asked to be exempt from the religious discrimination barrier for federally funded foster care and adoptive agencies. In South Carolina's case, Governor Henry McMaster had made the request on behalf of Miracle Hill Ministries, a Greenville-based agency that exclusively works with Protestant people. Miracle Hill makes its foster parents sign a doctrinal statement

professing Protestant beliefs, such as "We believe the Bible to be the only inspired, infallible, inerrant and authoritative Word of God." See Yonat Shimron, "New Rule Would Allow Foster Care, Adoption Agencies to Exclude on Religious Grounds," *Religious News Service*, November 1, 2019, https://religionnews.com/2019/11/01/new-rule-would-allow-foster-care-adoption-agen cies-to-exclude-on-religious-grounds. A few days after Texas sued, in November 2019, the Donald Trump administration announced plans to gut the HHS nondiscrimination rule. It would no longer protect the categories of gender identity, sexual orientation, and religion, arguing that the rule of law requires the government not to infringe upon religious freedom. The administration granted blanket waivers to Texas and two other states seeking them, South Carolina and Michigan. This meant that HHS's federal funding could flow freely to agencies that barred LGBTQ+ people from receiving their services, like foster care training and certification. HHS provides more grant money than any other federal agency; the Administration for Children and Families has a $70 billion budget alone. See "HHS Issues Proposed Rule to Align Grants Regulation with New Legislation, Nondiscrimination Laws, and Supreme Court Decisions," Department of Health and Human Services, November 1, 2019, https://public3.pagefreezer.com/browse/HHS .gov/31-12-2020T08:51/https://www.hhs.gov/about/news/2019/11/01/hhs-issues-proposed -rule-to-align-grants-regulation.html; "Budget," US Department of Health and Human Services, Administration for Children and Families, April 27, 2023, https://www.acf.hhs.gov/about /budget; Nathaniel Weixel, "Biden Administration Reverses Trump-Era Waivers of Nondiscrimination Protections," *The Hill*, November 18, 2021, https://thehill.com/policy/healthcare /582274-biden-administration-reverses-trump-era-waivers-of-nondiscrimination.

55. Oral arguments before the US Supreme Court in *Sharonell Fulton, et al. v. City of Philadelphia, Pennsylvania, et al.*, US Supreme Court, November 4, 2020, https://www .supremecourt.gov/oral_arguments/argument_transcripts/2020/19-123_o758.pdf.

56. Bernstein, xii.

57. Bernstein, 4.

58. *Wilder v. Bernstein*, Casemine, June 8, 1988, https://www.casemine.com/judgement /us/5914c13cadd7b049347b850d; *Wilder v. Sugarman*, Casetext, November 19, 1974, https:// casetext.com/case/wilder-v-sugarman.

59. Richard Severo, "Church Groups See Danger in Child-Care Bias Lawsuit," *New York Times*, March 16, 1975, https://timesmachine.nytimes.com/timesmachine/1975/03/16 /317523312.pdf; Bernstein, 30.

60. Sugarman was Jule Sugarman, then the city's human resources commissioner; when Blanche Bernstein took over that role later in the decade as the case dragged on, she became the lead defendant.

61. Severo, "Church Groups See Danger in Child-Care Bias Lawsuit."

62. Bernstein, 148.

63. Bernstein, 247.

64. Bernstein, 321.

65. Nina Bernstein, "Judge Approves Sweeping Settlement in Child Welfare Suit," *New York Times*, January 23, 1999, https://www.nytimes.com/1999/01/23/nyregion/judge-approves -sweeping-settlement-in-child welfare-suit.html.

66. "Opinion of the Court: Fulton et al. v. City of Philadelphia, Pennsylvania, et al.," Supreme Court of the United States, June 17, 2021, https://www.supremecourt.gov/opinions /20pdf/19-123_g3bi.pdf.

67. Julia Terruso, "Philadelphia Reaches $2 Million Settlement with Catholic Foster-Care Agency, Aiming to Prevent Future Challenges to LGBTQ Rights," *Philadelphia Inquirer*, November 22, 2021, https://www.inquirer.com/news/foster-care-philadelphia-catholic-church -lgbtq-settlement-supreme-court-20211122.html.

68. Perry, 16–17.

69. "CAFO 2022 Sponsorship Opportunities," Christian Alliance for Orphans, December 24, 2021, https://issuu.com/christianalliancefororphans/docs/cafo2022_sponsorship.

70. Joyce, xii.

71. Joyce, 42.

72. Joyce, 216; "Reminder—Ethiopia's Legislation Banning Intercountry Adoptions," US Department of State, Bureau of Consular Affairs, October 5, 2018, https://travel.state.gov /content/travel/en/News/Intercountry-Adoption-News/reminder-_-ethiopias-legislation-banning -intercountry-adoptions.html.

73. "Adoption Statistics," US Department of State, Bureau of Consular Affairs, accessed April 16, 2024, https://travel.state.gov/content/travel/en/Intercountry-Adoption/adopt_ref /adoption-statistics-esri.html?wcmmode=disabled.

74. Jamie Finn (@fosterthefamilyblog), "I understand that sometimes children need to be protected from their parents . . . ," September 13, 2022, https://www.instagram.com/p /Cid0_eUMGFm/?igshid=MmIxOGMzMTU=.

75. "Foster the Family Book Tour," Foster the Family Book, accessed April 16, 2024, https://www.fosterthefamilybook.com/the-book-tour.

Conclusion: Imagining a Better World for Children and Families

1. Except for a brief tangent on *Wuthering Heights*, please forgive me!

2. Publishers Marketplace search for US, Canadian, and UK deals only. More than this appear, but in some cases, this is because authors' previous books with "orphan" in the title are referenced.

3. "Chasing Eleanor," Publishers Marketplace, March 6, 2023, https://www.publishers marketplace.com/deals/ss.cgi?d=414064.

4. "Basil & Dahlia," Publishers Marketplace, January 24, 2023, https://www.publishers marketplace.com/deals/ss.cgi?d=408277.

5. "Rosie Frost & the Falcon Queen," Publishers Marketplace, October 17, 2022, https://www.publishersmarketplace.com/deals/ss.cgi?d=396880.

6. "The AFCARS Report: Preliminary Estimates," 2; "POP3 Race and Hispanic Origin Composition."

7. Roberts, *Torn Apart*, 27.

8. Deana Around Him, "American Indian and Alaska Native (AIAN) Children Are Overrepresented in Foster Care in States with the Largest Proportions of AIAN Children," Child Trends, November 8, 2022, https://www.childtrends.org/blog/american-indian-and

-alaska-native-aian-children-are-overrepresented-in-foster-care-in-states-with-the-largest-pro portions-of-aian-children.

9. Fong, 5.

10. "Disproportionality in Child Welfare," National Indian Child Welfare Association, October 2021, https://www.nicwa.org/wp-content/uploads/2021/12/NICWA_11_2021-Dis proportionality-Fact-Sheet.pdf.

11. Jan Hoffman, "Who Can Adopt a Native American Child? A Texas Couple vs. 573 Tribes," *New York Times*, June 5, 2019, https://www.nytimes.com/2019/06/05/health/navajo -children-custody-fight.html.

12. Rebecca Nagle, "Trojan Horse," *This Land*, September 20, 2021, https://crooked .com/podcast/6-trojan-horse.

13. Asgarian, "The Case for Child Welfare Abolition,"

14. Stephanie Clifford and Jessica Silver-Greenberg, "Foster Care as Punishment: The New Reality of 'Jane Crow,'" *New York Times*, July 21, 2017, https://www.nytimes .com/2017/07/21/nyregion/foster-care-nyc-jane-crow.html.

15. "The Hidden Bill for Foster Care," NPR, accessed April 16, 2024, https://www.npr .org/series/1078304434/the-hidden-bill-for-foster-care.

16. Joseph Shapiro, Teresa Wilitz, and Jessica Piper, "States Send Kids to Foster Care and Their Parents the Bill—Often One Too Big to Pay," NPR, December 27, 2021, https://www.npr.org/2021/12/27/1049811327/states-send-kids-to-foster-care-and-their-parents -the-bill-often-one-too-big-to-.

17. After this reporting, the Administration for Children and Family Services issued new federal guidelines stating that states did not have to require child support, but they have been spottily applied. See Joseph Shapiro, "The Federal Government Will Allow States to Stop Charging Families for Foster Care," NPR, July 1, 2022, https://www.npr .org/2022/07/01/1107848270/foster-care-child-support; Joseph Shapiro, "A Closer Look at the Practice of Billing Parents for Their Child's Foster Care," NPR, December 27, 2021, https://www.npr.org/2022/12/27/1145579344/a-closer-look-at-the-practice-of-billing -parents-for-their-childs-foster-care.

18. Asgarian, "The Case for Child Welfare Abolition"; "When the System Fails, Families My Pay the Ultimate Price," video posted to YouTube by *CBS Sunday Morning*, December 4, 2022, https://www.youtube.com/watch?v=bSC1IKHrKt4.

19. Roberts, *Torn Apart*, 144; Fong, 202.

20. "Adverse Childhood Experiences (ACEs)," Centers for Disease Control and Prevention," last updated June 29, 2023, https://www.cdc.gov/violenceprevention/aces/index.html.

21. "National Survey of Child and Adolescent Well-Being (NSCAW), No. 20: Adverse Child Experiences in NSCAW," US Department of Health and Human Services, Administration for Children and Families, August 8, 2013, https://www.acf.hhs.gov/opre/project /national-survey-child-and-adolescent-well-being-nscaw-1997-2014-and-2015-2024.

22. "Young Adults Formerly in Foster Care: Challenges and Solutions," Youth.gov, accessed April 16, 2024, https://youth.gov/youth-briefs/foster-care-youth-brief/challenges; Roberts, *Torn Apart*, 258–259.

23. Kristina Rosinsky, Megan Fischer, and Maggie Haas, "Child Welfare Financing SFY 2020," Child Trends, May 2023, https://cms.childtrends.org/wp-content/uploads/2023/04/ChildWelfareFinancingReport_ChildTrends_May2023.pdf, 1.

24. Rosinsky, Fischer, and Haas, "Child Welfare Financing SFY 2020," 4, 55, for definitions.

25. My interview with Joyce McMillan, July 11, 2023; "Sarah Powell Huntington House," Justice Involved Women Programs, National Institute of Corrections, accessed April 16, 2024, https://info.nicic.gov/jiwp/node/144.

26. My interview with Joyce McMillan, July 11, 2023.

27. My interview with Joyce McMillan, July 11, 2023.

28. "Status Map," National Coalition for a Civil Right to Counsel, accessed April 16, 2024, http://civilrighttocounsel.org/map.

29. My interview with Kathleen Creamer, June 2, 2023.

30. "About Us," Think of Us, accessed April 16, 2024, https://www.thinkofus.org/who-we-are/about-us.

31. "Our Portfolio," Think of Us, accessed April 16, 2024, https://www.thinkofus.org/our-work/portfolio.

32. Cancel, "I Will Never Forget That I Could Have Lived with People Who Loved Me."

33. "Why Should Child Protection Agencies Adopt a Kin-First Approach?," Casey Family Programs, August 12, 2020, https://www.casey.org/kin-first-approach.

34. "The AFCARS Report: Preliminary Estimates," 2.

35. Erica L. Green, "Can 'Kinship Care' Help the Child Welfare System? The White House Wants to Try," New York Times, October 13, 2022, https://www.nytimes.com/2022/10/13/us/politics/foster-children-biden-welfare.html.

36. Sharon McDaniel et al., "We're Building a New Path to Prioritize Kin," The Imprint, March 7, 2023, https://imprintnews.org/opinion/were-building-a-new-path-to-prioritize-kin/239153.

37. "Fact Sheet: Biden-Harris Administration Announces New Actions to Support Children and Families in Foster Care," White House, September 27, 2023, https://www.whitehouse.gov/briefing-room/statements-releases/2023/09/27/fact-sheet-biden-harris-administration-announces-new-actions-to-support-children-and-families-in-foster-care.

38. John Kelly, "White House Announces Slate of Actions on Child Welfare," The Imprint, September 27, 2013, https://imprintnews.org/youth-services-insider/biden-administration-announces-slate-actions-child welfare/244951.

39. "Fact Sheet: Biden-Harris Administration Announces New Actions to Support Children and Families in Foster Care."

40. "Children's Bureau," US Department of Health and Human Services, accessed April 16, 2024, https://www.acf.hhs.gov/cb.

41. Roberts, Torn Apart, 9.

42. Roberts, Torn Apart, 9.

43. Irin Carmon, "Dorothy Roberts Tried to Warn Us," *New York*, September 6, 2022, https://nymag.com/intelligencer/2022/09/dorothy-roberts-tried-to-warn-us.html.

44. Kenya Franklin and Shakira Paige, "New SCR Legislation Took Effect January 1st: What It Means for Parents," *Rise Magazine*, January 18, 2022, https://www.risemagazine.org/2022/01/what-new-scr-legislation-means-for-parents.

45. "Active Campaigns," JMAC for Families, accessed April 16, 2024, https://jmacforfamilies.org/active-campaigns.

46. "Framework for Evaluating Reformist Reforms v. Abolitionist Steps to End the Family Policing System," upEND Movement, accessed April 16, 2024, https://upendmovement.org/framework.

47. Jeanette Vega, email to author, July 17, 2023.

48. "Parents' Platform," *Rise Magazine*, accessed April 16, 2025, https://www.risemagazine.org/policy-and-advocacy.

49. My interview with Alan Dettlaff, April 23, 2023.

50. "We Can't Reform a Punishment System. We Must Imagine and Invest in Care and Healing," upEND Movement, 2023, https://upendmovement.org/wp-content/uploads/2023/02/upEND-one-page-2023.pdf; "About," upEND Movement, accessed April 16, 2024, https://upendmovement.org/about.

51. Asgarian, "The Case for Child Welfare Abolition."

52. "2023 Convening Schedule," upEND Movement, September 1, 2023, https://upendmovement.org/2023/09/01/how-we-endup-convening-2023-schedule.

53. "Transform Societal Conditions So Families and Communities Can Thrive," upEND Movement, accessed April 16, 2024, https://upendmovement.org/transform-societal-conditions-families-communities-can-thrive.

INDEX

Credit: Blake Martin

Kristen Martin is a writer and critic. Her work has appeared in the *New York Review of Books*, *New York Times Magazine*, *Washington Post*, *Atlantic*, *New Republic*, on NPR, and elsewhere. She received an MFA in nonfiction writing from Columbia University. *The Sun Won't Come Out Tomorrow* is her first book. She lives in Philadelphia, Pennsylvania.